Happy Birthday
Love

MW00812724

BROTHER BRIGHAM
CHALLENGES
THE SAINTS

Brigham Young, 1851. Photo courtesy of Archives of
The Church of Jesus Christ of Latter-day Saints.

The Collected Works of Hugh Nibley: Volume 13

BROTHER BRIGHAM CHALLENGES THE SAINTS

*Edited by Don E. Norton
and Shirley S. Ricks*

Deseret Book Company
Salt Lake City, Utah
and
Foundation for Ancient Research and Mormon Studies
Provo, Utah

The Collected Works of Hugh Nibley
Volumes published to date:

Old Testament and Related Studies
Enoch the Prophet
The World and the Prophets
Mormonism and Early Christianity
Lehi in the Desert/The World of the Jaredites/There Were Jaredites
An Approach to the Book of Mormon
Since Cumorah
The Prophetic Book of Mormon
Approaching Zion
The Ancient State
Tinkling Cymbals and Sounding Brass
Temple and Cosmos

© 1994 Hugh Nibley

Library of Congress Cataloging-in-Publication Data

Nibley, Hugh, 1910–
    Brother Brigham challenges the saints / Hugh Nibley; edited by Don E. Norton and Shirley S. Ricks.
        p.   cm.—(The Collected works of Hugh Nibley; vol. 13)
    Includes bibliographical references and indexes.
    ISBN 0–87579–818–7
    1. Mormon Church—Doctrines—History. 2. Young, Brigham, 1801–1877. 3. Church of Jesus Christ of Latter-day Saints—Doctrines—History. 4. Mormon Church—History. 5. Church of Jesus Christ of Latter-day Saints—History. I. Norton, Don E. II. Ricks, Shirley S. III. Foundation for Ancient Research and Mormon Studies. IV. Title. V. Series: Nibley, Hugh, 1910–   Works. 1986; v. 13.
    BX8635.2.N53   1993
    289.3'092—dc20   93–38393
                                                                          CIP

Printed in the United States of America

10   9   8   7   6   5   4   3   2   1

Contents

v

Key to Abbreviations

APOT	R. H. Charles, ed., *The Apocrypha and Pseudepigrapha of the Old Testament in English,* 2 vols. (Oxford: Clarendon, 1913)
CHC	*A Comprehensive History of The Church of Jesus Christ of Latter-day Saints*
CWHN	*Collected Works of Hugh Nibley*
HC	*History of The Church of Jesus Christ of Latter-day Saints*
JD	*Journal of Discourses*
JH	*Journal History*
MS	*The Latter-day Saints' Millennial Star*
PG	J.-P. Migne, *Patrologiae Cursus Completus . . . Series Graeca,* 161 vols. (Paris: Migne, 1847–66)
PL	J.-P. Migne, ed., *Patrologiae Cursus Completus . . . Series Latina,* 221 vols. (Paris: Migne, 1844–64)
TB	Babylonian Talmud
TPJS	*Teachings of the Prophet Joseph Smith*
WJS	Joseph Smith, *The Words of Joseph Smith,* compiled and edited by Andrew F. Ehat and Lyndon W. Cook (Provo, UT: Brigham Young University Religious Studies Center, 1980)

Foreword

Like many other Latter-day Saints, Hugh Nibley began reading full discourses of Brigham Young when the *Journal of Discourses* was reprinted in 1956 (volumes 1 through 19 contain more than 350 of Young's speeches). Just two years earlier, excerpts had become conveniently available in John A. Widtsoe's *Discourses of Brigham Young* (Deseret Book, 1954).

Nibley says his interest in Brigham Young was further piqued by conversations with his own grandfather, Charles W. Nibley, who knew Young personally, and by stories told by Young family members, notably Brigham's daughter Susa Young Gates and granddaughter Emma Lucy Gates Bowen. Nibley cites some of these stories in the essays in this volume.

Eduard Meyer, a renowned nineteenth-century German historian, writing early in this century on Mormon origins, also stimulated Nibley's interest in Joseph Smith's successor.

As those who have read Brigham Young's words know, the combination of his insight, articulateness, and candor is little short of stunning. Nibley calls him a "monumental figure," perhaps (after Joseph Smith) the most prominent mind of his century:

> No man ever spoke his mind more frankly on all subjects. All his days he strove to communicate his inmost feelings, unburdening himself without the aid of notes or preparation in a vigorous and forthright prose that was the purest antirhetoric. . . . [And] there never was a man more undeviatingly consistent and rational in thought and utterance. (pp. 307–8)

The Brigham Young that emerges from his discourses certainly contradicts the common and shortsighted image which his enemies, and all too often even Church historians, convey. Instead of the practical man of affairs, discourses reveal him as the epitome of the impractical man, an avid advocate of a less-work ethic (though his accomplishments are impressive); caring not a whit for wealth, having willinging left, no fewer than five times, all his possessions except the clothes on his back ("Just keep your dish right side up," he counseled), yet he ended his life in relative comfort. That a university should carry his name is entirely appropriate, for, as Nibley says, "No one ever thought harder than Brigham Young" or was more an advocate of general improvement of the mind and tastes—this despite only eleven days of formal education. "Yet what mastery of language! What vigorous and powerful prose! He knew exactly what he wanted to say, and he knew how to say it" (p. 486, n. 1).

There is good reason to reread Brigham Young regularly—especially on the topics featured in the four sections of this volume: environment, politics, education, and leadership. The timeliness of his counsel on these currently live topics will quickly become apparent to readers: "Brigham never gets stale," is how Nibley puts it. Nibley himself adds insights of his own which put Brigham in perspective.

When we asked Nibley if he could be quoted as saying, **"I feel like a mental midget to the side of Brigham Young,"** he replied, "Yes, you can say that—and you can put it in boldface."

Nibley's concerns with the environment span a time period of at least twenty years—"Man's Dominion" and "Brigham Young on the Environment" originally appeared in 1972; "Promised Lands" was delivered in 1992 to a group of lawyers. In "Man's Dominion, or Subduing the Earth," Nibley explores two opposing concepts of dominion— God's versus Satan's. God's command to have dominion over every living thing is a call to service, a test of responsibility, a rule of love, a cooperation with nature, whereas Satan's use of force for the sake of getting gain renders the earth uninhabitable. Brigham Young's views on the environment direct attention to man's responsibility to beautify the earth, to eradicate the influences of harmful substances, and to use restraint, that the earth may return to its paradisiacal glory. In "Stewardship of the Air," Nibley reminds us of the interdependence of the temporal and the spiritual—if one is corrupted, it corrupts the other. Man must learn to distinguish between necessity and greed. In "Promised Lands," Nibley questions the assumption that the American Indians should welcome our superior knowledge and technology.

Many of Nibley's views on politics and war, supplemented by writings from Brigham Young, were originally published in the seventies and even late sixties, but his masterful analysis of warfare in the Book of Mormon as it relates to modern-day principles of warfare described by Karl von Clausewitz was presented at a symposium on warfare in 1989. In this section on politics, Nibley describes the combat between good and evil. He delineates our personal responsibility to be involved in political activity, but admonishes us to keep politics in its proper perspective— legitimate concerns can "too easily [degenerate] into a sordid partisan competition of economic interest that can stifle the spirit of the gospel with deadly efficiency" (pp. 134–35). In this imperfect world, we are to live within the law; Brigham echoes Joseph Smith's recommendation: "Teach the people truth, teach them correct principles; show them what is for their greatest good and don't you think they will follow in that path? They will" (*JD* 12:257).

The true enemy or adversary is Satan, who promises "power and gain, backed up by trickery, violence, deception, and intimidation" (p. 192), and who exploits the two great weaknesses, covetousness and self-righteousness, demonstrated when men seek to contend, accuse, coerce, aspire, or flatter. In an observation as timely today as when he made it, Brigham Young recognizes the foolishness of identifying the enemy with outsiders: "There is not one man in this city nor in the Territory who hates the truth and the Latter-day Saints, whose influence I dread, no, not even the hundredth part, as I do a smooth, slick hypocrite who professes to be a Latter-day Saint" (*JD* 18:359).

Nibley's plea, backed by Brigham, is to renounce war as futile, to substitute trust and love for the overpowering temptation to fight, "to understand men and women as they are and not understand them as you are" (*JD* 8:37), to secede "not from the Constitution of the United States or the institutions of our country but from sin and the practice thereof" (*JD* 10:111), and to advance the work of salvation for the living and the dead. "In the end the most desperate military situation imaginable is still to be met with the spirit of peace and love" (p. 276).

Some of Nibley's writings on education date from the seventies, supplemented by thoughts on the mass media presented in 1991 to representatives of the LDS Church Communications Department. Here both Nibley and Brigham Young exhibit strong feelings about what is or is not appropriately labeled as "education." Both hold little stock in the professional per se, expecting that all should be experts where the gospel is concerned. Brigham's utmost concern is the improvement of the individual mind (in every field imaginable), for the benefit of all the Saints. For Brigham, it is impossible to separate intelligence, revelation, and hard work—"if the spirit may help in earthly learning, the mind is required to operate in celestial matters" (p. 326). Nibley decries the "education-for-success" philosophy rampant today—students "have been only too glad to settle for the outward show, the easy and flattering forms, trappings, and ceremonies of education. Worse still, they have chosen business-oriented, career-minded, degree-seeking programs in preference to the strenuous, critical, liberal, mind-stretching exercises that Brigham Young recommended" (p. 338). Students are too little interested in things of the mind yet are conversant in "(1) jobs and money, (2) cars, and (3) social activity—religious and romantic" (p. 374). In "Mediocre Meditations on the Media," Nibley discusses the *fulness* of knowledge: "the *fulness* is not that infinity of knowledge stretching into the eternities which we envisage in the eternities, but the *fulness* of what one is capable of receiving" (p. 385). Nibley and Brigham challenge us to become educated for fulfilling the Lord's purposes and preparing for his kingdom.

Nibley spoke in the late seventies on Brigham Young as a leader and continued to explore concepts of leadership in his now-famous "Leaders to Managers" BYU commencement address in 1983, his remarks on "Criticizing the Brethren" in 1989, and his "Exemplary Manhood" keynote address at BYU in 1991.

Clearly not sympathetic to criticism of the Church and its leaders, Nibley cites Joseph Smith, who even today is the main object of attack. Joseph places the responsibility to find out the truth squarely on our own shoulders: "Search the scriptures—search . . . and ask your Heavenly Father, in the name of His Son Jesus Christ, to manifest the truth unto you; . . . you will then know for yourselves and not for another. You will not then be dependent on man for the knowledge of God; nor will there be any room for speculation" (*TPJS*, 11–12). Brigham, too, delineates personal responsibility: "I have uniformly exhorted the people to obtain this living witness each for themselves; then no man on earth can lead them astray" (*JD* 6:100). Nibley explores Alma's struggle with dissenters—"the same shall ye not receive into my church" (Mosiah 26:28)—and further explains: "Excommunication was the limit of their authority and is the only power to punish which the Church has ever had. It is not the same power of excommunication claimed by the Roman church, where excommunication means the same as damnation. It is for God alone to judge and pronounce a sentence of eternal salvation or damnation" (p. 419).

According to Brigham, "The leader's business is to get people to want to do things, to place desirable objects before them, so that each will strive, entirely on his own, for that objective" (p. 459). Leadership consists of invitation rather than compulsion, of correcting one's own faults and gaining power over oneself. Leaders are movers, shakers, original, inventive, unpredictable, imaginative, and have a passion for equality and a desire to escape from mediocrity, while managers are safe, conservative, predictable, conforming, dedicated to the establishment, seeking promotion, perks, privilege, power, and rank. Nibley sees in the rise of management the decline of culture.

Nibley's respect and admiration for two great leaders of our time are a persistent theme in this volume: "I am thinking of the two greatest men of our dispensation, the one the devoted disciple and boundless admirer of the other— Joseph Smith and Brigham Young. They are practically out of reach as exemplary figures" (p. 517). Nibley's desire is that we emulate these remarkable individuals.

This volume (as well as the entire *Collected Works of Hugh Nibley*) is the result of countless hours of work by many individuals: Janet Carpenter, Glen Cooper, Karen Dick, James Fleugel, John Gee, Fran Clark Hafen, Andrew Hedges, Michael Lyon, Brent McNeely, Tyler Moulton, Phyllis Nibley, Kathy O'Brien, Stephen Ricks, Matthew Roper, James Tredway, and Natalie Whiting. At Deseret Book, the work has been expedited by Suzanne Brady, Tonya Facemyer, Devan Jensen, Patricia J. Parkinson, and Emily Watts.

DON NORTON
SHIRLEY S. RICKS
EDITORS

PART 1

Environment

1

Man's Dominion, or Subduing the Earth

Ever since the days of the Prophet Joseph, presidents of the Church have appealed to the Saints to be magnanimous and forbearing toward all of God's creatures. But in the great West where everything was up for grabs it was more than human nature could endure to be left out of the great grabbing game, especially when one happened to get there first, as the Mormons often did.

One morning just a week after we had moved into our house on Seventh North, as I was leaving for work, I found a group of shouting, arm-waving boys gathered around the big fir tree in the front yard. They had sticks and stones and in a state of high excitement were fiercely attacking the lowest branches of the tree, which hung to the ground. Why? I asked. There was a quail in the tree, they said in breathless zeal, a quail! Of course, said I, what is wrong with that? But don't you see, it is a live quail, a wild one! So they just *had* to kill it. They were on their way to the old Brigham Young

This article was printed as "Subduing the Earth" in Nibley on the Timely and the Timeless *(Provo: BYU Religious Studies Center, 1978), 85–89; it also appeared as "Man's Dominion,"* New Era 2 *(October 1972): 24–31, and* New Era 11 *(January-February 1981): 46–53.*

High School and were Boy Scouts. Does this story surprise you? What surprised me was when I later went to Chicago and saw squirrels running around the city parks in broad daylight—they would not last a day in Provo.

Like Varro's patrician friends, we have taught our children by precept and example that every living thing exists to be converted into cash, and that whatever would not yield a return should be quickly exterminated to make way for creatures that do. (We have referred to this elsewhere as the Mahan Principle—Moses 5:31.[1]) I have heard important Latter-day Saint leaders express this philosophy, and have seen bishops and stake presidents teaching their reluctant boys the delights of hunting for pleasure. The earth is our enemy, I was taught—does it not bring forth noxious weeds to afflict and torment man? And who cared if his allergies were the result of the Fall, man's own doing, and could be corrected only when he corrects himself? But one thing worried me: If God were to despise all things beneath him, as we do, where would that leave us? Inquiring about the issue today, one discovers that many Latter-day Saints feel that the time has come to put an end to the killing.

The contemporary reappraisal of man's relationship to his environment now confronts society at large with a question that has always been of major concern to the leaders of Israel, namely, What is man's dominion? The key scriptural passage on the subject reads: "And God blessed them, and God said unto them, be fruitful, and multiply, and replenish the earth, and subdue [*kivshū*] it: and have dominion over [*rədū b*] . . . every living thing that moveth upon the earth" (Genesis 1:28). The words *kivshū* and *rədū* both have a basic root-meaning of exerting pressure—that being, however, merely a point of departure for a whole spectrum of derivatives, so that scholars have translated the words according to individual taste and temperament to convey various ideas and types of dominion. Thus the dictionaries tell us that *radad*, with the basic meaning of trampling the earth, in Genesis 1:28, specifically means "to plow," while *kavash*, with the original idea of squeezing or hugging, can mean everything from "violate" to "cherish."[2]

In all the interpretations we are confronted by two opposing concepts of dominion that have always divided the human race. From the beginning men have been asked to choose between them. Thus the *Clementine Recognitions* tell us that Abel's claim to dominion was challenged by Cain, that Noah was challenged by the giants (the "Watchers" of Enoch's day), Abraham by Pharaoh, Isaac by the Philistines, Jacob by Esau, Moses by the magicians of Egypt, Christ by the adversary in person, Simon Peter by Simon Magus, the apostles by the whole world, and finally, in the last days, Christ by the anti-Christ again.[3] In each case the challenger argued from a position of strength and promised "all the kingdoms of the world" with all their power and glory to those who would worship and follow him, while the other offered the kingdom of heaven hereafter to those who worship the Lord and serve him only (Luke 4:5–8).

Each of the great leaders before entering upon his mission was allowed to make his own choice between the two ways, the case for each being presented personally to him by the highest authority on either side. Thus Adam, Enoch, Noah, Abraham, Moses, the ancient apostles, Joseph Smith, and, of course, the Lord himself were not only privileged to speak with God face to face, "even as a man talketh one with another" (Moses 7:4), but were also exposed to intimate and personal interviews, however harrowing and unsolicited, with the prince of darkness as well. Their opponents in each of the dispensations were also favored with direct ministrations from both sides, and each made his choice between enjoying power and dominion here or hereafter.

In commanding Adam to "be fruitful, and multiply," God also informed him that he had given the identical command to all his other creatures, and furthermore, that he was putting Adam in charge of things to see to it that his purposes were fulfilled. Specifically, he was to "replenish the earth, and subdue *it,* and to have dominion over" every *living* thing in the biosphere (Abraham 4:28). There are two clearly marked departments—the earth itself as a storehouse and source of life, which Adam is to keep replenished (*filled* is the word), and the creatures that move about on and over the earth, over which he is to have dominion. As Brigham Young explains it, while "subduing the earth" we must be about "multiplying those organisms of plants and animals God has designed shall dwell upon it,"[4] namely "all forms of life," each to multiply in its sphere and element and have joy therein.

As usual, it is the Prophet Joseph who sets the record straight with an inspired translation: "And it came to pass that after I, the Lord God, had driven them out, that Adam began to *till* the earth, and to have *dominion* over all the beasts of the field, and to eat his bread by the sweat of his brow" (Moses 5:1, emphasis added). Here, in the place of the "subdue" of the King James Version, we have explicitly the word "till" applied to the earth alone, while "dominion" is reserved for the animal kingdom. And what is dominion? After commanding every form of life to multiply for the express purpose of having joy, God gave the identical command to Adam, at the same time putting him in charge of the whole operation, making him *lord* over the whole earth and giving him *dominion* over everything on the face of the earth. Lordship and dominion are the same. The word *lord* is the usual English slurring of *hlafweard, hlaford,* the loaf-ward or keeper of the bread, because, according to the *Oxford English Dictionary,* "in its primary sense the word (which is absent from the other Teut[onic] lang[uage]s) denotes the head of a household in his relation to the servants and dependents who 'eat his bread.' . . . The development of sense has been largely influenced by the adoption of the word as the customary rendering of [the] L[atin] *dominus.*"

Which brings us in the dictionary to "dominion, . . . deriv[ative] of *domini-um,* property, ownership, f[rom] *dominus,* lord," specifically "the lord of the household," in his capacity of generous host, "*pater familias* and owner of the house [*domus*]." The title of dominus designated the Roman Emperor himself as the common benefactor of mankind inviting all the world to feast at his board. In short, lordship and *dominium* are the same thing, the responsibility of the master for the comfort and well-being of his dependents and guests; he is the generous host, the kind *pater familias* to whom all look for support. He is the lord who provides bread for all; but how? By tilling the earth that he may "eat his bread by the sweat of his brow" (cf. Genesis 3:19)—he is not a predator, a manipulator, or an exploiter of other creatures, but one who cooperates with nature as a diligent husbandman.

The ancients taught that Adam's dominion was nothing less than the priesthood, the power to act for God and in his place. The idea is that God, while retaining his unshakable throne in the heavens, extended his glory to a new world below in the work of the Creation, "then as the culmination of that work he created man to be in charge" (*limshol*) of all the beings he had created[5] with the understanding that

"from this time forth man must work to improve the earth
and preserve and take care of all that is in it, exactly as God
had done before."[6]

"The Spirit of the Lord and the keys of the priesthood,"
said Brigham Young, "hold power over all animated beings.
. . . In this dispensation the keys . . . will be restored."[7] God
is a god of the living (see Matthew 22:32) and gives Adam
dominion over every *living* thing, so that his rule ceases
where life ceases. A king's glory and success are measured
by the happiness, prosperity, and increase of his subjects,
even as the power and glory of God show forth, according
to the *Sefer Yetzirah,* in the exuberance of living things upon
the earth;[8] his "work and his glory" are to bestow the pre-
rogatives of divinity on those below him (Moses 1:39).
"From the hour in which I created the world it was my task
to bless my creatures," the Lord tells Abraham in making
the covenant of the priesthood with him; "from now on, the
bestowal of blessings is turned over to thee."[9] According to
a Jewish legend, as God put Adam and then Noah in charge
of all his creatures, he later put Abraham in charge, in order
that he might bestow his blessing on them.[10]

All creatures are duly overawed by the presence of
God's representatives and image: "Even the fierce beasts of
prey fear man," says the *Zohar,* "as long as he keeps his
covenant, his kingly dignity, and his eye fixed on God in
whose image he is."[11] For "God formed man in his own
heavenly form and made him to be Lord over them.
Whenever man stands upright and lifts his eyes toward
heaven, then all the animals raise their heads too, and look
to man, fearing and trembling in his presence." Throughout
history an indispensable fixture of royalty has everywhere
been the great animal park, paradise, or royal forest in
which majesty could display itself in the role of God on

earth, parent of the human race, and patron and protector of all lesser beings. In a word, the concept of man's dominion as a holy calling and high responsibility has been the common heritage of the human race throughout history.[12] God's rule is before all a rule of love: "I love my creatures far more than you ever could!" the Lord tells Esdras in a vision.[13] There is a tradition that Melchizedek, instructing Abraham in the things of the priesthood, explained to him that Noah earned his blessings by his charity to the animals, recalling how in the ark, "We did not sleep because all night we were setting food before this one and before that one." Taking this lesson to heart, Abraham himself made a sort of Garden of Eden near Hebron, and there practiced charity toward all creatures that thus he might "become possessor of heaven and earth."[14] Adam, according to many accounts, was the great friend and companion of all the animals when they lived together in perfect peace and happiness, and they continued true to him even after the Fall.[15] Indeed, "Adam was intimately acquainted with all the angels, all the seraphim [the spirits in heaven], and also with all the holy beasts, . . . before he came to this earth" so that he was peculiarly fitted in his priestly office to serve as mediator between the worlds as well as between higher and lower forms of life.[16]

The teaching of Israel laid the heaviest emphasis on responsibility. Because man is quite capable of exercising the awesome powers that have been entrusted to him as the very image of God, he must needs be an example to all, and if he fails in his trust, he can only bring upon himself the condemnation of God and the contempt of all creatures.[17] "When men lose *their* vicious dispositions," said the Prophet Joseph, "the lion and the lamb can dwell together."[18]

A favorite theme of Brigham Young was that the dominion God gives man is designed to test him, to enable him to
show to himself, his fellows, and all the heavens just how
he would act if entrusted with God's own power; if he does
not act in a godlike manner, he will never be entrusted with
a creation of his own worlds without end. So there is risk
involved: "The rule over the world is in the hands of God,"
says Ben Sirach, "and at the right time He setteth over it one
that is worthy"; but if that rule is ever exercised in an arbi-
trary or arrogant manner, it is quickly taken away and given
to someone else.[19] God tells Adam, "The beasts, over whom
thou didst rule, shall rise up in rebellion against thee, for
thou hast not kept my commandment";[20] all creatures are
quick to recognize the hand of the oppressor and impostor.

Some of the profoundest human commentary is contained in the vast and ancient corpus literature of the animal fables, a protest literature in which the beasts bring
accusation against the human race for their shabby performance in the days of their probation.[21] They are, moreover,
responsible for more than their own survival, for by God's
rule for the animals, "if humanity perishes, then all perish;
but if man lives, then all may live."[22] What kills men
destroys other forms of life as well, and having dragged
them down with us in the Fall ("On account of thee," they
say, "our natures have been transformed"[23]), we are answer-
able for them: "The Lord will not judge a single animal for
its treatment of man, but He will adjudge the souls of men
towards their beasts in this world, for men have a special
place."[24] A familiar early Jewish and Christian teaching was
that the animals will appear at the bar of God's judgment to
accuse those humans who have wronged them.[25] "Happy is
he who glorifies all the works of the Lord, but cursed is he
who offends the creation of the Lord; for nothing will go

unnoticed and unrecorded."[26] Jesus referred to God's intimate concern for all when he said of the sparrows, "not one of them is forgotten before God" (Luke 12:6), and has declared in these last days: "I, the Lord . . . make every man accountable, as a steward over earthly blessings, which I have made and prepared *for my creatures*" (D&C 104:13).

G. R. Driver has recently called attention to an important but forgotten teaching: "Few, if any, readers of the Old Testament seem to have noticed that, as our text stands and as it can only be read without violating normal standards of interpretation, they are committed to the strange doctrine of the resurrection not only of man and of birds and beasts but also of . . . 'gliding things innumerable' which swim in the sea."[27] Modern revelation confirms this: "For I, the Lord God, created all things, of which I have spoken, spiritually, before they were naturally upon the face of the earth; . . . in heaven created I them" (Moses 3:5). "Every tree . . . that is pleasant to the sight of man . . . became also a living soul. For it was spiritual in the day that I created it" (Moses 3:9).

"Always keep in view," Brigham Young exhorts us, "that the animal, vegetable, and mineral kingdoms—the earth and its fulness—will all, except the children of men, abide their creation—the law by which they were made, and will receive their exaltation."[28] We are all going to move together into the eternities, and even now look forward to "heaven, the paradise of God, the happiness of man, and of beasts, and of creeping things, and of the fowls of the air; that which is spiritual being in the likeness of that which is temporal; . . . the spirit of man in the likeness of his person, as also the spirit of the beast, and every other creature which God has created" (D&C 77:2). What an admonition to proceed with reverence and care! It is only because the Latter-day Saints are ignorant of these things, according to

President Young, that God has not already cursed them for their brutal and callous treatment of God's other creatures.[29]

Normative Judaism and Christianity, following the lead of Aristotle and the Doctors of Alexandria, have always rejected and resented the idea that animals might in any degree be classed with men, who alone, according to the perennial doctrine of the schools, enjoy the powers of speech and reason, the mark of divinity that sets them uniquely and absolutely apart. "Man is bound to treat dumb animals kindly and to abstain from unnecessary cruelty," an eminent churchman has recently written, "not because these animals possess any real rights (for only intelligent beings can have real rights) but because they are creatures of God."[30] The "Latter-day Saints," on the other hand, "do not take the view that animals have no reason, and cannot think. We have divine knowledge that each possesses a spirit in the likeness of its body, and that each was created spiritually before it was . . . given a body on the earth. Naturally, then, there is some measure of intelligence in members of the animal kingdom."[31] Animals do possess real rights, "for all things have an *equal* right to live[!]" as President Joseph F. Smith would say.[32] We are told that early Christian groups avoided the eating of meat, not as the flesh of irrational beasts, but as belonging to creatures having rational souls. Schopenhauer observed that the two most serious defects of Christian teaching are (1) the denial of spirits to all creatures but man, and (2) of life to all worlds but this one. These closely related doctrines have formed the common ground on which fundamentalism and scientism have joined hands, the former horrified at the thought of being related to lower creatures than man, the latter scorning any suggestion that we might be related to higher ones.[33]

God and Satan both presented plans of dominion to Adam and then to his son Cain. The father chose one plan, the son the other. It must be admitted that the second proposition was a very tempting offer and very skillfully presented—"Satan tempted me" is the stock excuse for giving in. But we must go back to Adam to see how clever the thing really is.

The story is told not only of Adam but of the other great patriarchs as well. Noah was confronted by the same party with the same proposition while he was working in his garden after the Flood.[34] Abraham too had an Eden and an altar, and while he was once calling upon God in prayer, Satan suddenly showed up with an insolent "Here I am!" and proceeded with his sales pitch.[35] Moses, like Christ, was tempted on a mountain, by the same person and with the same proposal: "If thou . . . wilt worship me, all shall be thine" (Moses 1:12–19; Luke 4:7). Adam is thus only the first; the elements of the story that follow are found in various combinations among the many texts of the growing Adam literature that is coming to light in our generation. The texts often take dramatic form, indicative of ritual origin.[36]

As Adam was praying one day, runs the story, a distinguished gentleman appeared on the scene and engaged him in conversation. There was nothing of the hippy or tramp about the stranger; he was well-dressed and came to Adam with cunning and smooth talk, as a true friend genuinely concerned for his welfare.[37] He began with some harmless generalities—the weather and the scenery: it was, he observed, a most glorious and beautiful world. This was, however, by way of leading up to his next point, which was that he happened to be the owner and proprietor of it all. Yes sir, as far as the eye could see it was all his, and he tolerated no nonsense in it: nobody dared make trouble where he was in charge. This was all hokum, of course; "Satan never owned the earth; he never made a particle of it," said Brigham Young; "his labor is not to create, but to destroy."[38] But to demonstrate his authority, when three strangers (usually described as angels)[39] appeared on the scene at this moment, he at once challenged them as trespassers, asking them if they had any money. He explained to Adam that everything in his world could be had for money,[40] and then got down to business. For the fellow was all business, a person of integrity, ready to keep his part of an agreement (the agreement always turns out to be a trap for the other party), pious and God-fearing,[41] dedicated to hard work—he works, in fact, "like a demon." He was there to offer Adam the chance of a lifetime to buy in on a scheme that would give him anything he wanted in this world. It was an ingenious and simple self-financing operation in which one would buy power with wealth and then more wealth with the power, until one might end up owning and controlling everything. The initial capital? It was right under their feet! You begin by taking the treasures of the earth and converting them to cash, gold, and silver; by exchanging them for the services of important people in key positions you end up running everything your way. What if your rule is one of blood and terror? "Better to reign in Hell," as Milton's Satan puts it, "than serve in Heaven."[42]

Satan's tempting proposition has been the theme of much popular legend and great literature. A transitional figure between the ritual and the literary is Pluto of Hades, the god of wealth: "All the riches of gems and precious metals hidden beneath the earth are his, but he owns no property above ground."[43] So he brutally kidnaps the fair Proserpine, who represents all the beauty and harmony of nature, to

establish his claim over the earth;[44] but the marriage is barren—Pluto can intimidate and coerce, but like his Egyptian
counterpart Seth he can neither beget nor create; what he
buys with the treasures of the earth is nothing but a rule of
blood and horror.[45] But Greek comedy and Roman satire
depict with agonizing frankness the irresistible success of
Pluto's program in a decadent world. In Aristophanes' last
play, *The Pluto,* Hermes the messenger of Zeus comes to
earth as a prophet to denounce mankind for having turned
from the worship of heaven to the worship of wealth or
Pluto: "You have all committed a great sin," he says, "and
must be destroyed." But seeing how well the people are living, he soon decides to change sides and asks for a job with
the establishment. Next, the high priest of Zeus, finding
himself unemployed, is forced to apply to Pluto for a job;
what is his surprise when he finds none other than Zeus
himself now working in the front office of Pluto, Inc.[46] The
cynical conclusion is that no one can resist Satan's bargain,
and in the history of the world very few people have. The
first to accept was Cain, who "loved Satan more than God,"
though at Satan's advice he continued to make offerings to
the Lord (Moses 5:18, 21). The "great secret" of success that
he learned from his new teacher was that he could get anything in this world by the calculated use of force, with no
need to be ashamed, since it could all be done in the sacred
name of freedom; instead of being appalled at the blood on
his hands, Cain "gloried in that which he had done, saying:
I am free; surely the flocks [wealth, *pecus, Vieh*] of my
brother falleth into my hands" (Moses 5:31–33). Cain slew
Abel not, as we like to think, in a fit of passion but with cold
calculation, "for the sake of getting gain" (Moses 5:50, 38).
He was all business. As for the victim, he was quite able to
take care of himself, and if he failed, that, by the rules of the

new game, was his hard luck: "Am I my brother's keeper?" Significantly enough, when this forthright, no-nonsense economy, unencumbered by enervating sentimentality, worked against Cain, he straightway became a "bleeding-heart" in his own behalf, and appealed for the mercy he would not give: "My punishment is greater than I can bear!" (Genesis 4:13). In making an example of Cain, God absolutely forbade the use of Cain's own methods against him: "Whoever slayeth thee, vengeance shall be taken on him sevenfold" (Moses 5:40; Genesis 4:15).

One of the best-known teachings of the Jews is that when man (Israel in particular) falls away from God, all nature becomes his enemy.[47] Modern revelation confirms this: when all the people became wicked in Enoch's day, "the earth trembled, and the mountains fled; . . . and the rivers of water were turned out of their course; and the roar of the lions was heard out of the wilderness" (Moses 7:13). Just so, in the last days "all the growing things will be blighted by the . . . great lawlessness, and plagues will come over all creatures of all the earth."[48] Where people refuse the gospel, according to Brigham Young, "that land eventually . . . will become desolate, forlorn, and forsaken," as nature refuses her bounties.[49]

The explanation of this all-out hostility is simple. "The animal, vegetable, and mineral kingdoms abide the law of their Creator; the whole earth and all things pertaining to it, except man, abide the law of their creation," while "man, who is the offspring of the Gods, will not become subject to the most reasonable and self-exalting principles."[50] With all things going in one direction, men, stubbornly going in the opposite direction, naturally find themselves in the position of one going the wrong way on the freeway during rush hour; the struggle to live becomes a fight *against* nature.

Having made himself allergic to almost everything by the Fall, man is given the choice of changing *his* nature so that the animal and vegetable creation will cease to afflict and torment him,[51] or else of waging a truceless war of extermination against all that annoys him until he renders the earth completely uninhabitable.

This second course is Cain's dominion. Satan, spitefully determined to destroy everything that God has commanded to live and multiply, began his earthly career by making war on the birds and fishes and systematically destroying the animals and trees. This, we are told, was because he was envious of the beautiful rapport that existed between Adam and the animals.[52] Next, under the administration of his pupil Cain, all the forests of the earth rapidly disappeared, while that hero wandered through the earth with his bow for 130 years, looking for anything to kill—"a human angel of death."[53] While Noah refused Satan's plan to divide up the world and rule with an iron hand,[54] his sons accepted it, each driving out from his property all the animals as trespassers, so that the beasts that had loved Noah began to fear and hate man.[55] In particular, Ham organized secret combinations "to work iniquity and to shed much blood, . . . and after this, they sinned against the beasts and birds, and all that moves and walks on the earth."[56] Next Ham's son Nimrod, the mighty hunter who boasted that no animal could escape his bow, turned that bow against men as well as animals and so subdued all things to his will, ruling all the earth with his inspired violence. He was the mortal enemy and rival of Abraham, and whereas Abraham gave Adam's blessing to the beasts, "Nimrod ordered thousands of . . . cattle brought, . . . and sacrificed them."[57] This he was able to do through possession of the garment of the priesthood that had once belonged to Adam and that Ham had stolen from Noah. Seeing him in this garment, all creatures willingly came and submitted to him, mistaking the dominion of Cain for the dominion of Adam.[58] From Nimrod, Esau, another hunter, inherited the garment but lost it to Jacob, from whom it passed down to Moses, who when it wore out replaced it with a garment of cotton or hair rather than skins to avoid the shedding of animal blood.[59]

These interesting old stories might be dismissed as literary oddities were it not that annals and chronicles of real history, "a continual scene of wickedness and abominations" (Moroni 2:18), are completely dominated by the Nimrod type. "The greatest acts of the mighty men" proclaim the nature of their dominion. "Before them the earth was a paradise," said Joseph Smith, "and behind them a desolate wilderness." There is another plan: "The designs of God, on the other hand," are that "the earth shall yield its increase, resume its paradisean glory, and become as the garden of the Lord."[60] Meanwhile, when "we see all the world trying to lord it over God's heritage," we can be sure that "it is in the spirit that the evil principle and power is trying to overcome and rule over the divine principle planted there. This constantly leads the children of men astray."[61] To render its appeal irresistible, the program is pushed by a clever rhetoric and high ethical tone; Babylon has never wanted for dedicated and highly paid apologists to justify the ways of those who "seek for power, and authority, and riches" (3 Nephi 6:15; Hebrews 13:26–28).

Man's dominion is a call to service, not a license to exterminate. It is precisely because men now prey upon each other and shed the blood and waste the flesh of other creatures without need that "the world lieth in sin" (D&C

49:19–21). Such, at least, is the teaching of the ancient Jews and of modern revelation.

Notes

1. Hugh W. Nibley, Approaching Zion (Salt Lake City: Deseret Book and F.A.R.M.S., 1989), CWHN 9:166, 276, 436.

2. The Septuagint renders the two words "rule throughout" (katakyrieusate) and "be first" or "govern" (archete). Both the Hebrew words have the two main ideas of (1) bringing pressure to bear, and (2) treading the earth and walking about on it. Very ancient parallels suggest that the original idea was that of the new master of the earth going about on his royal rounds of inspection and discovery, as we read in the Egyptian Coffin Texts, Spells 80, 132, 136. See also Adriaan de Buck, The Egyptian Coffin Texts, 7 vols. (Chicago: University of Chicago Press, 1938), 2:27–43, 152–57, 160–65.

3. Clementine Recognitions III, 61, in PG 1:1308. Each usurper claimed to be a "cosmocrator," or Ruler of the Universe.

4. JD 9:168.

5. Nicolas Sed, "Une cosmologie juive du haut moyen âge. La Běraytā di Maᶜaseh Berēšīt," Revue des etudes juives 124 (1965): 48–51.

6. Micha Josef bin Gorion, Die Sagen der Juden, 5 vols. (Frankfurt: Rütten and Loening, 1913), 1:83, 354.

7. Elden J. Watson, Manuscript History of Brigham Young 1846–1847 (Salt Lake City: Watson, 1971), 142–43 (26 April 1846).

8. Gérard Encausse, The Qabalah (Great Britain: Thorsons, 1977), 224–25.

9. Rabbi Nehemiah, in William G. Braude, The Midrash on Psalms, 2 vols. (New Haven: Yale University Press, 1959), Psalm 1:5 (cf. 1:8).

10. Bin Gorion, Die Sagen der Juden, 2:137, 424, citing a number of sources.

11. Cf. Zohar 13b.

12. Discussed by Hugh W. Nibley, "The Hierocentric State," in Western Political Quarterly 4 (1951): 235–44; reprinted in CWHN 10:110–23.

13. 4 Ezra 8:47, in R. H. Charles, Apocrypha and Pseudepigrapha of the Old Testament, 2 vols. (Oxford: Clarendon, 1964), 2:597.

14. Braude, The Midrash on Psalms, 37:1 (1:422–23); Midrash Proverbs 23:17a; bin Gorion, Die Sagen der Juden, 2:268–69, 428.

15. Book of Adam and Eve 8:3, in Charles, Apocrypha and Pseudepigrapha of the Old Testament, 2:135; Genesis 2:19–20.

16. Bin Gorion, Die Sagen der Juden, 2:288.

15. *Book of Adam and Eve* 8:3, in Charles, *Apocrypha and Pseudepigrapha of the Old Testament*, 2:135; Genesis 2:19–20.

16. Bin Gorion, *Die Sagen der Juden*, 2:288.

17. According to the Pure Brethren of Basra, ever since Cain slew Abel, the animals have followed the example of man; see the Arabic text in Fredrich Dieterici, *Thier und Mensch vor dem König der Genien* (Leipzig: Hinrichs, 1881), 36; cf. A. Vaillant, *Livre des Secrets d'Henoch* (Paris: Institut d'etudes slaves, 1952), 57–59, chap. 15 of the text. The teaching is attested to in very early times: L. Kákosy, "Ideas about the Fallen State of the World in Egyptian Religion: Decline of the Golden Age," *Acta Orientalia* 17 (1964): 205–16.

18. *TPJS*, 71.

19. Ben Sirach 10:4.

20. *Book of Adam and Eve*, 24:4, in Charles, *Apocrypha and Pseudepigrapha of the Old Testament*, 2:147.

21. Perhaps the most impressive treatment of the theme is the entire volume of Dieterici, *Thier und Mensch*.

22. Bin Gorion, *Die Sagen der Juden*, 1:198.

23. *Apocalypse of Moses* 11:2; *Jubilees* 3:28, in Charles, *Apocrypha and Pseudepigrapha of the Old Testament*, 2:16–17.

24. *Secrets of Enoch* 58:4–5, in ibid., 2:464; cf. Vaillant, *Livre des Secrets d'Henoch*, 57.

25. Vaillant, *Livre des Secrets d'Henoch*, 57.

26. Ibid.

27. G. R. Driver, "The Resurrection of Marine and Terrestrial Creatures," *Journal of Semitic Studies* 7 (1962): 12.

28. *JD* 8:191.

29. *JD* 15:227.

30. Francis J. Connell, "What about the Animals?" *American Ecclesiastical Review* 146 (1962): 270.

31. Joseph Fielding Smith, *Man, His Origin and Destiny* (Salt Lake City: Deseret Book, 1954), 194.

32. Joseph F. Smith, *Gospel Doctrine* (1970–71 Melchizedek Priesthood Manual), 2 vols. (Salt Lake City: Deseret Book, 1939), 1:372 (emphasis added).

33. On the problem of preserving man's uniqueness and dignity, cf. A. Lovejoy, *The Great Chain of Being* (Cambridge, MA: Harvard University Press, 1964), 121–23. Synesius, in *PG* 66:1289, 1292, recognizes both upward and downward relationships.

34. *Midrash Rabbah Noah* 36:3; bin Gorion, *Die Sagen der Juden*, 1:228.

35. Louis Ginzberg, *Legends of the Jews*, 6 vols. (Philadelphia: The

Jewish Publication Society of America, 1967), 1:270–72; *Testament of Abraham* 16:6–10; K. Kohler, "The Pre-Talmudic Haggada," *Jewish Quarterly Review* 7 (1895): 589.

36. Some of the old sources describing the confrontation of Adam and Satan are the *Testament of Adam*; various "Adam Books"; *The Lives of Adam and Eve*; *The Cave of Treasures*; *The Conflict of Adam and Eve with Satan*; sources in bin Gorion, *Die Sagen der Juden*, 1:92–94, 254–56; *Manichaean Hymn Book*; Thaʿlabī, *Qiṣaṣ al-Anbiyāʾ*; *Testament of Abraham*; *Apocalypse of Moses*; *Slavic Adam and Eve*; *Secrets of Enoch*; Theodosius, *Abbatôn*; *The Precious Jewel*; Midrash, etc.

37. Kohler, "Pre-Talmudic Haggada," 589.

38. *JD* 10:320.

39. They are the "Sent Ones" who come to instruct Adam.

40. The theme is dramatically treated in the *Testament of Job* 6–7, 22–23, where Satan says, "pay the price and take what you like!"

41. To Moses he even claims to be the son of God (Moses 1:19); he speaks only with reverence of the Father as his father.

42. John Milton, *Paradise Lost* 1:263.

43. Robert Graves, *The Greek Myths*, 2d ed. (Edinburgh: Penguin, 1955), 31e (1:122).

44. Homer, *Hymn to Demeter*, lines 16–21.

45. Graves, *The Greek Myths*, 31d-f (1:121–22); on Seth, Erik Hornung, review of J. Gwyn Griffiths, *The Origins of Osiris*, and H. Velde, *Seth, God of Confusion*, in *Orientalische Literaturzeitung* 65 (1970): 19; Siegfried Schott, *Sieg über Seth* (Leipzig: Hinrichs, 1929), 18.

46. Gilbert Murray, *Aristophanes* (New York: Oxford University Press, 1933), 206.

47. Discussed by Oscar Holtzmann, "Die Schafe werden sich in Wölfe verwandeln," *Zeitschrift für die Neutestamentliche Wissenschaft* 11 (1910): 231, 226–27.

48. *Apocalypse of Abraham* 29:16, in Charles, *Apocrypha and Pseudepigrapha of the Old Testament*, 704.

49. *MS* 38:344.

50. *JD* 9:246.

51. See *JD* 1:203: When man changes his nature, "every animal and creeping thing will be filled with peace; the soil of the earth will bring forth in its strength."

52. *Psalms of Thomas* I, 25–37, in C. R. C. Allberry, ed., *A Manichaean Song Book* (Stuttgart: Kohlhammer, 1938), 203–4; bin Gorion, *Die Sagen der Juden*, 1:151, on the destruction of the forest; ibid., on Satan's jealousy of the animals.

53. Bin Gorion, *Die Sagen der Juden*, 1:148–49, 151.

54. *Midrash Rabbah Noah* 36:3.

55. Bin Gorion, *Die Sagen der Juden*, 1:226.

56. *Jubilees* 8:23–24, in Charles, *Apocrypha and Pseudepigrapha of the Old Testament*, 2:22.

57. *Jewish Encyclopedia*, 12 vols. (New York: Funk and Wagnalls, 1905), 9:310.

58. *Pirkê de Rabbi Eleazer*, Gerald Friedlander, tr. (New York: Hermon, 1965), 175, chap. XXIV; Sperling and Simon, *Zohar*, 1:249–51, Noah 73b.

59. Robert Eisler, *Iēsous Basileus ou Basileusas*, 2 vols. (Heidelberg: Winters, 1929), 2:34.

60. *TPJS*, 248–49.

61. *JD* 9:107.

2

Brigham Young on the Environment

The Celestial Environment

Brigham Young is one of the few men in history who could claim the privilege of personally occupying, settling, and placing the stamp of his own personality on a large part of the earth's surface. He founded a hundred communities over hundreds of thousands of square miles of the continent; and after more than a century they are still in existence, some of them, in those places where the bulldozer and chain saw have not yet completed their devastation, still bearing visibly the marks of his genius. For Brigham was keenly aware of his unique opportunity to lay the foundations of a new civilization and of the awful responsibility that weighed upon anyone who presumed to alter the face of nature and create an environment in which generations yet unborn would be obliged to live.

It does not often fall to the lot of mortal men to set foot,

Printed in Truman Madsen and Charles D. Tate, eds., To the Glory of God: Mormon Essays on Great Issues—Environment, Commitment, Love, Peace, Youth, Man *(Salt Lake City: Deseret Book, 1972), 3–29.*

let alone to settle, in a land as fair and undefiled as in the
morning of Creation, but that part of the world into which
Brigham Young finally led the Mormons was such a land. It
was their privilege to lay the foundations of Zion in a
region of the globe that man had not visibly altered or
defiled, amid scenes of rare and startling beauty in a fresh
and unspoiled world. "You are here commencing anew," he
told the people. "The soil, the air, the water are all pure and
healthy. Do not suffer them to become polluted with
wickedness. Strive to preserve the elements from being contaminated by the filthy, wicked conduct and sayings of
those who pervert the intelligence God has bestowed upon
the human family."[1] For Brigham, moral and physical clean-
liness and pollution are no more to be separated than mind
and body: "Keep your valley pure, keep your towns as pure
as you possibly can, keep your hearts pure, and labour
what you can consistently, but not so as to injure yourselves. Be faithful in your religion. Be full of love and kindness towards each other."[2] There is nothing mysterious or
abstruse in this identifying of the defilement of man with
the defilement of nature. A Latter-day Saint pharmacologist
has recently written, "Pollution and environmental deteri-
oration are primarily moral and spiritual problems, rather
than problems of technology."[3]

At a time when "free as air" signified that a thing was
of negligible worth, Brigham Young was insisting that the
greatest physical asset the Saints possessed and one they
should treasure most highly was pure air. "What constitutes
health, wealth, joy, and peace? In the first place, good pure
air is the greatest sustainer of animal life."[4] "The Lord
blesses the land, the air and the water where the Saints are
permitted to live."[5] "We have the sweet mountain air, and a
healthy country. . . . What kind of air did *you* breathe, who

lived in eleven, twelve, and fourteen story houses in your native country?"[6] "Speaking of the elements and the creation of God, in their nature they are as pure as the heavens."[7] But since the earth is a place of testing, "every faculty bestowed upon man is subject to contamination—subject to be diverted from the purpose the Creator designed it to fill";[8] and it is so with all things in this world. Accordingly, "the strength, power, beauty, and glory that once adorned the form and constitution of man have vanished away before the blighting influences of inordinate appetite and love of this world."[9] The pressure is always on: "Our enemies . . . would like to see society in Utah polluted, and their civilization introduced; but it would be a woful day for the Israel of God, if such efforts were to be successful."[10]

Why should the enemy seek to pollute? There was an early Christian teaching, reported by Eusebius, that the evil spirits, being forever deprived of physical bodies, constantly go about in the world jealously seeking to defile and corrupt such bodies, glorying in foulness and putrefaction as they "move about in thick, polluted air," and make charnel houses and garbage dumps their favorite haunts,[11] until the earth cries out: "Wo, wo is me, the mother of men. . . . When shall I rest, and be cleansed from the filthiness which is gone forth out of me?" (Moses 7:48). Once in reply to that cry a vast outpouring of waters purged the earth, quite literally, of its filthiness.

It was an awesome task that the Mormons were undertaking in laying the foundations of Zion; it meant preparing a fit habitation for the Saints, an environment and an economy stable enough to last a thousand years, a setting worthy to receive and entertain the visits of heavenly beings, a place that in time the Lord himself would be pleased to call his permanent home! Yet Brigham did not hesitate for a moment to launch into the work with perfect confidence and astounding elan—before the Saints had been in the valley a single day, ditches, fields, and streets had been laid out and the water was running into garden patches.

Observers of the work that followed often remarked with awe that Brother Brigham seemed to know exactly what he was doing all the time. He did know, for this master builder and craftsman had been given the most perfect of models to work with, nothing less than the heavenly order as revealed to the Prophet Joseph. "We are trying to be the image of those who live in heaven; we are trying to pattern after them, to look like them, to walk and talk like them, to deal like them, and build up the kingdom of heaven as they have done."[12] Yes, but what is heaven really like? We know that too, according to Joseph F. Smith, a disciple of Brigham; for that we have only to look about us: "Heaven was the prototype of this beautiful creation when it came from the hand of the Creator, and was pronounced 'good.'"[13]

When Dr. Morrison compares this earth to "an exquisitely equipped spaceship" on which every human want has been anticipated and provided for,[14] he might be paraphrasing the scriptures that tell us that this earth has been prepared with "all things . . . made for the benefit and the use of man, both to please the eye and to gladden the heart; yea, for food and for raiment, for taste and for smell, to strengthen the body and to enliven the soul" (D&C 59:18–19). Or, as Brigham Young puts it, "All the creations are His work, and they are for His glory and for the benefit of the children of men; and all things are put into the possession of man for his comfort, improvement and consolation, and for his health, wealth, beauty and excellency."[15]

His words of a hundred years ago strongly suggest the

image of the spaceship today: "The earth is very good in and of itself, and has abided a celestial law, consequently we should not despise it, nor desire to leave it, but rather desire and strive to obey the same law that the earth abides."[16] "Our business is not merely to prepare to go to another planet. This is our home."[17] "We are for the kingdom of God, and are not going to the moon, nor to any other planet pertaining to this solar system. . . . This earth is the home he has prepared for us, and we are to prepare ourselves and our habitations for the celestial glory in store for the faithful."[18]

But if the work has already been done, all the physical arrangements completed, and the vessel a model of perfection at the time we set foot on the deck, what remains for us to do on it and with it? That is for us to find out first of all, according to Brigham, examining the structure with care, studying its nature and possibilities meticulously, considering well before we lay about us with gun, fire, and plow. "It is one of the most happifying subjects that can be named, for a person, or people, to have the privilege of gaining wisdom enough while in their mortal tabernacle . . . and understand the design of the Great Maker of this beautiful creation."[19] "Fields and mountains, trees and flowers, and all that fly, swim or move upon the ground are lessons for study in the great school of our heavenly Father, . . . [in what] is open before us in good books and in the great laboratory of nature."[20]

If the earth still retained its paradisiacal glory, we would be justified in asking, "What do we do now?" But that glory has departed, and the first step in the rebuilding of Zion is to help bring it back.

> Who placed the dark stain of sin upon this fair creation? Man. Who but man shall remove the foul blot, and

restore all things to their primeval purity and innocence? [That is a large order, an impossible assignment, and Brigham admits it.] But can he do this independent of heavenly aid? He can not. To aid him in this work heavenly grace is here.[21]

Fortunately it is God's work, in which he allows us to participate. "The greatest acts of the mighty men," said Joseph Smith, have been disastrous. "Before them the earth was a paradise, and behind them a desolate wilderness. . . . The designs of God, on the other hand, [are that] . . . the earth shall yield its increase, resume its paradisean glory, and become as the garden of the Lord."[22] It is a clear-cut and fundamental doctrine: "We believe . . . that Christ will reign personally upon the earth; and, that the earth will be renewed and receive its paradisiacal glory" (Tenth Article of Faith). That, however, according to the same Article of Faith, will be the last step of five in the rehabilitation of the earth, and, according to Brigham Young, it was to be a long hard pull: "Not many generations will pass away before the days of man will again return. But it will take generations to entirely eradicate the influences of deleterious substances. This must be done before we can attain our paradisaical [sic] state."[23]

But what about eternal progression? Is the best we can hope for a reversion to the primordial state of the earth? Man is not an intangible Ariel; he walks with solid tread and leaves his mark on everything he touches. God is quite aware of that—he planned it that way: "Behold, the Lord hath created the earth that it should be inhabited; and he hath created his children that they should possess it" (1 Nephi 17:36).

No one appreciated this better than the supremely solid and practical Brigham Young. Along with a deep-seated reverence for God's establishment, he had a New England Yankee's passion for "improvement." "What is this work?" he asks. "The improvement of the condition of the human family. This work must continue until the people who live on this earth are prepared to receive our coming Lord."[24] Day by day the prophet never tired in giving full and explicit instructions on just what the people should do to improve:

> There is a great work for the Saints to do. Progress, and improve upon, and make beautiful everything around you. Cultivate the earth and cultivate your minds. Build cities, adorn your habitations, make gardens, orchards, and vineyards, and render the earth so pleasant that when you look upon your labours you may do so with pleasure, and that angels may delight to come and visit your beautiful locations.[25]

For Brigham, improvement meant "to build in strength and stability, to beautify, to adorn, to embellish, to delight, and to cast a fragrance over the House of the Lord; with sweet instruments of music and melody."[26]

Specifically, the one way man can leave his mark on the whole face of nature without damage is to *plant,* and President Young ceaselessly counseled his people to do as Adam was commanded to do in Eden—when he dressed and tended the garden: Our work is "to beautify the whole face of the earth, until it shall become like the garden of Eden."[27] "The very object of our existence here is to handle the temporal elements of this world and subdue the earth, multiplying those organisms of plants and animals God has designed shall dwell upon it."[28]

Where men cannot foresee the distant effects of their actions on the environment because of the vastly complicated interrelationships of the balance of nature, what rule of action shall they follow? Brigham was never in doubt: the one sure guide for him was the feeling for beauty; he knew with Plato that the good, the true, and the beautiful are the same; that what looks and feels and sounds and tastes good is to that degree sound, useful, and trustworthy: "You watch your own feelings when you hear delightful sounds . . . or when you see anything beautiful. Are those feelings productive of misery? No, they produce happiness, peace and joy."[29] We can trust such feelings, for "every flower, shrub, and tree to beautify, and to gratify the taste and smell, and every sensation that gives to man joy and felicity are for the Saints who receive them from the Most High."[30] "Who gave the lower animals a love for those sweet sounds, which with magic power fill the air with harmony, and cheer and comfort the hearts of men, and so wonderfully affect the brute creation? It was the Lord, our heavenly Father, who gave the capacity to enjoy these sounds, and which *we* ought to do in His name, and to His glory."[31]

To the objection that some people have atrocious taste, Brigham has the answer. If taste, like mind and muscle, is a thing we are born with, it is no less a thing that we are under sacred obligation to cultivate and train properly. "We enjoy because we have sensibility. Promote this sensibility, seek to get more and more knowledge, more wisdom, and more understanding. . . . This will give us greater sensibility, and we shall know how to enjoy, and how to endure. I say, if you want to enjoy exquisitely, become a Latter-day Saint, and then live the doctrine of Jesus Christ."[32] Taste can be cultivated and so must be: "Let us . . . show to the world that we have talent and taste, and prove to the heavens that our minds are set on beauty and true excellence, so that we can become worthy to enjoy the society of angels."[33]

It is through "greater sensibility" that we both enjoy and

endure, for the appreciation of beauty is nothing less than the key to survival. Nature has so provided that we actually enjoy most doing and sensing the very things most conducive to our survival; we delight in performing the most vital functions of life, and so simply by enjoying ourselves, we build up more formidable defenses against the powers of destruction than any accumulation of scientific data or learned admonition could provide. We eat long before we are in danger of dying of hunger and drink long before reaching a critical stage of dehydration, simply because we enjoy eating and drinking. If we ate, drank, breathed, and slept only when persuaded by irrefutable scientific demonstration that if we did not do those things we would die, we would not be long in this world. So it is in all things, and creatures as weak and vulnerable as man must cultivate a salutary sense of what is lovely and desirable and what is wrong and threatening, a feeling that hits them long before they can tell just why a thing is to be welcomed or dreaded.

"When the Spirit of revelation from God inspires a man, his mind is opened to behold the beauty, order, and glory of the creation of this earth." How does such a one react when "a man says, 'I am going to make iron, and I will have the credit of making the first iron in the Territory.'" He can only feel that "the beauty and glory of this kind of proceeding is the blackest of darkness, and its comeliness as deformity."[34] Why so? Without being able to tell exactly why, we take immediate offense at such statements, made by men in high positions, as "I do not believe in conservation for conservation's sake," or "I do not believe in clean water for the sake of clean water." But we soon learn that our shocked first reaction is a healthy one; when the forest is reduced to the now proverbial one redwood, it is too late. What prevents such a catastrophe is not the logic of survival but the feelings of wrongness. "Are you not dissatisfied," asks Brigham Young, "and is there not bitterness in your feelings, the moment you find a kanyon put in the possession of an individual, and power given unto him to control the timber, wood, rock, grass, and, in short, all its facilities? Does there not something start up in your breast, that causes you to feel very uncomfortable?"[35] Brigham does not apologize for his feelings; the Puritan ethic, which he knew and despised so well, would salve its conscience by putting virtue on the side of the cash box and making a great show of abstemiousness not from greed but from the delights that God means us to have: "But the greater portion of the sectarian world consider it sacrilege to give way to any such pleasure as even to listen to sweet music, much more to dance to its delightful strains."[36] The voice of revelation has told the Saints, however, where to put their priorities: "And out of the ground made I, the Lord God, to grow every tree, naturally, that is pleasant to the sight of man; and man could behold it" (Moses 3:9). Trees were made in the first instance to be looked at and enjoyed; we are aware of that before research and experience show our intuition to be quite sound—but the feeling for beauty must come first if we are to survive.

Use All Gently

It behooves us as fortunate visitors in the King's palace to behave circumspectly, to look and admire, damage nothing, take nothing with us, and leave everything as nearly as possible as we found it. Restraint is the watchword in dealing with God's earth: The products of the earth are "to please the eye [that always comes first!] and to gladden the heart; yea, for food and for raiment, for taste and for smell, . . . to be used with judgment, not to excess, neither by extortion" (D&C 59:18–20). We may neither waste nor exploit what we find around us; Merriam-Webster defines *extortion* as the obtaining "from an unwilling or reluctant person by physical force, intimidation, or the abuse of legal or official authority."[37] We have a right to take what we need, but when we would extend that right to justify taking things we do not need, that is extortion, and is expressly forbidden: "It is our privilege and our duty," says Brigham Young, "to search all things upon the face of the earth, and learn what there is for man to enjoy, what God has ordained for the benefit and happiness of mankind, and then make use of it without sinning against him." [38] Sinning against him? "It is not our privilege to waste the Lord's substance."[39]

For "whatever you have, it is the Lord's. You own nothing, I own nothing. . . . The Lord has placed what I have in my hands, to see what I will do with it. . . . I have neither wife nor child, no wives and children; they are only committed to me, to see how I will treat them. If I am faithful, the time will come when they will be given to me."[40] The same applies to the world of nature, which we also hold in trust: "Not one particle of all that comprises this vast creation of God is our own. Everything we have has been bestowed upon us for our action, to see what we would do with it—whether we would use it for eternal life and exaltation or for eternal death and degradation."[41] We are being tested to demonstrate to the heavens, to ourselves, and to our fellows just how we would treat the things of a glorious and beautiful world if they were given to us as our very own.

Those who insist on "clinging to the earth" as if they owned it have forever disqualified themselves from receiving hereafter the mandate: "There is a vast eternity stretched out before you; now organize as you will."[42] We are placed in the position of a lover who is engaged to be married; if he cannot wait until he is properly wed, or if he displays an arrogant and brutal nature toward his promised bride, then the wedding had best be called off—he is not worthy of the prize.

"We should love the earth," says Brigham. "We should love the works which God has made. This is correct; but we should love them in the Lord."[43] We should look forward to a time when this earth "will be given to the Saints, when they and it are sanctified and glorified, and brought back into the presence of the Father and the Son."[44] But that time is not yet; the question is, Can we wait? "Why do men set their hearts upon them [material goods] in their present organized state? Why not lay a sure foundation to control them hereafter?"[45]

We may enjoy these things in anticipation, but in doing so we must display the spirit that shows we can be trusted: "It is the privilege of the Saints to enjoy every good thing, for the earth and its fulness belong to the Lord, and he has promised all to his faithful Saints; but it must be enjoyed without [the] spirit of covetousness and selfishness."[46] That is where all but a few fail the test: "The earth is organized for a glorious resurrection, and life and death are set before the people, true riches and false riches; and the whole world are gone after the false riches."[47]

To honor God's creation is a high moral principle with Brigham Young. First, it is God's wonderful work and bears his mark upon it, and man, try as he will, is in no position to improve on it.

> Man's machinery makes things alike; God's machinery gives to things which appear alike a pleasing difference. . . . Endless variety is stamped upon the works of God's hands. There are no two productions of nature,

whether animal, vegetable or mineral, that are exactly alike and all are crowned with a degree of polish and perfection that cannot be obtained by ignorant man in his most exquisite mechanical productions.[48]

Frankly, Brigham was not much impressed by "progress": "The civilized nations know how to make machinery, put up telegraph wires, &c., &c.; and in nearly all branches they are trying to cheat each other. . . . They have been cheating themselves for the golden god—the Mammon of this world."[49] They think it wonderful to "dwell amid the whirl of mental and physical energies, constantly taxed to their utmost tension in the selfish, unsatisfying and frenzied quest of worldly emolument, fame, power, and maddening draughts from the syren cup of pleasure."[50] Having "obtained the promise that he should be father of lives, in comparison with this, what did Abraham care about machinery, railroads, and other great mechanical productions?"[51]

In the second place, we should use extreme restraint, because it is immoral and foolish to destroy what we cannot replace. As Joseph F. Smith, Brigham Young's disciple, was wont to quote: "Take not away the life you cannot give, for all things have an equal right to live."[52] "Did you ever organize a tree, gold, silver, or any other kind of metal, or any other natural production? No, you have not yet attained to that power, and it will be ages before you do. Who owns all the elements with which we are commanded and permitted to operate? The Lord, and we are stewards over them."[53] By their own manipulations and sophistries, men get legal authority to destroy what they will of nature, but Brigham Young believed that "a man has no right with property, which, according to the laws of the land, legally belongs to him, if he does not want to use it . . . to do good to himself and his fellow-man."[54]

Not only have we no right to rifle the treasury that God has laid up for coming generations on the earth, but we can never justify such plunder on the plea of necessity. "If we have our hundreds or thousands, we may foster the idea that we have nothing more than we need; but such a notion is entirely erroneous, for our real wants are very limited. What do we absolutely need? I possess everything on the face of the earth that I need, as I appear before you on this stand. . . . I have everything that a man needs or can enjoy if he owned the whole world. If I were the king of the earth I could enjoy no more."[55] "When you have what you wish to eat and sufficient clothing to make you comfortable you have all that you need, I have all that I need."[56] "I do not desire to keep a particle of my property, except enough to protect me from a state of nudity."[57]

Paradoxically, we are learning to live *without* things so that we can learn to live *with* things. God wants us to "handle the gold and silver of the whole earth without having a desire for it, only as a means with which to gather Israel, redeem Zion, subdue and beautify the earth, and bring all things in readiness to live with God in heaven."[58] As long as we go on accumulating stuff in this life, we are playing the devil's game, for "there is no such thing as a man being truly rich until he has power over death, hell, the grave, and him that hath the power of death, which is the devil."[59] We will have a right to do as we please with our own only "when we can speak to the earth—to the native elements in boundless space, and say to them—'Be ye organized, and planted here, or there, and stay until I command you hence.'"[60]

Sin Is Waste

Brigham Young also had a Yankee passion for thrift, but it rested on a generous respect for the worth of things and not on a niggardly desire to possess them. When he says, "I do not know that, during thirty years past, I have worn a coat, hat, or garment of any kind, or owned a horse, carriage, &c., but what I asked the Lord whether I deserved it or not—Shall I use this? Is it mine to use, or not?"[61] he is expressing the highest degree of human concern and responsibility. "If I have horses, oxen, and possessions, they are the Lord's and not mine; and all I ask is for him to tell me what to do with them."[62] "Without the pure Spirit of the Lord Jesus Christ, we cannot enjoy the good things of life."[63] But with it we need never feel guilty: "It is the privilege of the Saints to enjoy every good thing, for the earth and its fulness belong to the Lord."[64] It is a magnanimous thrift that never hesitates to take and spend whatever is needed but under no circumstances will touch a molecule more. We may take all we need, because it is the Lord's, but wo to him who dares to take more—for it is the Lord's! This is the exact reverse of the world's economy. Who would expect our most competent businessman to proclaim as his slogan, "Never count the cost"? "If I am going to build a temple, I am not going to sit down and count the cost. I care not what it will cost."[65] "I have built a great many houses, and never counted the cost before I built them. I never wanted to know anything about it."[66] "I have built what I have built without asking how much they cost, or where I was to get the money to do it."[67] "When the Saints are required to embark in any public enterprise, the word should not be . . . 'What will it cost, and will it pay, etc.?' but, 'it is a work for the public good, and we can do it.'"[68] Strange as such a policy may seem, it is but the honest expression of the belief that God really does own everything and that he really will provide. "When we learn this lesson, where will be my interest and effort?" Certainly not in personal

acquisition: "Every man and woman has got to feel that not
one farthing of anything in their possession is rightfully
theirs."[69]

All waste on this earth becomes garbage—*waste* is in
fact the proper English word for garbage. To throw anything on the trash heap is to cast it aside in contempt; what
do we know about its true worth? Who are we to despise
what we do not understand? *"Never let anything go to waste.*
Be prudent, *save everything."*[70] Even sewage has its uses:
"Everything, also, which will fertilize our gardens and our
fields should be sedulously saved and wisely husbanded,
that nothing may be lost which contains the elements of
food and raiment for man and sustenance for beast."[71]
Brigham was aware of one of the basic facts of economy,
that man, whatever he may say, does not create or produce—he merely takes:

> Man cannot control the heavens; he cannot control
> the earth, nor the elements; he can fertilize and prepare
> the ground for the reception of seed; he can plant, water,
> till, and reap, . . . but, until his mind is opened by the
> Spirit of God, he cannot see that it is by a superior power
> that corn, wheat, and every kind of vegetation spring into
> life, and ripen for the sustenance of man and beast.[72]

Moreover, "we cannot own anything, in the strict sense of
the word, until we have power to bring into existence and
hold in existence, independent of all other powers."[73]

Since man cannot create, he must face up to the number
one fact of ecology that Brigham Young enunciated long
before even the scientific community began to take it seriously: "There is only so much property in the world. There
are the elements that belong to this globe, and no more. We
do not go to the moon to borrow; neither send to the sun or
any of the planets; all our commercial transactions must be

confined to this little earth and its wealth cannot be increased or diminished." To this he adds the observation—over one hundred years ago—that the resources of the earth are being placed out of our reach by an irreversible process of buying short-term prosperity on promissory notes that science will never be able to make good: "And though the improvements in the arts of life which have taken place within the memory of many now living are very wonderful, there is no question that extravagance has more than kept pace with them."[74] The dangerous policy of converting all into cash as quickly as possible is another expression of that lack of faith that will invest nothing in a hereafter: "It is all good, the air, the water, the gold and silver; the wheat, the fine flour, and the cattle upon a thousand hills are all good. . . . But that moment that men seek to build up themselves . . . and seek to hoard up riches, . . . it proves that their hearts are weaned from their God; *and their riches will perish in their fingers, and they with them.*"[75] It is natural for anyone to grab what he can get when he can get it, but "who will commit to that man or people the great things of the kingdom of God that are to be attained on this earth" when the time comes?[76]

Brigham in Action

On March 27, 1846, as the Saints were about to go forth on the first leg of their long journey west, we find President Young charging "the Captains particularly to instruct their respective divisions, to be very careful about setting the Prairie or woods on fire, . . . to prohibit all discharge of fire arms in the Camp and to keep their guns and pistols out of sight."[77] On May 6, 1847, as the first company moved out, he reported in his journal: "Traveled 19 miles. The prairie appeared black being covered with immense herds of buffalo." May 7th. "I preached in Camp and advised the brethren not to kill any more buffalo or other game until the meat was needed."[78] To appreciate the farsightedness of the man, let us recall that twenty years after he gave this warning against fires, the youthful Mark Twain sat in a canoe on Lake Tahoe and watched with delight as the flames spread from his *own* campfire to set all the woods ablaze in a holocaust that destroyed everything "as far as the eye could reach the lofty mountain-fronts."[79] All he could think of was the splendor of the spectacle, for in his eyes the forests of the West were inexhaustible, and men could do as they pleased with them.

As to the buffalo, on a single day in the year 1884 Buffalo Bill killed 285 of them and left their carcasses rotting on the plains. In the following two years the last of the great herds disappeared, but William Cody instead of going to jail became a national hero.[80] So far were the Americans, forty years after Brigham Young's admonition, from feeling the necessity of exercising the restraint which he felt so urgent in our contacts with nature.

All who attended, at President Young's invitation, the great 24th of July celebrations at Brighton "were requested to show their tickets at the gate" to the canyon road. The tickets were free, and on them was printed: "All persons are forbidden to make or kindle fires at any place in the kanyon, except on the camp ground."[81] A hundred years later people in Utah still resent limitations on campfires as an infringement on their God-given freedom. The prophet ended his 24th of July speech with a ritual admonition "to put out their fires and vacate this ground, for I intend to tarry . . . until the rest are gone, and see that the fires are all well put out."[82] The event at Brighton was magnificent enough to get coverage in the eminent *New York Herald,* and the reporter who described the doings in the year 1860 tells how at dawn of the following day, after all the wagons had gone home and the dust had settled on the canyon road, he beheld a singular spectacle: "By nine o'clock the last team had left the camping-ground," but one man remained behind "to see that all fires were extinguished." And who should that man be but Brigham Young: " 'The Prophet' left the last, satisfied that all was right, and that his disciples had enjoyed themselves to their hearts' content; and thus ended the great celebration of 1860."[83]

Reverence for Everything

What guided and prescribed the teachings and acts of this great man in all his earthly dealings seems to be before all else his constant awareness of being in the presence of the Divine. To the picnicker at Brighton, he said, "Here are the stupendous works of the God of Nature, though all do not appreciate His wisdom as manifested in his works. . . . I could sit here for a month and reflect on the mercies of our God."[84] Everything around him reminds him of what is holy:

> It is seldom that I rise before a congregation without feeling a child-like timidity; if I live to the age of Methusaleh I do not know that I shall outgrow it. There are reasons for this which I understand. . . . This mortality shrinks before that portion of divinity which we inherit from our Father. This is the cause of my timidity.[85]

"Where is the man who can rise to address children without feeling this same modesty?"[86]

This same reverence, which the Greeks called *aidos*, for Brigham Young extends to all things; for if life is holy, for him "there is not a particle of element which is not filled with life, and all space is filled with element."[87] "Well, how many lives are there in this grain of corn? They are

innumerable, and this same infinity is manifest through all
the creations of God."[88] "There is life in all matter, throughout the vast extent of all the eternities; it is in the rock, the
sand, the dust, in water, air."[89]

This vitalism, supported by interesting and ingenious
physical speculations that we cannot go into here, was
something that Brigham Young felt very strongly. He laid
special emphasis on the importance of human esteem for
the animal world, for one of the peculiar doctrines of the
Latter-day Saints is that animals are living souls destined to
participate in the resurrection as they did in the premortal
existence. "Learn to control yourselves and that which is
immediately around you, and always keep in view that the
animal, vegetable, and mineral kingdoms—the earth and its
fulness—will all, except the children of men, abide their creation—the law by which they were made, and will receive
their exaltation."[90] "Every tree . . . that is pleasant to the
sight of man . . . became also a living soul. For it was spiritual in the day that I created it; for it remaineth in the sphere
in which I, God, created it. . . . Every beast of the field, . . .
they were also living souls" (Moses 3:9, 19). The four beasts
of Revelation are symbolic animals, but they denote "the
paradise of God," that very real "happiness of man, and of
beasts, and of creeping things, and of the fowls of the air;
that which is spiritual being in the likeness of that which is
temporal; and that which is temporal in the likeness of that
which is spiritual; the spirit of man in the likeness of his
person, as also the spirit of beast, and every other creature
which God has created" (D&C 77:2).

Granted there are different levels and degrees that exist
within as well as between species, still it is the privilege of
every form of life to multiply in its sphere and element and
have joy therein. Adam's dominion was a charge to see to it

that all went well with God's creatures; it was not a license to exterminate them:

> Every living creature that moveth . . . and every winged fowl after his kind, . . . I, God, saw that all things which I had created were good. And I, God, blessed them, saying: Be fruitful, and multiply, and fill the waters in the sea; and let [the] fowl multiply in the earth; . . . and everything which creepeth upon the earth. (Moses 2:21–22, 25)

There is a forgotten teaching of the early Jews and Christians that the dominion that God gave to Adam in Eden over his other creatures was nothing less than the holy priesthood, the power to act in God's stead. In making his covenant with Abraham, God is represented as saying to him, "When God created Adam, he blessed him, and man lived in this blessing, until the generation of the Flood came and destroyed that blessing. When Noah came forth from the ark God saw that the world was bereft of any blessing and blessed them anew through Noah. This blessing continued until Abraham came and increased it still more."[91] To Adam he said, "From now on it is all given over into your hand, and they [the creatures] will fear you as they fear me."[92] Accordingly, Adam enjoys God's authority only insofar as he exercises it as God himself would, with perfect love and understanding.

The *Zohar* says, "When men transgress the precepts of the Torah, their visages change, and they fear the other creatures and tremble before them; the beasts of the field obtain dominion over men because they do not see any more in them the true supernal image."[93] Adam's calling, says an equally venerable source, was to take care of the animals, not to dispose of them as his property. The spirits of all beasts have their proper paradise, and at the judgment man will have to give an exact accounting of how he has treated them.[94] "Man by his sovereignty over nature resembles God," says an early Christian writing, "but he enjoys that authority only as long as he behaves in a godlike manner."[95] Only in a noble, generous, and forbearing spirit can the powers of the priesthood be exercised (D&C 121:36–46), and to that spirit in us all creatures have a right to appeal.

When the famous missionary Mildred Cable visited the inhabitants of a remote oasis in the Gobi Desert, she found they did not still their hunger by eating the doves that visited the place in large numbers, since "to trap and eat a pigeon would be contrary to all right feeling, and the oasis dweller's standard of ethics would not admit that a gentle, harmless, self-constituted guest like a wild bird could be deceived, slain and devoured. 'The Princely Man,' he would say, 'is not a betrayer of trust.'"[96] God will justify the taking of animal life to sustain man's want, but he reserves a special blessing for those who place their own nobility before their necessity.

This is strikingly illustrated in Brigham Young's declarations regarding the meanest, most repulsive and destructive of creatures—the crickets of the plague. "Last season when the grasshoppers came on my crops, I said, 'Nibble away, I may as well feed you as to have my neighbors do it; I have sown plenty, and you have not raised any yourselves.' And when harvest came you would not have known that there had been a grasshopper there." The moral of this, he says, is "Pay attention to what the Lord requires of you and let the balance go."[97] Years later it came again: "According to present appearances, next year [1868] we may expect grasshoppers to eat up nearly all our crops. But if we have provisions enough to last us another year, we can say to the grasshoppers—these creatures of God—you are welcome. I have never yet had a feeling to drive them from one plant in my garden; but I look upon them as the armies of the Lord."[98]

The Day of the Destroyer

Because of the Fall, man has become the enemy of his own environment, at odds with the whole creation, allergic to all manner of things good in themselves that afflict and torment him: "The animal, vegetable, and mineral kingdoms abide the law of their Creator; the whole earth and all things pertaining to it, except man, abide the law of their creation."[99] Conflict is inevitable, with man stubbornly refusing to become subject to the most sensible and self-exalting principles, determined to subdue the earth in his way. "We see all the world trying to lord it over God's heritage. It is in the spirit that the evil principle and power is trying to overcome and rule over the divine principle planted there. This constantly leads the children of men astray."[100] So there is a fundamental conflict here, and it goes back to the beginning. It is said that Satan approached Adam with certain propositions that he later presented to Cain, Noah, Abraham, and Job,[101] in which he set forth his plan for running things: (1) He claimed all of God's earth, "most glorious and beautiful" from end to end for his own; (2) then he put up everything in it for sale to anyone who had the money; (3) and finally he revealed the source of power and dominion under his system: it all rested on possession of the treasures of the earth, with which one can buy any military and political power necessary to rule, or rather misrule, among the children of men. William W. Phelps told the story in simple verse:

> This earth was once a garden place,
> With all her glories common,

And men did live a holy race,
And worship Jesus face to face,
In Adam-ondi-Ahman.

That was long ago, when "Enoch walked with God, above the pow'r of mammon,"[102] but it was this power of mammon that changed the whole picture. Two fatal flaws stand between us and that time foreseen by Brother Taylor, "when all the earth in glorious bloom, affords the Saints a holy home,"[103] and the situation is explained with perfect clarity in the Doctrine and Covenants, where we are told (1) that "the beasts of the field and the fowls of the air, and that which cometh of the earth, is ordained for the use of man for food and for raiment, and that he might have in abundance" (D&C 49:19). We may take what we need, but (2) "wo be unto man that sheddeth blood or that wasteth flesh and hath no need" (D&C 49:21). We may not take more than we need. (3) Above all, we may not use this substance to exercise control and dominion over each other. "But it is not given that one man should possess that which is above another, wherefore the world lieth in sin" (D&C 49:20). The sweeping indictment against the whole world gets down to fundamentals: "Before the blighting influences of inordinate appetite and love of this world . . . the strength, power, beauty, and glory that once adorned the form and constitution of man have vanished away."[104] Zion has ever been supplanted by Babylon, which is ever bent on converting the treasures of God's world into the "substance . . . of an idol, which waxeth old and shall perish in Babylon, even Babylon the great, which shall fall" (D&C 1:16); while with Zion the earth is to "be renewed and receive its paradisiacal glory" (Tenth Article of Faith).

The issue between the old and the new was drawn when Joseph Smith changed the up-and-coming name of

Commerce, Illinois, to Nauvoo, "the Beautiful," and at Far West rebuked the speculators who would retain the techniques of Babylon in building Zion:

> Brethren, we are gathering to this buitiful land, to build up "Zion.". . . . But since I have been here I perseive the spirit of selfishness. Covetousness exists in the hearts of the Saints. . . . Here are those who begin to spread out buying up all the land they are able to do, to the exclusion of the poorer ones who are not so much blessed with this worlds goods, thinking to ley foundations for themselves only, looking to their own individual familys, and those who are to follow them.[105]

Most Americans call this "vision," but the prophet Joseph had another word for it:

> Now I want to tell you, that Zion cannot be built up in eny such way. . . . I see signs put out, Beer signs, speculative scheems are being introduced. This is the ways of the world—*Babylon* indeed, and I tell you in the name of the God of Israel, if thare is not repentance . . . and a turning from such ungodlyness, covetousness and self will, you will be Broken up and scattered from this choice land to the four winds of Heaven.[106]

Within a short time this prophecy was fulfilled to the letter, and only the faithful remnant of the Church went west.

What happened there? A generation later Brigham Young addressed the conference of the Saints: "Have we separated ourselves from the nations? Yes. And what else have we done? Ask ourselves the question. Have we not brought Babylon with us? Are we not promoting Babylon in our midst? Are we not fostering the spirit of Babylon that is now abroad on the face of the whole earth? I ask myself this question, and I answer, Yes, yes, . . . we have too much of Babylon in our midst."[107]

> One man has his eye on a gold mine, . . . another for
> selling his cattle, . . . another to get a farm, or building here
> and there, and trading and trafficking with each other, just
> like Babylon. . . . Babylon is here, and we are following in
> the footsteps of the inhabitants of the earth, who are in a
> perfect sea of confusion. Do you know this? You ought to,
> for there are none of you but what see it daily.[108]

And what has this to do with the environment? That
whole economy was based on seizing and selling the treasures of the earth beyond one's own personal needs—the
land itself, the minerals, water, soil, forests, grass; all are
converted into means of making or purchasing the long list
of unnecessary wares that John the Revelator sets forth as
the quintessence of Babylon, whose "merchants were the
great men of the earth" (Revelation 18:23). In the process,
their beauty and value are destroyed, the short-lived finished product soon joining the earlier industrial wastes to
cumber the earth with refuse. Why are we so foolish? For
the same reason the Nephites were, because "Satan had
great power, . . . tempting them to seek for power, and
authority, and riches, and the vain things of the world" (3
Nephi 6:15). The "love of this world" is not an appreciation
of the wonderful things that are in it but the desire to possess it here and now, before we have shown that we can
deal lovingly and wisely. The voice of Brother Brigham still
pleads: "Do not obey the lusts of the flesh, the lusts of the
eye, and the grovelling grasping after property."[109]

The history of America during the first hundred years
of Mormonism was largely the history of the frontier, and
most Americans still like to imagine themselves living in a
land of inexhaustible resources in which everything is "up
for grabs." Brigham Young exposed and denounced that
myth from the beginning, though he recognized its powerful

appeal: "We want to go where we can have plenty of range for our stock, . . . mount our horses, and ride over the prairies, and say, I am Lord of all I survey, . . . that we can get the whole world in a string after us, and have it all in our own possession, by and bye. . . . This is the object many have. . . . Elders of Israel are greedy after the things of this world."[110] "Some want to be separated far from their neighbors, and own all the land around them, saying 'all is right, all is peace.'"[111] They simply are following the example of the adversary, who glories in his kingdom and his greatness where none dare molest or make afraid. But that illusion is not for the Saints: "Let all learn that the earth is not ours."[112]

"Satan . . . never owned the earth; he never made a particle of it; his labor is not to create, but to destroy."[113] Yet it is he who puts it all up for sale and thereby achieves his work of confusion and destruction: "The riches of the world are natural, and common to the human family, but who governs and controls them?"[114] "The earth is here, and the fullness thereof is here. It was made for man; and one man was not made to trample his fellowman under his feet" through the possession of it.[115] "Light, intelligence, good, that which is of God, creates, fashions, forms, builds up, brings into existence, beautifies, makes excellent, glorifies, extends and increases." But that is not the easy road to power; it is easier to doubt than to believe, to tear down a pioneer monument than to restore it, to set a fire than to put one out, so that "that which is not of God burns, destroys, cuts down, ruins. . . . Light and intelligence lead people to the fountain of truth; while the opposite principle says, 'Don't believe a word, don't do a thing; burn up and destroy.'"[116] It is a fundamental maxim of the Jews that wherever Satan as Mastemah rules on earth, he induces men "to sin against birds, and beasts, and reptiles, and fish, and to devour one another's flesh, and drink the blood."[117] When Israel and mankind sin, nature itself is thrown into confusion, so that the violent destructions that overtake the wicked are of their own making (Moses 7:13). Brigham illustrated this principle from his own experience, describing how those parts of the land from which the Saints had been driven have since become poor and unproductive, "desolate, forlorn, and forsaken."[118] In the end, as the wise rabbis saw, it is pollution that makes the earth uninhabitable: "When you completely defile the land," Israel is told, "then I will no longer dwell in it; and then before long *you* can no longer dwell in it!"[119] For Babylon is the city dump, a "hold of every foul spirit, and a cage of every unclean and hateful bird" (Revelation 18:2). And so the warning goes out, "Not many years hence they shall not be left to pollute mine heritage" (D&C 105:15). "There remaineth a scourge and judgment to be poured out upon the children of Zion. For shall the children of the kingdom pollute my holy land?" (D&C 84:58–59). The process goes on while Satan operates with "wealth . . . used . . . out of its legitimate channel" to "subvert every wholesome law of God and man."[120]

But all is not lost.

> The Spirit of the Lord and keys of the priesthood hold power over all animated beings. When Father Adam transgressed the law, he did not fall at once from the presence of the Lord. . . . Men continued to sin and degenerate from generation to generation. . . . During this time the earth and all creation groaned in sin, and enmity increased, and the lives of men and beasts decreased. . . . In this dispensation the keys . . . will be restored, and we are to return into the favor and presence of the Lord. . . . Cease hostility with the serpents and lay aside all enmity and treat all animals kindly.[121]

It is not too late to heed this wisest of counselors: "Let

me love the world as He loves it, to make it beautiful, and glorify the name of my Father in heaven. It does not matter whether I or anybody else owns it, if we only work to beautify it and make it glorious, it is all right."[122]

Notes

1. *JD* 8:79.
2. *JD* 8:80.
3. A. B. Morrison, "Our Deteriorating Environment," *Ensign* 1 (August 1971): 69.
4. *MS* 22:738.
5. *JD* 10:222.
6. *JD* 1:78.
7. *JD* 8:341.
8. *JD* 6:94.
9. *JD* 12:118.
10. *MS* 27:205–6.
11. Eusebius, *Praeparatio Evangelica* V, 2, in *PG* 21:313.
12. *JD* 9:170.
13. *JD* 23:175.
14. Morrison, "Our Deteriorating Environment," 65; cf. *TPJS*, 248.
15. *JD* 13:151.
16. *JD* 2:302–3.
17. *JD* 8:297.
18. *JD* 8:293–94.
19. *JD* 1:111.
20. *JD* 9:370.
21. *JD* 10:301.
22. *TPJS*, 248–49.
23. *JD* 8:64.
24. *JD* 19:46.
25. *JD* 8:83.
26. *MS* 10:86.
27. *JD* 1:254.
28. *JD* 9:168.
29. *JD* 12:314.
30. *JD* 9:244.
31. *JD* 1:48.
32. *JD* 18:246–47.
33. *JD* 11:305.

34. *JD* 9:256–57.
35. *JD* 1:210.
36. *JD* 1:48.
37. *Webster's Third New International Dictionary* (Springfield, MA: Merriam, 1971).
38. *JD* 9:243.
39. *JD* 11:136.
40. *JD* 10:298.
41. *JD* 8:67.
42. *JD* 8:341.
43. *JD* 11:112.
44. *JD* 15:127.
45. *JD* 1:272.
46. *JD* 8:82.
47. *JD* 1:274.
48. *JD* 9:369–70.
49. *MS* 22:741.
50. *MS* 20:218.
51. *JD* 8:63.
52. Joseph F. Smith, *Gospel Doctrine* (Salt Lake City: Deseret Book, 1939), 1:371–72.
53. *JD* 4:29.
54. *JD* 1:252.
55. *MS* 32:818–19.
56. *JD* 13:302.
57. *JD* 4:55.
58. *JD* 3:160.
59. *JD* 1:271.
60. *JD* 1:269.
61. *JD* 8:343.
62. *JD* 6:46.
63. *JD* 8:82.
64. *JD* 8:82.
65. *JD* 8:355.
66. *JD* 8:335.
67. *JD* 17:158.
68. *JD* 10:362.
69. *JD* 4:29.
70. *JD* 1:250.
71. *JD* 11:130.
72. *JD* 3:119.
73. *JD* 8:118.

74. *JD* 13:304.

75. *JD* 1:272–73 (emphasis added).

76. *JD* 8:295.

77. Elden J. Watson, *Manuscript History of Brigham Young, 1846–1847* (Salt Lake City: Watson, 1971), 109 (27 March 1846).

78. Ibid., 88 (6 May 1847).

79. Mark Twain (S. L. Clemens), *Roughing It*, 2 vols. (Hartford, CT: American, 1901), 1:190–92.

80. On the passing of the buffalo, see final chapters of J. W. Shultz, *My Life among the Indians* (Boston: Houghton Mifflin, 1906), esp. chap. 34.

81. *MS* 18:674.

82. *MS* 18:679.

83. *MS* 22:702.

84. *MS* 18:675.

85. *JD* 13:139.

86. *JD* 13:170.

87. *JD* 3:277.

88. *JD* 15:138.

89. *JD* 3:277.

90. *JD* 8:191.

91. *Midrash Psalms* 1:5; cf. other Midrash passages in Micha Josef bin Gorion, *Die Sagen der Juden*, 5 vols. (Frankfurt: Rutten and Loening, 1914), 2:137, 424.

92. Bin Gorion, *Die Sagen der Juden*, 1:83.

93. *Zohar*, Noah 71a.

94. *2 Enoch* 58:4–6.

95. V. Aptowitzer, "La création de l'homme," *Revue des etudes juives* 75 (1922): 4–6, citing St. Ephraim and other early Christian and Jewish teachers on the subject.

96. Mildred Cable and Francesca French, *The Gobi Desert* (New York: Macmillan, 1944), 114.

97. *JD* 3:159.

98. *JD* 12:121.

99. *JD* 9:246.

100. *JD* 9:107.

101. For Satan's confrontation with Adam, see bin Gorion, *Die Sagen der Juden*, 1:255. Satan's shrewd business propositions were also repeated in the case of Noah; see *Midrash Rabbah Noah* 36:3, in H. Reedman and Maurice Simon, *Midrash Rabbah*, 10 vol. (London: Soncino, 1961), 1:290; cf. bin Gorion, *Die Sagen der Juden*, 1:226. The *Testament of Job* 23:3 follows the story of Abraham; particularly

enlightening is the conversation between Satan and the wife of Job, wherein he explains to her that "you can have anything in this world for money!"

102. William W. Phelps, "Adam-ondi-Ahman," in *Hymns of The Church of Jesus Christ of Latter-day Saints* (Salt Lake City: The Church of Jesus Christ of Latter-day Saints, 1985), no. 49.

103. Ibid.

104. *JD* 12:118.

105. Edward Stevenson, *Life and History of Elder Edward Stevenson* (n.d.), 40–41; cf. J. Grant Stevenson in "The Life of Edward Stevenson," master's thesis, Brigham Young University, 1955, 43.

106. Ibid.

107. *JD* 17:38.

108. *JD* 17:41.

109. *JD* 8:125.

110. *JD* 1:164.

111. *JD* 1:107.

112. *JD* 8:342.

113. *JD* 10:320.

114. *JD* 1:268.

115. *JD* 19:46.

116. *JD* 13:241.

117. *1 Enoch* 7:5–6; *Jubilees* 7:24, in *APOT* 2:192, 24, respectively.

118. *MS* 38:344.

119. See TB *Sabbath* 33a.

120. *JD* 10:3.

121. Watson, *Brigham Young Manuscript History 1846–1847*, 142–43 (26 April 1846).

122. *JD* 2:308.

3

Stewardship of the Air

Let me say at the outset that after forty years of breathing the miasmic exhalations of Geneva, I must admit that things are definitely better under Mr. [Joseph] Cannon's supervision than they were in the days of U.S. Steel. We have all heard arguments on both sides in this affair. Recently Mr. Cannon publicly injected a religious note into the discussion with his declaration that the reborn steel mill is a child of divine intervention, an act of providence.

The connection between the sacred and profane is entirely a proper one, and I welcome the excuse for a philosophical discourse. For as we learn even from the Word of Wisdom, body and mind—the temporal and the spiritual— are inseparable, and to corrupt the one is to corrupt the other. Inevitably our surroundings become a faithful reflection of our mentality and vice versa. The right people, according to Brigham Young, could convert hell to heaven, and the wrong ones heaven to hell. "Every faculty bestowed upon man is subject to contamination—subject to be diverted from the purpose the Creator designed it to fill."[1] This principle meets us in the law of Moses: "Ye shall

---

This talk was given 16 February 1989 in Provo, Utah, as part of a Clean Air Symposium at Brigham Young University.

not pollute the land wherein ye are: for blood it defileth the
land. . . . Defile not therefore the land which ye shall inhabit,
wherein I dwell: for I the Lord dwell among the children of
Israel" (Numbers 35:33–34). And today we are told that "the
whole world lieth in sin, and groaneth under darkness and
under the bondage of sin. . . . For shall the children of the
kingdom pollute my holy land?" (D&C 84:49, 59). "I have
promised . . . their restoration to the land of Zion. . . .
Nevertheless, if they pollute their inheritances, they shall be
thrown down; for I will not spare them if they pollute their
inheritances" (D&C 103:13–14).

Brigham Young explains:

> You are here commencing anew. The soil, the air, the
> water are all pure and healthy. Do not suffer them to
> become polluted with wickedness. Strive to preserve the
> elements from being contaminated by the filthy, wicked
> conduct and sayings of those who pervert the intelligence
> God has bestowed upon the human family.[2]

And this is now brought home to us in the great bicentennial address of President Kimball:

> But when I review the performance of this people in
> comparison with what is expected, I am appalled and
> frightened. Iniquity seems to abound. The Destroyer
> seems to be taking full advantage of the time remaining
> to him in this, the great day of his power. . . . I have the
> feeling that the good earth can hardly bear our presence
> upon it. . . . The Brethren constantly cry out against that
> which is intolerable in the sight of the Lord: against pol-
> lution of mind, body, *and our surroundings.*[3]

Brother Brigham states the problem in terms of a flat-
out contest between the most vital necessity of life and pure
greed, a principle as old as the human record, rooted in a
fundamental fact of nature: "The world is after riches.

Riches is the god they worship. . . . What constitutes health, wealth, joy, and peace? In the first place, *good pure air* is the greatest sustainer of animal life."[4] "The Lord blesses the land, the air, and the water where the Saints are permitted to live."[5]

As is well known, all metals are lifeless crystals arranged on a hexagonal plan which can grow only by accretion from without—they are, so to speak, expansive, acquisitive, and dead by nature. On the other hand, all organic life favors pentagonal forms (with the Fibonacci progression) and grows from within, reproducing itself in the life process.

Throughout the human experience that strange dichotomy between the organic and inorganic meets us in parable, history, myth, and folklore. Brother Kimball referred expressly to the Destroyer. There is no more ancient, pervasive, or persistent tradition than that of the adversary, the Prince of Darkness, most often and most widely described as the lord of the underworld who sits in his Stygian realm upon all the mineral treasures of the earth, worked by toiling slaves amidst foul and pestilential vapors. Many years ago Jakob Grimm made a long study of the subject. Our lord of the underworld rules under many names—Satan, Loki, Mammon, Mulciber, Hephaestus, etc.; and his workers are the gnomes, trolls, kobolds, the dwarfs, and other grimy, hard-working creatures. The model is plainly taken from prehistoric mining regions such as the immensely old Varna works in Yugoslavia and others in Asia Minor and Cyprus. For the classical writers, Spain was his kingdom, with its blighted regions of mines, smelters, and foundries—all worked by starving, filthy, driven slaves, converting the landscape into barren wastes of slag and stunted vegetation.

Cyprus was early stripped of its forests to provide fuel for the copper and silver smelters.[6] Plato tells us that Attica in his day had become "the skeleton of a body wasted by disease." The abundant forests were gone; gone were the food for animals and the storage for water. "In the old days," he says, "the water was not lost, as it is today, by running off a barren ground to the sea."[7] Though that enlightened city passed an ordinance against throwing garbage into the streets as early as 500 B.C., today 2,500 years later Athens is strangling in smog, which is literally destroying those glories of Plato's day which have survived until the present.

The big boss is best known by far under his names of Pluto and Plutus, the one denoting his function as the lord of the underworld and the other as the god of riches.[8] The best-known public appearance of Pluto is his rape of Proserpine, the most famous rape in song and story.[9] She is the daughter of Demeter, Mother Earth, and represents everything that is fresh, beautiful, green, young, and growing. Pluto, in his black *quadriga* or black stretch limousine, sweeps out of his subterranean realm amidst choking clouds of sulphur dioxide, carbon monoxide, and assorted particles, and snatches Proserpine away from the scene to go down and live with him as a very rich but unhappy bride. In northern mythology when the maiden goes down to live below, her name is changed to Hell. With her departure all the upper world becomes as dull and gloomy as Pluto's own busy factories, foundries, and smelters. This makes Pluto's claim to rule over the earth complete. He takes the treasures of the earth and with them creates the wealth and the armaments that enable him to rule through the ages with blood and horror.

The psychological side of the legends is significant. The

Pluto figure is shunned and avoided by men; no ancient tribe claimed him as an ancestor. No cult paid him honor, for all the fear and dread his power inspired. His uncompromising enemy is Dikē—justice or righteousness. Theognis of Megara, a ruined aristocrat, lamenting his lost fortune, sings the praise of "Plutus, thou fairest of gods and most desirable of all things, through thee even the basest man can become a pillar of society" (*esthlos aner*).[10] Shakespeare says the same when he has Timon of Athens, after losing his fabulous wealth, tell us how gold can make "black white, foul fair, wrong right, base noble, old young, coward valiant,"[11] how it can turn scoundrels to senators; and, most to the point, how it can transmute the foulest stench into the balms and spices of an April day. Plutus is always selfish, always reluctant to share what he has with his brother (Hyginus). His gifts to mankind are dullness of intellect (*anoia*), boundless self-importance amounting to self-adoration (*megalauchia*), and *hybris*—that arrogance which guarantees ultimate ruin.

In a fable told in Phaedrus, we are told that when Hercules, after completing his philanthropic labors among men, was received into heaven, all the heroes and demigods gathered round to congratulate him on his arrival. When Plutus came to greet him he promptly turned his back on him. This shocked them all, and when he was asked why he did it, Hercules replied, "Because he makes men base and corrupts everything he touches."[12] But the best-known trait of Plutus to the ancients was his blindness, which is the main theme of the philosophers and poets. There is no proportion between merit and mischief, reward and deserts, right and wrong when Plutus bestows his gifts.

At first, in archaic times, Plutus was an agrarian figure, the reward of the hardworking farmer, but with advancing civilization he was given a new persona, wealth as such and no questions asked. "Plutus has become the common guide of life," writes the poet Antiphanes, "because people think it will get them everything, and they are not particular how." When the schoolmen started to make the rules in late antiquity, they ordered Arete (virtue, honesty) to step down and yield her place to Pluto.

It is easy to recognize in Pluto the Cain figure. Cain began as a farmer; but when following Satan's instructions, he made use of that great secret of how to murder and get gain, the earth refused him her strength, and he became a wanderer. Since time immemorial that homeless tribe (the land of Nod means land of unsettled nomad) is designated throughout the East by the name *Qayin*, meaning a wandering metal-worker, the mark of his trade and his tribe being the face blackened at the forge; he is a skillful maker and peddler of weapons and jewels, the twin destroyers and corrupters of mankind. Long ago, Eusebius, called the father of church history, tells of an early Christian tradition that the evil spirits which constantly seek to defile and corrupt human society "move about in thick polluted air," as a most fitting environment for their work. In a passage from a famous Hermetic work, the *Korē Kosmu* 23, the Air complains to the Creator, "O Master, I myself am made thick and polluted, and by the stench of dead things from the dump I reek to heaven, so that I breed sickness, and have ceased to be wholesome; and when I look down from above I see things which are too awful to behold."

Of the Sagas of the North, the one best known to us, thanks to Wagner, is the *Nibelungenlied*. The Nibelungs were hideous dwarfs who mined, smelted, and forged deep within the earth. They possessed the Rheingold, which gave any possessor infinite power but forced him to renounce love and doomed him to destruction. Freia, the goddess of youth, was bartered for the gold and carried by the giants; whereupon the earth was covered with a pall of smoke, and all things, including the gods, began to age and wither. Note the Proserpine parallel. The story is an endless procession of tricks, lies, and murders for power and gain. We are introduced into a world of ringing hammers, glowing forges, warped and deformed dwarfs plotting their dirty tricks and murders, brainless giants knocking each other's brains out, men and women of high society plotting and poisoning, all of them after the same Rheingold—because the Rheingold of course made its owner the ruler of the universe. A recent production of the "Ring" in Germany, in which the protagonists are steel and munitions barons, departs not a jot from Wagner's intent.

The most famous passage relevant to our subject is from another medieval epic, the opening refrain from Macbeth: "Fair is foul, and foul is fair: Hover through the fog and filthy air."[13] Shakespeare must have got the idea from the Bible, which calls Satan the Prince of the Air but also the Prince of Darkness—that kind of air. He is also called the Prince of this World, who promises power and gain to all who will make a pact with him. The theme of Shakespeare's tragedy is fraud and deception as a means of obtaining power and control; in the closing lines Macbeth admits that he has been taken in: "I . . . begin to doubt the equivocation of the fiend that lies like truth,"[14] i.e., the double-talk of the promoter that put him on top, the rhetoric of Madison Avenue: "And be these juggling fiends no more believed that palter with us in a double sense; that keep the word of promise to our ear, and break it to our hope!"[15] The worst thing about the "filthy air" is that it turns out to be a smokescreen; Macbeth is led on and put off from day to day until he is done in. It is a smooth, white-collar scam such as Macbeth half suspected from the beginning: "But 'tis strange; And oftentimes, to win us to our harm, The instruments of darkness tell us truths, Win us with honest trifles, to betray's In deepest consequence."[16] What kind of honest trifles? Such pleasant bits as those pacifying public relations assurances, "We are not monsters or ogres, we are people just like you. We love our families just like you, we go to church too!" Or to quote the scriptures, "I am no devil" (2 Nephi 28:22). That, of course, is all perfectly true—the workers are not the culprits but the pawns of owners, who use them to justify profitable pollution while hiring as few workers as possible and paying them as little as possible.

Not only Wagner but Ibsen, Shaw, and others call attention to the moral dilemma that beset the nineteenth-century industrial society, as it does ours today. When getting gain entails the destruction and degrading of life, what should we do? Undershaft, Shaw's super tycoon, replies with the simple motto, "Unashamed." The great fortunes that made America a world-class power were paid for by mill towns in which life was very near to hell. But the owners lived far away, and starving immigrants desperately competing for jobs were willing to submit to anything.

No more vivid description of that world can be found than one written in 1855 by a prominent Latter-day Saint living in England. I thought of his essay last fall. Looking toward Provo from Redwood Road where it enters the valley at an elevation to the west, I paused to behold the dense, murky, brown fog jammed against the mountains right behind the Brigham Young University by the prevailing winds, and I remembered the opening lines of the composition,

> All nature smiles, and teems with health and bright-
> ness and fragrance, where you are, but over the valley

before you rests an awful, impenetrable, dark, black
cloud, . . . approximating to a realization of your ideal of
the "dark valley of the shadow of death.". . . You walk
down the hillside, and, as you enter the thick, dark cloud,
. . . you feel no more the invigorating influences [of the
sun], . . . a sense of oppressiveness falls upon you, and
you realize, to your unmistakable discomfort, that the
darkness around [you] can not only be seen, but felt and
tasted. Suddenly, to your great astonishment, you discover that this dreary spot is inhabited by human
beings![17]

He contrasts the situation with that of the Latter-day Saints
"spreading themselves on the face of the earth, and carefully cultivating it," invigorated by "the pure, bracing air,
[and with it] health."[18]

For one hundred years, Utah Valley was idyllic.
Agrarian economies, as we know, are the stablest on earth.
They have existed for thousands of years throughout the
world and are still going strong. Industrial economies, on
the other hand, though surprisingly ancient, are expansive,
acquisitive, extractive, unstable, speculative, competitive,
destructive. In England it meant the Deserted Village, and
the vast futility of empire. It has kept any attempts at
achieving a stable American civilization off balance for 200
years.

Our Latter-day Saint philosopher of the 1850s tells us
what he found when he entered the factory town: "Over-
population—filth, want of employment, destitution, moral
degradation, physical degeneracy, disease, and untimely
death."[19] Who would ever have thought 135 years ago that
this would be an accurate description of our inner cities
today?

Men of science viewing such scenes deplore as possibly
the worst aspect of the whole thing the fact that people can

adapt themselves to such a life, especially if the alternative is starvation. How much can people live with? Do you recall the last sentence of Orwell's novel *1984?* "He loved Big Brother." Or how people could go on for years resigned to daily life in the Gulag Archipelago? Or how the prisoner of Chilon finally refuses to leave his rat-infested dungeon because he has become accustomed to it? Jake Garn says that we should all learn to live with corporate pollution lest we jeopardize the profits of big business. But where do you draw the line? How much cigarette smoke should we tolerate, for example?

This brings up the question of degree or intent. To return to our ancients, Aristotle tells us that there are two kinds of goods which we are after in this life, goods of first intent and goods of second intent.[20] Goods of second intent are good because they help us obtain other things. Thus a pencil, a watch, shoes, a hammer, a stove, etc., are all useful for obtaining something beyond their own value. Goods of first intent, on the other hand, are good in themselves and need no excuse; they are not the means but the goal. Thus millions of people take the plane to Hawaii—the plane is a good of second intent and gets us there; but the delights of the islands are goods of first intent, whose enjoyment needs no explanation or excuse. People crave them for what they are and actually need them more than any of the amenities. Goods of first intent: "All things which come of the earth . . . are made for the benefit and the use of man, both to please the eye and to gladden the heart, . . . for taste and for smell, to strengthen the body and to enliven the soul" (D&C 59:18–19). Utah Valley, without the steel mill, offers treasures of first intent. The mill is not beautiful and for most of us has precious little utility. What is it then? It is a good of *third intent*, the one and only thing which is not good of itself and not useful of itself but is prized above all else—it is money. Letters to the editor have been quite frank in telling us to wake up and realize that those dark clouds to the west mean just one thing—money.

Clear examples of third intent lie all around us today. Take the town of Beatty, Nevada, for example. "The residents here," says the news report, "are dusting off the welcome mat for something the rest of the country abhors: a dump to house nuclear waste which will remain 'hot' for tens of thousands of years. . . . Despite protests by Governor Richard Bryan and others, . . . Beatty residents say they would welcome the dump, if handled properly, because it would mean an economic boost." Only in southern Utah could we top such eagerness to sacrifice forever values both of first and second intent for number three, a quick monetary shot in the arm. Where else but in Utah would you ever find an *Anti*-Wilderness Society, composed of mining, lumber, and cattle interests? What? Making war on the lingering remnants of our precious wilderness already in full retreat, as people by the millions buy vans and camping gear and take off to our overcrowded parks and national forests in forlorn search of remaining open spaces? Of course the object of the league is not to destroy the wilderness—those are the very men who like to play Wild West; their behavior is explained by one word—money.

Another example to convince you that there is such a thing as that ruinous good of third intent: A Houston financier bought the Pacific Lumber Company in 1985 by selling high-yield, high-risk corporate notes through Drexel Burnam Lambert, specialists in what some people call "junk bonds." To pay off the $795 million debt, they were logging the largest stand of virgin redwoods remaining. Instead of cutting some trees, the company was felling all the trees in selected tracts. Maximum harvesting of these trees, many over 1,000 years old, was to satisfy debts incurred. Needless to say, "spokesmen for the company" assured us that this was only common industry practice, and was not environmentally unsound.

They say production can be sustained indefinitely under current plans. Just wait 1,000 years and the clear-cut will grow right back again. Here one of earth's supreme goods of first intent, unsurpassed anywhere in its haunting magnificence, exists merely to pay off junk bonds, third intent pure and simple. Not long ago a governor of California, championing the cause of those who were bent on turning all the groves into cash, uttered the famous one-liner: When you have seen one redwood, you have seen them all.

I grant you that the product of the operation is useful, a good of second intent; but how carefully do we balance the value of one against the other? Should whales be slaughtered to make useful soap and shoe polish? Should the sacred Blue Canyon of the Hopis be strip-mined to light millions of bulbs glorifying the gambling dives of Las Vegas?

When U.S. Steel moved in during World War II, advertising its vastly profitable operations as a selfless patriotic contribution toward making America strong and free, the people cheerfully accepted the inconvenience. After World War II, a new excuse was needed for uncontrolled pollution, and the smelters came up with the slogan, "The Solution to Pollution is Diffusion." There would be taller smokestacks. But being still further pressed, they took the bull by the horns with a campaign brazenly proclaiming, "Mining is Beautiful!" adding "when it creates a common heritage." Brigham Young never ceased telling the Saints that the one thing that would disrupt the civilization of Deseret was mining in the Territory. What the company called a common heritage was temporary jobs for "Chicanos, Blacks, Native Americans, and sons and daughters of the immigrants," but I strongly suspect that the miners were as little aware of the heritage as the stock holders and owners were.

"Oh what a powerful argument human *self-interest* is!" says Tertullian.[21] Here is a bold headline: "Timber Spokeswoman: Environmentalists Gag Free Enterprise." But here is another by Jack Anderson: "Timber Firms Ax Free Enterprise."[22]

Within the past ten days we have had a classic example of the overpowering argument of third intent. Last autumn Congress finally got through a bill against the fierce opposition of the billboard interests, tightening restrictions on the industry. Billboards are not ornamental, and they are not useful; they are strictly goods of third intent. For years now, enlightened communities throughout the land have put increasing controls on the things. But what do we find now in Utah Valley? The *Provo Daily Herald* displayed a picture of "officials cutting the ribbon on a new billboard campaign," which is to adorn Provo and Orem with a rash of new giant signs, "hoping to encourage Utah County residents to keep dollars here." At the same time we learned that the authorities are planning to attract more retirees to the state. The people I know who have moved to Provo from both coasts have done so expressly to get away from the ticky-tacky urban clutter of billboards, remembering the mountains and the clear, blue sky of their childhood—and we offer them billboards cunningly placed where the eye cannot avoid their impudent and offensive intrusion. And we think that is going to make us richer?

The first reply to complaints when the mill reopened

was, "If you don't like it, then why don't you just move out?" Again we have Brigham's reply, "This is our home."[23] "This earth is the home he has prepared for us, and we are to prepare ourselves and our habitations for the celestial glory in store for the faithful."[24] "This is the habitation of the Saints; this is the earth that will be given to the Saints."[25] Again we have the support of the ancients. The earth, says Aristotle, was made to be a home for man, permanently, and for that he must achieve a stable balance with nature, harmonious and pleasant to all. Cicero echoes this sentiment when he says that the earth is a fit home for both gods and men, and man has his part to play in taking good care of the garden. This must be a stable, eternal order with man at the top of the animal scale, held most responsible if things go wrong.[26]

Notice that all these references are to one's local home as well as earthly habitation. They are now one—where do you move when pollution is universal? Now the dispute takes on a wholly new direction. It is a new ball game. Heretofore we have always heard that air is free, and it is a free country, and business cashed in on the boundless ocean as a free dumping ground for industrial garbage. But then Heyerdahl found his rafts floating in displays of garbage even in the remote vastness of the mid-Pacific and the mid-Atlantic. Last year we all held our noses as we watched the three-month odyssey of a scow loaded with 3,000 tons of waste, which it tried in vain to dump surreptitiously in various places. That no longer goes. If the ocean is finite, how much more so the limited airspace of the valley, an even less proper receptacle for tons of industrial filth, that must be inhaled by 250,000 people with every breath (taking in between 10,000 and 12,000 liters of air every day).

For nigh on two hundred years, smoke-blackened skies

were joyfully hailed as the sign of prosperity and progress, and still we hear the pious protests, "Are you against progress? Do you want to turn back the clock?" Again the answer should be seriously considered.

Before the late war [World War II], one could not buy a watch that did not have a phosphorescent dial. The things were immensely convenient and economical, indispensable. We could not live without them, and their manufacture gave employment to thousands of poor people, for it was largely handwork. In spite of all those great benefits and blessings touted by the industry, you cannot buy one of those watches today. We have actually turned back the clock on progress, made a technological retreat, trashed an indispensable commodity. But it took Jane Addams a whole generation to bring about that drastic change. Her argument was the naively simple one that making phosphorescent watches killed people, since the worker had to tip the tiny phosphorus-bearing brushes with her tongue, dooming her to the deadly phossey-jaw. But of course the disease took years to show up, and so for long years that was the franchise of the industry to continue. This is an extreme case, but the same delaying tactics are followed everywhere. You will recognize the likeness to the effects of breathing Geneva air. Maybe not so drastic, and not so quick, but granting the same license to pollute and jeopardize health.

But the problem is more serious than that. Every passing month brings forth new evidence from around the world that the physical danger entailed in the operation of such plants as Geneva is far greater than anyone had heretofore realized. The contribution of such combustion centers to acid rain, greenhouse effect, and damaged ozone is irreversible. An entire issue of the *National Geographic*

(December 1988) asks on the cover, "Can Man Save This Fragile Earth?"[27] We have long known that there is something wrong, if only by the duck test: if it looks bad, tastes bad, smells bad, and sounds bad in duplicitous argument, then it must be bad.

"The respect that makes calamity of so long life" is always the time element, allowing for endless obfuscation: No definitive proof, requires further study, experts disagree, a complicated problem, we are doing everything in our power, or we have done everything in our power (meaning in both cases we can't do more and intend to go on stalling), we are leaning over backwards, studying the problem, we are bringing in our experts to reject the findings, only a small sampling, figures out of date, taking it under advisement, etc. Along with this goes a swelling liturgy of praise for the benign effects, the lofty intent, and boundless benefits of the operation.

Imagine an official offering a sizable sum of money to a local institution with which I am associated. The head of that group says he would thankfully receive the generous donation the moment the company was ready to show him a letter from the EPA stating that EPA emissions standards, low as they are, were being observed at the plant. Being a lawyer, he knows the real nature of the offer and puts his finger on the spot, and there the matter ends.

A far better gift than cash handouts to our nature-loving Boy Scouts, and school children, and to the freedom-loving citizens attending the festival in July, would be "the clear blue sky [arching] over the vales of the free,"[28] the clearer the freer, including freedom from respiratory complications in later life. But of course there is one serious drawback to that. The clear blue skies cost much more than the highly publicized handouts.

I could be accused of being prejudiced and extremist, but I would not have taken my position at all if I was not forced into it by the bristling headlines that have suddenly emerged on every side; and the issue never would have reached the covers and front pages of staid conservative journals had it not been thrust upon *them* by the crushing accumulation of evidence sounding alarm in all quarters. I was brought up in an alarmist atmosphere first by my grandparents, then by the Axis Powers, and now by a sea of frightening statistics; but especially the scriptures kept me thinking. After hearing Jack Anderson this morning, I feel that if anything, I am much too complacent.

I do not worry very much about Geneva anymore; it is only a small fumarole at the base of a mighty volcano which is now shuddering and groaning ominously. Brother Anderson said that he hears the great waterfall roaring just ahead. So let us both end with the Book of Mormon:

> For behold, ye do love money. . . . O ye pollutions, . . . who sell yourselves for that which will canker, why have ye polluted the holy church of God? . . . Why do ye build up your secret abominations to get gain, and cause that widows should mourn before the Lord, and also orphans, . . . and also the blood of their fathers and their husbands to cry unto the Lord . . . for vengeance upon your heads? Behold, the sword of vengeance hangeth over you; and the time soon cometh that he avengeth the blood of the saints upon you, for he will not suffer their cries any longer. (Mormon 8:37–41)

The following letter to the editor was written immediately after the original presentation:

February 16, 1989

Editor
The Daily Herald
1555 North 200 West
Provo, Utah 84601

Dear Sir:

People often say they do not understand me. They say
it so often that I should have the sense to shut up in public.
And now I have gone and done it again. Since it is a
preacher's duty to make himself understood, when he fails
he owes his hearers an apology. And I fail every time I step
into the past, where I prefer to spend my days. There my
students lose me. The past simply does not exist for us
today, except in old costume movies revived on TV. So the
idea of the age-old confrontation between agriculture and
industry in days long past rings no bells.

For example, nothing is more beyond dispute than that
people who worked in mines and mills have throughout
history been underpaid and overworked, living in unspeakably dismal conditions. Most of them right down to modern times have, in fact, been slaves. I have written feelingly
about them. But to interpret the above statement as a
description of the workers at Geneva, where friends and relatives of mine have worked from the beginning at far better wages than I ever received, is about as far as misunderstanding can go. And to say that it depicts them as hideous
and deformed dwarves, forging the fatal Rheingold, either
makes me the world's worst communicator or denotes a
hair-trigger predisposition to jump at conclusions.

Then why did I bring up the subject at all? We have here
a discussion that has reached something like a stalemate.
Each side accuses the other of being insufficiently informed,

and both are right. I have the advantage of being equally uninformed on both sides, and look on only as a spectator. But what I see is a drama of immense age and impact, something that has been quite fundamental to the scenario of life on this afflicted globe. We are told that in cases like this, one cannot know too much about the subject; and in an impulsive moment, acting on that unproven premise, I agreed to bring ancient instances into the discussion. That was a mistake. It is rash and foolhardy to go out for the recondite and esoteric stuff unless you are prepared to take it all the way, which is hardly to be done in half an hour.

Recently, indignant citizens have been reminding me of "what has made this country great." Unfortunately they can only tell me what has made it rich—a very different thing, as Socrates would tell you. Every time the Nephites got rich they stopped being great. What has made us rich in the first instance is vast, natural resources. Just an hour before sounding off, I listened to Jack Anderson tell how the Japanese, with none of our fabulous resources, are able to run rings around us in almost every department, getting very rich indeed by all-out work and dedication. But that is not real greatness—the soaring Dow-Jones is not forever. To me the austerity, the "plain living and high thinking" of old New England, the devout wisdom of the Founding Fathers, and the studious and courtly ways of a handful of Southern gentlemen showed us the way to be great—a way we have not followed.

Time did not allow me to give the conclusion to the talk, which was to declare that I no longer worry much about Geneva, that the only time it really got to me was on those sweet spring nights when every breath from the west reminded me of what I was missing. Unfortunately, breathing was not optional or I could have escaped that prejudice too. Today I see in Geneva a smoking fumarole at the base of a mighty volcano which is just about to blow—Jack Anderson's talk left me in little doubt about that. I take small comfort in the conviction that before long circumstances are going to settle the problem for us.

Sincerely,

Hugh Nibley

Notes

1. *JD* 6:94.

2. *JD* 8:79.

3. Spencer W. Kimball, "The False Gods We Worship," *Ensign* 6 (June 1976): 4 (emphasis added).

4. *MS* 22:738 (emphasis added).

5. *JD* 10:222.

6. Strabo, *The Geography of Strabo* XIV, 6, 5.

7. Plato, *Critias* 111A-D.

8. Ernst Wüst, "Puton," in *Paulys Realencyclopädie der Classischen Altertumswissenschaft*, 23 vols. (Stuttgart: Druckenmüller and Waldsee, 1951), 21:1:998–99.

9. Ibid., 21:1:1000.

10. J. Zwicker, "Plutos," in ibid., 21:1:1035.

11. William Shakespeare, *Timon of Athens*, act IV, scene iii, lines 28–29.

12. Phaedrus, *Fables* IV, 12.

13. William Shakespeare, *Macbeth*, act I, scene i, lines 14–15.

14. Ibid., act V, scene v, lines 49–51.

15. Ibid., act V, scene viii, lines 25–28.

16. Ibid., act I, scene iii, lines 137–41.

17. *MS* 17:337.

18. *MS* 17:338.

19. *MS* 17:338.

20. Aristotle, *Metaphysics* V, 2, 3–4.

21. Tertullian, *De Spectaculis* II, 89–90.

22. Jack Anderson, *Provo Daily Herald*, 2 January 1985, 21.

23. *JD* 8:297.

24. *JD* 8:294.

25. *JD* 15:127.

26. Cf. Cicero, *De Natura Deorum* II, 39; 45; 53.

27. *National Geographic* 174 (December 1988): front cover.

28. Charles W. Penrose, "O Ye Mountains High," in *Hymns of The Church of Jesus Christ of Latter-day Saints* (Salt Lake City: The Church of Jesus Christ of Latter-day Saints, 1985), no. 34, verse 1.

4

Promised Lands

Another World

When I first came to Provo shortly after World War II, I was approached by Brother Virgil Bushman, who had been called to revive the mission to the Hopi Indians after it had languished during the war. He urged me to go with him and promised me that I would see an ancient world probably much like the kind I would like to have found in the ancient Near East. I eagerly complied, and on a cold, bleak morning in March we approached the Third Mesa from the west. The landscape was utterly desolate, nothing in sight but sand and rock. Brother Bushman assured me that these were the fields of the Hopi. The men would come down every morning afoot or on their donkeys to walk out into the sand for a few miles. There with a stick they pushed down five kernels of corn twenty inches into the sand, hoping that it would strike the underground moisture from the Denebito Wash.

Each stalk of corn would grow only two feet or so and never bear more than a single ear of corn. This was their

---

This address, originally entitled "The Value of the Land," was given on 9 October 1992 at the J. Reuben Clark Law School to an assembled group of lawyers.

staff of life, their security, their capital. And yet they had
survived all the rigors of nature and the fierce pressure of
white intruders since the sixteenth century. Later I learned
that Sister Theresa Harvey's house in Walpi on the First
Mesa had been the first one measured by the new tree-ring
dating method and was found to be over 800 years old.

I was stunned by what I saw as we came through a low
arch at dawn out onto the spectacle of a splendid drama in
progress. Here, on a high, bleak rock, surrounded by nothing but what we would call total desolation in all directions,
was a full-scale drama in progress in the grand manner of
the Ancients. The only witnesses were a few shivering little
kids and some hunched-up old people on stone benches.
Everything was being carried out with meticulous care; all
the costumes were fresh and new; there was nothing that
could be bought in a store, nothing artificial—all the dyes,
woven stuff, and properties were taken from nature.

What an immense effort and dedication this represented! And for what? These were the only people in the
world that still took the trouble to do what the human race
had been doing for many millennia—celebrating the great
life-cycle of the year, the creation, the dispensations. I told
Brother Bushman that there should be fifty-two dancers,
and that is exactly what there were. Fifty-two was not only
the sacred number of the Asiatics and the Aztecs, but it was
also the set number of dancers in the archaic Greek chorus.
The dancing place was the bare plot which the Greeks
called the *konistra,* the sand patch where this world came in
contact with the other, at the crucial periods of the year.
That was the time when the *orcus mundi* was open—*mundus
patet*; that is, when the mouth of the other world was open
and the spirits of the ancestors attended the rites. By the
altar, of course, was the *sipapuni,* the mouth of the lower

world, the *orcus mundi*, at which the spirits from above and below could meet with their relatives upon the earth. This was the essential year-rite, found throughout the world from the earliest times. On either side of the altar was a small evergreen, adorned like a Christmas tree with prayer feathers, for as in countless ancient societies these dramas were sacred. I have written extensively on this theme, which is called "Patternism,"[1] but we can't go into it now. Suffice it to say, it was a miracle of survival, commonly recognized as the only surviving instance of the fully celebrated year-cycle.

Almost the first house one comes to in mounting up the climb to Hotevila where this was taking place was the dwelling of Tom and Belle Kuyushva. Tom was a Kikmongui, an honored elder, the nearest thing to a chief among these egalitarian and independent people, who have always eschewed any type of power structure. He wore all the splendid regalia—the silver and turquoise of an honored person—and was present in the seat of honor several years before, when Brother Bushman gave his first sermon. Brother Bushman spoke only about twenty minutes, and at the end, old Tom, who knew not a word of English, came up and asked to be baptized. Brother Bushman explained, "But you have only just barely heard me speak!" "But I know it's true," said Tom, who was ninety years old (incidentally, all his life he had been thoroughly immersed in the doctrines and customs of his people). He pointed to his breast and said, "I know it's true in here."

He was soon baptized and became an elder, and we should note that he and Brother Bushman had to go clear to Gallup to find enough water for baptizing. That's how desolate the land was; there was what they called Jacob's Well in Oraibi, but the water was poisonous. There was indeed a spring in Hotevila, which gave the place its name. The WPA wanted, by installing a pump, to relieve the women of Polacca from the trouble of going down the long trail to the water and fetching it up again on their heads. This was vigorously opposed by all. Were these people insane to reject such a convenience? Not at all. It was a way of life that your ancestors and mine had practiced for thousands of years since the days of Rebekah at the well. When the U.S. government wanted to install electric lines in Hotevila, the people repeatedly took down the poles. The government officials would put them up again, and the people would take them down again—they actually rejected the blessings of electricity and a ready water supply. I talk about these things to show how different their ways were from ours.

Since this is Homecoming Week, I may suggest a parallel. All the time my children were growing up, it was a special thrill for all of us to go out in front of the house during Homecoming Week to watch the lighting of the "Y"—the long, zigzag trail of flickering torches creeping up the mountain (a good 1000 feet), dividing and slowly enclosing the giant emblem with mysterious flickering orange flames, until the final glory. It was exciting, strenuous, thoroughly unnecessary, and everybody loved it. How silly, how wasteful, how impractical! Now we just throw a light switch and it's all done—as convenient and inspiring as lighting a billboard. That is the difference between our cultures. The torches on the mountainside served no practical purpose whatever, but the water trail up the mountain had been an absolute necessity for many centuries; what greater imperative than to preserve the operation just as it is, where an act of drudgery becomes an act of devotion and even fun? Pumps can and do break down.

The day after that first dance in Hotevila was Easter

Sunday. I was met in New Oraibi by a delegation of Hopi men who announced that they had just been in a session with the Mennonite, Baptist, and Methodist missionaries who had explained to them exactly why our Book of Mormon tells very much the same story as their own traditions. The explanation was this: When the great chief Tuba (for whom Tuba City was named) became a Mormon, he went to Salt Lake City to marry his wives in the temple there. While he was there, Joseph Smith got hold of him and pumped him for all the secrets of the Hopi. Then he sat down and wrote it all down in what became the Book of Mormon. It was not hard for me to set them straight simply by throwing out a few dates. The point of this story is the promise of common ground that we have with this strange people—the Book of Mormon is their story.

There is considerable general knowledge about certain salient traits of the Hopi which are not peculiar to them but characteristic of almost all Indians. The first of these is the way they see all things together. "I was seeing in a sacred manner the shapes of all things in the spirit," says Black Elk, "and the shape of all shapes as they must live together like one being. And I saw that the hoop of my people was one of the many hoops that made one circle, wide as daylight and as starlight, and in the center grew one mighty flowering tree to shelter all the children of one mother and one father. And I saw that it was holy."[2] Here we have that peculiar idiom which makes the Indian a total alien to our own culture. The culture is completely religious and therefore completely consistent. If you wrote an essay on Hopi farming, it would be an essay on Hopi religion; on Hopi hunting, it would be an essay on Hopi religion; an essay on Hopi family life, it would be an essay on Hopi religion; on Hopi games the same—on everything they do and think is their religion. As they see all things as a whole, all joined in a single divine pattern, like a great sand painting, so they feel that all who share a common life should act together. I have often heard them say that when they join the Church, it will be all together—as soon as we set them the example. This mysterious but very real oneness is beautifully expressed in our scriptures, which might have been written by Black Elk: "And now behold, all things have their likeness, and all things are created and made to bear record of me, both things which are temporal and things which are spiritual; things which are in the heavens above, and things which are on the earth, and things which are in the earth, and things which are under the earth, both above and beneath: all things bear record of me" (Moses 6:63). The Hopis have not only survived but prospered on their desolate mesas, the last place on earth anyone would covet. We find it foolish that they constantly protest the slightest change in the way of doing things—but it all hangs together, just as our projects continually fall apart as we insist on sanctifying growth and change.

From the beginning there was conflict between those who were willing to be ingratiating and comply to pressure from the U.S. government and those who rigidly opposed it. The one party was labeled "progressive," of course, and the other who called themselves the "traditionals" were called the "Hostiles." The leader of the traditional party in Oraibi was Tewaqueptewa, about whom many stories were told. I have talked with him often and bought many Kachina dolls, which he made of strictly native materials and sold for a dollar and a half apiece, never more or less. The anthropologists were fighting among themselves for these dolls, for which they could get high prices, and yet the great chief was practically giving them away. We just can't understand a thing like that. In 1906 there was a showdown between the progressives and Tewaqueptewa's party. They settled in a sensible fashion by a tug-of-war, the losing party going off to Moenkopi. Tewaqueptewa's daughter, Mina Lansa, was entrusted with the national treasures, always kept by a woman. Her husband, John Lansa, was the leader of the traditionalists.

One evening as it was getting dark I was passing by their house, the northernmost house in Old Oraibi, when Mina came out and beckoned me vigorously to come in. I wondered what I had done wrong, because new infringements of the whites were causing considerable tension. In the house the chief elders were seated all around the room. A small kitchen table and chair were in the middle of the room and a coal oil lamp was on the table. Mina told me to sit on the chair; then she went out of the room and soon returned with a bundle, something heavy wrapped in a blanket. She put it on the table and then unwrapped it. It was the holy tablet, the Hopi Stone, no less, the most sacred possession of the people. I knew what I was expected to do and started talking.

By an interesting coincidence I had spent the previous week in Cedar City with President William Palmer, a patriarch as well as stake president, who taught anthropology in the college there. He had been initiated into the Paiute tribe, and took me out to their sacred place in the plain southwest of Parowan. The building of the highway had put an end to the rites of initiation that once took place there, but President Palmer described the teachings and ordinances as far as was permitted. In particular he told the story of the descent of the Lord from heaven as if at that place, an event much like that described in 3 Nephi.

Tobats was the God of all Creation; his son Shinob was

the peacemaker full of love and eternally young. One day the Evil One Un-nu-pit killed Shinob. At once a great darkness fell upon "Tu-weap," the whole earth. It was absolute blackness for three days. In this chaos and confusion everyone was groping around in howling and lamentation. Finally, a voice from the top of the mountain spoke; it was Tobats the Father. He told them to move about with outstretched arms, calling out to each other, and joining hands with whoever one touched. Thus they formed lines, and the lines were instructed to join with each other; people in the lines were to cry out for husbands and wives and children until all families had reformed. Then the noise ceased, and a voice told them to climb the mountain or mesa where Tobats was. They worked their way up the mountain, toiling in human chains and finally forming a huge circular formation on the top, with Tobats in the middle. Well, Tobats said he would shoot an arrow straight up (this is the well-known Indian and world-wide theme of the arrow chain to heaven). His arrow produced a tiny spark of light; but the second arrow brought light, which grew like an explosion until it flooded all the land. The blackbird and the flicker have been honored ever since because their feathers were used for the arrows—they are perpetual reminders of the great event.[3] And thus the Indians typically reedit, according to the tribe and the land, those stories whose origin is lost in a distant past.

There were many things on the Hopi Stone that are never shown in the sketchy reproductions of it, but the main items were the wanderings of the people and upheavals of nature, the arrow-chain to heaven and the light descending from the clouds. I started to explain things in terms of what I had learned from President Palmer a few days before. As I talked the elders began whispering among themselves with some animation. Suddenly Mina snatched the stone from the table, clutched it tightly, and said excitedly, "You are a smart man—but you don't know everything!" Was I on the right track? I suspect so, because some years later, in 1965, when I was wandering in the sad desolation of Oraibi, now emptier than ever, I was approached again with an invitation to come to the house and see the Hopi Stone again. When I got there, there was confusion and excitement; something had happened. We would have to call it off. Everyone was going to where the meeting of the Tribal Council had just been held. The Tribal Council was a creation of the BIA, compliant to the will of the powers of the East, whose authority the traditionalists had never recognized. They had just that day leased a tract of the sacred Black Mesa to the Peabody Coal Company. The company had generously offered to provide trailer houses for the entire tribe if they would move to Los Angeles. A more colossal culture gap could not be imagined.

Here it is necessary to speak of that strange passion for the *land* with which all Indians seem to be obsessed. This state of mind can best be explained by reference to the Book of Mormon. In his great sermon to the Nephites the Lord declares, "Behold, the covenant which I have made with my people is not all fulfilled" (3 Nephi 15:8). "And behold, *this is the land of your inheritance; and the Father hath given it unto you*" (3 Nephi 15:13). Again he tells them to "write these sayings after I am gone, . . . that these sayings which ye shall write shall be . . . manifested unto the Gentiles, that through the fulness of the Gentiles, the remnant of their seed, who shall be scattered forth upon the face of the earth because of their unbelief, may be brought in" (3 Nephi 16:4). We are to take note of what they have written, and it is this: "Verily, verily, I say unto you, thus hath the Father *commanded* me—that I should give unto *this people this land for their inheritance*" (3 Nephi 16:16). The Hopi Stone, beautifully done on highly polished porphyr, is such a writing as the Nephites were ordered to make—a deed to the land. The Lord concludes with a final repetition: "And the Father hath commanded me that I should give unto you this land, for your inheritance. . . . And if the Gentiles do not repent . . . after they have scattered my people, . . . the sword of my justice shall hang over them at that day" (3 Nephi 20:14–15, 20).

What could be clearer? This land has been given to that particular branch of Israel as an inheritance for their children in perpetuity—it is their sacred obligation to hold it for their children; they cannot possibly sell it or allow it to be taken from them. That would be unthinkable, and that we never seem to understand.

Never the Twain Shall Meet

It would be hard to imagine two cultures more opposed than our own and that of the Indians. Typical of the total misunderstanding that still prevails is a statement by Ronald Vertrees, president of the Customs Clearing House, a Denver-based drilling supply firm, in a letter to the Navajo tribal council protesting favored treatment of the council in hiring Navajos on their own reservation. "'Given the historical facts, we consider ourselves to be members of the conquering and superior race and you to be members of the vanquished and inferior race. We hold your land and property to be spoils of war, ours by right of conquest. Through the generosity of our people, you have been given a reservation where you may prance and dance as you please, obeying your kings and worshipping your false gods.' . . . Contacted Monday, Vertrees said he has no

regrets about sending the letter," which appeared conspicuously in the *Salt Lake Tribune*, January 17, 1986, and elicited
no comment.[4] As is well known and often noted, the Treaty
of Guadalupe Hidalgo in 1848 recognized the sovereignty
of the Indian Nations. Between 1876 and 1893, trading
posts, missions, and schools were established—for profit. It
was the Presbyterians and not business or government that
built the small hospital. One day I picked up an old Navajo
woman who had just finished making a blanket at her
hogan near the sacred Blue Canyon (since dismantled by
Peabody); we went to the trading station at Tuba City,
where the man offered her $5 for her beautiful blanket. I
was standing by, witnessed the deal, and instantly offered
to buy the blanket. The man was furious—he had to sell it
to me for $10 instead of the $100 he could have got. I gave
the old lady another $5 and we parted happily, though I
have felt guilty ever since. Later I went back but found the
hogan deserted—the Navajos had been driven out.

At the turn of the century, schooling was compulsory
for Hopi boys, who were forced to cut their hair and forbidden to speak Hopi. Those elders who protested were
labeled the Hostiles. In 1891 and 1894 the Hostiles were
rounded up, arrested by U.S. troops, and imprisoned for a
time. In 1906 young people were sent to Carlisle Indian
School in the East, smaller children were sent to Keams
Canyon, and the Kikmongui, the most influential men, were
sent to the Sherman Indian School in California. When
Albert B. Fall became Secretary of the Interior in 1921, a
familiar plot was played out. The name of Albert Fall
should still ring a bell—Teapot Dome Oil and the scandals
of the Harding Administration. Standard Oil had discovered the oil on the reservations in 1921, and Fall went all out
to take over. "Along with various schemes to defraud the

Indians of their land, oil, and mineral rights would be injected a plan by Fall's Commissioner of Indian Affairs, Charles H. Burke, to deny the Indian what freedom of religion he still enjoyed."[5] "Freedom of Religion, as provided for in the Bill of Rights, rarely, until recent times, was even considered as applying to religions of the Indians of the United States [and today we still deny them peyote]. In fact, . . . it was government policy to aid missionaries in converting the Indians to one or another of the Christian denominations [and, incidentally, turned them against the Mormons]. Definite stipulations curtailing Indian freedom of religion were contained in the official Bureau of Indian Affairs regulations, often referred to as its 'Religious Crimes Code.'"[6] The suppression of the Sun Dance ceremony at the instance of missionaries and government officials "led to the enactment of a regulation which, although aimed particularly at the Sun Dance, concluded that 'all similar dances and so-called religious ceremonies, shall be considered 'Indian Offenses,' punishable by 'incarceration in the agency prison for a period not exceeding thirty days.'"[7]

"In 1922 . . . the Senate . . . pass[ed] the so-called Bursum bill, taking the most valuable agricultural lands of the Pueblo Indians of New Mexico."[8] In the following year Commissioner Burke wrote to all Indians: "I feel that something must be done to stop the neglect of stock, crops, gardens, and home interests caused by these dances or by celebrations, pow wows, and gatherings of any kind that take the time of the Indians for many days. . . . No good comes from your 'give-away' custom at dances and it should be stopped. . . . You do yourselves and your families great injustice when at dances you give away money and other property, perhaps clothing [had he never heard of Christmas?]. . . . I could issue an order against these useless and harmful performances, but I would much rather have you give them up of your own free will. . . . I urge you . . . to hold no gatherings in the months when the seed time, cultivation, and harvest need your attention, and at other times to meet for only a short period and have no drugs, intoxicants, or gambling and no dancing that Superintendent does not approve. If at the end of one year the reports which I receive show . . . that you reject this plea then some other course will have to be taken."[9] Need we recall that God commanded Moses to lead the people in the great feasts at the seed time, cultivation, and harvest? Just as he commanded them to waste their time resting on the Sabbath?

Three hundred and seventy formal treaties with the Indians, which by the Constitution are the law of the land, have nearly all been violated as ninety percent of the land has been taken from them. The Dawes Act of 1887 was held as a liberating gesture, for it allowed individual Indians to own the land privately and, best of all, to sell it, which was the purpose of the whole thing, of course. In 1934 the Indian Reorganization Act set up the tribal councils for a democratic representation. The Indian votes *No* by not voting at all—after all the *Yes* votes are counted, it is assumed that the rest vote *No*, since all must vote. Oliver Lefarge explained that to the Commission, but they went ahead and installed Tribal Councils with the tiniest possible number of Indians approving—the *No*-votes did not count.

In 1946 the Indian Claims Act compensated Indians in money for their lands but deprived them of all title. The government could claim to be acting in good faith, since we sincerely believed that *anything* could be honestly and fairly had if *enough* money was offered for it. The most vicious proviso of the Act allowed lawyers to receive ten percent of the fee that was paid, and an army of lawyers descended from all sides to help the Indians settle the compulsory compensation. The Utes did not want the money—they wanted the land, and they still say so. But Ernest L. Wilkinson was able to make a settlement for $30 million, collected his ten percent, and came to Provo trailing clouds of glory and talking loudly of Manifest Destiny.

I got to know him quite well, beginning with our clash at the very first faculty meeting. He had given a degree to a friend in Washington, and some of the faculty protested that degrees should be bestowed or at least approved by colleges, such being the immemorial practice of universities. Well, a paper was circulated to that effect, and some people signed it. Wilkinson stormed into that first faculty meeting in a towering rage: This has nothing to do with right or wrong, whether it was moral or immoral is irrelevant. The only question is, was it *legal*? Who would dare question him on a point of law? Who signed this protest? I had signed it, so I stood up, and I was the only one. "Come and see me in my office!" I did, and we became good friends—being a lawyer, he was not at all upset by adversarial confrontation; in fact, he enjoyed it. I was his home teacher at the time, and he started out at the "Y" by familiarizing himself with the students with a fireside at his house, followed by other such firesides, some of which I attended. The theme of his discussion in all of these was, "What is the difference between being dishonest and being shrewd?" He illustrated each time by his own case. When he was in Washington fresh out of law school, he was looking for a job, and so found himself in Senator King's office. The senator was not there, but the secretary allowed him to use the phone for what he said was an urgent call. It was urgent indeed, for he called up the office of Justice Charles Evans Hughes and said, "This

is Senator King's office speaking. I would like to recommend a certain young man, etc., of high qualifications to
work for the Justice." And so he became a clerk to the celebrated Chief Justice Charles Evans Hughes—not dishonest,
just shrewd.

At the second faculty meeting we got another shocker.
The family that owned the farm on Temple Hill where
President Wilkinson wanted the land for expansion refused
to sell. President W. would appeal to eminent domain, but it
was his introductory remark that rocked us: "I never yet
saw a contract I couldn't break," he boasted. I mention this
because this has been our ace-card in dealing with the
Indians through the years—aptness in breaking and ignor-
ing contracts.

When I got out of the army in 1946, I made a beeline for
the Colorado Plateau, lived with a ranch family in
Hurricane, and traveled all over the area on roads at that
time marked on the maps with such inviting admonitions
as "Do not enter without guides," and "Carry water," and
"Make inquiries." The impressive thing was the utter desolation into which the Indians had been turned out to starve,
like the scapegoat in the desert. But before long the same
vast area was buzzing with activity. Helicopters and specially equipped trucks were everywhere looking for uranium. Promptly a decree from Washington forbade any
Hopi to go out of sight of his mesa. That was a hard one to
enforce, so it was followed up by another that in order to
operate, one would have to have at least ten million dollars
capital. So the Hopis were out of it.

What a turnabout! For all those years they had nothing
we wanted—having turned them out from any valuables
they happened to be sitting on; but now even this desolate
place had the very things we wanted most of all. We on the

other hand always believed quite sincerely that what the Indians most wanted and needed must surely be our superior knowledge and technology. Technology was all we had to offer after all, but, as we have seen, they refused that—even vital water pumps for Polacca were turned down, and attempts to electrify Hotevila in 1984 and 1986 were deliberately wrecked—we would say vandalized, which is exactly how the Indians viewed our activities on the land. The supreme irony is that our technology will not work without their energy, locked up in the coal, the oil, the natural gas, the uranium, and the water, which we are exhausting at a record rate. You are probably familiar with the so-called Hopi-Navajo controversy. I have watched Hopi and Navajo barter in total silence, since neither understood the other's language, and in perfect amity. They would meet and celebrate their pow-wows together, and everybody had a great time. But that has stopped since the discovery of coal and oil on the sacred Black Mesa—controversy has been stirred up between them, though the Hopis have been perfectly content to let the Navajos graze on the northern areas as they have for generations. The game has been to push the Navajos off land which the Hopis do not use and so let the Big Boys move into it. I heard Barry Goldwater declare on TV that if the Navajos did not move out of their homes, he, as commander of the Arizona National Guard, would send in his helicopter gunships and drive them out. Our little Vietnam. Finally, the so-called Trilateral Commission of energy and military interests has recommended that the entire Colorado Plateau be set aside as a "National Sacrifice Area," in which the coal, oil, uranium, natural gas, timber, and water could be extracted, the power developed in huge coal-burning plants immune to EPA regulation against pollution, with power lines, railroad lines, slurry lines crossing the area to take the final product to the great cities of the coast and to animate the million light bulbs that are the glory of Las Vegas. It was a sacrifice area because there would be no obligation whatever to observe any niceties in extracting the stuff and especially to restoring any of the landscape after it had been ruined. Naturally in this scheme the Hopis have been considered nothing but a primitive obstruction—hence the generous offer to move them all to the dire inner city of Los Angeles.

The Two Ways

The ancient doctrine of the Two Ways is a lively one with the Hopis. A thing is either Hopi or Ka-Hopi. When I first went there they spoke of *three ways,* those of the Hopi, the Pahana, and the Momona—the Mormons, which in the early days were manifestly not typically Pahana, who in fact were constantly denouncing them to the Indians. But one of the best Indian men I know told me very recently that the Indians no longer consider the Mormons their friends. And it is not hard to understand why. There is a bitter joke among the Navajo today: "What is the Peabody Corporation?" Answer, "A bunch of Mormon lawyers getting rich." A list of the nineteen principal corporations seeking the wealth of the Colorado Plateau in order of the money invested begins with Pacific Gas and Electric, with the controlling stock owned by the Rothschild family. We go down the list of awesome and familiar names such as the City Bank of New York controlling the Public Service Company of New Mexico; number four in the list is the Arizona Public Service Corporation with its huge coal-burning power plants selling electricity far and wide, the main investor being the Latter-day Saint Church. We go on to Standard Oil of Ohio, controlled by British Petroleum

Ltd.; the Gulf Corporation, by the Mellon and Hunt families; Utah International, by General Electric; Peabody Coal Company, by Equitable Life of New York; El Paso Gas, Coal and Power, by the Latter-day Saint Church; and so on to Shell Oil, Mobile Oil (Bankers Trust of New York, Hess family, John Paul Getty, Manufacturers Hanover Bank; Citibank, J. P. Morgan).

Is all this for the Indians' own good? When the Navajos asked for an increase in the royalties they were receiving for their coal from $.15 a ton to $1.50 a ton, they were roundly denounced, according to the *New York Times,* by Mormon lawyers, so specified, for jeopardizing the sanctity of a contract—had they no shame?

With increasing interest in the Indians and a considerable, growing literature on the subject, the Mormons are regularly given a black eye in books and articles—a black eye which they would not deserve if they would only pay a little more attention to their scriptures. There is one common ground, one common need, between us and them, and it is the Book of Mormon. Consider how much it tells us about the present situation. First of all, we accept the Great Spirit—we do not consider the Indians heathen. King Lamoni mistook the visiting superman Ammon for the Great Spirit, a mistake which his descendants have made more than once, to their loss. To his servants he said, "I know that [this] is the Great Spirit; and he has come down at this time to preserve your lives" (Alma 18:4). But Ammon explained that he was not the Great Spirit: "Believest thou that there is a God?" (Alma 18:24). Lamoni: "I do not know what that meaneth" (Alma 18:25), or What are you talking about? Ammon: "Believest thou that there is a Great Spirit? And he said, Yea. And Ammon said *This is God, . . .* this Great Spirit . . . is God [who] created all things" (Alma

18:26–28). Can we not safely say that we believe on that same Great Spirit who is God, just as we believe in Allah when we understand who he is? Our missionaries in Lebanon had no other name for him.

In the second place we believe the one thing which the Indians are constantly emphasizing, that all things are spiritual; to be carnally minded, says the Book of Mormon, is death, but to be spiritually minded is eternal life. Carnal mindedness embraces those four things which both Nephis declare will destroy any society, namely seeking for power, gain, popularity, and the lusts of the flesh (1 Nephi 22:23; 3 Nephi 6:15). For particulars see your local TV guide. In the third place is their attitude to nature, which is their livelihood, beautifully summed up in Doctrine and Covenants 49: "For behold, the beasts of the field and the fowls of the air, and that which cometh of the earth, is ordained for the use of man for food and for raiment, and that he might have in abundance. But it is not given that one man should possess that which is above another, wherefore the world lieth in sin. And wo unto man that sheddeth blood or that wasteth flesh and hath no need" (D&C 49:19–21). This is the creed of the Hopi which so shocks us. If you live on a soaring rock 200 yards long and 50 yards wide with a hundred other families, you will find little room to accumulate the things of this world.

What we are speaking of is that ideal society described in the Book of Mormon as being established by the Lord in person, to succeed and fulfill the Law of Moses, that society which we should both emulate. Quoting from 4 Nephi, "And there were no contentions and disputations among them [the Hopi, as we all know, are a peaceable people and do everything to avoid violence—are we that way?], and every man did deal justly one with another [no money, no law courts]. And they had all things [in] common among them ["if one has corn we all have corn"]; therefore there were not rich and poor, bond and free, but they were all made free, and partakers of the heavenly gift. . . . And the Lord did prosper them exceedingly in the *land*; Yea, insomuch that they did build cities" (4 Nephi 1:2–3, 7). But it wasn't easy—they had to work at it exactly as the Hopis do, meticulously carrying out all the prescribed functions. These are, it is true, mere "forms and observances," but they "point their minds forward," as with the Nephites—did not old Tom in Hotevila instantly recognize and accept the gospel because he was the most thoroughly trained man of the village in his own religion? "And they did not walk any more after the performances and ordinances of the law of Moses; but they did walk after the commandments which they had received from their Lord and their God, continuing in fasting and prayer, and in meeting together oft both to pray and to hear the word of the Lord. . . . And . . . there was no contention among all the people, in all the land" (4 Nephi 1:12–13). To this day and against fearful cultural and economic opposition, the Hopis persist in their fasting and their prayers; they meet together unfailingly to pray each week—all the villages come together for ceremonies at one place. There the Baho-feathers are always in evidence, for they are the call to prayer. But the dances are also accompanied by sermons, teaching things of life and death, even as temple sessions of the Latter-day Saints in the early days were followed by dancing,[10] and as the great celebrations of Israel as ordered by Moses always required rejoicing and dancing to the sound of the timbrel, the sackbut, and the drum. I have seen such happy ring dances of Jewish elders performed near the Wailing Wall in Jerusalem while members of our Latter-day Saint tour group expressed lively disapproval of such undignified goings-on. In the times of upheaval and destruction, the legends tell us, the Hopi have survived by coming together on the mountain-tops and singing together, uniting their voices in praise, until the evil passes. Even so I can still hear my grand-mother fervidly singing, "When thy judgments spread destruction, keep us safe on Zion's hill; singing praises, singing praises, songs of glory unto thee," etc.[11] That goes back to the Jaredites and their sing-ins while they crossed the violent ocean (Ether 6:9).

After two hundred years the Nephites relaxed and reverted to the easier program of privatization: "And from that time forth they did have their goods and their sub-stance no more common among them. And they began to be divided into classes; [business was booming] and they began to build up churches unto themselves to get gain, and began to deny the true church of Christ. . . . And yet they did deny the more parts of his gospel. . . . And this church did multiply exceedingly . . . because of the power of Satan who did get hold upon their hearts" (4 Nephi 1:25–28). This is surely an ominous statement. The people claimed to worship Christ, and they did have parts of the gospel, but Satan was their inspiration. We will consider their condition later, but first let us ask whether there is any chance at all of our two cultures merging with their present teachings intact. In the Doctrine and Covenants we read that "My gospel shall go unto the Lamanites" (D&C 28:8) and all nations through the Book of Mormon. "And this was their [the Nephites'] faith—that my gospel . . . might come unto their brethren the Lamanites, and also all that had become Lamanites because of their dissensions" (D&C 10:48). That broad and inclusive term includes a rich ethnic mix, specified in the Book of Mormon as Nephites,

Zoramites, Mulekites, Jaredites, and others who may have become Lamanites; there are as well broad implications of other people, including "former inhabitants of this continent" (Joseph Smith–History 1:34), making contacts. "They did leave a blessing upon this land in their prayers [how very Indian!]. . . . And now, behold, according to their faith in their prayers [also very Indian, that obsessive faith in prayer itself] will I bring *this part* of my gospel to the knowledge of my people" (D&C 10:50, 52).

Would not that have a disruptive effect on their established traditions? On the contrary, it would strengthen them: "Behold, I do not bring it to destroy that which they *have* received, but to build it up. And for this cause have I said: If this generation [of Lamanites] harden not their hearts, I will establish my church among them" (D&C 10:52–53). But what effect will this have on the members of the restored Church—if the Indians have nothing to lose by joining the Church, do the church members stand in any danger of contamination? Not at all! "Now I do not say this to destroy my church, but I say this to build up my church; Therefore, whosoever belongeth to my Church *need not fear*, for such shall inherit the kingdom of heaven. But it is they who do not fear me, neither keep my commandments but build up churches unto themselves to *get gain*, yea, and all those that do wickedly and build up the kingdom of the devil— . . . it is they that I will disturb" (D&C 10:54–56).

We need the resources of "backward people" for raw materials as we need their markets for expansion. It is the old imperialist game, with energy as the good of first intent. But they don't need anything we have, neither our goods nor our money; all they want is the land. For that matter, our own people are soon glutted with the products of the ever-expanding corporate giants. Nothing amazed me more in the remote backwaters of the Fayyum in Egypt, among villages unchanged for five or six thousand years (and looking and acting very much like Hopi villages, incidentally), in this most stable of all civilizations to see the landscape dominated by enormous American billboards, "Come to Marlboro Country!" The Americans won't take any more of the poison stuff, so now it must be forced on the poor backward Egyptians; and so now we too must be prodded, wheedled, shamed, and beguiled into buying more stuff by enormously costly and ingenious sales campaigns; every ten minutes our absorption in the soap or sport or documentary is interrupted with a "message" demanding our instant and undivided attention. No wonder we have lost all capacity for concentration or critical thought, and, above all, reflection and meditation, preeminent Indian skills.

In 1540 when Pedro de Tovar came up to Bear Chief, who was standing to greet him on the rise at Old Oraibi, the chief reached out his hand to establish the visitor's identity by offering him the sacred handclasp, the *nachwach*—was he really the promised White Brother? Naturally, the Spaniard, who had come looking for gold and nothing else, thought he was asking for money and placed a gold coin in his hand. Have you any signs or tokens? asked the chief. Yes, I have money, replied the visitor. From that moment the Hopis knew it was not the one they were looking for,[12] and to this day they have never been converted to Christianity. We are most fortunate in possessing Satan's game-plan, which he gave away in a fit of temper in the Garden of Eden. The perennial source of wealth, the treasures of the earth, are to be controlled by the convenient symbols of a money economy, gold and silver; these are used to buy up kings and presidents, armies and navies, popes and priests. They are controlled by "secret combinations, to get power and gain" (Ether 8:22; cf. 8:18–19), and the result is rule by violence. Adam rejected the plan, but Cain bought into it, and so became "master of this great secret, that I may murder and get gain" (Moses 5:31)—the great design which at last is nearing fulfillment in our day of converting all living things into marketable commodities.[13]

We may be puzzled about the Indian's insistence in viewing all things, including the earth itself, as alive, though it is a doctrine clearly taught by Joseph Smith, Brigham Young, and other of our prophets. We say a human is worth more than an owl, but, as Black Elk puts it, what do we care for humans? To reverence life is to reverence all life. "I could see that the Wasichus did not care for each other the way our people did before the nation's hoop was broken. They would take everything from each other if they could, and so there were some who had more of everything than they could use, while crowds of people had nothing at all and maybe were starving."[14]

The first revelation in the Doctrine and Covenants puts us into the picture which the Indian sees of us: "Every man walketh in his own way, and after the image of his own god, whose image is in the likeness of the world, and whose substance is that of an idol, which waxeth old and shall perish in Babylon, even Babylon the great, which shall fall. . . . The hour is not yet, but is nigh at hand, when peace shall be taken [away] from the earth, and the devil shall have power over his own dominion" (D&C 1:16, 35).

And so we get to the ultimate prophecies, which we also share with the Indians.

> And I command you that ye shall write these sayings after I am gone. . . . But wo . . . unto the unbelieving of the Gentiles . . . [who] have scattered my people . . . and have . . . trodden [them underfoot]. . . . At that day when the

Gentiles shall sin against my gospel, and shall reject the fulness of my gospel, and *shall be lifted up in the pride of their hearts above all nations, and above all the people of the whole earth*, and shall be filled with all manner of lyings, and of deceits, and of mischiefs, and . . . hypocrisy, and murders, and priestcrafts, and whoredoms, and of secret abominations [again consult your *TV Guide*]. (3 Nephi 16:4, 8–10)

Note that lying comes first in the list, a judgment that few will dispute today.[15] "If they shall do all those things, and shall reject the fulness of my gospel, . . . I will bring the fulness of my gospel from among them. And then will I remember my covenant which I have made unto my people . . . and I will bring my gospel unto them. . . . The Gentiles shall not have power over you; . . . and ye shall come unto the knowledge of the fulness of my gospel. But if the Gentiles will repent and return unto me, . . . behold, they shall be numbered among my people, O house of Israel. And I will not suffer my people . . . [to] tread them down" (3 Nephi 16:10–14). There is an ominous note here which we cannot pursue.

The promise is repeated in the last speech to the Nephites: "Verily, verily, I say unto you, thus hath the Father commanded me—that I should give unto this people this land for their inheritance" (3 Nephi 16:16). "And it shall come to pass that all lyings, and deceivings, and envyings, and strifes, and priestcrafts, and whoredoms shall be done away. . . . But if they will repent . . . I will establish my church among them, and they shall come in unto the covenant and be numbered among this the remnant of Jacob, unto whom I have given this land for an inheritance; And they shall assist my people, the remnant of Jacob, and also as many of the house of Israel as shall come, that they may build a city, which shall be called the New Jerusalem" (3 Nephi 21:19, 22–24). Throughout these explicit prophecies it is the Gentiles who join "the Lamanites and those who have become Lamanites," not the other way around. If we are to be saved, we must move in their direction.

Notes

1. See *CWHN* 4:21–22, 366–67, 383; 6:xv, 295–310, 506; 8:247–48, 301–2, 317–18.

2. *Black Elk Speaks*, as told through John G. Neihardt (Lincoln, NB: University of Nebraska Press, 1988), 43.

3. William R. Palmer, *Two Pahute Indian Legends: "Why the Grand Canyon Was Made" and "The Three Days of Darkness"* (Cheney, WA: Citizen Journal Press, 1987), 21–22.

4. "Racial Navaho Letter Prompts Removal of Subcontractor," *Salt Lake Tribune*, 17 January 1986.

5. Harry C. James, *Pages from Hopi History* (Tucson: University of Arizona Press, 1974), 185.

6. Ibid.

7. Ibid., 185–86.

8. Ibid., 186.

9. Ibid., 187–88.

10. Heber C. Kimball Journal, cited in Elden J. Watson, *Brigham Young Addresses 1836–1849*, vol. 1 (n.p., 1979): "Pres. Young called the attention of the whole company, and gave them a message . . . that this temple [Nauvoo] was a holy place, and that when we danced we danced unto the Lord, and that no person would be allowed to come on to this floor, and afterwards mingle with the wicked. . . . He strongly impressed upon the mind of those present the impropriety of mingling again with the wicked after having come in here, and taken upon them the covenants" (1 January 1846).

11. William Williams, "Guide Us, O Thou Great Jehovah," in *Hymns of The Church of Jesus Christ of Latter-day Saints* (Salt Lake City: The Church of Jesus Christ of Latter-day Saints, 1985), no. 83, verse 3.

12. Frank Waters, *Book of the Hopi* (New York: Ballantine Books, 1963), 308–9.

13. Jerry Mander, *In the Absence of the Sacred: The Failure of Technology and the Survival of the Indian Nations* (San Francisco, CA: Sierra Club Books, 1991); regarding Hopis, see 268–86.

14. *Black Elk Speaks*, 217.

15. Paul Gray, "Lies, Lies, Lies," *Time* (5 October 1992): 32–38.

PART 2

Politics

5

In the Party but Not of the Party

This is an assigned topic, continuing by request the theme of "Beyond Politics," which was the subject of a talk three years ago [1973], and was given as a personal excuse for bypassing political activity. But the First Presidency tells us that we should be active in the field. And so the question arises, Why should the Saints, endowed with knowledge from on high, bother with a petty and sordid business? It is to that question that I now address myself. We must needs get into the action because we have no choice. Consider a classic story and example.

Behold Paul going up to the temple at the time of pilgrimage (cf. Acts 21:1). He is spotted by some Jews from a town in Asia Minor where he had stirred things up, and they try to stop him—"He is bringing Greeks into the temple!" they scream as they try to drag him away (cf. Acts 21:28). As a result, the entire *polis* flared up in instant rioting in the manner of Near Eastern cities to this day. The word *polis* is significant here, since it designates the community in its political aspects. As a result the temple gates were actually closed during the pilgrimage.

This BYU Academics Lecture was given 3 June 1976.

Jerusalem at this time was an occupied city, and the man in charge of keeping peace for the Romans was the tribune Lysias, a freedman who had worked his way up the hard way and didn't want to lose his job and his head. Personally leading a formidable group of soldiers and centurions to the spot, he arrested Paul and began to ask questions and take names. But there was so much shouting with everybody yelling at once that he couldn't go on, so he took Paul back to the headquarters heavily guarded, for the screaming mob followed them through the streets all the way. At the Castellum (which has recently been discovered and partly restored—an impressive structure), he asked Paul whether he was not a certain Egyptian, a very much wanted leader of the Sicarii, a political action group then hiding out in the desert. The Sicarii carried little knives (*sikkin*) under their shirts and would use them in liquidating undesirables. Paul said no, he was, on the contrary, of an important city, and he asked for permission to address the crowd.

From the balcony he talked in Hebrew, so that only the troublemakers understood him. He said he too had once been a Zealot like them (that is the word used, as we all know, to designate a party of political extremists). He told them the story of his conversion and explained his mission to the whole world. The result was more rioting, with Paul being dragged back into the office, where the tribune was determined to clear things up among all these conflicting claims by examining Paul under the lash. As he was being bound, Paul asked a centurion if it was customary to beat Roman citizens without even giving them a hearing. The worried centurion lost no time in reporting to the tribune, who questioned Paul about his citizenship. To get out of a ticklish situation, Lysias passed the buck to the high priests and the council of the Jews. Paul began by proclaiming innocence and was hit in the mouth. Paul's instant reaction was to call the man a damned hypocrite; but when they told him not to talk that way to a high priest, he immediately apologized, and then in telling his story cleverly achieved a deadlock between the Pharisees and the Sadducees by throwing their favorite apple of discord—the resurrection—into their midst. The result was not just a disputation among the scribes but another four-star riot which brought the Roman troops back to rescue Paul, who was about to be torn apart.

Next, forty fanatics conspired to get Paul out of Roman hands long enough to murder him, the chief priests and elders agreeing to the plot. But Paul's nephew overheard things and hurried to tell Paul at the Castellum. Paul called a centurion and said that his nephew had news which would interest the top man. It would indeed. It behooved the tribune to check on every threat and rumor in this powder-keg of a city. What the commander wanted most at that point was to get Paul out of there. So there was a change of venue, and Paul went with a very impressive escort to Caesarea on the coast with a letter declaring him absolutely innocent and passing the buck to Felix, the Roman governor of the whole province. Paul was kept there in custody in Herod's palace, which now served as a praetorium or military headquarters. Hard on his heels came the delegation from Jerusalem, the high priests and important elders, bringing a high-powered Roman lawyer with them. He reminded Felix in court that he was responsible for law and order, that Paul was stirring up the whole nation; nay, as ring leader of a sect which was troubling the peace of the entire empire, he had crowned his criminal activity by causing a disturbance at the national shrine of the Jews. In his defense Paul, addressing Felix, who sat as "judge unto this nation" (Acts 24:10), stated that there was no disturbance at all until the people from Asia started making trouble in Jerusalem, and that the council itself had found him guiltless. Felix said he would have to wait for Lysias the tribune to come and confirm all this. While Paul was being kept under house arrest, Felix's wife, Drusilla, who was a Christian, drew Paul and her husband into some gospel conversations in which Paul's moral fervor alarmed the governor, whose principles were not above reproach. He kept Paul for two years, hoping for a payoff from the Christians (he knew about their organization from his wife).

Before he could collect anything, Felix was replaced by Porcius Festus, a personal friend of Claudius the emperor, who was out to achieve another step in his *gradus honorum* by keeping Rome's most difficult province under control— for if there was one thing the emperor did not want, it was more trouble in Judea. Festus began his term with a courtesy visit to Jerusalem, where the dignitaries joined in asking him to send Paul back to that city—for there was another plot to murder him as soon as he was out of Roman hands. But Festus properly pointed out that since the administrative headquarters were at Caesarea, it would be better for them all to come there. In the Roman magisterium, legislative, executive, and judicial authority all resided in a single exalted official. Paul declared in the court that he had broken no laws of (1) the Jews, (2) the temple, or (3) the Romans. To keep the Jews satisfied, Festus asked Paul if he wouldn't be willing to go to Jerusalem. "Why?" said Paul. "I am standing now before Caesar's judgment seat, the only proper court for this case; I am innocent, and I appeal to Caesar." Conferring with legal council, Festus saw his chance to get rid of Paul by sending him to Rome.

Soon after, Herod Agrippa, the king of the Jews, came with his wife to pay a courtesy call on the new governor; and among other things, Festus raised the case of Paul, whose position was now extremely dangerous, for Herod Agrippa was a personal friend of the emperor Claudius, with whom he had been to school, and had been made king of the Jews by the helping hand of the Roman Tenth Legion. Because Herod was only half Jewish, the desire of his life was to be accepted by the people as their legitimate ruler. So here we have Herod eager to gratify the Romans and the Jews, Festus supporting him as his best chance of controlling the populace, and the only thing that would quiet them was to appease the rowdy factions; and the only thing that would satisfy *them* was Paul's head. Paul was to be the fall guy. The governor gave a magnificent reception for Agrippa and Bernice, and Paul was brought in as part of the entertainment. As Professor Garrod has shown, the standard form of entertainment at high-class Roman parties was listening to rhetorical recitals, as we listen to music.[1] Paul was part of the show and played his part very skillfully by an oration that put everybody into high good humor. He flattered Herod as the great authority on all Jewish matters, and Festus as the model judge and governor. When Festus joked that Paul had become balmy with too much study, they all laughed; and when Agrippa topped that by saying that Paul had almost converted him, they laughed even louder. When the high-ups and their wives talked it over among themselves, they agreed that there was nothing wrong with Paul, but to Caesar he must go. So the little nobody who got some hoods mad at him in the streets of a provincial town in Asia Minor ends up with personal letters to the emperor of the world—the Oecumene (cf. Acts 21–26).

These are typical episodes from Paul's missionary career, in which we find him perpetually in *political* hot water. Why? Because only under such strange circumstances could he accomplish his mission. What was that mission? At the time of his conversion Ananias said: "Brother Saul, receive thy sight. . . . The God of our fathers has chosen thee. . . . For thou shalt be his witness unto all men of what thou hast seen and heard" (Acts 22:13–15). "And the night following the Lord stood by him, and said, Be of good cheer, Paul: for as thou hast testified of me in Jerusalem, so must thou bear witness also at Rome" (Acts 23:11)—two completely corrupt cities. (How often does the Lord apply the word "corrupt" to our modern world in his first words to the Prophet Joseph? [Joseph Smith–History 1:19].) "I am Jesus whom thou persecutest. . . . But rise, and stand upon thy feet: for I have appeared unto thee *for this purpose,* to make thee a minister and a witness. . . . I will appear unto thee; Delivering thee from the people, and from the Gentiles, unto whom now I send thee" (Acts 26:15–17; emphasis added). Why send him to the people and the gentiles if he has to be delivered from them? "To open their eyes, and to *turn* them from darkness to light, and from the power of Satan unto God" (Acts 26:18; emphasis added).

That was his mission: He had to go down into the gutter if he was to get anybody out of it! And you can be sure that Satan is not going to relinquish his power over anybody without a fight!

In all of this the attentive student of Church history recognizes familiar overtones. If we shift the drama from its setting of Olympian grandeur and unlimited wealth amidst the accumulated glories of immemorial antiquity to the plain, homespun backwoods theater of the American frontier of the nineteenth century, stretching from western New York to the Great Salt Lake, we find the plot and the characters strangely intact. The Prophet Joseph and the brethren go forth to preach; religious leaders raise up mobs against them; ambitious politicians see a chance to get into the act; the military are drawn in to quell or excite popular unrest, their leaders acting under the instruction of judges and governors until the case goes right on up to the president himself. Forty-six times Joseph Smith appeared before the magistrates. The mobs were both political and religious, led by ministers, who as often as not were military officers, working in cooperation with murderous extremist conspiracies, while the *haute monde* (high mannered) was kept agog in Europe and America by a sensation-mongering press. Everywhere the elders went, their itinerary was marked by rioting and arrest, and almost never were they proven guilty of any illegal behavior.

We will recall that the ancient apostles went through the same routine and for the same reason, going forth "as sheep among wolves" to "turn the world upside down," as the charge ran against them. Like the missionaries in this dispensation, the nature of their activity naturally involved them in showdowns with every level of society. This is what we call being "in the world," where they had to go in order to call people "out of the world." Exactly the same applied to the Lord himself. The complicated threads of his trial and execution are still being untangled, but it is always the same cast of characters and the same reaction; and from the human side the story is predominantly political in nature.

Earlier, Daniel and his friends held high political office and served well, but they ran afoul of leaders of religion and jealous political rivals, who stirred up the king and the nation against them to encompass their death. This was possible because of the unflinching religious and moral position they took, which made them conspicuously peculiar and a standing rebuke to the society at large—and also made possible trumped-up charges against them. It was very effective but a very dangerous form of publicity for their cause.

Still earlier, the prophets all achieved maximum attention from the highest to the lowest of the people by addressing the crowds in the streets and at the temple or in the desert, or chatting intimately with kings upon their thrones—and by preserving their peculiar aloofness and persisting in their unwelcome message, courting and often achieving martyrdom. Moses, brought up at the court of the pharaoh and intimate with the chieftains of the desert, was a political as well as a religious leader, for the law he gave to Israel was their civil as well as their religious code. Abraham the wanderer was constantly making contacts and contracts with kinglets, priests, sheikhs, and individual landowners (most of whom took advantage of him), but everywhere preaching the gospel as Abraham the missionary. The friend of God and the friend of man, in a hysterically insecure and restless world (drought was the ruling influence), he always did the fair and politic thing, and paid the highest price for his independence—he would deal and bargain, but he would not join up. Enoch came as a missionary, "a strange thing in the land; a wild man hath come among us" (Moses 6:38)—great publicity. So they came forth to hear him and were at first alarmed by his teaching; then "all men were offended" (Moses 6:37) by it; but he began to make converts and draw them off, founded his own church, then his own city, and finally brought all those who would follow him *out* of the world. That was Paul's assignment also: "To open their eyes, and to turn them from darkness to light, and from the power of Satan unto God" (Acts 26:18).

All these men were "in the world but not of the world"—up to their neck in politics, yet maddeningly aloof from political commitment to any party or faction. It is very much a political drama, this restoration of the gospel. It seems so astonishingly uniform regardless of time or place that one must ask, Can this be a part of God's plan for the salvation of the human race, this steady immersing of God's chosen messengers in human affairs at their most distracting, tumultuous, and corrupt level? The answer is found in what are structurally the strangest passages in the scriptures, sections that are more suggestive of a graphically worked-out diagram than ordinary narrative or doctrine.

I refer to chapters 14, 15, and 17 of the Gospel of John and chapter 19 of 3 Nephi. The summary of all our relationships to other beings is given in these chapters from the lips of the Savior. Chapter 17 is a prayer, and it corresponds to another prayer delivered by the Lord in the Book of Mormon, 3 Nephi 19:20–23 and 28–29. Those six short verses contain no less than 70 personal pronouns; of the three chapters in John, chapter 14 (thirty-one verses) contains 165 personal pronouns; chapter 15 (twenty-seven verses) contains 136; and chapter 17 (only twenty-six verses) contains 166—in all some 467 personal pronouns in three short chapters!

In Nephi's version the whole relationship of every man to every other person in the universe is set forth using a vocabulary of just 32 words: 10 personal pronouns repeated 70 times, 6 prepositions, 7 verbs, 4 participles, and only 5 nouns: "Father," "Holy Ghost," "world," "words," and "faith." From this tiny packet the whole system is set forth. The structure uses personal pronouns as bricks, with prepositions and a few

verbs as mortar. The few nouns are the all-important indication to show what all those pronouns refer to.

This is what we find in the three chapters of John: There
are seven parties working on seven different levels: Father,
Son, Holy Ghost, apostles, Saints, the world, the prince of
this world—each of the first five acting on behalf of all those
below:

> The Father is greater than I. (cf. John 15:1)

> You have not chosen me, but I have chosen you. (cf.
> John 15:4–5)

> I am the vine, you are the branches; if I am in you
> you will bear fruit. (cf. John 15:16)

The upper five are in upward motion. This is expressed
in terms of glory:

> And the glory which thou gavest me I have given
> them; that they may be one, even as we are one. (John
> 17:22)

> Herein is my Father glorified, that ye bear much fruit;
> so shall ye be my disciples. (John 15:8)

> This is my work and my glory—to bring to pass the
> immortality and eternal life of man. (Moses 1:39)

Those above strive to raise up the others to their own
level:

By teaching:

> The word which ye hear is not mine, but the Father's
> which sent me. (John 14:24)

By testifying:

> I will send him [the Holy Ghost] from the presence of

my Father; he will go forth from my Father to testify of me, and when you hear him, you [in turn] will testify for you were with me in the beginning. (cf. John 15:26–27)

The teachings are commandments, instructions (John 14:21); and they who receive them respond by *believing* and *doing:*

> Believe me that I am in the Father, and the Father in me: or else believe me for the very works' sake. . . . He that believeth on me, the works that I do shall he do also. (John 14:11–12)

> Ye are my friends, if you do whatsoever I command you. (John 15:14)

Also, those who accept the teachings from the apostles must do the same works:

> If they have kept my saying, they will keep yours also. (cf. John 15:20)

Having accepted the word, it is vitally important that they "remain," "abide," and "persevere" in it:

> If you abide [*meinete*] in me and my sayings also abide in you, whatever you ask will be given. (cf. John 15:7)

The steps are summed up in a single verse:

> Ye have not chosen me, but I have chosen you, and ordained [set apart] you, that ye should go and bring forth fruit, and that your fruit should remain: that whatsoever ye shall ask of the Father in my name, he may give it you. (John 15:16)

All have a piece of the action, and all engaged in this activity form a single community in which the binding and motivating force from top to bottom is *love:*

If ye love me, keep my commandments. (John 14:15)

He that hath my commandments, and keepeth them, he it is that loveth me: and he that loveth me shall be loved of my Father, and I will love him. (John 14:21)

If a man love me, he will keep my words: and my Father will love him, and we will come unto him, and make our abode [remain] with him. (John 14:23)

He that loveth me not keepeth not my sayings. (John 14:24)

As the Father hath loved me, so have I loved you: continue ye in my love. [How?] If ye keep my commandments, ye shall abide in my love; even as I have kept my Father's commandments, and abide in his love. (John 15:9–10)

They must pass it on down:

This is my commandment, That ye love one another, as I have loved you. (John 15:12)

By this love they "abide in" each other. They are "in each other"—a complete identity, which results in the parties concerned becoming completely *one*:

At that day ye shall know that I am in my Father, and ye in me, and I in you. (John 14:20)

Abide in me, and I in you. (John 15:4)

Holy Father, keep through thine own name those whom thou hast given me, that they may be one, as we are. (John 17:11)

Neither pray I for these [the apostles] alone, but for them also which shall believe on me through their word;

That they all may be one; as thou, Father, art in me, and I
in thee, that they also may be one in us. . . . And the glory
which thou gavest me I have given them; that they may
be one, even as we are one: I in them, and thou in me,
that they may be made perfect in one. (John 17:20–23)

This oneness is characterized by a perfect reciprocity:

Whatsoever ye shall ask in my name, that will I do,
that the Father may be glorified in the Son. (John 14:13)

The Son is glorified in the Father:

Herein is my Father glorified that *ye* bear much fruit.
(John 15:8; emphasis added)

And all mine are thine, and thine are mine; and I am
glorified in them. (John 17:10)

The five levels at the top form an unbroken continuum,
"a single universe of discourse," as Cherbonnier puts it,[2]
which does not embrace the two lowest levels: the world
and the prince of the world operate on their own principles
on the other side of a great gulf. Here visitors from above
are not welcome; they are treated as trespassers and offend-
ers—despised, rejected, persecuted wherever they go.

The Lord shows himself in his true nature to the
Apostles, but not to the World. (cf. John 14:22)

[When the Comforter comes in his place], the world
cannot receive [him], because it seeth him not, neither
knoweth him. (John 14:16–17)

[The Lord leaves his peace with the saints,] not as the
world giveth [peace], give I unto you. (John 14:27)

Hereafter I will not talk much with you: for the

prince of this world cometh, and hath nothing in me.
(John 14:30)

Yet a little while, and the world seeth me no more.
(John 14:19)

This dangerous and hostile territory was the scene of
Christ's earthly mission. Why? For the same reason Paul
was sent there—to testify to a benighted world and give
them a chance:

If I had not come and spoken unto them, they had
not had sin: but now they have no cloke for their sin. . . .
That the word might be fulfilled that is written in their
law, They hated me without a cause. [He gives them a
chance to accept or reject not only himself but the Father.]
But now have they both seen and hated both me and my
Father. [For] he that hateth me hateth my Father also.
(John 15:22, 25, 24, 23)

The apostles are included in the scheme:

If the world hate you, ye know that it hated me
before it hated you. (John 15:18)

If they have persecuted me, they will also persecute
you. (John 15:20)

All these things will they do unto you for my name's
sake, because they know not him that sent me (John
15:21) [even as they do not know and cannot receive the
Holy Ghost (cf. John 14:17); this is the complete reversal
of the celestial order of love].

In leaving the world behind, the Lord leaves the apostles
there to carry on the work—the same work he did; and their
prospects are equally gloomy:

As thou hast sent me into the world, even so have I
also sent them into the world. (John 17:18)

And now I am no more in the world, but these are in the world. (John 17:11)

I pray not that thou shouldest take them out of the world, but that thou shouldest keep them from the evil [they must face it]. (John 17:15)

All are in the world together:

That they all may be one; as thou, Father, art in me, and I in thee, that they also may be one in us: that the world may believe that thou hast sent me (John 17:21).

In short, the saints must be *in* the world to do their dangerous work of recruiting other saints *out* of the world:

If ye were of the world, the world would love his own . . . but I have chosen you out of the world, therefore the world hateth you. (John 15:19)

I pray not for the world, but for them which thou hast given me. (John 17:9)

I have given them thy word; and the world hath hated them, because they are not of the world, even as I am not of the world. (John 17:14)

Those on both sides of the line are of the same human family: some make the crossing over, but for them to do that they must hear and accept the word. "I have chosen you, and ordained you, that ye should go and bring forth fruit" (John 15:16). The world supplies the fruit; flee from Babylon is the call—but bring others with you!

All these things may seem perfectly obvious once they are pointed out, but we tend easily to forget them and identify with the world by the simple process of following the way of least resistance. Once in the world, even the angels are tempted.

The posture of "sheep among wolves" is a difficult one to maintain: In fact, in most cases the sheep were "turned into wolves." Almost invariably the easy way, offering "the flesh-pots of Egypt" or "the precious things" at Jerusalem is the winner against the hard way of life in the wilderness. The famous ancient hymn of *The Pearl*, the story of the "Watchers," the tragedy of many a fallen age and saint, all admonish us to beware:

> When anyone heareth the word of the kingdom, and understandeth it not, then cometh the wicked one, and catcheth away that which was sown in his heart. . . . He that received the seed into stony places . . . hath he not root in himself, but dureth for a while: for when tribulation or persecution ariseth because of the word, by and by he is offended. He also that received seed among the thorns, . . . the care of this world [*merimna tou aionos*— "concern for temporal affairs"], and the deceitfulness of riches, choke the word, and he becometh unfruitful. (Matthew 13:19–22)

The gospel goes its own way: it may never commit itself wholly to one faction or another. Once it does, endowing that faction or party with religious sanction and moral supremacy, infinite mischief is done. Let us see what happened in the ancient church: I have written a good deal on the subject and will cash in on it now. But first an important background note, showing how men in every age have been decoyed away from the real contest, a sad and miserable sideshow that is ever engaging the energies and emotions of mankind in the sort of futile contention that is Satan's masterpiece. We give here the official formulas of royal power for ancient rulers from Pharaoh to the Byzantine emperors, the kings of France, the khans of Asia, popes, caliphs, etc., and conclude:

It is clear and unequivocal in each case: (1) the monarch rules over *all* men; (2) it is God who has ordered him to do so and, significantly, none claims authority as originating with himself, but even the proudest claims to be but the humble instrument of heaven; (3) it is thus his sacred duty and mission in the world to extend his dominion over the whole earth, and all his wars are holy wars; and (4) to resist him is a crime and sacrilege deserving no other fate than extermination. The most obvious corollary of this doctrine is that there can be only one true ruler on earth. "The eternal command of God is this," wrote Mangu Khan to Louis IX, "in heaven there is but one eternal God; on earth, there is no other master than Chingis Khan, the Son of God."[3]

This is the world's answer to John 14, 15, and 17: a hierarchy of fear and compulsion. This political imperative polarizes human society.[4]

Highly characteristic of the hierocentric doctrine [of the old sacral state] is an utter abhorrence of all that lies outside the system. The world inevitably falls into two parts, the heavenly kingdom and the outer darkness, a world of monsters and abortions. Whoever is not of the *frithr* is a *nithung*, without rights and without humanity. All who do not willingly submit to Alexander or Constantine are, according to Dio Chrysostom and Eusebius, mad beasts to be hunted down and exterminated. For the Roman, all the world is either *ager pacatus* or *ager hosticus*, says Varro,[5] the only alternative to submission being outrageous rebellion. Anyone who resents the Roman yoke is a guilty slave, says Claudian, who should be consumed by remorse of conscience.[6] For the Moslem, all the world is either *Dār al-Islām* or *Dār al-Ḥarb*, the latter being any spot in the world that has refused to pay tribute and thereby made itself guilty of rebellion, because everything in the world without exception is the legitimate property of the Moslems.[7] We have already noted the claim of the khans that whoever resisted them

were guilty of crime against God. To Attila, those who
resisted his yoke were runaway slaves,[8] and the Assyrian
kings constantly declare that whoever will not take and
keep an oath to them must needs be exterminated as
"wicked people" and "rebels." In a word, "the world
without the 'Kingdom' remains in its state of primordial
rebellion," and all who do not recognize the divine king
are truly "children of destruction."[9]

Thus the whole world has been engaged in a counterfeit
version of the combat between good and evil in which Shiz
and Coriantumr, Lamanites and Nephites destroy each
other in the illusion that it is good guys fighting bad guys.
This is a constant tendency in politics, against which Elder
Wallace F. Bennett warns us in a forceful statement in the
Ensign, discussing the necessity of compromise, a thing
which many Latter-day Saints consider a threat to their
integrity.[10] But see what effect that hypnotic polarization
had on the ancient church, completing its ruin in the fourth
century:

> The Church Fathers, diligently reconstructing history
> in retrospect, made it appear that the church and Rome
> had always been one. . . . "One Empire was set up over
> all the earth, and all men became brothers, having one
> Father—God, and one Mother—true piety."[11]

The cultural background or national heritage had such a
strong attraction that the Christians identified themselves
wholly with their culture.[12]

> Thus Western Civilization was nursed in the schools
> on a legend of Western Goodness: *Hic est Ausonia*, the
> Western World of clean, fresh, simple, unspoiled pio-
> neers. This fiction became the very cornerstone of the offi-
> cial Vergilian doctrine of *Romanitas*—Rome was great
> because Rome was good.[13] The emperors who after the
> second century took the names of Pius and Felix were

giving expression "to the old Roman belief in the close association between piety and good fortune,"[14] while indulging in the ingrained Roman vice, blatantly paraded throughout the whole of Latin literature, of dwelling with a kind of morbid fascination on one's own simple goodness. School boys have been told for centuries that the Romans were a simple, severe, and virtuous folk, with a near monopoly on *pietas* and *fides,* because, forsooth, the Romans themselves always said so, though almost every page of the record contradicts the claim.[15] What better demonstration for the effectiveness of the official propaganda? Teachers and orators drilled the essentials of Western goodness into their pupils and auditors until, by the fourth century, when hardly a speck of ancient virtue remained, men could talk of nothing but that virtue.[16] They go right on sinning, Salvian reports, in the sublime conviction that no matter how vilely they may act, or how nobly the barbarians behave, God must necessarily bless them and curse the barbarians for being what they are. Yet Salvian himself shows how well the lesson has been taught when he stoutly affirms that, after all, *no* barbarian can be really virtuous![17]

In this view it is always the others who are the bad guys.

Just as all obedient subjects are embraced in a single shining community, so all outsiders are necessarily members of a single conspiracy of evil, a pestilential congregation of vapors of such uniform defilement that none can be ever so slightly tinged with its complexion without being wholly involved in its corruption.[18] A favorite passage with the churchmen of the period was that which declared that to err in the slightest point of the law is to break the whole law.[19]

It must be our side or nothing:

All virtue is comprised in the fact of membership in Our Group; all vice consists in not belonging.[20] It can be shown by a most convenient syllogism that since God is on our side we cannot show any degree of toleration for any opposition without incurring infinite guilt.[21] In the fourth century everybody was officiously rushing to the defense of God;[22] but John Chrysostom's pious declaration that we must avenge insults to God while patiently bearing insults to ourselves is put in its proper rhetorical light by the assumption of Hilary that an insult to himself is an insult to God.[23] Therein lies the great usefulness of the doctrine of guilt and innocence by association that became so popular in the fourth century: one does not need to quibble; there is no such thing as being partly wrong or merely mistaken; the painful virtue of forbearance and the labor of investigation no longer embarrass the champions of one-package loyalty. No matter how nobly and austerely heretics may live, for Augustine they are still Antichrist—all of them, equally and indiscriminately;[24] their virtues are really vices, their virginity carnality, their reason unreason, their patience in persecution mere insolence; any cruelty shown them is not really cruelty but kindness.[25] Chrysostom goes even further: the most grossly immoral atheist is actually better off than an upright believer who slips up on one point, since though both go to hell, the atheist has at least the satisfaction of having gratified his lust on earth. Why not? Is not heresy in any degree a crime against God? And is not any crime against God an infinite sin?[26]

The insidious thing about such immoral conclusions is that they are quite logical. The cruelty of the times, says Alföldi, "cannot fully be explained by the corruption of the age; . . . the spirit of the fourth century has its part to play. The victory of abstract ways of thinking, the universal triumph of theory, knows no half-measures; punishment, like everything else, must be a hundred percent, but even this seems inadequate."[27] Compromise is now out of the question: God, who once let his sun shine upon the just and the unjust, and let the wheat and tares grow together, now insists that the unjust should cease to exist, that only wheat should grow in the earth, and that only sheep should inhabit it.[28] In all seriousness the Emperor Justinian announced to the churchmen his intention of forcing the devil himself to join the true church, and thus achieving in the world that perfect unity "which Pythagoras and Plato taught."[29]

We have just noted the use of absolutes in clerical polemic. The results were what might have been expected, but the ferocity of party conflict within the church as described by the writers of the fourth and fifth centuries exceeds the wildest imaginings. Even those men, St. Basil reports, who had fought the uphill fight for decency and striven conscientiously through the years to be just and fair with others, in the end found themselves forced to surrender and become just like the rest, who were all engaged in a frantic game of testing each other's loyalty.[30] The result, he says, is that the Church is entirely leaderless, everyone wants to give orders, but no one will take them; the self-appointed have grabbed what they could and broken up the church in a spirit of such savage, unbridled hatred and universal mistrust that the only remaining principle of unity anywhere is a common desire to do harm: men will cooperate only where cooperation is the most effective means of doing injury to others.[31] It was characteristic of the Age of Constantine, says Burckhardt, "that a man could be intensely devout and at the same time grossly immoral." [There was nothing contradictory in that—men had simply discarded personal integrity for a much easier group loyalty.] "Who can swim against the tide of custom?" cries Augustine.[32]

You can swim in the river, but how long can you resist the current? And how do you achieve unity in such a system? Not by persuasion but simply by winning:

The emperor's formula for establishing perfect unity and loyalty in the church and the Empire was that plan which the clergy themselves constantly urged upon him and his successors, importunately demanding that he proscribe, banish, and anathematize whoever withheld allegiance from their particular parties. The *Vita Constantini* tells how the Emperor attempted to end each crisis by outlawing all opposition, thereby inevitably sowing the seeds of the next crisis. But how could one expect a simple soldier to question the proposition that compulsory loyalty is the secret of universal peace, when it was being pressed upon him by all the cleverest men of the age? "The barbarians reverence God, because they fear my power," he had declared, and everyone had applauded his doctrine of compulsory reverence.[33]

But it didn't work. No sooner had Constantine removed his last civil and military opponents than the issue between his Christian and pagan subjects became acute. No sooner had he "given profound peace and security to the Church" by restraining her pagan opponents than the churchmen started accusing each other of heresy with a wild abandon that surpassed—as the Emperor himself observed—any performance of the heathen.[34] No sooner had his successors removed the last heretic and received the undying thanks of the church, than the *true* believers were at each others' throats. St. Ambrose notes that it is harder to make orthodox Christians live together in peace than it is to eliminate heretics.[35] The problem was never solved, for the doctrine of absolute, one-package loyalty would allow no compromise.[36]

This year [1976] the subject of the annual session of the American Academy of Religion was restitution, i.e., restoration, a fitting theme for the Bicentennial, it was thought— the restoration of the gospel in America! What short memories we have! Restoration was a very naughty word just a few years ago, but the concept is now being recognized as fundamental to Christian preaching. Speakers pointed out that every church has thought of itself as returning to pure primitive Christianity, but in a *spiritual* sense, i.e., it was really a reformation of the church. In a survey of the whole problem, Samuel S. Hill, Jr. decides that the most tangible form of restoration,

> Institutional Restitution, is exemplified almost perfectly by the Church of Jesus Christ of Latter-Day [*sic*] Saints, the Mormon people, and stands as the most radical or revolutionary of all the American enterprises aiming toward building the Church on earth to correspond to the exact specifications disclosed in the divine revelation . . . [in] the conviction that their institutional form is *the* form intended by Christ. Mormonism presents so many angles for seeing this point that it can hardly be missed.[37]

What follows is a remarkably fair and accurate statement of the Mormon position, concluding: "Intact, it is neither Catholic nor Protestant, though of course emphatically Christian. One has to say finally that it is not classifiable with any other branch of Christianity, since it is its unique self, quite distinct—and of course separate—from all traditional ecclesiasticism. Mormonism is a separatist social and religious modality, because its base is the one institution which possesses the authority of the Restored Gospel."[38] "Clearly the Latter-day Saints live by a unique and significantly different theology separating them from all other Christians."[39] "Mormonism introduces something without precedent and in the process modifies the old."[40]

The points to note here are (1) that Mormonism, though "emphatically Christian," is *neither* Catholic or Protestant, and (2) that it defies identification with or absorption by any other movement. It is an astonishing phenomenon: Here you can be a loyal follower of Christ without being either Catholic or Protestant. During World War II if you were a Christian you had to have either "P" or "C" on your dog-tags. "Look bud," said the angry quartermaster, "if you're not Catholic, you're Protestant, and that's all there is to it." They could not conceive of anything else. But Mormonism does not commit us to either Shiz or Coriantumr. The same applies in politics. For many years if you were not a Republican, you had to be Democrat; if you were not right wing, you had to be left wing; if you were not "conservative," you had to be "liberal." Last week someone wrote in the *Universe* quite smugly noting that we do not allow radical speakers at the BYU, but if Mormonism is "the most radical or revolutionary of all American enterprises" in religion, then every day we can hear more radical speeches on the campus than anywhere else in the nation. And indeed if you listen carefully to a gospel sermon and then to the most extreme leftist and rightist discourses, you will be impressed how tame, insipid, and shallow the latter are; they never go beyond a few shop-worn clichés and mechanically repeated economic formulas as the cure for everything. They are dull and tedious by comparison with the gospel, their impact fleeting and superficial. What difference does it make? The case of Constantine should convince us that we cannot get rid of radicals even if it was worth the trouble. Only consider that a short time ago a Communist speaker addressed the student body in the Marriott Center! For no less an authority than the late Mr. H. L. Hunt has publicly declared Mr. William Buckley to be a Communist, no less. And the most popular author with BYU students is a woman [Ayn Rand] whose writings are as wildly radical as any produced in this century.

But the gospel opens our minds to the eternities! That is another matter, another dimension, another world. Thus says President Kimball in the current issue of the *Ensign*:

The Lord who created and has power over all the earth created many other earths as well, even "worlds without number" (Moses 1:33); and when this man received the oath and covenant of the priesthood (D&C 84:33–44), he received a promise from the Lord of "all that my Father hath" (D&C 84:38). To set aside all these great promises in favor of a chest of gold and a sense of carnal security is a mistake in perspective of colossal proportions. To think that he has settled for so little is a saddening and pitiful prospect indeed; the souls of men are far more precious than this.[41]

How could anything as trivial as human politics subvert our minds from the gospel? The danger lies in the fact that nothing is easier than to identify one's own political, economic, dietary, cosmological, aesthetic, etc., ideas with the gospel, both to please one's own vanity and to flatten the opposition. Therefore, our prophet was truly inspired when he told the priesthood at the last general conference to avoid "even the implication" of associating the Church with any political party, policy, or name.[42] After all, political obligation does have a hold on us: "Let such things be done by the voice of the people," says the Book of Mormon (cf. Alma 2:3; Mosiah 29:25–26). We must join our voices to others. But it is a *limited* hold:

> All covenants, contracts, bonds, obligations, oaths, vows, performances, connections, associations [including political], or expectations, that are not made and entered into and sealed by the Holy Spirit of promise . . . are of no efficacy, virtue, or force in and after the resurrection from the dead; for all contracts that are not made unto this end have an end when men are dead. (D&C 132:7)

We are in such associations, but they do not absorb our whole lives or our real nature—we are not *of* them in their essence. Nothing is more fluid than political activity, which only too rarely has but its sole objective the next election in view. At best it is an expedient, unstable, overemotional, shifting, contriving sort of thing but indispensable under certain conditions. The genius of our Constitution is that it puts us under obligation to participate, while striving for a minimum of government influence: "Congress shall make *no* law" is the key idea.

But who is there to step in when men use the law or absence of law as a device for tricking others, cheating, and taking advantage of the public and each other, forming those "secret combinations for power and gain" which the Book of Mormon says were the undoing of both the Jaredites and the Nephites? Of course men want to be let alone, "free from governmental interference," in such operations; but their activities are even now made known to us, "shown unto you," says Moroni, "that thereby ye may repent of *your* sins, and suffer not that these murderous combinations shall get above you, which are built up to get power and gain—and the work, yea, even the work of destruction come upon you, yea, even the sword of the justice of the Eternal God, . . . to your overthrow and destruction if ye shall *suffer* these things to be" (Ether 8:23). The key word is "suffer"; we may not stand idly by under such conditions. Nor can we live sheltered lives and still do the work for which we were sent into the world: "As sheep among wolves"—is that sheltered?

Our leaders urge us to be active in politics—and yet think it very important to keep the Church *out* of politics. Is this a contradiction? Consider:

Brigham Young encouraged the people to dance, even while proclaiming, "Dancing [is] no part of our worship."[43]

He says, "I labor for my own dear self," and in the same

breath adds that men have no right to work for themselves.[44]

We practice shrewd economics even while being told to take no thought of what we shall eat or wear.

We should constantly be storing our minds with knowledge, yet take no thought of what we are to say when we teach the gospel.

We are told to be provident and thrifty—but to ask and trust our Heavenly Father for our daily bread.

We are told to be industrious and independent, yet "if the laborer in Zion labor for money, he shall perish" (cf. 2 Nephi 26:31).

We are told to go to with our might—and consider the lilies of the field who toil not neither do they spin.

We are told to hold the Sabbath most sacred as a day of rest, yet it is the day on which many of us work hardest.

We are told to acquire worldly learning and told that worldly learning is nothing.

Joseph Smith said he would have nothing to do with politics and ran for president!

The Savior, speaking with the woman at the well, was thirsty and asked for a drink, and even as he was drinking she asked him for a drink, because he told her that he could give her water of which whoever drank would never thirst again.

We could go on and on, but what is wrong here? Nothing. If we were to examine each of the above apparent paradoxes, we would find them all falling into the pattern of Moses' declarations, both uttered on the same occasion and as it were in the same breath. First he said, "Now, for this cause I know that man is nothing, which thing I never had supposed" (Moses 1:10). And then he adds: "But now mine own eyes have beheld God; . . . his glory was upon me; and I beheld his face, for I was transfigured before him. . . . I am a son of God, in the similitude of his Only Begotten" (Moses 1:11, 13). Which is it? Is man nothing or everything? It all depends on which existence we behold him in, temporal or eternal.

It should be plain to anyone that each of these statements has two parts and applies to two levels of existence. The world, including the Christian world, does not acknowledge that other level of existence as a tangible reality—but Latter-day Saints do. It is not only a real world, in the end it is the only world with which we are wholly concerned. The gospel takes up where the concerns of this world leave off. Robert Heinlein begins a story thus: "All of them should have been very happy—their problems were solved: the poor they no longer had with them [note the scriptural language]; the sick, the lame, the halt, and the blind were historic memories; the ancient causes of war no longer obtained; they had more freedom than Man has ever enjoyed. All of them *should* have been happy."[45] The point was that they were miserable to the point of insanity. Does it take an angel from heaven to tell us that when people are sick, the problem at hand is to make them well? That when they are hungry, the problem is to feed them? That when they are poor, the problem is to get the necessities of life? We don't need the gospel for that. The gospel takes up where all these things leave off. Even Aristotle, in the *Nicomachean Ethics I,* knew that merely to live is not the problem, but to live well. Science is helping us put forth our hand to partake of the tree of life and possibly live forever—its ultimate goal; but that is the ultimate disaster unless we have something to live for. There are certain Christian societies (thinking of one church in particular) who are good, kind people, observe the Word of Wisdom far more strictly than we do, and send out their benevolent medical missionaries: they take their people up to the threshold of the gospel—and leave them there. The dominant conflicting political ideologies of our time are economic by nature, whether Marxist or capitalist in their leanings; but the student of the gospel finds himself like Samuel the Lamanite, standing aloof above the teeming multitude high on the wall, giving them his parting warning as the deadly missiles from all sides fall ineffectually around him: "Wo unto this great city, for . . . the more part of this great city, that will harden their hearts against me" (Helaman 13:12). ("We are, *on the whole*, an idolatrous people," says President Kimball.)[46] "Ye do not remember the Lord your God, . . . but ye do always remember your riches" (Helaman 13:22). (The economy, the economy, always the economy!) "For this cause hath the Lord caused that a curse should come upon the land, and also upon your riches, and this because of your iniquities" (Helaman 13:23).

When the Lord first appeared to the Nephites after his resurrection he identified himself to them as he had to the apostles, and then commanded them all to be baptized again (3 Nephi 11:15, 21); for he was coming back to teach them, and they had to be all cleaned up to stand in his presence. After preliminary instructions he told them, "Go ye unto your homes, and ponder upon the things which I have said . . . and prepare your minds for the morrow, and I come unto you again" (3 Nephi 17:3). Then he asked if there were any sick among them or any with physical handicaps or deformities of any kind—"and he did heal them every one" (3 Nephi 17:7). Then he fed them until they were all filled (cf. 3 Nephi 18:9). Does this complete his mission? No, it is only the setting of the stage, getting ready for school, as it were. Now at last they were ready to *begin* their lessons in the gospel—right at the point where the teachings of men leave off. After all our physical wants are satisfied, what comes next? What do people do in such situations? That is the dilemma of Mr. Heinlein's men of the future after science has solved all their problems—the answer he gives in his latest work is simply that they would go on enjoying unlimited sex:[47] but our generation has had enough experience to know that nothing is more pitiful or forlorn than that.

But note well that before Christ took up the real substance of the gospel with the people, he saw to it that all their temporal wants were supplied; without that, these would have proved a distraction. Taking care of such matters is not the essence of the gospel, but it is an indispensable preliminary to it. As soon as we have done those sensible and humane things which God has commanded us to do for our neighbors and ourselves, then and only then will we be in a position to ask that our minds be opened to the mysteries.

So now I hope I can begin to see politics in its proper perspective. While we are in the world it is a legitimate concern, it belongs indeed at its best—like medicine, teaching, social work, and the arts—to the idealistic, philanthropic, sociable, and lovable sphere of activity to which sectarian religion also belongs; and as long as ninety percent of our fellows are engaging in it (actively or passively), we can do no less, ever mindful of its ephemeral, fallible, all-too-human nature. Like golf, it is a game into which a man can put his whole soul without dedicating his life to it, which can engage his total concentration for a few hours a week, and then be put in proper perspective, even held in contempt, for the rest of the time. Its weakness is that it all too easily degenerates into a sordid partisan competition of economic interests that can stifle the spirit of the gospel with deadly efficiency. May the Lord preserve us from that.

Notes

1. Heathcote W. Garrod, *The Oxford Book of Latin Verse* (Oxford: Clarendon, 1944), xxxvii, xliii.

2. Edmond LaB. Cherbonnier, "The Logic of Biblical Anthropomorphism," *Harvard Theological Review* 55 (1962): 198.

3. Hugh W. Nibley, "The Hierocentric State," *Western Political Quarterly* 4 (1951): 234; reprinted in *CWHN* 10:109.

4. The following block quotation is from Nibley, "The Hierocentric State," 244–45; in *CWHN* 10:123.

5. Varro, *De Lingua Latina* V, 33.

6. Claudius Claudianus, *The Gothic War* 355.

7. Ernst F. K. Rosenmueller, *Institutiones Iuris Mohammedani circa Bellum contra Eos Qui ab Islamo Sunt Alieni* (Leipzig: Barth, 1825), nos. 13, 16, 22, 27, 38, 47–48, 55.

8. Jordanes, *Gothic History* 52.

9. Robert Eisler, *Iēsous Basileus ou Basileusas*, 2 vols. (Heidelberg: Winter, 1930), 2:625; August von Gall, *Basileia tou Theou* (Heidelberg: Winter, 1926), 241–42.

10. Wallace F. Bennett, "I Have a Question," *Ensign* 6 (June 1976): 63.

11. Eusebius, *De Laudibus Constantini* 16, in *PG* 20:1421–29; cf. Prudentius, *Contra Symmachum* II, 578–95 and 634–40. Cf. Hugh W. Nibley, "The Unsolved Loyalty Problem: Our Western Heritage," *Western Political Quarterly* 6 (1953): 643; reprinted in *CWHN* 10:210.

12. The following block quotation is from Nibley, "Unsolved Loyalty Problem," 638; in *CWHN* 203–4.

13. Charles N. Cochrane, *Christianity and Classical Culture* (Oxford: Clarendon, 1944), 65–72.

14. Joseph Vogt, *Constantin der Grosse und sein Jahrhundert* (Munich: Münchner, 1949), 59.

15. Catullus beautifully illustrates both these points; cf. R. M. Henry, "*Pietas* and *Fides* in Catullus," *Hermathena* 75 (1950): 63–68.

16. E.g., Prudentius, *Contra Orationem Symmachi* II, 488–91 and 503–23; Aldo Marsili, "Roma nella poesia di Claudiano. Romanità occidentale contrapposta a quella orientale," *Antiquitas* 1 (1946): 11–13.

17. Salvianus, *On the Government of God* VII, 2–3, in *PL* 53:130–32; V, 2–4, in *PL* 53:91–96.

18. For Claudius Claudianus, *The Gothic War*, passim, all who deny humble submission to Rome are faithless destroyers of peace, mad, demented, feeble-minded, insane, *praedones, proditores, scellerati, presuntuosi, superbi, barbari, clienti, audacii false inerti, impii, rabiosi, perfidi,* and so forth; see Marsili, "Roma nella poesia di Claudiano," 17–18.

19. Cf. Nibley, "Unsolved Loyalty Problem," 644; in *CWHN* 10:210.

20. Thus Optatus, *De Schismate Donatistarum* (*On the Donatist Schism*) II, 13, in *PL* 11:966, can show that "the true Church cannot be cruel," since "dum sanat, vulnerat" (it causes pain while healing), ibid., in *PL* 11:1020.

21. Lucifer of Carales, *De Non Conveniendo cum Haeresibus*, in *PL* 13:768–70, 774, 777, 787, 791.

22. The common-sense republicanism of Tiberius Caesar had been prompted by the sentiment "deorum injuriae dis curae" (the gods' injuries are matters of concern to the gods).

23. John Chrysostom, *Homilia in Joannem* (*Homily on John*) LIV, 4, in *PG* 59:301.

24. Augustine, *Enarrationes in Psalmos* (*Narrations on Psalms*) 62:15, in *PL* 36:684–85.

25. Augustine, *Contra Julianum Pelagianum* (*Against Julian Pelagius*) IV, 30–31, in *PL* 44:753–54, 763: "Unbelievers do evil even when they do good."

26. John Chrysostom, *De Virginitate* 5, in *PG* 48:536–37.

27. András Alföldi, *A Conflict of Ideas in the Late Roman Empire, the Clash between the Senate and Valentinian*, tr. Harold Mattingly (Oxford: Clarendon, 1952), 40.

28. John Chrysostom, *Exposition on Psalm 50*, in *PG* 55:530; John Chrysostom, *Homilia in Isaiam 6:1* (*Homily on Isaiah 6:1*) IV, 1–2, in *PG* 56:121.

29. Cf. Nibley, "Unsolved Loyalty Problem," 646; in *CWHN* 10:211–12.

30. Basil, *De Spiritu Sancto* (*On the Holy Ghost*) 76–77, in *PG* 32:213–17.

31. Ibid.

32. Nibley, "Unsolved Loyalty Problem," 647; in *CWHN* 10:213–14.

33. Cf. Nibley, "Unsolved Loyalty Problem," 647–48; in *CWHN* 10:214; Sozomen, *Ecclesiastical History* II, 28, in *PG* 67:1013–17.

34. The Emperor's famous letter is quoted in Eusebius, *Life of Constantine* II, 71, in *PG* 20:1044–45.

35. Ambrose, *Epistles* 12, in *PL* 16:988–89.

36. Cf. Nibley, "Unsolved Loyalty Problem," 48; in *CWHN* 10:214.

37. Samuel S. Hill, "A Typology of American Restitutionism: From

Frontier Revivalism and Mormonism to the Jesus Movement," *Journal of the American Academy of Religion* 44 (1976): 69.

38. Ibid.

39. Ibid., 70.

40. Ibid., 71.

41. Spencer W. Kimball, "The False Gods We Worship," *Ensign* 6 (June 1976): 5.

42. Spencer W. Kimball, "Boys Need Heroes Close By," *Ensign* 6 (May 1976): 46.

43. *JD* 1:30.

44. *JD* 14:101.

45. Robert A. Heinlein, *Beyond This Horizon* (Reading: Fantasy, 1948), 1 (emphasis added).

46. Kimball, "False Gods We Worship," 6.

47. Robert A. Heinlein, *Time Enough for Love* (New York: Putnam's Sons, 1973).

6

Brigham Young as a Statesman

We could talk about something with a glamorous title, but then as Brigham Young told us yesterday,[1] How do you know I'm telling you the truth? How do you know that I'm not deceiving you? How do you know I'm not pulling your leg? How do you know I'm not deceiving myself? What do I know about what happened thousands and thousands of years ago?[2] The best way for me to stay in business is to avoid situations in which my real knowledge might be put to the test, and some of us become extremely skillful at that. I'm going to talk about Brigham Young today. After all, this is Brigham Young University, and the one thing we have to be proud of is the name of Brigham Young. The best way we can honor that name is not with bronze statues and plaques and the usual velour and Victorian bric-a-brac, status symbols for the dead, but to heed his sayings, to heed his teachings. He gave them as eternal teachings, based on eternal principles—very practical, very up-to-date. You can judge for yourself just how timeless and up-to-date they are.

First of all, Brigham Young the leader was Brigham

This address was given 7 June 1967 at Brigham Young University.

Young the statesman because of what he had done. He had led his people out away all by themselves; they were entirely independent; they had to govern themselves. He had to know all about government, because he was in charge. And so here we have a man, whether he would or not, in charge of a state.

> You may judge whether there has been a labour upon me, when you reflect that I realize that God holds me responsible for the salvation and safety of this people. You hold me responsible, every one of you, as standing between you and God, to guide you safely—to dictate and direct the affairs of this Church and kingdom; and then you may judge whether my mind labours or not. My mind becomes tired, and so do your minds, if you are Saints.[3]

They, too, had to work, and the thing that would get the Saints through was using their brains, not using their voices or their muscles, necessarily. He says, of himself,

> It is the man who works hard, who sweats over the rock, and goes to the kanyons for lumber, that I count more worthy of good food and dress than I am. But do not I labour? Yes, with my mind. Can any man tell what labour there is upon me? [Of course, the labor, the real burden of responsibility, of administration. It is a terrible thing when you have all the responsibility and take it.] No, not a man can begin to tell what I feel for the Latter-day Saints in this Territory, throughout the mountains and the world—what I feel for their salvation and preservation. They have to be looked after and cared for; and all this more particularly rests upon me. My brethren love to share with me all that the Lord puts upon them; but in the day of trouble they look to me to secure them and point out a way for their escape.[4]

He had to know about government, and his leadership went over into government. "When God calls a man to pre-

side, He gives him wisdom to preside, so heap the blame on
me. . . . I was the designer of that Hall, and I am ashamed
of it, it is too small [i.e., he built his first assembly house,
and it was too small; the man says, "All right, I am responsible"]; to do credit to this body of men, let them build a
Hall that will contain 15,000 persons"—so he started on the
tabernacle that very month.[5] He is the noble character, the
nobleman seeking the benefit of all around him, trying to
bring his servants—if you please, his tenants—to his knowledge; to receive like blessings that he enjoys, to dispense his
wisdom and talents among them, and to make them equal
with himself. This is the person—the great political leader.
This is very much, of course, like the discourse of Pericles.
"As old as I am now [he said when he was 73], I expect that
if I should see a wagon in the mud, my shoulder would be
first to the wheel to lift it out."[6] And that was true. He was
always helping; he was always right in there.

A correspondent from the New York newspapers went
up to the 24th of July picnic at Alta—it was Brighton in
those days—in 1860, and he gives a very moving description. When the show was all over, when some three thousand wagons had gone down the canyon on the specially
made road, and the dust had settled, late in the evening
there was one figure still left in the camp, going around
with a bucket dowsing all the campfires—and that was
Brigham Young, the last man left, to make sure that all the
fires were out.[7] This is a careful man, who doesn't want to
waste, doesn't want to destroy, wants to preserve, to see
that everything is done right. He was a marvelous figure.

After all, these people had broken with the civilization
in which they lived; they'd been pushed out, and the Lord
required that of them. It was necessary, but they were very
much aware of the fact of having been cut off and being by

themselves. And Brigham had led them out; he'd led them out of the world. This meant that their attitude to politics, especially national politics, would be conditioned by this feeling of aloofness—they had no real part in it, one way or the other. But we'll see how. "[The] world [is] bound in the dim light of king-craft, money-craft, and serfdom."[8] He says, "[Our life is] tame and uninteresting to those who dwell amid the whirl of mental and physical energies, constantly taxed to their utmost tension in the selfish, unsatisfying and frenzied quest of worldly emolument, fame, power, and maddening draughts from the syren cup of pleasure."[9] What style the man has! As I say, he never wrote a note, never followed anything at all, just spoke strictly from the cuff. And as we'll see tomorrow,[10] he spent but eleven days at school—the only formal education he ever had.[11] Yet he has one of the most vigorous, terse, powerful prose styles of any American. And he could also be very eloquent. "[We] are so remote from the high-wrought excitement . . . [and] little prone to deem mere property, rank, titles, and office the highest prizes for human effort."[12] We don't take those things seriously anymore. We are out of that rat-race, and we are glad of it. "How easy it is for the love of the world to take possession of the hearts of the human family! How easy it is for their minds to become darkened by the god of this world, and become like the eyes of the fool, which are in the ends of earth, seeking for gold and silver, and the riches, grandeur, popularity, and titles of this world"[13]—all the things people look for. You notice how up-to-date these things are too. "When I see them grovelling in the dust; longing, craving, desiring, contending for the things of this life, I think, O foolish men, to set your hearts on the things of this life! To-day they are seeking after the honors and glories of the world, and by the time the sun is hidden by the western mountains the breath is gone out of their nostrils, they sink to their mother earth."[14] What a lesson this is for us now.

So he had taken the Saints out, and when he saw the Nauvoo Temple burning he said, "Good, the best thing that could happen; take it, Father, it's yours. I'm glad of it." He never looked back.[15] Five times his own house was taken from him, as well as his farm and everything he'd built up. He said he never thought of it; "Finest thing in the world," he says. "Out for more."[16] Now there are certain principles, and therefore certain attitudes. He regards the state as a necessary evil: "Necessary, but evil." "Every system of civil polity invented by men, like their religious creeds, has been proved by experiment wholly inadequate to check the downward tendency of the human race."[17] He certainly takes a dim view, and so this is his advice. "As for politics, we care nothing about them one way or the other, although we are a political people; but it is for the right."[18] "It is the Kingdom of God or nothing with us."[19] The Latter-day Saints were now isolated where they wouldn't have to make this choice, and would be able to think in the unified sense, just of the kingdom of God, not being identified with one party or another. He hammers at that all the time.

He sent a general epistle to all the missionaries:

> Amid all the revolutions that are taking place among the nations, the elders will ever pursue an undeviating course in being subject to the government, wherever they may be [be subject to the government, respect the government,wherever you are], and sustain the same by all their precepts to the Saints, having nothing to do with political questions which engender strife, remembering that the weapons of their warfare are not carnal but spiritual, and that the Gospel which they preach is not of man but from heaven.[20]

Maintain this aloofness; keep out of it; don't get down into that business—that is what he tells them. They're spreading the gospel. Wherever you live, however, you must be subject to the government. And so, he says, "Revenue laws should embrace a penalty." The fact that a collector dislikes to enforce his collections should cease to be an excuse. Tax collectors in Utah didn't want to collect, so they were being lax. The people were abundantly able to pay their taxes, and if they failed or neglected to do so, the law should be enforced against them. We're still bound to live by it—it's the only way we can get along. Then he explains that politics is not a primary concern, because of its partisan nature. Primarily, "we do not send these elders forth for political purposes; we have nothing to do with the political world."[21] Had Joseph Smith made political capital of his religion and calling and raised up a political party, he doubtless would have become celebrated and renowned in the world as a great man and a great leader. But he didn't do that. "Are there any Democrats, any Whigs, any Methodists, and Baptists, or anything like the parties and sects of the day among us? No. What is there?"[22] He could still say that in 1857; nobody wanted to be here then when the heat was on. "Those who want to do the will of their Father in heaven—and when they can know his will, and their faith is one—their hope is one, they are one in all things."[23] "The world complain[s] of us with regard to our politics. . . . [They say why don't you take sides?] And enquire, 'are there any Democrats here? Are there any Republicans here?' We do not care who rules; we are satisfied with God, who setteth up one man, and casteth down another."[24] They had to send Brother Babbitt to Congress to do business for them, but Brigham did that reluctantly; he didn't like the idea of Babbitt being there, and he said of Babbitt in conference, "If we could keep him here a few months, and in our councils a few years, I think that he would despise litigation as he would the gates of hell. If we had him here, we would wrap him up in the Spirit and power of God, and send him to preach glad tidings to the nations of the earth, instead of his being engaged in the low and beggarly business of petti-fogging,"[25] which was Brigham's idea of Congress. Regional rivalry and factionalism were the order of the day:

> Clubs, societies, or firms are apt to clash more or less and run into sectional differences and sectional feelings. This I do not want. When we say we will do a good thing, I want the whole community to be of one heart and of one mind in that matter.[26]

> Here is a great bone of contention with regard to political affairs. The world say[s]; "Why do not these Latter-day Saints get up their mass meetings and sustain this, that or the other man, and be like other people in the political point of view?" Why do we not sustain these advocates who are now in the field, and join, and be one with some one or other of the political parties of the country? We have no desire to do so, that is the reason.[27]

He said that, of course, when he was old. The Saints were a unique and peculiar people, separated from these things. But they had reason; it was very wise to keep out of this because of what was happening. As soon as the Saints were driven off, then arose the terrible mobs, "bleeding Kansas and Missouri," and all the issues; and then the mounting partisanship, the fierce party politics, and the savage loss of self-control crystallized around the issue of slavery—this was a good thing to be out of. In 1845, before the Saints had come to Utah (and Brigham Young had taken over after the death of Joseph Smith), he said, "A crisis of extraordinary and thrilling interest has arrived. . . . The ranklings of violence and intolerance, . . . of settled vengeance, and blood guiltiness cannot long be suppressed."[28] These were the feelings. After all, "bloody Kansas" and the "bushwackers" and the "jayhawkers" of Missouri were far worse in their depredations after the Saints left. They did far more mobbing and burning of each other than they ever did to the Saints. And this went on for twenty-five years after. "Settled vengeance, and blood guiltiness cannot long be suppressed. . . . Every sensible man in the nation has felt . . . the dreadful vortex into which partizan ambition [people exploiting interest for their own purpose], contempt of the poor, and trampling down the just as things of nought, were fast leading the nation."[29] Then he says (this is his theory),

> There has been a progressive revolution since the close of the [Revolutionary] war, but not in virtue, justice, uprightness, and truth. It has become quite a custom, and by custom it has the force of law, for one party to mob another, to tear down and destroy Catholic churches, drive citizens from the ballot box, . . . and persecute, plunder, drive from their possessions, and kill a great people. Revolution in the United States is progressing [this is in 1854]; but to the true spirit of Democracy and the science of government, the Revolution I refer to is strictly opposed.[30]

It's going the wrong way; this is nothing for us to get mixed up in. Very closely allied to this party spirit is the national feeling, and he said we should avoid that. "[Since the time of Nimrod,] physical force, conquest, and oppression have been the characteristic of every period of the world's history."[31] He's right. And this feeling, this attitude of aloofness, added to the other peculiarities of the moment, in a sense deepened the common charge of treason:

Do you blame the wicked for being mad? [I don't
blame them; they look at us in our peculiar position, and
you can hardly expect any other reaction!] No. They
desire to rule, to hold the reins of government on this
earth; they have held them a great while. I do not blame
them for being suspicious of us; men in high standing are
suspicious of us, hence the frequent cry, "Treason, treason, we are going to have trouble with the people in
Utah."[32]

He has a lot to say about that. But his theory of government is that all earthly government is imperfect, because all
earthly things are imperfect since the Fall. "Don't get carried
away by them—they are not eternal." Necessary, yes, but
every government is makeshift. "Every government in the
world has the seeds of its own destruction within itself," he
says, and he means that.[33] It can be a good thing and a necessary thing, but it is all tending toward one end. It's like the
human system itself. There are remedies, there are various
ways of life, there are various regimes you can follow to
enjoy life and be healthy, but this isn't your eternal life. We
haven't been resurrected yet. We're all tending toward one
end. And it's so with governments. "Why are they thus led
to sow the seeds of their own destruction?" he asks.
"Because the kingdoms of this world are not designed to
stand."[34] "Every government lays the foundation of its own
downfall,"[35] and "I am so far from believing that any government upon this earth has constitutions and laws that are
perfect, that I do not even believe that there is a single revelation, among the many God has given to the Church, that is
perfect in its fulness."[36] Don't expect governments to be perfect, he says; even our revelations are not perfect. "The revelations of God contain correct doctrine and principle, so far
as they go; but it is impossible for the poor, weak, low, grovelling, sinful inhabitants of the earth to receive a revelation

from the Almighty in all its perfections."[37] And how would you expect such poor, weak, low, grovelling, and sinful inhabitants of the earth to set up for themselves a model government that would last forever? You're not going to get it, Brigham says, so don't fool yourselves.

"With all the excellency, and all the carefulness and correctness exhibited in the formation of constitutions and laws, they have the seeds of destruction within themselves. In the laws of every government now on this earth, there are certain principles in their constitutions that will ere long sap the foundations of their existence."[38] It wasn't many years before we had the great Civil War, because of certain defects in the Constitution itself, which allowed all sorts of conflicts and interpretations. So it was with Israel—was it good for Israel to have a king? Yes, it was, because that is what they sought for. "Was it the Lord's choice that they should have an earthly king? No, it was not His mind and will, but it was the will of the people, consequently, He brought about circumstances to give them kings and rulers, according to their desire, and to bring judgments upon them."[39]

"If we must have an organization after the order and wishes of those who are ignorant of the things of God, we must have political and municipal organizations. Kingdoms are organized to suit the conditions of the people, whether the government is that of the people, in the hands of a few individuals, or centred in one."[40] So this is his attitude toward government in general: Don't put your trust in it, and don't look to it for salvation. "Our experience has demonstrated the simple fact [and this corollary grows out of that] that in enacting laws, the fewer they are, when well-executed, the better they are for the people. Multiplying laws would not add to our peace or union. If we did not know how to govern and control ourselves that would be a broken reed to lean upon."[41]

A principle of leadership: Let us control ourselves. So Brigham gives some general principles of correct government. "The Priesthood of the Son of God [Is the world ready for that? No], which we have in our midst, is a perfect order and system of government, and this alone can deliver the human family from all the evils which now afflict its members, and insure them happiness and felicity hereafter."[42] "I do not know that we should want any sheriff, marshals, constables, magistrates, jurors, judges or governors."[43] And this was established because the word of God would govern and control every person as an individual. "That Kingdom grows out of the Church of Jesus Christ of Latter-day Saints, but it is not the Church [talking about the kingdom of God], for a man may be a legislator in that body which will issue laws to sustain the inhabitants of the earth in their individual rights, and still not belong to the Church of Jesus Christ at all."[44] He was talking about a model plan of government.

The trouble is that we are not perfect. Isn't that a sad thing? "I have not yet attained to perfect confidence in myself in all circumstances, neither has God in me, for were such the case, He would answer every request I made of Him, every wish of mine would be answered to the letter."[45] "There are a thousand circumstances I cannot help or control that are thrown around me without any action of my choice."[46] He admits that he is at the mercy of circumstances, and so are the rulers of the world. "Do you think that I would have let my brother die, if I had the power the Lord has? Would I have let Jedediah [go] behind the veil, had I had that power? No; though in that I might have gone contrary to the wishes of the Almighty. For want of the knowledge which the Lord has, if I had power I might bring injury upon myself and this people."[47] If he used power without the Lord's knowledge, he would bring injury upon himself and his people, so it was good that he didn't have it! "Could I in the flesh become as perfect as God in the spirit, I could not stay on the earth with my friends to hold close communion with them and speak with them face to face as men speak to each other."[48] "If I were perfect the Lord would take me to Paradise quicker than you would be willing to have me go there. I want to stay with you; and I expect to be just perfect enough to lead you on—to still know a little more than you know."[49] That's all he expects, but don't look for perfection in human government or the things of this world.

So what follows from this? "I endeavor to look upon [mankind] as an angel would, having compassion, long-suffering, and forbearance towards them. How many times can I forgive a brother? . . . I think I could forgive a brother seventy times seven in one day."[50] "It is no more natural for your lungs to expand and contract in breathing than it is for you to wish others to be like yourselves. . . . [And this is the thing you've got to get over with.] All of these classes act according to their faith and traditions, and each one of them says, 'If you are not as I am, you are not right.' This is just as natural as it is to breathe vital air. I wish this trait in the Saints to be done away. I want the Elders of Israel to learn to take people as they are."[51] It is one of his principles of leadership. "Just as soon as our eyes are turned away from watching ourselves, to see whether we do right, we begin to see faults in our neighbors; this is the great difficulty, and our minds become more and more blinded until we become entirely darkened."[52] "It matters not what your neighbours do, look to your God with all your heart, instead of watching your neighbours, and there will be no danger of your leaving the true path."[53] This is a powerful thing; he said this on a number of occasions: "The spirit that seeks only to accuse, that can only delight itself in the failings and errors of mankind, so born of hell as only to find delight in the defects of humanity—. . . it is the very work of Satan, and his servants."[54] So don't accuse—never accuse. "People cannot judge themselves as they can others, nor look upon their own conduct as they do the conduct of others. Cease looking at others; cease to judge each other." Yes, "but they, through their traditions, can judge every person but themselves: they can weigh every person in their scale of justice; but they never think of trying themselves."[55] "There is one principle I wish to urge upon the Saints in a way that it may remain with them—that is, to understand men and women as they are, and not understand them as you are."[56] "Judge not each other rashly, for you will find that ninety-nine wrongs out of a hundred committed by men are done more in ignorance than from a design to do wrong."[57]

Brigham Young keeps at suspicion, judging, etc.—the very basic things—all the time. "Do not be so full of religion as to look upon every little overt act that others may commit as being the unpardonable sin that will place them beyond the reach of redemption and the favours of our God."[58] "In this Territory are people gathered from almost all nations, where they have been differently educated, differently traditioned, and differently ruled. How, then, can we expect them to look, to act, and to have sentiments, faith, and customs precisely alike? I do not expect to see any such thing, but I endeavor to look upon them as an angel would, having compassion, long-suffering, and forbearance towards them."[59] Here's a very good psychological insight; this is typical Brigham Young. He knows the answer here.

He says, "You may see, or think you see, a thousand faults in your brethren; yet they are organized as you are; they are flesh of your flesh, bone of your bone; they are of your Father who is in heaven: we are all his children, and should be satisfied with each other as far as possible. The main difficulty in the hearts of those who are dissatisfied is, they are not satisfied with themselves."[60] When you start attributing your misfortune to the wickedness of others, that's your subconscious at work. Brigham Young was a marvelous psychologist; you could write a whole book about that aspect of him. If anyone gets so excited about someone else's wickedness, he's not satisfied with himself. He's fallen short.

> Let compassion reign in our bosoms. Try to comprehend how weak we are, how we are organized, how the spirit and the flesh are continually at war.[61]

> Be kind to all as our Father in heaven is kind. He sends His rain upon the just and the unjust; and gives the sun to shine upon the evil and the good. So let our goodness extend to all the works of His hands, where we can; but do not yield to the spirit and influence of evil.[62]

> How often it is said—"Such a person has done wrong, and he cannot be a Saint, or he would not do so." How do you know? We hear some swear and lie; they trample upon the rights of their neighbor, break the Sabbath by staying away from meeting, riding about the city, hunting horses and cattle, or working in the kanyons. Do not judge such persons, for you do not know the design of the Lord concerning them; therefore, do not say they are not Saints. What shall we do with them? Bear with them.[63]

"May the Lord God Almighty bless the Saints, and every one who will permit his blessings to come upon them. I am under the same obligations to bless sinners as I am to bless Saints, if they will receive my blessings."[64] "Do we despise them? No; we pity them. 'Pity them?' Yes, pity them. [He's talking about the people that were persecuting them.] They are flesh of your flesh, bone of your bone. God 'hath made of one blood all nations of men for to dwell on all the face of the earth.'"[65] "Forgive them, not only seven times, but seventy times seven in a day, if their hearts are fully set to do right. Let us make it a point to pass over their weaknesses and say, 'God bless you in trying to be better in time to come,' and act as wise stewards in the kingdom of God. . . . Do not throw away a man or a woman, old or young."[66] "Do you expect to see a perfect man? Not while you stay here[!]"[67] "Much of Joseph's policy in temporal things was different from my ideas of the way to manage them."[68] Brigham Young never managed things the way Joseph did. He was a businessman; Joseph wasn't. "He did the best he could, and I do the best I can."[69] We must always give others the benefit of the doubt.

> We are not capacitated to receive in one day, nor in one year, the knowledge and experience calculated to make us perfect Saints, but we learn from time to time, from day to day, consequently we are to have compassion one upon another, to look upon each other as we would wish others to look upon us, and to remember that we are frail mortal beings, and that we can be changed for the better only by the Gospel of salvation.[70]

"Oh fools! not to understand that those you condemn are the workmanship of God, as well as yourselves! God overlooks their weaknesses; and so far as they do good, they are as acceptable as we are."[71] This is our Brigham Young again, running true to form. "It's not our calling to accuse or punish the wicked [you remember that Mormon says the same thing; cf. Mormon 3:15; 4:5]. Surely, the justice of God will overtake the wicked, and it is by the wicked that the wicked are punished."

> Would you like to empty these vials [of God's wrath] upon the heads of the nations, and take vengeance upon those who have so cruelly persecuted you? Do you delight in the sufferings of your fellow-beings? Jesus died for those very beings. Have you ever realized that the blood of Jesus, the Son of God, was voluntarily shed for those very characters, as well as for us? Do you not think that he has feeling for them? Yes, his mercy yearns over the nation that has striven for a score of years to rid the earth of the Priesthood of the Son of God and to destroy the last Saint. He has mercy upon them, he bears with them, he pleads with them by his Spirit, and occasionally sends his angels to administer to them. Marvel not, then, that I pray for every soul that can be saved. Are they yet upon saving ground? Many of them can yet be saved, if they will turn to the Lord.[72]

As you know, they were cast out; but what were their ties to the country? This great strife, this great political partisanship, these terrible fights going on, this mounting crisis back home—what were the guiding stars of Brigham Young's policy? First was the Constitution. Accept that. "I do not lift my voice against the great and glorious Government guaranteed to every citizen by our Constitution, but against those corrupt administrators who trample the Constitution and just laws under their feet."[73]

> Do we wish to be free from the United States Constitution? No. There is not a word in it but what we can subscribe to with all our hearts. Do we wish to be free from the laws of the United States? No. They are as good laws as we can ask for. Neither do we wish for any better laws than are the most of those enacted in Missouri and Illinois [they had wonderful laws in Missouri and Illinois,

too]. What, then, was the difficulty with this people? Magistrates, sheriffs, constables, military officers, &c., walked those laws under their feet.[74]

The signers of the Declaration of Independence and the framers of the Constitution were inspired from on high to do that work. But was that which was given to them perfect, not admitting of any addition whatever? No. . . . They laid the foundation, and it was for after generations to rear the superstructure upon it. It is a progressive—a gradual work. If the framers of the Constitution and the inhabitants of the United States had walked humbly before God, . . . the nation would now have been free from a multitude of place-hunters who live upon its vitals.[75]

If they had, there would have been a consistent growth, but as Brigham said, the revolution had been downwards instead. Then here's the famous passage—which he refers to often—about the Constitution being rescued: "I expect to see the day when the Elders of Israel will protect and sustain civil and religious liberty and every constitutional right bequeathed to us by our fathers, and spread those rights abroad in connection with the Gospel for the salvation of all nations. I shall see this whether I live or die."[76]

"Protect and sustain civil and religious liberty and every constitutional right." "How long will it be before the words of the prophet Joseph will be fulfilled? He said if the Constitution of the United States were saved at all it must be done by this people."[77] "When the Constitution . . . hangs, as it were, upon a single thread, they will have to call for the 'Mormon' Elders to save it from utter destruction; and they will step forth and do it."[78] "Will the Constitution be destroyed? No: it will be held inviolate by this people; and, as Joseph Smith said, 'The time will come when the destiny of the nation will hang upon a single thread [the original quotation of Joseph Smith does not mention the Constitution]. At that critical juncture, this people will step forth and save it from the threatened destruction.' It will be so."[79]

"The present Constitution, with a few alterations of a trifling nature, is just as good as we want; and if it is sustained on this land of Joseph, it will be done by us and our posterity. Our national brethren do not know how to do it."[80] Brigham supports the federal government on this principle. "The American Government is second to none in the world in influence and power, and far before all others in liberal and free institutions. . . . It was in this government, formed by men inspired of God, although at the time they knew it not."[81] "We love the Constitution of our country; it is all we could ask; . . . we love the Federal Government, and the laws of Congress."[82] "To accuse us of being unfriendly to the Government [and, of course, this was the constant charge], is to accuse us of hostility to our religion, for no item of inspiration is held more sacred with us than the Constitution under which she acts."[83] "The General Constitution of our country is good, and a wholesome government could be framed upon it, for it was dictated by the invisible operations of the Almighty; he moved upon Columbus to launch forth upon the trackless deep."[84] "We have no difficulties with our Government: we never have had any difficulties with any government under which we have lived."[85] "The Latter-day Saints live and always have lived in a land of law, and, if they have transgressed the law, shame on a community, like the people that live under the Government of the United States, to persecute them instead of prosecuting them."[86] If they've broken the law they should be prosecuted.

But that wasn't the way it was done—persecuting them instead of prosecuting them. It was perfectly legal and all right for them to be prosecuted. "An instance cannot be found upon the records of any court in the United States where the leaders of this people have been legally convicted of a breach of law and order."[87] Not one instance. "There is not another nation under heaven but this, in whose midst the Book of Mormon could have been brought forth. The Lord has been operating for centuries to prepare the way for the coming forth of the contents of that Book from the bowels of the earth."[88] It would have had an easier time in other countries, but it would have been against the will and policy of their various state religions. The restoration could have been suppressed by law. In this country it could not be suppressed by law. Persecution, yes. Mobs, yes. But that wasn't the government; that wasn't the country—it was the way people were misbehaving. This was what the Mormons always had to deal with. They never had any trouble with laws, government, or anything like that; all those ran beautifully.

"This is my country. I am a native-born American citizen. My father fought for the liberty we ought to have enjoyed in the States, and we shall yet see the day when we shall enjoy it."[89] But what do you do when the whole country has turned against you for religious reasons? The declaration of 1897, asking why Christians couldn't fellowship with the Mormons, was purely for religious reasons, and not for social reasons.[90] To paraphrase: "We think the social plan of the Mormons is wonderful: their organization, their progress, their economy—all that is marvelous. We have nothing to hold against them. It is their doctrine—their degrading belief in revelation, their belief in prophets, the degrading doctrine of God, the Book of Mormon, belief in angels—it is all those things we can't go along with." The reasons the churches of America refused to allow their members to "fellowship," as they put it, with the Mormons were purely doctrinal and had nothing to do with anything else. This declaration was signed by other religious leaders in America and was officially accepted. It was first introduced by the Congregationalists, then the Methodists took it over, then came the Baptists, and also the Episcopalians— all for religious reasons, for specific Mormon beliefs.

"Now, we left the United States with the intention of planting our feet in the Great Basin, which then belonged to Mexico. Before we left Nauvoo we wrote to the governors of every State and Territory in the Union, requesting them to give us an asylum within their borders. We received five answers, and these refused to listen to our petition. I have now in my possession copies of those letters."[91] So they refused to let them stay.

> Before we left Nauvoo, not less than two United States' senators came to receive a pledge from us that we would leave the United States; and then, while we were doing our best to leave their borders, the poor, low, degraded curses sent a requisition for five hundred of our men to go and fight their battles! That was President Polk; and he is now weltering in hell with old Zachary Taylor, where the present administrators will soon be, if they do not repent.[92]

First, officials refused to let the Latter-day Saints stay, ordering them out; then they refused to let them depart in peace! Once the Mormons departed and succeeded against all expectations, "We are obliged to maintain our rights; for every blackleg, horse thief, counterfeiter, and abominable character are united with the hireling priests and lying editors and wicked leaders of our Government to falsely accuse the 'Mormons,' with a view to our destruction."[93]

Finally the wicked followed the Saints west, setting up gambling shops, drinking and carousing, stirring up strife, hatching up law suits, hunting out disaffected spirits, and then lecturing the people on morality, wishing them to become like other communities. Only after they had done everything they could—and the Mormons had done nothing to oppose—did they finally let the Mormons alone. No, now they tried to involve them in all sorts of intrigues. Here is a typical case. They sent a governor. And then some miserable scamp got into a fuss with the Indians and got killed. So the governor ordered out the militia to kill off the Indians. The brethren, naturally, were required to go along, but knowing the white men to be the aggressors, they did not want to turn out and, like General Harney, kill the "enemy." So they said, "We shall not go." Then the governor said, "Ah, they've committed treason!" He would send an army to Utah to shoot and hang. "Our enemies are determined to bring us into collision with the Government."[94] Brigham had no argument with the government—the perfect government. Nothing was better for this life than the Constitution. "You are not going to find anything better to go by," said Brigham. But, "Our enemies are determined to bring us into collision with the Government, so they can kill us; but they shall not come here."[95]

"Joseph Smith, in forty-seven prosecutions was never proven guilty of one violation of the laws of his country. They accused him of treason, because he would not fellowship their wickedness."[96] "Now, as we are accused of secession, my counsel to this congregation is to secede, what from? From the Constitution of the United States? No. From the institutions of our country? No. Well then, what from?

From sin and the practice thereof. That is my counsel to this congregation and to the whole world."[97]

Brigham Young explains further:

> We have got to be called treasoners by our enemies. Joseph was taken up six times, if I remember rightly, on the charge of treason. Once he was brought into court by some enemies who thought they could prove that he had committed adultery, and that they termed treason. At another time our brethren wanted to vote in Davies County, Missouri, and said they would cast their votes and have their rights with other citizens; whereupon Joseph was taken up for treason. Another time, he was taken up on a charge of high treason; and when he came before the grand jury, his enemies wanted to prove that he had more than one wife, asserting that that was high treason.[98]

Anything to get the Saints into trouble, and that sort of thing had been going on all along. Thus they faced the problem of security; they had not been listened to. Certain people were out to get them, and the press was never quiet. Always, stirrings were going on. Brigham said in 1853: "I have been frequently asked, what is going to be the result of these troubles? I answer—*The result will be good.*"[99] "He will not suffer the Priesthood to be again driven from the earth. They may massacre men, women, and children; but the Lord will not suffer them to destroy the Priesthood."[100] "Up to this time we have carried the world upon our backs. Joseph did it in his day, besides carrying this whole people, and now all this is upon my back, with my family to provide for at the same time and we will carry it all, and bear off the Kingdom of God."[101] "This is my confidence in my God. I am no more concerned about this people's suffering unto death, than I am concerned about the sun's falling out of its orbit and ceasing to shine on this earth again."[102]

"I am aware [he sounds like Demosthenes] that you will want to know what will be the result of the present movement against us [Johnston's Army in 1857]. 'Mormonism' will take an almighty stride into influence and power, while our enemies will sink and become weaker and weaker, and be no more; and I know it just as well now as I shall five years hence."[103] A year after this he stood up in conference and said, "I thank God for the United States Army—I'm two million dollars richer than one year ago." Yet it had looked as though the Saints would be destroyed. When he heard of the army's coming, he got in his buggy with his old colored servant, Abel, and they whipped the horses and came down to Provo as fast as they could. He held a conference. He said, "The Army's coming in. They're going to camp down here. You just double the price of everything. Charge what you can get for your eggs; if they want to raise their own chickens and vegetables, fine, they're welcome to do so. Meanwhile, put on the screws." And they did! And so the Army paid through the nose for the luxury of conquering Utah.[104]

Brigham Young said of the intentions of the Church's enemies, "The waves of civilization, to use their own figure, will then surge right up against the walls of barbarism, in which we are entrenched, and wash them down. We as a religion can then be wiped out, and no longer offend the fastidious tastes and senses of the priests and politicians of this enlightened age." Well, we shall see. "Now they are seeking again to break up this people. God will hold them in derision."[105] This was in 1870. Again and again there were the plots, and we often forget that the most dangerous plots were hatched in the 1870s. Brigham had one formula for survival: "If this people will serve Him with all their heart, mind, and strength, they have nothing to fear from this time henceforth and forever," he told them in 1853.[106] "In doing this, no power under the heavens can disturb this people."[107] "If we will only practise what we profess, I tell you we are at the defiance of all hell."[108] "And now I prophesy that, if this people will live their religion, the God of heaven will fight their battles, bring them off victorious over all their enemies, and give to them the kingdom."[109]

In 1857, Brigham Young said, "I will prophesy a little, and I will say that my word shall be as true as any word ever spoken from the heavens. If this people, called Latter-day Saints, will live to the truth, the thread of oppression which is cut will never be united again."[110] And it never has been since then. We'd better live up to it now. "As the Lord live, if this people will be faithful in the performance of every duty [this is ten years later], they will never come upon a field of battle to fight their enemies."[111] "If we will stand up as men and women of God, the yoke shall never be placed upon our necks again."[112] What is the warfare of the Saints?

> With some the question arises, Are we in danger from our enemies [the year after Johnston's Army]? No; there is no danger, only in our neglecting the duties of a Saint. Are we in danger now? No. Have we been? No. Shall we be? No, we shall not. It has been written that many should be slain for the testimony of Jesus; and, in my humble opinion, there have already been enough slain to fulfil that prophecy.[113]

"Now, brethren, can we fight against and subdue *ourselves?* That is the greatest difficulty we ever encountered, and the most arduous warfare we ever engaged in."[114] "In this probation, we have evil to contend with, and we must overcome it in ourselves, or we shall never overcome it anywhere else."[115] "As to being afflicted, never fear that: only fear that you are not living as well as you might, and then there is no danger."[116]

We are never going to destroy the enemies of God by the evil passions that are in us—never, no never. When those who profess to be Saints contend against the enemies of God through passion or selfwill, it is then man against man, evil against evil, the powers of darkness against the powers of darkness. But when men who are sanctified, purified, do anything, they will do it with a coolness as if conversing at their firesides with each other.[117]

You will be whipped until you have the Spirit of the Lord Jesus Christ sufficiently to love your brethren and sisters freely, men, women, and children; until you can live at peace with yourselves, and with every family around you; until you can treat every child [this was during Walker's War] as though it were the tender offspring of your own body, every man as your brother, and every woman as your sister; and until the young persons treat the old with that respect due to parents.[118]

All right, that is victory.

Let us go down into the cabin and do up our praying in fair weather. That is what "Mormonism" teaches me; and when it is dark as midnight darkness, when there is not one particle of feeling in my heart to pray, shall I then say, I will not pray? [This is Brigham, the leader.] No, but get down knees, bend yourselves upon the floor, and mouth, open; tongue, speak; and we will see what will come forth, and you shall worship the Lord God of Israel, even when you feel as though you could not say a word in His favor. That is the victory we have to gain; that is the warfare we have to wage. It is between the spirit and the body; they are inseparably connected.[119]

So who is the enemy?

As to the struggle that is going on between the Latter-day Saints and the world, have we any struggle with them? No. Have we any contention? No, not in the least. Have we any battle to fight? No, none at all. Are we to marshal our armies to contend against them? No. Here are the words of truth; we go forth and declare them to the ends of the earth; it is our mission and all we have to do. They may war against us, they may marshal their forces and their armies. God rules, I fear them not. If I preserve myself in the truth, I am all right.[120]

Who hinders you from being happy? from praying, and serving the Lord as much as you please? Who hinders you from doing all the good in your power to do? Who is there here, to mar in any way the peace of any Saint that lives in these peaceful valleys? No one. It is for us to keep our own gardens clean, and see we do not harbor evil in our own hearts.[121]

How do we deal with them then? "One of the nicest things in the world is to let an enemy alone entirely, and it mortifies him to death."[122]

Woe to those who fight against it [Joseph Smith's testimony]. What will we do to them? Nothing at all, but preach the Gospel. They may lie about us as they please. If we will faithfully mind our own concerns, live our religion, do good to all men, preach the Gospel to the nations of the earth, gather up the honest in heart, build up and establish Zion in the earth, send the Gospel to the House of Israel, and live and serve God in all things, all will be well with us, we have no cause for fear in the least.[123]

"If there are any hearts or spirits in this city, or elsewhere, that are fearfully wondering whether or not we are going to be destroyed, . . . I will say to all such trembling souls, You need entertain no such fears. You need have only one fear, and that is with regard to yourselves."[124] And so he continues:

> If I do not enjoy all I anticipated, if my happiness is not as complete as I anticipated, if the light of the Holy Spirit is not in my heart to that degree which I expected it would be [many of the saints being disappointed], if I have not obtained all I anticipated when I was down in yonder world, mingled with the wicked, *the cause is in myself*, in my own heart, in my own disposition, in the weakness of human nature; it is my own will that prevents me from enjoying all I anticipated, and more.[125]

> As for the weaknesses of human nature, we have plenty of them; weakness and sin are with us constantly; they are sown in the mortal body, and extend from the crown of the head to the souls of the feet. We need not go to our neighbors for sin, to palliate all our crimes, for we ourselves have plenty of it; we need not crave weakness from our fellow man, we have our own share of it; it is for us to trust in the Lord, and endeavor to deliver ourselves from the effects of sin, plead with every person to take the same course, and propose and plan every possible means to become friends of God, that we may thereby become friends of sinners, and receive a great reward in a day to come.[126]

Brigham doesn't like retaliation to arms. "I sometimes felt, before the move, like taking the sword and slaying my enemies, until they were wasted away. But the Lord did not design this, and we have remained in peace and quietness."[127] "We could wipe the few enemies now in our borders out of existence in a very short time, if I would give the word to do so."[128] "We could circumscribe their camps and kill every man, woman and child of them. This is what others have done, and if we were to do it, what better are we than the wicked and the ungodly?"[129] "The cause of human improvement is not in the least advanced by the dreadful war which now convulses our unhappy country [this was 1863]."[130] "War is instigated by wickedness—it is the consequence of a nation's sin."[131] "Never try to destroy a man. It is our mission to save the people, not to destroy them. The least, the most inferior spirit now upon the earth, in our capacity, is worth worlds."[132]

> We do not want to stand here and talk about war [Johnston's Army was entering]. There is nothing so repugnant to my feelings as to injure or destroy. But what is upon us? Nothing, only another manifestation of the opposition of the Devil to the kingdom of God. War has been declared against the Saints over twenty-seven years, and our enemies have only fallen back so as to gain strength and pretexts for making another attack. Will that spirit increase? If it does, and we love our religion, let me tell you that we will increase faster than our enemies will.[133]

All war can do is destroy. "Let a few incendiaries go through a city and put the torch here and there, and the city is destroyed—the labor of years, perhaps of centuries, is wasted. Does this make great men of them? Perhaps they think so. If they can destroy a city or a nation they think they will gain a great name. They will not."[134]

War is futile. "A large share of the ingenuity of the world is taxed to invent weapons of war. What a set of fools!"[135] "There is a spirit that prompts the nations to prepare for war, desolation, and bloodshed—to waste each other away. Do they realize it? No."[136]

> According to my definition of the word, there is not a strictly and fully civilized community now upon the earth. Is there murder by wholesale to be found in a strictly and fully civilized community? Will a community of civilized nations rise up one against another, nation

against nation, and kingdom against kingdom, using against each other every destructive invention that can be brought to bear in their wars?[137]

"Much of the skill, ingenuity, and ability of the Christian nations are now devoted to manufacturing instruments of death. [And of course it's truer today than it was then!] May we be saved from the effects of them! As I often tell you, if we are faithful, the Lord will fight our battles much better than we can ourselves."[138]

When the nations have for years turned much of their attention to manufacturing instruments of death [of course this was in 1860, and this is just before the six weeks war broke out—wasn't it between Prussia and Denmark, and then between Prussia and Austria], they have sooner or later used those instruments. Our nation, England, France, Germany, Austria, Italy, and other nations have for years exercised their inventive skill, and expended much means in inventing and fabricating instruments of death [little did he realize what was coming!]. . . . From the authority of all history, the deadly weapons now stored up and being manufactured will be used until the people are wasted away, and there is no help for it. The spirit of revolution goes on through the nations: it never goes back.[139]

"Does it justify the slaying of men, women, and children that otherwise would have remained at home in peace, because a great army is doing the work? No: the guilty will be damned for it."[140]

Some Christian nations lately went to war with each other [this is in 1859, and he is referring to the Crimean War (1853–56)]. What for? Pride—to please a selfish, worldly, carnal, wicked heart. And the priests, the majority of them being of the same faith, on both sides the line of battle prayed to the same God for success in slaying the opposing army.[141]

The destruction of property and life during the war [the Civil War] has been enormous; but I am satisfied that the destruction of the love of virtue—the love of every exalted principle of honor, and of political and social government—has been greater, comparatively, than the destruction of property and life. Religious societies abound in the nation. Although it never was more wicked than at the present time, it is strange to say that it never was more religious in profession.[142]

Brigham says more about the futility of armaments. Here is his policy, and it seems rather demanding. He applied it, too.

Whenever the time comes that you hate an object, or a thing, try and heap blessings on the object, and it will be well for you, for it will take away those feelings. . . . When I see a man commit folly in his weakness, am I to stretch forth my hand to destroy that man? No! But I will pull him out of the pit if I can.[143]

Why do you not say, if you have a mind to abuse, abuse away? . . . Let every heart be firm and every one say, I will never contend any more with a man for property. I will not be cruel to my fellow-creature, but I will do all the good I can, and as little evil as possible. Now where would be the wrong of taking this course?[144]

You will find it unwise to quarrel with your neighbour for differences of opinion, or for his course of conduct, but simply be concerned to always do right, and rest assured that each one the world over, will attain to precisely that amount of intelligence, happiness, and glory, or the reverse, which he has lived for.[145]

How about a policy of nonresistance, then? He says, "When men are oppressed, it is in their own hearts and feelings: it is not because oppression comes upon them from any other quarter, than that they are dissatisfied. They are not satisfied with themselves."[146] That is the trouble. Of course that is the psychology of feeling oppressed. We are told that during the worst times of the persecution, in Nauvoo, etc., the Saints were never so happy. Those who went through it never felt better. "Our enemies are unremitting in their labors and vigilance, and with a zeal worthy of a better cause. It is interesting to watch the fruitlessness of their labors."[147] "Interesting to watch," he says—nonresistance. "But these things [the excesses of the army of occupation in 1859; they were pretty bad] are most excellent tests of the patience and forbearance of the Saints, and are such as would not be quietly endured by any other people."[148]

> They talk about overthrowing us, and obliterating our peculiarities which are so obnoxious to them. . . . They have schemed, planned and devised mischief against us in secret, . . . and, in fact, done everything against us that they could [and he knew a great deal of what was going on]; . . . but notwithstanding all this, have they been able to rob us of the enjoyments of our religion and of peace?[149]

> The *Vedette* [the newspaper, printed at Fort Douglas, that had just changed hands] has been unusually bitter of late, since the change of editors—too bitter to hold out very long. . . . If we would quarrel with them, or notice them, it would be encouraging; . . . but it is very annoying, after they have exhausted every invective, and every species of vituperation and slander, to find no spot so vulnerable that they can cause us . . . to even express the most trifling anger or vexation.[150]

And that settles it.

> I must be patient with them, as the Lord is patient with me; as the Lord is merciful to me, I will be merciful to others; as He continues to be merciful to me, consequently

I must continue, in long-suffering, to be merciful to others; patiently waiting, with all diligence, until the people will believe.[151]

Since the Jews are now front-line news, let us review Brigham's interesting prophecies on them. "Let me here say a word to the Jews [this is an interesting story, because I've heard my grandmother tell about this many times]. We do not want you to believe our doctrine. If any professing to be Jews should do so, it would prove that they are not Jews. A Jew cannot now believe in Jesus Christ. Brother Neibaur [who was sitting on the stand then], who thinks he is a Jew, is a good Latter-day Saint; he has not any of the blood of Judah in his veins."[152] Grandpa Neibaur went home that day, stormed into the house, threw down his hat, and said, "Brigham doesn't know everything!" I guess he was very proud of being a Jew.

> The decree has gone forth from the Almighty that they cannot have the benefit of the atonement until they gather to Jerusalem, for they said, let His blood be upon us and upon our children, consequently, they cannot believe in him until his second coming. We have a great desire for their welfare, and are looking for the time soon to come when they will gather to Jerusalem, build up the city and the land of Palestine, and prepare for the coming of the Messiah. When he comes again, he will not come as he did when the Jews rejected him; neither will he appear first at Jerusalem when he makes his second appearance on the earth; but he will appear first on the land where he commenced his work in the beginning, and planted the garden of Eden, and that was done in the land of America. When the Savior visits Jerusalem, and the Jews look upon him, and see the wounds in his hands and in his side and in his feet, they will then know that they have persecuted and put to death the true Messiah, and then they will acknowledge him, but not till then.

They have confounded his first and second coming,
expecting his first coming to be as a mighty prince
instead of as a servant. They will go back by and by to
Jerusalem and own their Lord and Master. We have no
feelings against them. I wish they were all gentlemen,
men of heart and brain, and knew precisely how the Lord
looks upon them.[153]

"Jerusalem is not to be redeemed by the soft still voice
of the preacher of the Gospel of peace."[154] This is interesting
too, because everything he says here is diametrically
opposed to what the whole Christian world was preaching
about the restoration of Jerusalem. I wrote a long article in a
Jewish encyclopedia on this particular subject.[155] All the
Christian churches were climbing all over each other in
their eagerness to get back to Jerusalem and establish the
Jews. The Mormons would take no part in that, because it's
the Jews' show, not ours. Jerusalem is not—and moreover
the Latter-day Saints didn't think it was—to be redeemed
by evangelism or anything similar; it would have to be by
the shedding of blood and in other ways.

Look how things have gone: "Jerusalem is not to be
redeemed by the soft still voice of the preacher of the
Gospel of peace. Why? Because they were once the blessed
of the Lord, the chosen of the Lord, the promised seed. . . .
Jerusalem is not to be redeemed by our going there and
preaching to the inhabitants," as every other Christian
church has been doing.[156] That's what that Crimean War was
about—the holy places; the French and the Russians
claimed the right to protect them and send their missionaries, the Franciscans. Every other church thought that, but
not the Latter-day Saints:

> Jerusalem is not to be redeemed by our going there
> and preaching to the inhabitants. It will be redeemed by

the high hand of the Almighty. It will be given into the possession of the ancient Israelites by the power of God, and by the pouring out of His judgments. . . . The people who are the most ready to receive the Gospel are those who have lived without it from the days of Noah to this time [the Jews had never heard it. The Jews] . . . will be the last of all the seed of Abraham to have the privilege of receiving the New and Everlasting Covenant. You may hand out to them gold, you may feed and clothe them, but it is impossible to convert the Jews, until the Lord God Almighty does it.[157]

By and by the Jews will be gathered to the land of their fathers, and the ten tribes, who wandered into the north, will be gathered home, and the blood of Ephraim, the second son of Joseph, who was sold into Egypt, which is to be found in every kingdom and nation under heaven, will be gathered from among the Gentiles, and the Gentiles [notice, the blood of Ephraim is largely us] who will receive and adhere to the principles of the gospel will be adopted and initiated into the family of Father Abraham [receive the covenant by adoption], and Jesus will reign over His own and Satan will reign over his own. This will be the result.[158]

"Build up Zion, redeem the House of Israel, and perhaps assist (though I do not think there will be any need of it) to gather the Jews to Jerusalem and prepare for the coming of the Son of Man."[159] The Jews can take care of themselves. "God has removed the kingdom from Jerusalem again to Zion, and here he will wind up the scene."[160] "This American continent will be Zion; for it is so spoken of by the prophets. Jerusalem will be rebuilt and will be the place of gathering, and the tribe of Judah will gather there; but this continent of America is the land of Zion."[161] He is very clear. "Here are the Lamanites, another example. Their wickedness was not so great as those who slew the Son of

God. . . . Still, the curse will be removed from them before it will be removed from the children of Judah; and they will become 'a white and delightsome people.'"[162]

These interesting things will happen, and they have followed this pattern and not that predicted by the whole Christian world, in its wisdom. Brigham Young's Indian problems (remember, his main problems were with the Indians) are very important, because they are an excellent measure of his statesmanship. His policy applies to any international or cultural conflict.

> I certainly believe that the present affliction, which has come upon us from the Indians, is a consequence of the wickedness which dwells in the hearts of some of our brethren. . . . I believe that the Lord permits them to chasten us at the present time to convince us that we have to overcome the vindictive feelings which we have harbored towards that poor, down-trodden branch of the house of Israel [the Indians definitely have a case].[163]

Brigham says in 1853 of Walker's War,

> And when the Indians make war on us, the mob only had power to drive the Saints to their duty, and to remember the Lord their God, and that is all the Indians can do. This people are worldly-minded, they want to get rich in earthly substance, and are apt to forget their God, the pit from which they were dug, and the rock from which they were hewn, every man turning to his own way. Seemingly the Lord is chastening us until we turn and do His will. . . . There will always be Indians or somebody else to chastise you.[164]

Talking about polygamy, Brigham says, "There will always be more cats coming out of the bag." "You'll get rid of polygamy"; that will cease to be an issue, but he says, "There will always be cats coming out of the bag to scandalize the world."[165] Of course it's the Negro question today.

It will always be something like that. Expect it. "There will always be Indians or somebody else to chastise you, until you come to that spot; so amen to the present Indian trouble, for it is all right. I am just as willing the rebellious of this people should be kicked, and cuffed, and mobbed, and hunted by the Indians, as not, for I have preached to them until I am tired."[166] Don't do as they do. "People do not realize what they have done by driving us into the midst of the Lamanites. [It's the best thing that could happen for both of us.]"[167] "Shall we do as the Lamanites do? No. I forbid it in the name of the Lord Jesus Christ—I forbid any elder or member in this church slaying an innocent Lamanite, any more than he would slay an innocent white man."[168]

I wish to impress them with the necessity of treating the Indians with kindness, and to refrain from harboring that revengeful, vindictive feeling that many indulge in. I am convinced that as long as we harbor in us feelings towards them, so long they will be our enemies, and the Lord will suffer them to afflict us. But now their game has gone, and they are left to starve. It is our duty to feed them. The Lord has given us ability to cultivate the ground and reap bountiful harvests. We have an abundance of food for ourselves and for the stranger. It is our duty to feed these poor ignorant Indians; we are living on their possessions and at their homes [so what else can we expect?]. Do we wish to do right? You answer, yes. Then let the Lamanites come back to their homes, where they were born and brought up. This is the land that they and their fathers have walked over and called their own; and they have just as good a right to call it theirs to-day as any people have to call any land their own. The Indians are far oftener, if not always, when differences of education and habits are included, more sinned against than sinners.[169]

[Take] these wild Indians; we call them savages; we call them heathens. Let yourselves be divested of prejudice . . . and let your minds be in open vision before the Almighty, seeing things as they are, [and] you will find that that very people know just as much about the Lord as anybody else.[170]

[The demands of the Indians] should be met with a spirit of liberality on the part of the General Government. . . . I have uniformly pursued a friendly course of policy towards them, feeling convinced, that independent of the question of exercising humanity towards so degraded and ignorant a race of people, it was manifestly more economical, and less expensive, to feed and clothe, than to fight them. . . . Doubtless, a vast deal of patience and forbearance would be required to carry out this policy, even if the Indians should consent to try it.[171]

Toward the Indians, continue to exercise patience, charity, and forbearance; pray for them, and teach them also. We exhort you to feed and clothe them as heretofore, but never lose an opportunity of teaching them to work. Let us impart freely of such as have received.

I am sorry that some of our brethren have been killed by the Indians, but am far more sorry that some of the Indians have been slain by the brethren [imagine that!]. I have often said, and I say again, if any person is to be killed for stealing, let that one be a white man, and not an Indian, for the white men know better, while Indians do not; and you must lay aside your angry feelings towards them, and cease wishing to kill them. . . . Any man who cheats a Lamanite should be dealt with more severely than for cheating a *white* man.[172]

The last few days the emissaries of darkness have been exulting in the creation of another Indian outbreak. [They would always raise these outbreaks and then blame them on the Mormons.] Another Indian outbreak incident, of course, by the Mormons. This time the plot was laid at Deep Creek. Our brethren, the Lamanites, had nothing to do with it. Thus far it has resulted in dispatching troops from California, Camp Douglas and other points to the seat of war. This shows how the ring in Salt Lake works to stir up.

He claims there was actually a ring. The Saints' enemies had it very carefully worked out, and they never missed a chance. Think of the opposition; think of the fighting. There was tremendous power behind that opposition. He continues to comment on the Indian policy. How did he deal with a military minority?

> I have saved the Government hundreds of thousands of dollars, by keeping the Indians peaceable in Utah. Hundreds of miles have the Indians travelled to see me, to know whether they might use up the emigrants, saying—"They have killed many of us, and they damn you and damn us, and shall we stand it?" I have always told them to hold on, to stop shedding blood, and to live in peace. . . . It is more than I can do to keep the Indians still under such outrageous treatment.[173]

> There has been much prejudice raised against us on account of Indian depredations, notwithstanding the great trouble and expense to which we have been subjected in preventing them, and without which no person could have travelled across these mountains and plains. [If we hadn't held the Indians down], what is the reason the Indians have acted so badly? Because of the practice, with many emigrants, of killing the Indians wherever they could find them. . . . In this, there is one man in the Senate of the United States who, I think, agrees with me, if there is nobody else; and that one is General Sam Houston. [He was a great friend of Brigham Young's.] He has had experience, and has good sense. You will find as

fine natural talent among these Indians as among any people; and often, when one of them, who has as kind a heart and good appearance as need be, walks up to an emigrant camp with kindly feelings, he is shot down.[174]

What a fine way to receive people. What can you expect of the Indians? "Has there been one treaty with the Indians fulfilled in good faith by the Government? If there is one, I wish you would let me know."[175] He was satisfied that among the redmen of the mountains and forests you could find as many good and honest persons as among the Anglo-Saxons.

The Indian policy, then, was one of coexistence. Of Chief Walker, Brigham said,

> How many times have I been asked in the past week what I intend to do with [Chief] Walker? I say, Let him alone, severely. I have not made war on the Indians, nor am I calculating to do it. My policy is to give them presents, and be kind to them. Instead of being Walker's enemy, I have sent him a great pile of tobacco to smoke when he is lonely in the mountains. He is now at war with the only friends he has upon this earth, and I want him to have some tobacco to smoke. . . . Let the Lord extend the hand of benevolence to brother Walker [and he always called him "Brother Walker"], and he will make you do it by other means than exhortations given in mildness. This very same Indian Walker has a mission upon him, and I do not blame him for what he is now doing: he is helping me to do the will of the Lord to this people, he is doing with a chastening rod what I have failed to accomplish with soft words, while I have been handing out my substance, feeding the hungry, comforting the sick. But this has no effect upon this people at all, my counsel has not been needed, so the Lord is making brother Walker an instrument to help me, and perhaps the means that he will use will have their due effect.[176]

I tell you, [Brother] Walker has not been the cause of the Indian war. But the Lord will work out the salvation of his people, if they do as they are told. I tell the brethren who live out from this city that the Indians are friendly and wish to make treaties.[177]

As human beings, the Indians also had weaknesses, and Brigham Young was not a sentimental fool. We should neither underestimate them nor imitate their weaknesses. "The Elders of Israel are either so fluctuating in their feelings, so unstable in their ways, or so ignorant of the Indian character, that the least mark of friendship manifested by these treacherous red men will lull all their fears."[178] Don't let that happen. Remember, they play the game, the same game you do. They're human beings too. Throw them entirely off their guard saying, "It is all right." Wait a minute.

The Indians are very much as *they* say the whites are, that is, uncertain—not to be trusted [because they don't trust us]. The whites *may* be uncertain, *but I know* the Indians are. [And so] I dislike to trust them far [right now, so don't be completely disarmed; don't let your good will become sentimentality.] When we first entered Utah, we were prepared to meet all the Indians in these mountains, and kill every soul of them if we had been obliged to do so. [Fortunately we didn't have to do any of that.] This preparation secured us peace [for the time they needed it]. I would rather take my chance to-day for good treatment among Indians, than I would white men.[179]

If the inhabitants of this Territory . . . had never condescended to reduce themselves to the practices of the Indians . . . [this is not your culture at all. This is a good thing; he recognized that there is a difference. Don't act like them. In that case, if they hadn't done that, so many of our people went off and tried to act like Indians] there

never would have been any trouble between us and our
red neighbors. [This is the key to the whole of it.][180]

To Walker, the chief, whom all California and New
Mexico dreaded, I said, "It will just as sure kill as the
world, if you live as we live." Said he, "I want as good as
Brigham, I want to eat as he does." Said I, "Eat then, but it
will kill you." I told the same to Arapeen, Walker's
brother, [if you adopt our diet and our way of life, it will
kill you].[181]

You're not for that, Brigham said. "I am suspicious
that this people do not possess the faith they should have,
therefore I calculate to carry with me proper weapons of
defence."[182] It's a lamentable thing, regrettable, but if we
lack the faith, it's the next best thing.

But, lest you should not have faith, we have caused
to be done that which has been done, in having this
people prepared for any emergency that should arise. My
advice is *be on the watch all the time*. Do not lie down, and
go to sleep, and say all is well, lest in an hour when you
think not, sudden destruction overtake you.[183]

This, of course, was in the midst of an Indian war, over-
confidence in the other extreme. "You cannot, with *my consent*, go to any place, unless it is to a city, that is, or [to a
place that] will be walled in."[184] He recommended that the
Saints wall the cities—we still have Cedar Fort; Lehi was a
walled town. The last remnants of the wall still stand.
Payson was the last one of the walled cities.

"You are so instructed," he said during 1853, "to see if
you will do as you are told. Let your dwelling house be a
perfect fort. From the day I lived where brother Joseph
Smith lived, I have been fortified all the time so as to resist
twenty men, if they should come to my house in the night,
with an intent to molest my family, assault my person, or

destroy my property."[185] He'd had enough experience with Joseph Smith to know that you had to be ready for the enemy. "But there's no place for alarmism," he counsels; "I know this people have suffered more by the contemplation of trouble, than they have when actually passing through it. As they have magnified future trouble almost infinitely beyond its real dimensions, so they have imagined to themselves a greater heaven than they can find in Zion, at its present stage of progression."[186] But things can be overdone in both extremes. There were many manic depressives among the Saints, who got panicky at the least sign of danger, thinking the Millennium should be here when things started going well. Some members surmised that they were going to have trouble; they needed not expect any trouble except they took a course to bring it on themselves. They needed never expect to see sorrow unless their own conduct, conversation, or acts brought it on them. "On the other hand, they no sooner discover an Indian in an hostile attitude, than the hue and cry is *'We shall all be murdered immediately.'*"[187] As soon as an Indian started behaving himself, they immediately went off guard and became all lovey-dovey, and opened themselves wide open to this man, who still suspected them. He didn't know how to deal with these strange, volatile people. On the other hand, as soon as the Indian frowned, what happened? The human cried, "*'We shall all be murdered immediately.'* That is the kind of stability, the kind of unshaken self-command, the style of generalship and wisdom manifested by Elders in Israel."[188]

This was the kind of man to have for a leader. Brigham Young also commented on the race crisis. As you can imagine, he believed strongly in the brotherhood and equality of man. It was an important principle with him, because we're living in that third dimension which makes the gospel. He lived in a third-dimensional world; we live in a two-dimensional world. That's why we have difficulty representing the gospel very well; we'll always fail because ours is two-dimensional. The gospel has another dimension that other religions don't have. You can't interpret this dimension to other people unless they want to see it. One must see it in stereo. Brigham Young saw the world, the cosmos, in stereo. He saw that other dimension which leaders of the world today don't see, which we don't see ourselves. It's rare, but when you do see it, it's a real image, a real thing. When you live in that dimension, everything looks entirely different. He seems to be a man from another planet, a strange man that could do and say these things. He seemed to be equal to anything; he seemed to carry it off so easily. Of course the fact that he had a tremendous physique may have helped too. But he was very calm. When he was fifteen years older than I am, he didn't have a gray hair. He died at the age of seventy-seven of a ruptured appendix, a thing that could be easily prevented and taken care of today, but doctors didn't know what to do about it then. And they had nothing for mountain fever. They had nothing for the various diseases and plagues which the Saints suffered from, and Brigham had them again and again, yet he survived and accepted everything with his sweet, calm nature.

We're always given a picture of Brigham Young the hard driver, because we can't consider a person accomplishing what he did without being a bulldozer. He was anything but a bulldozer. He was the kindest gentleman. I know this from his wives, his daughters, his grand-daughters. I've heard it again and again from my grandmother; Brigham Young came into the house to be met there by a big feast for the President. He wanted bread and milk, his favorite dish, and he settled for that, while everybody else had the banquet. Everybody else had a good time; then he would dance until 3:00 in the morning. They said he was the last figure dowsing the campfire in the canyons, but when the Saints first went up there, he welcomed them all. Then some character appeared with a bugle and a list of events, and Brigham charged him. Brigham said they could blow the bugle all they wanted, but he'd do what he wanted to, so they started dancing. When at 10:00 the bugle blew, Brigham said, "Well, I'm going to go on dancing," and so they all went on dancing until 3:00 in the morning.[189] He didn't like regimentation. He liked variety, differentness, everybody being themselves. What a marvelous man.

Notes

1. See "Brigham Young as a Leader," an address delivered on 6 June 1967 at Brigham Young University, pages 449–90 in this volume.

2. Cf. *JD* 17:51; 14:205.

3. *JD* 6:174.

4. *JD* 5:99.

5. *MS* 15:386.

6. *JD* 16:113.

7. *MS* 22:702.

8. *MS* 14:216.

9. *MS* 20:218.

10. Nibley's address delivered on 8 June 1967 at Brigham Young University was "Brigham Young as an Educator."

11. *JD* 13:149, 176.

12. *MS* 20:218.

13. *JD* 1:335.

14. *JD* 15:18.

15. Cf. *JD* 8:203.

16. Cf. *JD* 2:18–20; 3:5–6.

17. *MS* 17:675.

18. *JD* 31:573.

19. *JD* 31:573.

20. *JD* 13:215.

21. *JD* 12:33–34.

22. *JD* 5:228.

23. *JD* 5:229.
24. *JD* 10:329.
25. *JD* 1:361.
26. *JD* 10:204.
27. *JD* 15:123.
28. *MS* 6:197.
29. *MS* 6:197.
30. *JD* 7:9.
31. *MS* 17:674.
32. *JD* 4:38.
33. Cf. *JD* 4:267.
34. *JD* 4:267.
35. *JD* 14:93.
36. *JD* 2:314.
37. *JD* 2:314.
38. *JD* 4:267.
39. *JD* 3:257 (emphasis added).
40. *JD* 15:161.
41. Cf. *JD* 14:83: "'Must we not have law?' We have plenty of it, and sometimes we have a little too much. Legislators make too many laws; they make so many that the people do not know anything about them. Wise legislators will never make more laws than the people can understand."
42. *JD* 13:242.
43. *JD* 15:161.
44. *JD* 2:310.
45. *JD* 4:284.
46. *JD* 9:105.
47. *JD* 4:284.
48. *JD* 10:223.
49. *JD* 10:212.
50. *JD* 7:134.
51. *JD* 9:121, 123.
52. *JD* 3:195.
53. *JD* 8:177.
54. *MS* 8:45.
55. *JD* 6:71.
56. *JD* 8:37.
57. *JD* 10:232.
58. *JD* 7:136.
59. *JD* 7:134.
60. *JD* 8:287.

61. *JD* 3:247.
62. *JD* 12:220.
63. *JD* 1:339.
64. *JD* 8:261.
65. *JD* 8:136.
66. *JD* 8:368.
67. *JD* 8:367.
68. *JD* 8:16.
69. *JD* 8:16.
70. *JD* 3:363.
71. *JD* 8:148.
72. *JD* 8:124.
73. *JD* 5:232.
74. *JD* 5:351.
75. *JD* 7:14.
76. *JD* 11:262–63.
77. *JD* 12:204.
78. *JD* 2:182.
79. *JD* 7:15.
80. *JD* 8:324.
81. *JD* 2:170.
82. *JD* 2:182.
83. *JD* 2:175.
84. *JD* 7:13.
85. *JD* 5:124.
86. *JD* 9:331.
87. *JD* 9:331.
88. *JD* 11:17.
89. *JD* 8:279.
90. League for Social Service, *Ten Reasons Why Christians Cannot Fellowship the Mormon Church* (Salt Lake City, UT: Kinsman, 1897).
91. Cf. *JD* 11:17–18: "When we were driven from Nauvoo, our Elders went to the East to lay our case before the judges, governors, and rulers of the different States to ask for any asylum; but none was offered us."
92. *JD* 5:231–32.
93. *JD* 5:350.
94. *JD* 5:234.
95. *JD* 5:234.
96. *JD* 10:111.
97. *JD* 10:111.
98. *JD* 5:234.

99. *JD* 1:164.
100. *JD* 2:184.
101. *JD* 2:317.
102. *JD* 4:26.
103. *JD* 5:235.
104. Cf. *JD* 8:356–57.
105. *JD* 13:335.
106. *JD* 1:78.
107. *JD* 1:78.
108. *JD* 2:186.
109. *JD* 5:167.
110. *JD* 5:332.
111. *JD* 11:134.
112. *JD* 5:332.
113. *JD* 7:56.
114. *JD* 6:315.
115. *JD* 6:99.
116. *JD* 5:258.
117. *JD* 8:325.
118. *JD* 1:169.
119. *JD* 3:207.
120. *JD* 18:360.
121. *JD* 2:95.
122. *JD* 19:70.
123. *JD* 19:5.
124. *JD* 19:3.
125. *JD* 1:311.
126. *JD* 1:360.
127. *JD* 8:150.
128. *JD* 5:351.
129. *JD* 11:264.
130. *JD* 10:250.
131. *JD* 10:230.
132. *JD* 9:124.
133. *JD* 5:340.
134. *JD* 10:315.
135. *JD* 8:324.
136. *JD* 8:174.
137. *JD* 8:6–7.
138. *JD* 8:325.
139. *JD* 8:157.
140. *JD* 7:137.

141. *JD* 7:134.
142. *JD* 12:120.
143. *MS* 13:258.
144. *JD* 1:32–33.
145. *MS* 17:120.
146. *JD* 6:328.
147. *MS* 33:170.
148. *JD* 21:303.
149. *JD* 27:637.
150. *JD* 27:206.
151. *JD* 15:45 (supplement).
152. *JD* 11:279.
153. *JD* 11:279.
154. *JD* 2:142.
155. Hugh W. Nibley, "Jerusalem: In Christianity," in *Encyclopedia Judaica*, 16 vols. (Jerusalem: Macmillan, 1972), 9:1570–75.
156. *JD* 2:141–42.
157. *JD* 2:141–42.
158. *JD* 12:38.
159. *JD* 11:294.
160. *JD* 8:195.
161. *JD* 5:4.
162. *JD* 2:143.
163. *JD* 11:263.
164. *JD* 1:169.
165. Cf. *JD* 1:188–89.
166. *JD* 1:169.
167. *JD* 5:236.
168. *JD* 11:265.
169. *JD* 11:263–64.
170. *JD* 3:87.
171. *MS* 17:261.
172. *MS* 16:188.
173. *JD* 5:236.
174. *JD* 7:58.
175. *JD* 10:108.
176. *JD* 1:168–69.
177. *JD* 6:327.
178. *JD* 1:163.
179. *JD* 1:105.
180. *JD* 6:327.
181. *JD* 14:87.

182. *JD* 1:106.
183. *JD* 1:107.
184. *JD* 1:77.
185. *JD* 1:167.
186. *JD* 1:314–15.
187. *JD* 1:163.
188. *JD* 1:163.
189. *MS* 18:673–80; 22:699–702.

7

Brigham Young and the Enemy

It would be hard to find in history another man who spent as many days of his life surrounded by determined, implacable, and dangerous enemies as did Brigham Young: "Forty-five years ago," he recalled in the last year of his life, "they were determined to kill the Prophet Joseph. I have lain upon the floor scores and scores of nights ready to receive the mob who sought his life. This persecution commenced with a little neighborhood, then a town, then a county, then a State, and the people of the United States; and by and by other nations will be just as bitter towards us, . . . as many of the people of our own nation now are."[1] There was never any indication that things would improve: "The enemies of God and truth do not love us any better this year than they did last year, nor will their love for us increase in the year that is to come."[2] The enemy was within and without: "It was pro-slavery men that pointed the bayonet at me and my brethren in Missouri, and said, 'Damn you we will kill you,'"[3] and yet "our difficulties and persecutions have always arisen from men right in our midst."[4]

After the death of the Prophet Joseph Smith, all their

This text was originally printed in The Young Democrat, *privately printed leaflets, edited by Omar Kadar and published in two separate parts in 1970.*

hatred and virulence were concentrated against Brigham Young. It is no exaggeration when he says in 1860, "All the army, with its teamsters, hangers-on, and followers, with the judges, and nearly all the rest of the civil officers, amounting to some seventeen thousand men, have been searching diligently for three years to bring one act to light that would criminate me."[5]

The Helpless Enemy

Faced with such terrifying hostility on all sides with preachers and editors in all the land calling for his blood, what was Brigham to do? Answer: He put his faith in God and smilingly went on his way; he absolutely refused to be in any way alarmed or upset no matter what the enemy was up to:

> As to the struggle that is going on between the Latter-day Saints and the world, have we any struggle with them? No. Have we any contention? No, not in the least. Have we any battle to fight? No, none at all. Are we to marshal our armies to contend against them? No. Here are the words of truth; we go forth and declare them to the ends of the earth; it is our mission and all we have to do. They may war against us, they may marshal their forces and their armies. God rules, I fear them not. If I preserve myself in the truth, I am all right.[6]

In 1858 when crickets, Indians, drought, and the U.S. Army were threatening the Saints at once, President Young told the people: "With some the question arises, Are we in danger from our enemies? . . . No; Have we been? No. Shall we be? No, we shall not."[7] Two years later, after a series of terrible tensions and crises, he could say, "Let our worst wish toward our worst enemies be that we may see the time when they will be obliged to do right."[8] And later: "I love my friends, and as for my enemies, I pray for them daily;

and, if they do not believe I would do them good, let them call at my house, when they are hungry, and I will feed them."[9]

How could the man be so coolly sure of himself in the face of appalling dangers? It was not a pose—no one knew better than Brother Brigham how real and intimate the dangers were. The event, contrary to all expectation, fully justified his prophetic certitude; he knew all along where the real danger lay and where it did *not* lie: "They can do us no harm—they can do nothing against the truth. The Lord will make the wicked and the ungodly and their acts accomplish his design."[10] "The wicked cannot do anything against the truth. Every move they make to crush the kingdom of God will be attended with the single blessings of the Almighty for its further extension and ultimate triumph."[11] "How easy it is for the Almighty to direct the steps of our enemies, until they fall off the precipice and are dashed in pieces, without the efforts of his servants."[12] "Do not be afraid: The enemies of God and his Christ will be divided and subdivided all the time. . . . Wherefore have no fears in the least."[13] He was speaking to the fearful Saints who had seen one formidable campaign after another mounted against them, but he knew with a perfect assurance that such assaults would never prevail: "They will struggle and strive, and plan and devise, saying, Let us take this course, and that course; and they will struggle until they will come to a stop as though they were against a mountain of solid rock. They will do all they can to break us up, and even destroy us; this has been the case now for the last forty-five years."[14]

And if the Saints only knew it, that is good news for them: "We have received enough to understand that the wicked are a rod in the hands of God to chasten his children. If you do not [understand that], it is time that you had learned it, for it is even so; if we are chastened, it is for a purpose. . . . But were we ever destroyed? No, neither will God permit us to be, so long as we are desirous of being his servants, and of doing the work given us to do."[15] It is with absolute certitude of prophecy that Brigham Young declares: "As the Lord live[s], if this people will be faithful in the performance of every duty, they will never come upon a field of battle to fight their enemies."[16]

This is a prophecy peculiar to the last days; in former times the wicked have prevailed, but this time God has set their bounds: "The wicked have succeeded in doing so [destroying the Saints] in former ages; but this kingdom they cannot destroy, because this is the last dispensation— because this is the fulness of times."[17]

Therefore what is there to worry about? "Do you think that the Lord will suffer his people to be hungry and starve to death, to go naked and freeze to death, or to go house-less, if they serve him with an undivided heart? No he never will—never, no, never."[18] Nothing but good can happen to the righteous: "Shall we speak evil of others? No. Why? Because the result of their treatment towards us has made us better and greater than we could have been other-wise. . . . Let us thank God, and speak evil of none."[19]

The Real Danger

In all these promises there is always an "if" clause; to be safe from enemies there are certain things the people must do, and it is in neglecting these things that the real danger lies. What are those things? In the first place, they are never required to fight against anybody: "It is written that the Lord will destroy the wicked, and He has done so by bringing about circumstances to cause them to destroy themselves."[20] Or, in the words of Mormon, "But, behold, the judgments of God will overtake the wicked; and it is by the wicked that the wicked are punished" (Mormon 4:5). No one knew this better than Brigham, who had seen it happen time and again: "The enemies of God . . . will be divided and subdivided all the time,"[21] for they love each other no better than they love us. For one thing, to fight against the world is futile: "We have not the influence and power necessary to refute the falsehoods circulated about us. We depend on God, who sits in the heavens."[22]

Brigham recognizes that such restraint is hard and demanding, for it is human nature to strike back; but that is just the test to which we are being subjected in all this: "May God help us to search our own hearts, to find out whether we are obedient or disobedient . . . and let the enemies of this kingdom do what they please, for God will overrule all things for the special benefit of his people."[23]

The Adversary in Action

For Brigham Young, Satan is a very real quantity, and of course he is an enemy—the enemy. "Evil is here; the Devil reigns on the earth, and has held dominion on it for thousands of years."[24] His power is not weakening for his time is not yet come; on the contrary, "as the kingdom of God rises and advances upon the earth, so will the power of Satan increase to impede its progress until God shall purge that power from the earth."[25] "Has the world become more enlightened in the things of God? No, it has not; and the enmity that did exist, exists still, and has grown, increased and strengthened, and this warfare between the power of the devil and the power of Jesus Christ will continue until Jesus obtains possession of the kingdom."[26] How and by whom his power will be brought to an end is clearly stated in the scriptures—and it will not be by us. He is quite beyond our power to cope with: "The enemy, this potent foe that we have to contend with, we know but little about him, very little."[27] So far from being able of ourselves to match his power, Brigham finds it "a marvel to me that you have lived up to so much as you have, considering the power of the enemy upon the earth. . . . I do not fully comprehend the awful power and influence Satan has upon the earth, but I understand enough to know that it is a marvel that the Latter-day Saints are so good as they are."[28] It is all we can do to break even, let alone conquer: "Let me say to the Latter-day Saints that they stand upon slippery places. They do not all fully know the paths they walk in, they do not all perfectly understand their own ways and doings, many do not altogether realize their own weaknesses, do not understand the power of the devil and how liable they are to be decoyed one hair's breadth, to begin with, from the line of truth."[29]

The only power Satan has is the power to destroy—"that is just what the devil can do, but he never can build anything";[30] he is a cheat and a fraud, and all the power he has over us is what we give him; he rules not by virtue of his real self but by the image he cultivates and the rewards he promises of power and gain, backed up by trickery, violence, deception, and intimidation. When we say, "Destroy them, or they will destroy you!" we are playing it his way, for with such a program, however the game turns out, there will be destruction. By him, "the whole world is contaminated with a spirit to remember evil and forget the good," and when we are animated by hatred of anything it is "because the power of the tempter has control over you, and because the world is full of evil principles, and you have adhered to them."[31] He has power to contaminate our bodies,[32] but that is enough, since he works through the weakness of the flesh. He is always looking for an opening: "There are invisible agencies around us in sufficient numbers to encourage the slightest disposition they may discover in us to forsake the true way, and fan into a flame the slightest spark of discontent and unbelief. The spirits of the ancient Gadiantons are around us."[33] Anything will do: "The devil does not care how much religion there is on the earth; he is a great preacher, and to all appearance a great gentleman. . . . It is popular now-a-days to be religious, it has become the seasoning to a great deal of rascality, hypocrisy and crime."[34] With him it is never a matter of black and white, virtue vs. vice, the good guys vs. the bad guys—he wasn't born yesterday: "In teaching false doctrine there always will be more or less of truth mixed with it. . . . The enemy, the serpent, who beguiled our first mother, told some truth."[35]

The awful power that Satan possesses on this earth is given him by God. This has given rise to the favorite proposition of the philosophers that God is either weak because he cannot prevent evil, or vicious because he does not want to, an argument which conventional Christianity finds unanswerable. But it all makes sense to Brigham Young: "To say that sin is necessary is an unusual saying. Sin is in the world, but it is not necessary that we should sin, because sin is in the world; but, to the contrary, it is necessary that we should resist sin, and for this purpose is sin necessary. . . . Sin is co-eternal with righteousness, for it must needs be that there is an opposition in all things."[36] The idea that sin should be put within the reach of all who want it is by no means the same thing as saying that all are obliged to sin all the way. Satan's prime mission is to test us: "This is a world in which we are to prove ourselves. The lifetime of man is a day of trial, wherein we may prove to God, in our darkness, in our weakness, and where the enemy reigns, that we are our Father's friends, and that we receive light from him and are worthy to be leaders of our children."[37] It would be hard to find a better summary of the teachings of the ancient Christian and Jewish sectaries of the desert than that. Experience with the Missouri mob gave solid support to a doctrine which of itself seems paradoxical—that devils are necessary and useful: "Consequently we could not have got along so well and so rapidly without those mobocrats. And if mobbers should happen to come here do not look too sour at them, for we need them. We could not build up the kingdom of God without the aid of devils, they must help to do it. They persecute and drive us from city to city, from place to place, until we learn the difference between the power of God and the power of the devil."[38] The uses of adversity was a favorite theme with Brigham Young: "But we cannot clear ourselves from the power of Satan; we must know what it is to be tried and tempted, for no man or woman can be exalted upon any other principle."[39] "Could we do without the devils? No, we could not get along without them. They are here, and they suggest this, that, and the other."[40] Any thought of total victory and annihilation of the enemy is out of the question, since his presence is necessary to God's plan, as the wicked Lamanites were to the healthy existence of the Nephites. "I would not bring a railing accusation against [the Devil], for he is fulfilling his office and calling manfully."[41] If we only let him alone it is he who is the dupe: "I have often thought of the foolishness of the devil, notwithstanding all his cunning; yet he is much of a gentleman, when compared with many that serve him."[42] The ultimate in damnation is to fall under his miserable fraudulent power: "What Joseph meant by being damned was that people will go into the spirit world without the Priesthood, and consequently they are under the power of Satan, and will have to be redeemed, or else they will be forever under his power."[43] In the end all the power he has is what we concede to him: "A person, to become an angel of the Devil, has first to be a good Saint, and then deny the Lord who bought him"[44] (i.e., refuse redemption when it is offered him). "Has the devil the power to afflict, and cast the spirit into torment? No!"[45] His control is strictly through the flesh. Say, how then does it work? By striking the flesh where it is most vulnerable, by threatening its very existence, by withholding its means of subsistence and survival. "You take my life," said Shylock, "when you do take the means whereby I live"—he being a notoriously greedy and unscrupulous money-lender.[46] As "the prince of the world," Satan commands the treasures of the earth, and with them he is able to carry on his rule of blood and terror.

Brigham Young and Joseph Smith constantly reiterated warnings against what they considered to be the two really dangerous weaknesses in the Mormon character, the damaged spots in the wall through which Satan could always enter most readily; these two were covetousness and self-righteousness.

Covetousness: The Number One Weapon

Covetousness takes the lead; it is the most formidable obstacle to the progress of the Saints and furnishes Satan with the most effective weapon in his arsenal. When the Church was only a year old, the Prophet Joseph said that "God had often sealed up the heavens because of covetousness in the Church."[47] What is covetousness? Simply wanting to get rich—for millions the American (and the Greek

and the Roman and the Babylonian and the Spanish, etc.)
dream. "Brethren," said Joseph Smith,

> we are gathering to this beautiful land, to build up Zion.
> . . . But since I have been here I perceive the spirit of self-
> ishness. Covetousness exists in the hearts of the Saints.
> . . . Here are those who begin to spread out buying up all
> the land they are able to [get] to the exclusion of the
> poorer ones who are not so much blessed with this
> world's goods, thinking to lay foundations for them-
> selves, only looking to their own individual families, and
> those who are to follow them. Now I want to tell you,
> that Zion cannot be built up in any such way. . . . I see
> signs put out, beer signs, speculative schemes are being
> introduced. This is the way of the world, Babylon indeed,
> and I tell you in the name of the God of Israel, if there is
> not repentance . . . and a turning from such ungodliness,
> covetousness, and self-will you will be broken up and
> scattered from this choice land to the four winds of
> heaven.[48]

In due time they were indeed driven out, and many
years later Brigham Young explained why, as he often did:
"I hope to God that we never will have the privilege of
stopping and making ourselves rich while we grind the face
of the poor; but let us be driven from State to State until we
can take what we have got and dispose of it according to
the dictation of the spirit of revelation from the Lord."[49] Was
it as bad as that? It was:

> The covetousness of some of this people has grieved
> me, and it has caused my spirit to weep and mourn to
> observe their greediness, their cheating and lying, their
> scheming in every possible way to wring a picayune out
> of this man, or that woman. I can put my finger upon
> owners of little shops in this city, who will lie to you for
> half an hour on a stretch, who will, if you send a child to

their shops to buy a yard of ribbon that is worth ten cents, charge the child fifteen or twenty cents for it.[50]

The sermons of Brigham Young are full of such obser-vations: all were guilty, the farmers as well as the mer-chants. "I see some men so greedy after the things of the world, that they will take their grain from the mouths of innocent, helpless women and children who are suffering for food, and sell it to gentile merchants to speculate upon."[51] "The poor are filled with idolatry as well as the rich, and covet the means of those who have helped them; the rich, also, have the same spirit of idolatry, and stick to what they have."[52] "The vile practice of stealing cattle and other property . . . has been encouraged by covetous, selfish men, who have refused to use their property for their own good, or the community's."[53] So after these words of wrath and warning, drought, crickets, Indians, and the U.S. Army struck all at once, and every house in the valley was pre-pared for burning. Then it was that Brigham declared, "If we love our improvements and property better than we love the lives of our brethren, the Lord will lead us in a way to waste us instead of our property. Can you understand that it is better to lose property than the lives of men, women, and children? But if we are so wedded to our prop-erty that we would rather fight for it than sacrifice it, if required, for our religion, then we are in a condition to be wasted, and our property would go into the hands of our enemies."[54]

At the height of danger, with the Army actually descending on the valley, the prophet declared: "I am more afraid of covetousness in our Elders than I am of the hordes of hell. Have we men out now of that class? I believe so. I am afraid of such spirits; for they are more powerful and injurious to this people than all hell with them outside of

our borders. All our enemies in the United States or in the
world, and all hell with them marshalled against us, could
not do us the injury that covetousness in the hearts of this
people could do us; for it is idolatry."⁵⁵ So there was a real
danger—the only thing that Brigham really feared.

> Could our brethren stay in Jackson County,
> Missouri? No, no. Why? They had not learned "a" con-
> cerning Zion; and we have been traveling now forty-two
> years, and have we learned our a, b, c? . . . I will say,
> scarcely. Have we seen it as a people? How long shall we
> travel, how long shall we live, how long shall God wait
> for us to sanctify ourselves and become one in the Lord,
> in our actions and in our ways for the building up of the
> kingdom of God, that he can bless us?⁵⁶

The pattern was to be that of ancient Zion: "And the
Lord called his people Zion, because they were of one heart
and one mind, and dwelt in righteousness; and there was
no poor among them" (Moses 7:18). When the Saints entered the Salt Lake Valley, Brigham Young, remembering
the admonitions of the Prophet Joseph and the experience
of four or five previous settlements (hopeful foundations of
Zion), laid down the principle that "no man should buy or
sell land. Every man should have his land measured off to
him for city and farming purposes"—the one thing to be
avoided was speculation.⁵⁷ Likewise, "there would be no
private ownership in the streams [that come out of the
canyons]; that wood and timber would be regarded as community property."⁵⁸

Such doctrine was hardly calculated to be popular with
everybody; it was in fact a test of the Saints, and the writing on the wall became increasingly plain: "Through the
selfishness of some, which is idolatry, through their covetousness, which is the same, and the lustful desire of their

minds, they were cast out and driven from their homes."[59]
After Nauvoo it would seem that they should begin to learn
their lesson, and at

> Winter Quarters, the Lord gave to me a revelation. . . . I
> talked it to my brethren; I would throw out a few words
> here, and a few words there, to my first counselor to my
> second counselor and the Twelve Apostles, [Were they
> ready for the revelation?] but with the exception of one
> or two of the Twelve, it would not touch a man. . . . I
> would have given it if the people had been prepared. . . .
> But I could not touch them. One would say, "I am for
> California," another one, "I am for gold," and I am for
> this and I am for that.[60]

Down through the years the prophet pleaded with the
people. He tells us how in 1851 he could not bring himself
to address a body of Saints departing from the valley: "I
was sick at the sight of so many of the saints running to
California, chiefly after the God of this world, and was
unable to address them."[61] "I pray you in Christ's stead," he
pleaded, "to let gold hunting alone, and pray the Lord to
cover it up in our region of country that it cannot be found.
Those among us who are anxious to find rich gold deposits,
are equally anxious to destroy themselves."[62] As early as
1848 he reports, "Some few have caught the gold fever; I
counseled such and all the saints to remain in these valleys
of the mountains . . . against the days of famine and pestilence with which the earth would be visited."[63] But gold
fever was only one aspect of the disease, whose progress
may be noted down through the years:

1853: "This people are gathering much substance
around them, which is a principle of heaven—a principle
of Zion, but there is a fear within us lest it cause us to forget our God and our religion."[64] "A man has no right with

property, which, according to the laws of the land, legally belongs to him, if he does not want to use it."[65]

1855: "Again, it is known to all that a great many of the poor are as bad as those who have property. . . . They are just as covetous and craving in their feelings as are the rich who hoard up their means and keep it from the honest poor. . . . There are many who live in this city without labor . . . and you have neighbors near you who steal your wood."[66]

1856: "The mass of the people are all asleep together, craving after the world, running after wickedness, desiring this, that, and the other, which is not for their good."[67]

1862: "While we should be diligent and industrious . . . we should not suffer a covetous and grasping spirit to take possession of us. It is lamentable to see the ignorance manifested by many of this people in that respect, for no man who possesses the wealth of wisdom, would worship the wealth of mammon."[68]

1864: "If this people can at the same time possess riches and glorify God, then we want them to be rich"[69]—but that is a very big "if"; few have ever pulled it off.

1866: "I am sorry that this people are worldly-minded; . . . they love the world, and covet their fine horses [cars today]; their affections are upon them, and upon their farms, upon their property, their houses and possessions."[70]

1874: "Have we separated ourselves from the nations? Yes. And what else have we done? Ask yourselves the question. Have we not brought Babylon with us? Are we not promoting Babylon here in our midst? Are we not fostering the spirit of Babylon that is now abroad on the face of the whole earth? I ask myself this question, and I answer, Yes, yes, . . . we have too much of Babylon in our midst."[71] "What is the general expression through our community? It is that the Latter-day Saints are drifting as fast as they can into idolatry, drifting into the spirit of the world and into pride and vanity. . . . We wish the wealth or things of the world; we think about them morning, noon and night; they are first in our minds when we awake in the morning, and the last thing before we go to sleep at night."[72]

> We have gone just as far as we can be permitted to go in the road on which we are now traveling. One man has his eye on a gold mine, another is for a silver mine, another is for marketing his flour or his wheat, another for selling his cattle, another to raise cattle, another to get a farm, or building here and there, and trading and trafficking with each other, just like Babylon. . . . Babylon is here, and we are following in the footsteps of the inhabitants of the earth, who are in a perfect sea of confusion. Do you know this? You ought to, for there are none of you but what see it daily; . . . the Latter-day Saint trying to take advantage of their brethren. There are Elders in this Church who would take the widow's last cow, for five dollars, and then kneel down and thank God for the fine bargain they had made.[73]

Fighting Fire with Non-fire

In dealing with this particular enemy, the enemy of all righteousness, the first rule is never to use his methods, for if we do he has already won. He does not care which "side" we are on as long as we act like devils, just as God does not care which side we are on if we keep the great commandments: he held up as the shining example that of a Samaritan who was not a member of the Church, was not even of Israel, and contrasted his behavior ("Go and do thou likewise"; Luke 10:37) to that of two devout and active churchmen who wanted nothing to do with a drunken bum lying unconscious in the gutter.

"We are never going to destroy the enemies of God by the evil passions that are in us—never, no never. When those who profess to be Saints contend against the enemies of God through passion or selfwill, it is then man against man, evil against evil, the powers of darkness against the powers of darkness."[74] We do *not* fight fire with fire or match hate with hate. "No man or people possessing wisdom will give vent to wrath, for that is calculated to weaken, to destroy, to blot out of existence. When the Supreme Ruler of the universe wishes to destroy a nation, he takes away their wisdom . . . and they are filled with wrath: they give way to their anger, and thus lay the foundation of their own destruction."[75] "If we are permitted to rule, govern, and control, in the first place we must control our passions until they are in perfect subjection to us."[76] As a stimulant, anger has no long-term value: "The Lord said, 'Hold on.' He can fight our battles far better than we can. Anger towards them [the enemy] is a poor, miserable feeling; and I am trying to get rid of it."[77] Brigham Young was a forceful and formidable man who was often provoked and knew what anger was—but he also knew it was wrong: "I will say, there is not a man in this house who has a more indomitable and unyielding temper than myself. But there is not a man in the world who cannot overcome his passion, if he will struggle earnestly to do so. If you find passion coming on you, go off to some place where you cannot be heard; . . . struggle till it leaves you; and pray for strength to overcome."[78] "When evil arises within me let me throw a cloak over it, subdue it instead of acting it out upon the false presumption that I am honest and no hypocrite. Let not thy tongue give utterance to the evil that is in thine heart. . . . So far I believe in being a hypocrite."[79] The trouble with feeding and yielding to anger is that it is altogether too easy: "Cast all bitterness out of your own hearts—all anger, wrath, strife, covetousness, and lust, and sanctify the Lord God in your hearts, that you may enjoy the Holy Ghost."[80] That is the real victory, as the Prophet Joseph put it: "We shall go on from victory to victory, and from conquest to conquest; our evil passions will be subdued, our prejudices depart; we shall find no room in our bosoms for hatred."[81] In this it is ourself we fight all the time, and no one else: "It is natural for me to contend, and if I am opposed to oppose in return, and if a sharp word is spoken to me to give a sharp word back, I have done so but rarely. It is wrong, and we must subdue the inclination."[82] As one of the great leaders of all time, Brigham Young understood why this was so: "No man ever did, or ever will rule judiciously on this earth, with honor to himself and glory to his God, unless he first learn to rule and control himself."[83]

If you want to meet the enemy head-on, here he is. "This is what I call resisting the devil, and he flees from me I strive to not speak evil, to not feel evil, and if I do, to keep it to myself until it is gone from me, and not let it pass my lips. . . . 'Had I not better let it out than to keep it rankling within me?' No. I will keep bad feelings under and actually smother them to death, then they are gone."[84] They do not fester in the subconscious, because they simply vanish: hatred is vanquished only when it turns to love. Must the battle always be within ourselves? Where else? "With all the power I possess, I cannot prevent a man from cursing and swearing if he is disposed to do so."[85] Whom can he command? Himself. "If I did not feel like praying, . . . I should say, 'Brigham, get down here, on your knees, bow your body down before the throne of Him who rules in the heavens, and stay there until you can feel to supplicate at that throne of grace erected for sinners.'"[86]

If you feel that you are tempted not to open your mouth to the Lord, and as though the heavens are brass over your heads and the earth iron beneath your feet, and that everything is closed up, and you feel that it would be a sin for you to pray, then walk up to the devil and say, Mr. Devil, get out of my way; and if you feel that you cannot get down upon your knees for fear you will swear, say, get down knees; and if they don't feel right when they are down, put something under them, some sharp sticks, for instance, and say, knees come to it.[87]

When it is dark as midnight darkness, when there is not one particle of feeling in my heart to pray, shall I then say, I will not pray? No, but get down knees, bend yourselves upon the floor, and mouth, open; tongue, speak; and we will see what will come forth, and you shall worship the Lord God of Israel, even when you feel as though you could not say a word in his favor. That is the victory we have to gain; that is the warfare we have to wage. It is between the spirit and the body; they are inseparably connected.[88]

Note well the protagonists in the great contest: nothing is easier when our plans and ambitions miscarry than to blame our misfortunes on the wickedness of others and cry, "The enemy has done this!" He has, indeed—but I gave him the power. At general conference in 1859, President Young "advised the Latter-day Saints . . . when tempted and buffeted, to keep their mouths closed, instead of diffusing abroad that which the Evil One puts into their hearts . . . [and] to keep the bad feelings to themselves."[89] Surely there is no better way to come to grips with the enemy, and surely there is no closer close combat than this: "never let anger arise in your hearts. No, Brigham, never let anger arise in your heart, never, never!"[90] That takes a bit of doing, but that makes it worthwhile. "If you are in the kanyon and your cattle are likely to fill you with wrath, fill your mouth with India-rubber and keep it close that the words cannot get out. Do not say a word to grieve the Spirit of God."[91]

Brigham on War

Such being the nature of our warfare, it follows that real warfare, resorting to overt violence directed against others, defeats the whole purpose of our earthly existence. Heaven is "the peaceable kingdom" from which Satan was thrust "in a twinkling" the moment he resorted to violence. War, utterly wasteful as it is, has the vast appeal of shifting one's own guilt, of all of which we relieve ourselves as soon as the shooting begins. Brigham Young understood the psychology of war very well: "The main difficulty in the hearts of those who are dissatisfied is, they are not satisfied with themselves."[92] As for the deadly enemies of the Church, "They are not angry with me or with you; and the professors of Christianity, the priests, are not angry with us, but they are filled with wrath and indignation with themselves, and with the Almighty."[93] "I wish this fact to sink into your hearts, that when men or women have doubts, they also have fear; and when they have fear, they are in danger of what? Of themselves."[94] "Our own evils make for us danger; and if chastisement comes upon us, it is the result of our own unrighteous acts."[95] "Just as soon as our eyes are turned away from watching ourselves, to see whether we do right, we begin to see faults in our neighbors; this is the great difficulty, and our minds become more and more blinded until we become entirely darkened."[96] "We need not go to our neighbors for sin, to palliate all our crimes, for we ourselves have plenty of it; we need not crave weakness from our fellow man, we have our own share of it; it is for us to trust in the Lord, and endeavor to deliver ourselves from the effects of sin . . . to become friends of God, that we may thereby become friends of sinners, and receive a great reward in a day to come."[97] "If you want a revolution go to work to improve yourselves and give your minds something to act upon instead of looking at the faults of others."[98] Above all, we must not attribute our distress to the wickedness of others, however convenient and flattering that may be: "I must be happy for myself. I must live my religion for myself, and enjoy the light of truth for myself, and when I do that all hell cannot deprive me of it, nor of its fruits."[99] Where is the enemy? For the righteous there is no enemy! It was Joseph Smith who said, "A man is his own tormentor and his own condemner. . . . The torment of disappointment in the mind of man is as exquisite as a lake burning with fire and brimstone."[100] And who are the disappointed ones? Ambitious men and women who have failed to make the grade—who have aspired to power and coveted the things of the world and lost them; Satan, thus appointed, is the great archetype, but his spirit infects all of us: "All is before them [the LDS]; they have nothing to do but enjoy themselves, and yet their spirits are unhappy, uneasy, and discontented; they want more, and are inclined to retain what they do have, unlawfully. . . . Brethren, let us . . . not be children all of the days of our lives, but let us . . . become men and women before the Lord."[101] What is the cure? "Self-argument is the most effectual argument that can be used. Let each person argue himself into the belief that God will grant to him his request in righteousness."[102] Brigham Young was a sound psychologist.

Even in the midst of the shooting, President Young stuck to his principles: "Are we in danger from our enemies? No; there is no danger, only in our neglecting the duties of a Saint."[103] "Now, brethren, can we fight against and subdue *ourselves*? That is the greatest difficulty we ever encountered, and the most arduous warfare we ever engaged in."[104] "If there are any hearts or spirits in this city, or elsewhere, that are fearfully wondering whether or not we are going to be destroyed, . . . I will say to all such trembling souls, You need entertain no such fears. You need have only one fear, and that is with regard to yourselves."[105]

The Mormons, believing that all living beings are immortal and in the end indestructible, were sensibly admonished by their great leader: "Never try to destroy a man. It is our mission to save the people, not to destroy them. The least, the most inferior spirit now upon the earth, in our capacity, is worth worlds."[106] And so from the *Boston Atlas* it is reported that the Mormons were "busy about their own affairs, and never intermeddled in the concerns of their neighbors. They were exceedingly peaceful and adverse to strife, quarrels and violence."[107] As he was leading the flight from Nauvoo, Brigham Young was visited, he says, by the Prophet Joseph in a dream, with the repeated instruction to "tell the brethren to keep their hearts open to conviction, so that when the Holy Ghost comes to them, their hearts will be ready to receive it. They can tell the Spirit of the Lord," it was explained, "from all other spirits; it will whisper peace and joy to their souls; it will take malice, hatred, strife and all evil from their hearts."[108] And this was at the very culmination of mob violence. Just before his death, the Prophet Joseph had prophesied that though wars would come "it will not be by sword or gun that this kingdom will roll on,"[109] and he reassured the Saints: "So long as men are under the law of God, they have no fears—they do not scare themselves."[110]

In a declaration of February 27, 1845, the followers of Emmett were invited "to stand forth with the servants of

God and in the majesty and strength and greatness of the everlasting priesthood rescue the earth from violence, oppression and wickedness."[111] This is not done by force of arm, even in the face of Johnston's Army: "But, says one, 'I want to fight.' Do all such persons know that they are not right? If they will examine their hearts, they will find a wicked anger and a malice there; and they cannot get into the kingdom of God with those feelings."[112] No man was ever threatened with firearms more constantly than Joseph Smith, yet he would not carry a weapon: "He that arms himself with gun, sword, or pistol, except in the defense of truth, will sometimes be sorry for it. I never carry any weapon with me bigger than my penknife. When I was dragged before the cannon and muskets in Missouri, I was unarmed. God will always protect me until my mission is fulfilled."[113] "I sometimes felt," Brigham confesses, "before the move, like taking the sword and slaying my enemies, until they were wasted away. But the Lord did not design this, and we have remained in peace and quietness."[114] "Had we the power, would we hold the wicked down and whip them? No; for, except in self-defence, it is our duty to plead with them and offer them the terms of life and salvation—to give them all the opportunity God has designed them to have."[115] "Are we prepared to receive the blessings, and let the fighting alone?" he asked the next year. "I do not much believe in fighting, and my faith is to escape such a calamity as to war and fight with either friends or enemies."[116]

What then? "I have asked the Lord to mete out justice to those who have oppressed us, and the Lord will take his own time and way for doing this. It is in His hands, and not in mine, and I am glad of it, for I could not deal with the wicked as they should be dealt with."[117] This is not to say that great and strenuous efforts are not demanded of us: "We have got to take the ground by force. Yes, by the *mental* force of faith, and by good works, the march forth of the Gospel will increase, spread, grow and prosper, until the nations of the earth will feel that Jesus has the right to rule King of nations as he does King of Saints."[118] But that is the hard way; the other is easier: "Some of the Elders would much rather fight for their religion than live it. If any one thinks to get into the kingdom by fighting . . . they will find themselves mistaken."[119] "The devil and his associates" are going in due time to be "driven from the earth, and he and his clan are bound and thrust down to hell, and a seal put upon them." How is that to be done? Not by us, of course, though we prepare the way for it by overcoming every sin in ourselves so that God can "bring forth righteousness, salvation, and deliverance to the house of Israel."[120] In the last year of his life President Young delivered a dire threat against the enemies of Zion: "Woe to those who fight against it. What will we do to them? Nothing at all, but preach the Gospel. They may lie about us as they please. If we will faithfully mind our own concerns, live our religion, do good to all men, . . . we have no cause for fear in the least."[121]

These are the last days, the days of wickedness and vengeance, when war becomes the order of the day: "Some may have cried peace, but the Saints and the world will have little peace from henceforth. Let this not hinder us from going to the Stakes; for God has told us to flee. . . . Wars are at hand; we must not delay; but are not required to sacrifice. . . . Look to the Presidency and receive instructions. Every man who is afraid, covetous, will be taken in a snare. The time is coming when no man will have any peace but in Zion and her stakes."[122] Thus said Joseph Smith in

1839. And still earlier the issue was made clear by the voice of prophecy: "*Destruction*, to the eye of the spiritual beholder, seems to be written by the finger of an invisible hand, in large capitals, upon almost every thing we behold."[123] No one has described the world situation better than Brigham Young, whose words would not be out of place in today's newspaper. "Great improvements are making in the art of killing folks," he commented away back in 1847, "and it is getting to be a very popular idea, that it is better to load guns with cotton than powder." After a satirical comment on the beauty and convenience of the new killing device, he concludes with a stinger: "This may be joyful news to those who have plenty of cotton."[124]

The danger of growing armaments was one on which he frequently commented: "A large share of the ingenuity of the world is taxed to invent weapons of war. What a set of fools!"[125] Today by far the greater part of our vast military budget is spent on research. Brigham does not approve of that sort of thing: "Much of the skill, ingenuity, and ability of the Christian nations are now devoted to manufacturing instruments of death. May we be saved from the effects of them! As I often tell you, if we are faithful, the Lord will fight our battles much better than we can ourselves."[126]

In the midst of the mobs, he told the Saints, "One plowshare will do more to drive off the mob than two guns."[127] The hardest thing is not to take to weapons when we feel threatened: "Imagined danger always produces the most trouble," he reflected from long experience with the mobs;[128] counter-action is no solution to violence: "I should have more fear in consequence of the ignorant and foolish audacity of the Elders, than of their being afraid. I should fear they would rush into danger like an unthinking horse into battle. So I will not find fault with regard to their courage.

On that point I am a coward myself, and if people would do as I tell them, I would not only save my own life, but theirs likewise."[129]

As he saw the great Civil War approaching, he observed, "It is a remarkable fact, that the flames of civil war are kindling in that portion of the United States from which the Saints were first driven by a reckless mob. That same spirit, . . . by the tacit consent of the nation, has diffused itself through the land, and sealed the doom of that mighty republic."[130] That was in 1855, but even ten years before, the prophet knew that "The ranklings of violence and intolerance, . . . of settled vengeance, and blood guiltiness cannot long be suppressed. . . . Every sensible man in the nation has felt . . . the dreadful vortex into which partizan ambition, contempt of the poor, and trampling down the just as things of nought, were fast leading this nation."[131] From his experience with the U.S. Army in Utah, he reflected in 1859, "A standing army in time of peace in a republican government is more dangerous to the liberties of the people than to any foreign foe, and is a terrible and dangerous tax upon the prosperity of the country."[132] In the midst of the Civil War he observed, "The cause of human improvement is not in the least advanced by the dreadful war which now convulses our unhappy country. . . . According to accounts, in all probability not less than one million men . . . have gone to the silent grave in this useless war . . . and all to gratify the caprice of a few."[133]

And after the war: "The destruction of property and life during the war has been enormous; but I am satisfied that the destruction of the love of virtue—the love of every exalted principle of honor, and of political and social government—has been greater, comparatively, than the destruction of property and life. Religious societies abound in the nation. Although it never was more wicked than at the present time, it is strange to say that it never was more religious in profession. Religion is the ruling power."[134] It was the usual postwar surge of churchgoing, and not long after, Brigham commented on the result: "I will say with regard to the so-called Christian world, and the moral reform of which they talk so much, that they are an utter failure, so far as stemming of the tide of evil among men is concerned; and if this Gospel that Jesus has revealed in the latter days does not do it, it will not be done."[135] And that was not to be for quite a while: "If we could, we would hide ourselves away from the scenes that will take place; but this we cannot do."[136] "Shall we have a warfare? We shall; we will war and contend for the right, and trust in our God until righteousness is established upon the earth, until peace shall [reign] everywhere, until the children of men shall lay down the weapons of their warfare and cease to exhaust their ability and ingenuity in forming weapons of destruction to slay their fellow men, until . . . their energies be directed to beautifying the earth and making it the garden of Eden."[137]

And what part will the Saints have in the war? "Is there war in our religion? No, neither war nor blood-shed."[138] "Of one thing I am sure: God never institutes war; God is not the author of confusion or of war; they are the results of the acts of the children of men. Confusion and war necessarily come as the results of the foolish acts and policy of men; but they do *not* come because God desires they should come."[139] "War is instigated by wickedness—it is the consequence of a nation's sin."[140] "Follow after peace," said Joseph Smith, "that you may be the children of our Heavenly Father."[141] "When you find a spirit that wants bloodshed—murder, the same is not of God, but is of the devil."[142] "I never did harm any man," he said at the end of his life, "since I was born in the world. My voice is always for peace."[143] Brigham takes it from there: "There is no need for war and bloodshed, for the earth is large enough for all. The elements of which this earth is composed are all around it."[144] He tells how during the mobbing he dreamed of shooting an enemy: "I felt so bad because I had shot a man, that I awoke and was thankful that it was but a dream."[145]

As a great constructive and original spirit, Brigham was appalled by the totally negative nature of warfare (Omar Bradley claimed that war is waste):

> Look at the world. The feeling among mankind is "we will rule or ruin." An architect may build a splendid habitation, and in so doing do a good work; but a poor fool can come along and with the touch of a torch destroy it. Let a few incendiaries go through a city and put the torch here and there, and the city is destroyed—the labor of years, perhaps of centuries, is wasted. Does this make great men of them? Perhaps they think so. If they can destroy a city or a nation they think they will get a great name. They will not.[146]

"Our traditions have been such that we are not apt to look upon war between two nations as murder. . . . Does it justify the slaying of men, women, and children that otherwise would have remained at home in peace, because a great army is doing the work? No: the guilty will be damned for it."[147] "According to my definition of the word, there is not a strictly and fully civilized community now upon the earth. Is there murder by wholesale to be found in a strictly civilized community? Will a community of civilized nations rise up one against another, nation against nation, and kingdom against kingdom, using against each other every destructive invention that can be brought to bear in their wars?"[148] "There is a spirit that prompts the nations to prepare for war, desolation, and bloodshed—to waste each other away. Do they realize it? No."[149]

> When the nations have for years turned much of their attention to manufacturing instruments of death, they have sooner or later used those instruments. Our nation, England, France, Germany, Austria, Italy, and other nations have for years exercised their inventive skill, and expended much means in inventing and fabricating instruments of death. . . . From the authority of all history, the deadly weapons now stored up and being manufactured will be used until the people are wasted away, and there is no help for it. The spirit of revolution goes on through the nations: it never goes back.[150]

"You will see that the wisdom of the wise among the nations will perish and be taken from them. They will fall into difficulties, and they will not be able to tell the reason, nor point a way to avert them any more than they can now in this land. They can fight, quarrel, contend and destroy each other, but they do not know how to make peace. So it will be with the inhabitants of the earth."[151]

Brigham Young's Indian Policy

When one thinks of Brigham Young, one thinks of the pioneers; and when one thinks of the enemies of the pioneers, one thinks of the Indians. Brigham Young's policy was an acid test of his ability to deal with an enemy by refusing to treat him like an enemy. Nothing could be more drastic than a policy of kindness towards a clever, tough, tricky, unscrupulous and determined enemy. This is not the place to discuss it; a few quotations will do. Even before the Saints came to the valley,

> I felt that it was wrong to indulge in feelings of hostility and bloodshed toward the Indian, the descendants of

Israel, who might kill a cow, an ox or even a horse; to them the deer, the buffalo, the cherry and plum tree or strawberry bed were free. It was their mode of living to kill and eat. . . . I realized there were men among us who would steal, who knew better, whose traditions and earliest teachings were all against it. Yet such would find fellowship with those who would shoot an Indian for stealing.[152]

1850: To the people in Salt Lake:

As to fighting with and killing the Indians, there was no necessity for it, if the brethren acted wisely in their intercourse with them; and [I] warned the brethren that if they killed Indians for stealing, they would have to answer for it. [I] also proposed for their consideration the following question: "Why should men have a disposition to kill a destitute, naked Indian, who may steal a shirt or a horse, and think it no harm, when they never think of meting out a like retribution to a white man who steals, although he has been taught better from infancy?"[153]

1853: "I am sorry that some of our brethren have been killed by the Indians, but am far more sorry that some of the Indians have been slain by the brethren. I have often said, and I say again, if any person is to be killed for stealing, let that one be a white man, and not an Indian, for white men know better, while Indians do not; and you must lay aside your angry feelings toward them, and cease wishing to kill them."[154]

1854: Demands of the Indians "should be met with a spirit of liberality on the part of the General Government. . . . I have uniformly pursued a friendly course of policy towards them, feeling convinced, that independent of the question of exercising humanity towards so degraded and ignorant a race of people, it was manifestly more economical, and less expensive, to feed and clothe, than to fight them."[155]

1857: "To reflect their angry words and acts, and kill them for every trivial [offense], as is the usual course pursued towards them by the whites . . . will never cause them to appreciate the blessings of civilized society, nor influence them to seek its benefits, but will . . . drive them to the opposite extreme. . . . Therefore let us . . . exhibit a superior understanding, a larger comprehension of right, forbearance and honor. Be just, brethren, in your dealings with them; no matter what course they may pursue towards you, never retaliate a wrong."[156] This forbearance works both ways, of course: "Hundreds of miles have the Indians travelled to see me, to know whether they might use up the emigrants, saying—'They have killed many of us; and they damn you and damn us, and shall we stand it?' I have always told them to hold on, to stop shedding blood, and to live in peace."[157]

1865: The reality of the Indian danger must never be forgotten: "If we make no efforts to guard our towns, our houses, our cities, our wives and children, will the Lord guard them for us? He will not. . . . I do not know that there is one person in the Territory who would refuse to perform military duty."[158] But this in no wise justifies any aggressive or vengeful action.

1866: "I wish to impress them with the necessity of treating the Indians with kindness, and to refrain from harboring that revengeful, vindictive feeling that many indulge in. I am convinced that as long as we harbor in us such feelings towards them, so long they will be our enemies, and the Lord will suffer them to afflict us."[159] It is the old Book of Mormon theme: one can never hope to get rid of his enemies by destroying them: "I certainly believe that the present affliction, which has come upon us from the Indians, is a consequence of the wickedness which dwells in the hearts of some of our brethren. . . . I believe that the Lord permits them to chasten us . . . to convince us that we have to overcome the vindictive feelings which we have harbored towards that poor, down-trodden branch of the house of Israel."[160]

Locating the Enemy

There is an enemy, the enemy of all righteousness—but he is a disembodied spirit. How do we come to grips with him, according to Brigham Young? Very intimately and immediately; he enters, or seeks to enter, right into us individually—there we can meet him hand to hand and eye to eye, within our own minds and bodies. But we cannot engage him by attacking other human beings, no matter how full of the devil they may be. The futility of trying to combat Satan in the persons of those whom we deem to be his human representatives is rendered complete by the circumstance that there is evil as well as good in all of us, and while every man can know for himself what is good and evil in himself, he cannot possibly distinguish with any accuracy what is good and evil in others. "Pray always, that you may come off conqueror," the Lord told Joseph Smith, "yea, that you may conquer Satan, and that you may escape the hands of the servants of Satan" (D&C 10:5). We can conquer Satan, and the evil we know in ourselves, but the best we can hope for is to escape evil's servants, whoever they are: "Satan has great hold upon their hearts; he stirreth them up to iniquity against that which is good" (D&C 10:20). But who are they? The Lord continues: "But as you cannot always judge the righteous, or as you cannot always tell the wicked from the righteous, therefore I say unto you, hold your peace until I shall see fit to make all things known unto the world concerning the matter" (D&C 10:37).

If our greatest prophet, with his admittedly uncanny knowledge of human nature (his worst enemies grant him that), could not always tell the wicked from the righteous, who are we to set up human targets? Being full of evil ourselves, we are in no position to judge: "Where is the man that is free from vanity?" said the Prophet Joseph. "None ever were perfect, but Jesus."[161] "We are called ignorant," said Brother Brigham. "So we are: but what of it? Are not all ignorant? I rather think so."[162] Before the Church was two years old, Joseph admonished the brethren to "be patient as they had a considerable distance (to go). . . . Until we have perfect love we are liable to fall."[163] This awareness of our universal weakness is basic to an understanding of how to deal with the enemy: "There are no persons without evil passions to embitter their lives. Mankind are revengeful, passionate, hateful, and devilish in their dispositions. This we inherit through the fall, and the grace of God is designed to enable us to overcome it. The grace of God is bestowed upon all . . . to overcome the evil that is in them, and to save all."[164]

Nothing can frustrate the operation of the grace of God like self-righteousness: "For man, what is he; he is but dung upon the earth," says the Prophet Joseph, using the strongest terms and concluding, "There is one thing under the sun which I have learned and that is that the righteousness of man is sin because it exacteth over much."[165] "As long as they live in the flesh no being on this earth, of the posterity of Adam, can be free from the power of the devil."[166] "Every son and daughter of Adam that has come into this world has been subject to sin."[167] "We are naturally prone to wander from that which is good, and to receive every species of iniquity; we must get rid of this disposition, and the Gospel of salvation is expressly for the purpose of

changing it."[168] "The best man that ever lived on this earth
only just made out to save himself through the grace of
God."[169] "We are not capacitated to receive in one day, nor
in one year, the knowledge and experience calculated to
make us perfect Saints, but we learn from time to time, from
day to day, consequently we are to have compassion one
upon another."[170]

"And who are the sinners? We are all sinners."[171] Since
this is so, one cannot identify the sinners and the righteous
as members of this or that society or party or nation.
Indeed, on the principle that the greater the blessing the
greater the obligation, the Latter-day Saints are by no means
singularly righteous: "You are constantly taught to live your
religion for to-day," says President Young to the Saints.
"Can you not live it for one hour?"[172] At the very beginning
Joseph Smith viewed the condition of the Saints with alarm:
"If the fountain of our tears be not dried up, we will still
weep for Zion . . . and for the wrath of heaven, which
awaits her if she repents not."[173] Soon after, Brigham Young
recalls, "I left Kirtland in consequence of the fury of the
mob and the spirit that prevailed in the apostates, who had
threatened to destroy me."[174] Sidney Rigdon and others also
fled "because of the mobocratic spirit prevailing in the
bosoms of the apostates."[175]

There is nothing worse than a Saint turned bad, and
shortly before the death of Joseph, Brigham Young said,
"Our difficulties and persecutions have always arisen from
men right in our midst."[176] We have the best and the worst,
is one of Brigham's themes: "I have told the people many a
time, if they want anything done, no matter how mean,
they can find men here who can do it, if they are to be found
on the earth."[177] "We are not all, as yet, fully sanctified by
the truth. . . . The Gospel net still gathereth fish of every

kind, . . . the flock has some goats intermingled with sheep
of various grades, and that day of separation has not yet
arrived."[178] "'Will everybody be damned except the Latter-
day Saints?' 'Yes,' said Joseph, 'and many of them, unless
they take a different course from what they are now taking.'"[179] "I have seen months and months, in this city, when
I could have wept like a whipt child to see the awful stupidity of the people in not realizing the blessings bestowed
upon them."[180]

> You need, figuratively, to have it rain pitchforks,
> tines downwards, from this pulpit, Sunday after Sunday.
> . . . You need to have the thunders of the Almighty and
> the forked lightnings of truth sent upon you, to wake you
> up out of your lethargy. . . . Comparatively speaking,
> they should have their ears cuffed and be roughly
> handled, be kicked out doors, and then kicked into it
> again. Most of the Elders who preach in this stand ought
> to be kicked out of it, and then kicked into it again, until
> they overhaul themselves and find out what is the matter
> with them.[181]

If the righteous have evil in them and the Saints are by
no means without it, the wicked are not without a measure
of good:

> Some may imagine and really believe that I am
> opposed to the great majority of the inhabitants of the
> earth—to the religious and political parties of the day;
> but it is not so. To individuals, as such, I am not opposed.
> The doctrine I preach is not opposed to an individual
> upon the earth. If I am opposed to anything, it is to sin. . . .
> I do not feel opposed to an individual on the earth. I have
> not any enmity in my heart, or at least I should not have.
> If I have, I am thus far wrong. If we harbor vindictive-
> ness, hatred, malice, and a spirit that produces evil within
> us, we are so far given up to the power of evil.[182]

And that is what Satan wants; he cares not against whom our anger is directed. "Boast not over the misery of your fellow-men. God will fulfill his purposes. . . . There are moral Christians among the heathen, among the Hindoos, and among all nations. God has laid a plan to save all such. His name be praised!"[183] There are wonderful people in the world—"a gentleman or lady, that is, one who is a true gentleman or a true lady . . . would border very closely on an angel."[184] We should not be hasty in judging the world: "It appears to the Elders, and to those who go from the Saints into the world, that it is growing wicked faster than it really is."[185]

It is foolish to identify the enemy with the outsiders: "There is not one man in this city nor in the Territory who hates the truth and the Latter-day Saints, whose influence I dread, no, not even the hundredth part, as I do a smooth, slick hypocrite who professes to be a Latter-day Saint."[186] "[Our religion] does not send a portion of the people to howl in torment for ever and ever, but it reaches after the last son and daughter of Adam and Eve, and will pluck them from the prison, unlock the doors, and burst the bonds and bring forth every soul who will receive salvation."[187]

If it is folly to identify the enemy with outsiders, many of whom are righteous; shall we seek them out among the less desirable elements within the Church? By no means. "We have a great many gars, sharks, sheepheads, lampereels, and every other kind of fish that is to be found, in the pond; the Gospel net has gathered them up, and what may you expect from such a mess?"[188] "We have men who are dishonest, and are as yet obliged to have them; for the net gathers in the good and the bad. We have the meanest and the best mixed together."[189] "It is acknowledged all the time that there are evil doers here. . . . I am not going to give up the ship, or forsake my religion, because there are those who do evil."[190] "There are many who swear occasionally; others get drunk, &c. Do you not know it? O fools and slow of heart to understand your own existence! But many indulge in such practices, and some will stumble here and there; and we must keep pulling them out of the mire and washing them all the time. Will they be consigned to eternal damnation for such conduct? . . . They are the workmanship of God's hands—brothers to Jesus."[191]

And here is an extreme case: "I see men before me, in this house that have no right to be here. They are as corrupt in their hearts as they can be, and we take them by the hand and call them brother."[192] Why such concessions to wickedness? "We are as yet obliged to have devils in our community, we could not build up the kingdom without them. . . . We must have those amongst us who will steal our fence poles, who will go and steal hay from their neighbor's hay stack. . . . It is essentially necessary to have such characters here."[193] "We are under obligation, through the filial feeling and ties of humanity, to more or less fellowship those who do evil. We must endure this until the Lord shall see fit to separate the wheat from the chaff."[194] "I am under the same obligations to bless sinners as I am to bless Saints, if they will receive my blessings."[195] "But we had better gather nine that are unworthy than to neglect the tenth if he is worthy. If they come here, apostatize and turn our enemies, they are in the hands of God, and what they do will be to them everlasting life or everlasting condemnation."[196] But neither the life nor the condemnation is ours to give.

In this Brigham was following as usual in the footsteps of the first prophet, his beloved Joseph, who said, "We have thieves among us, adulterers, liars, hypocrites,"[197] and

observed, "I have learned in my travels that man is treacherous and selfish, but few excepted."[198] What do we do with
such people? Nothing. Here is a remarkable reflection:
Joseph Smith publicly stated that Sidney Rigdon's faults
included "selfishness and independence of mind. . . . But
notwithstanding these things, he is a very great and good
man."[199] How could such a defective creature be at the same
time a very great and good man? We all, as it were, have a
foot in both camps, and the moral of it all, for both the
prophets, is that we must have charity: "You may see, or
think you see, a thousand faults in your brethren; yet they
are organized as you are; they are flesh of your flesh, bone
of your bone; they are of your Father who is in heaven: we
are all his children, and should be satisfied with each other
as far as possible."[200]

"There is one principle I wish to urge upon the Saints in
a way that it may remain with them—that is, to understand
men and women as they are, and not understand them as
you are."[201] "If brethren and sisters are overtaken in fault,
your hearts should be filled with kindness—with brotherly,
angelic feeling—to overlook their faults as far as possible."[202] "The doctrine which we have embraced takes away
the stony hearts."[203] "We are to have compassion one upon
another, to look upon each other as we would wish others
to look upon us, and to remember that we are frail mortal
beings, and that we can be changed for the better only by
the Gospel of salvation."[204] It is for God to judge, condemn,
punish, reward, give life and take it, but not for men. He
will forgive whom he will forgive, but of us he required to
forgive all men. "If others ought to do right, we more. Be
full of love and compassion to your fellow-beings, full of
kindness, such as human beings can possess, for that is our
business."[205] "I am very thankful that it is *not* our province,

in our present condition, to judge the world; it if were, we would ruin everything. We have not sufficient wisdom, our minds are not filled with the knowledge and power of God; the spirit needs to contend with the flesh a little more."[206]

"We must . . . learn to bring the whole man—all the passions, sympathies, and feelings in subjection to the spirit. Our spirits are warring against the flesh, and the flesh against our spirits; and all we have to do is to let the spirits that have come from our Father in heaven reign triumphant."[207] Meantime, "because of our weaknesses, . . . we shall have to bear with one another until we become stronger and wiser."[208] "All of us are in the hands of that God. We are all His children. We are his sons and daughters naturally, and by the principles of eternal life. We are brethren and sisters."[209]

The Slough of Self-Righteousness

These lessons have always been hard for the Latter-day Saints to learn, and it is clear from the words of Brigham Young that we still have a long way to go. There are a few absolute and categorical "Thou Shalt Nots" in the scriptures which we are far from taking to heart: we have been told that under no circumstances are we to contend, accuse, coerce, aspire, or flatter. These practices will be readily recognized as standard procedure in getting to the top in our modern competitive society. What all of them have in common is a feeling of self-righteousness.

Next to covetousness it was self-righteousness against which Joseph and Brigham most urgently warned the Saints. "Let not any man publish his own righteousness," said the Prophet Joseph (not even, one might, add, in testimony meeting).[210] "Don't be limited in your views with regard to your neighbor's virtue, but beware of self-righteousness, and be limited in the estimate of your own virtues. . . . You must enlarge your souls towards each other. . . . As you increase in innocence and virtue, as you increase in goodness, let your hearts expand, let them be enlarged towards others. . . . You must not be contracted, but you must be liberal in your feelings."[211] "Christ was condemned by the self-righteous Jews because He took sinners into His society."[212] "All the religious world is boasting of righteousness: it is the doctrine of the devil to retard the human mind, and hinder our progress, by filling us with self-righteousness. . . . We are full of selfishness; the devil flatters us that we are very righteous, when we are feeding on the faults of others."[213] Here surely is the greatest threat of communism: it puts us to sleep and paralyzes our minds in the comforting assurance that we are the good people, and it is they and not we who need to repent. Brigham Young has much to say on each of the topics just mentioned. Taking them briefly in order:

Do not contend "There shall be no disputations among you, as there have hitherto been; neither shall there be disputations among you concerning the points of my doctrine, as there have hitherto been. For verily, verily I say unto you, he that hath the spirit of contention is not of me, but is of the devil, who is the father of contention, and he stirreth up the hearts of men to contend with anger, one with another. . . . But this is my doctrine, that such things should be done away" (3 Nephi 11:28–30). Even so, Joseph Smith warned the brethren at the beginning: "Let the Elders be exceedingly careful about unnecessarily disturbing and harrowing up the feelings of the people. Remember that your business is to preach the Gospel in all humility. . . . Avoid contentions and vain disputes with men of corrupt minds, who do not desire to know the truth."[214] "Let contention, *all* contention cease," said Brigham Young; "cease finding fault with and casting reflections upon those who are not exactly with us."[215]

"Contention is not my calling; it is no part of the Gospel of Christ; that is peace, life, light, and salvation."[216] This does not mean that one cannot speak his mind: "I would rather be chopped to pieces at night, and resurrected in the morning, each day throughout a period of three-score years and ten, than be deprived of speaking freely, or be afraid of doing so. I *will* speak for my rights."[217] We are commanded "to bear down in pure testimony" (cf. Alma 4:19), letting our conversation be only "Yea, yea; [and] Nay, nay: for whatsoever is more than these cometh of evil" (Matthew 5:37; cf. 3 Nephi 12:37). Each man speaks for himself—he cannot transmit his testimony to others, let alone force it on them, but he can bear it to them and let the Spirit of God speak to the others. "We deem it a just principle," said Joseph Smith, "and it is one the force of which we believe ought to be duly considered by every individual, that *all* men are created equal, and that all have the privilege of thinking for themselves upon *all* matters relative to conscience. Consequently, then, we are not disposed, had we the power, to deprive any one of exercising that free independence of mind which heaven has so graciously bestowed upon the human family as one of its choicest gifts."[218]

It is not necessary that free and open discussion lead to contention, but that is usually the result, thanks to the normal tendency of *accusing:* "While one portion of the human race is judging and condemning the other without mercy, the Great Parent of the universe looks upon the whole of the human family with a fatherly care and paternal regard . . . without any of those contracted feelings that influence the children of men. . . . He will award judgment or mercy to all

nations according to . . . His inscrutable designs in relation
to the human family."[219] Accusing goes along with judging,
condemning, and "counselling one's fellow men" (cf. D&C
1:19), all of which God has strictly forbidden to us—they are
his business alone, according to his inscrutable designs, and
in that office "he employeth no servant, . . . for he cannot be
deceived" (2 Nephi 9:41), as all the rest of us can. "Remember
to cast no reflections, nor throw out any bitter sayings," the
Prophet Joseph admonished.[220] "Do not watch for iniquity in
each other, if you do you will not get an endowment, for God
will not bestow it on such."[221] Speaking of those who went
about "denouncing all who disagree with them in opinion,"
the prophet said, "I charged the Saints not to follow the
example of the adversary in accusing the brethren. . . . If
you will not accuse me, I will not accuse you." Then he said
a remarkable thing, namely that Ham was cursed because
he became an accuser: "What many call sin is not sin. . . . I
referred to the curse of Ham for laughing at Noah, while in
his wine, but doing no harm."[222] Those, whether they are
members of the Church or not, who accuse their brethren
place "themselves in the seat of Satan, who is emphatically
called 'the accuser of the brethren.'"[223] (*Diabolos* means
"accuser.")

Even though the special gift of the priesthood is the discerning of spirits, "no person through the discerning of
spirits can bring a charge against another, they must be
proven guilty by positive evidence, or they stand clear."[224]
No matter how wicked others may be, it is not our business
to take them on: "The spirits of good men cannot interfere
with the wicked beyond their prescribed bounds, for
Michael, the Archangel, dared not bring a railing accusation
against the devil, but said, 'The Lord rebuke thee, Satan.'"[225]
"Mankind will persist in self-justification until all their

iniquity is exposed. . . . Hear the warning voice of God, lest
Zion fall. . . . The brethren in Kirtland . . . greatly fear for
you."[226]

Brigham Young takes up the theme:

> There is one virtue, attribute, or principle, which, if
> cherished and practiced by the Saints, would prove sal-
> vation to thousands upon thousands. I allude to charity,
> or love, from which proceed forgiveness, longsuffering,
> kindness, and patience. But the short-sightedness and
> weakness in some are marvelous. . . . People come here
> from different parts of the earth to make this their
> adopted country, and the old residents expect them to at
> once conform to and adopt their manners, customs, and
> traditions. . . . In other words, "If every man, woman, and
> child does not act, think, and see as I do, they are sin-
> ners." It is very necessary that we have charity that will
> cover a multitude of what we may suppose to be sins.[227]

He repeats the words of the Prophet Joseph: "Bring no railing accusation against your brethren, . . . for the principle is
of the devil; he is called the accuser of the brethren."[228]

He tells of "a gang of about a dozen Baptist ministers"
who tried to break up gambling activities on a riverboat on
which Brigham and other brethren were travelling: "I told
them if there had been gambling, the gamblers had minded
their own business and behaved like gentlemen, for there
had been no disorder on board, . . . and if *they* pretended to
be ministers of the Gospel of Jesus Christ, their conduct
belied their profession."[229] This is consistent with the principle "I can tell you that I would rather have the practice of
a good moral religion without any faith at all in a Supreme
Being, than to have faith in a Supreme Being without any
moral good action."[230] Believing in correct doctrine does not
sanctify one's actions. But no one is in a position to accuse:
"You may see, or think you see, a thousand faults in your

brethren; yet they are organized as you are. . . . The main difficulty in the hearts of those who are dissatisfied is, they are not satisfied with themselves."[231]

Experience shows that the arch accusers are invariably very ambitious men whose accomplishments have not equalled their ambitions. "No person has a right to say to another, 'Why do you eat wheat bread, corn bread, or no bread at all? why do you eat potatoes, or why do you not eat them? why do you walk, or why do you sit down? why do you read this or that book? or why do you go to the right or the left?' . . . If the Elders of Israel could understand this a little better, we would like it, for the simple reason that if they had power given them now they manifest the same weaknesses in the exercise thereof as any other people."[232]

As to those who reject the gospel, "what will be their condemnation? Let the Lord judge."[233] "Remember this O ye man because he is not baptized."[234] "There is one thing that we are too much guilty of, and that is, evil speaking of our neighbors."[235] "Shall we speak evil of others? No. Why? Because the result of their treatment towards us has made us better and greater than we could have been otherwise. . . . Let us thank God, and speak evil of none."[236] Beware of making anyone an offender for a word: "Our Christian brethren almost deny the existence of a God; but it is in word only; they do not feel it in their hearts, they do not mean any such thing."[237] Atheists and gentiles are none of our business, but what about those nearer to home? "The greatest trial this people are under the necessity of bearing is to hold fellowship with false brethren"—but hold it they must.[238]

"I think it can be shown that the great majority of difficulties between brethren, arises from misunderstandings rather than from malice and a wicked heart, and instead of talking the matter over with each other in a saint-like spirit, they will contend with each other until a real fault is created, and they have brought a sin upon themselves."[239] "Let the Elders of this Church go forth and preach that every person who does not become as they are will have to suffer the wrath of God, and go down to hell, . . . and I would not give the ashes of a rye-straw for all they will do. It is good for nothing: there is no life in it—there is no soul in it";[240] it is Satan's game of accusing, and it is all negative. This was the spirit of those who came bursting with self-righteousness, to expose and correct the vices of the Utah Mormons. On September 29, 1851, Brigham Young wrote to President Fillmore: "Is it true that officers coming here by virtue of any appointment by the President, have *private instructions* . . . to watch for iniquity, . . . and make a man 'an offender for a word,' to spy out our liberties, and, by manifold misrepresentations, seek to prejudice the minds of the people against us?"[241]

In the end, it is our own weakness and ignorance that makes the business of accusing so false and futile: "God has commenced His kingdom on the earth. How intricate it is, and how difficult for a man to understand if he be not enlightened by the Spirit of God!"[242] "It requires all the atonement of Christ, the mercy of the Father, the pity of angels and the grace of the Lord Jesus Christ to be with us always, and then to do the very best we possibly can, to get rid of this sin within us."[243] "It matters not," therefore, "what your neighbours do, look to your God with all your heart, instead of watching your neighbours, and there will be no danger of your leaving the true path."[244]

Coercion has no place in the gospel, where power is exercised "only by persuasion" (D&C 121:41). "These tribes of Indians . . . war with each other, and try to destroy each

other; and why do they do it? Why, 'you are not as righteous as I am, and I want to bring you over to my holy
faith.'"[245] And the so-called civilized nations take up arms
"to subdue you heathens, and bring you over to our more
enlightened customs and religion."[246]

> Now, suppose that we were to issue our edicts to the
> whole world of mankind for them to obey the Gospel we
> preach, and had the power to compel them to obey, could
> we do it according to the dictates of our religion? We
> could not. We could invite them, and could tell them
> how, but we could not say, and maintain the faith that we
> have embraced, you must bow down . . . and submit to
> the ordinances of the kingdom of God. . . . But if we
> become Godlike, we will be just as full of charity as he is.
> We would let pagans worship as they please, and to the
> Christians and Mahommedans [sic], and all sects and par-
> ties in the world we would say, "Do just as you please,
> for your volition is free, and you must act upon it for
> yourselves before the heavens." Our religion will not per-
> mit us to command or force any man or woman to obey
> the Gospel we have embraced.[247]

"I have thought a great many times I was very thankful
I was not the Lord Almighty. I should be consuming my
enemies. How I should contend against those who hate me.
I am glad I am not the Lord."[248]

> Do not you wish sometimes you had power to pinch
> their ears? Do not you wish you had power to stop them
> in their mad career? Let the Lord Almighty do this. You
> think his eye is upon the work of his hands? It is. His ears
> are open to the prayers of his children, . . . and when we
> as a people possess the abundance of that patience, that
> longsuffering and forbearance that we need, to possess
> the privileges and the power that the Lord has in reserve
> for his people, we will receive to our utmost satisfaction.
> We shall not have it now. The Lord says, "I can not give it
> to you now."[249]

An *aspiring spirit* is alien to any man who had the Spirit of the Lord, and yet in the past has been very marked among leading Latter-day Saints. It was responsible, Joseph Smith maintained, for all the persecutions brought upon the Church. "President Smith continued by speaking of the difficulties he had to surmount ever since the commencement of the work, in consequence of aspiring men. 'Great big Elders,' as he called them, who cause him much trouble. . . . He said he had been trampled under foot by aspiring Elders, for all were infected with that spirit. . . . He said he had a subtle devil to deal with, and could only curb him by being humble."[250] "Beware of pride, and not seek to excel one above another. . . . Must the new ones begin to exalt themselves . . . as several of the quorum have done? . . . It is an eternal principle: . . . That man who rises up to condemn others . . . is in the high road to apostasy."[251]

It is the most natural thing in the world: "We have learned by sad experience that it is the nature and disposition of almost all men, as soon as they get a little authority, . . . to exercise unrighteous dominion," not realizing that the power of the priesthood must flow "without compulsory means" (D&C 121:39, 46). "We have history enough," says Brigham Young, "to prove that when men have the power their motto is, 'You shall.' But there is no such thing in the economy of heaven."[252] "Gather the Saints, but do not *flatter;* invite, but do not urge, and by no means compel anyone."[253] "There are men who . . . wish to destroy every power in Heaven and on earth that they do not hold themselves. This is the spirit of Satan that was made so visibly manifest in Heaven and which proved his overthrow, and he now afflicts this people with it; he wants to dictate and rule every principle and power that leads to exaltation and eternal life."[254]

Notice that the lofty objective—exaltation and eternal life—does not justify any personal ambition, any more than hard work justifies power and gain as an objective. After the death of Joseph Smith, many had ambition: "This wild spirit of ambition has repeatedly manifested itself to us by many communications received from various sources," wrote Brigham Young in the winter of 1845, "suggesting schemes of blood and empire, as if the work of the Lord was intended for personal aggrandisement."[255] Many justified their personal ambitions on the grounds that after all they were doing it all for the Church: "Where you find a man who wishes to steady the ark of God, without being called to do so, you will find a dark spot in him. The man full of light and intelligence discerns that God steadies his own ark, dictates his own affairs, guides his people, controls his kingdom, governs nations, and holds the hearts of all living in his hands"—he asks no assistance of us, though we eagerly justify our plans of conquest and career by dedicating them to God.[256] It is the wicked who "desire to rule, to hold the reins of government on this earth. . . . I do not blame them for being suspicious of us; men in high standing are suspicious of us, hence the frequent cry, 'Treason, treason, we are going to have trouble with the people in Utah.'"[257]

An insidious form of compulsion is the oath, against which Joseph Smith and Brigham Young issued strong warnings. "Swear not at all" (Matthew 5:34; cf. 3 Nephi 12:34), the Savior said, explaining that since we have no control over the future—even to influence our own stature or hair color—we have no business committing ourselves to future situations which we cannot control or even foresee. "Let our covenant be that of the Everlasting Covenant, as is contained in the Holy Writ," said Joseph Smith. "Pure friendship always becomes weakened the very moment you undertake to make it stronger by penal oaths and secrecy. . . . Our religion is between us and our God."[258] We do not take an oath to men. Brigham Young tells of how when he was a boy he absolutely refused to take a temperance pledge, not because he did not believe in temperance, but because he did, and felt that the pledge would only be an insult.[259] "Many times I have a feeling to bring this people under a covenant," he said at the 24th of July celebration at Big Cottonwood in 1856,

> but a doubt as to the propriety of doing so operates as a check upon that feeling. While the toasts were being read . . . it was strongly in my mind to ask, will you live your religion from this time, henceforth and forever? and to bring the people under covenant. But they are already under one, and my feelings are, I would rather they would not make covenants, than to make them and break them. Live your religion; . . . deal justly with your own conscience and with one another, and do right from henceforth, and you shall be blessed.[260]

On another occasion he says, "I will not call upon you to enter into a covenant to do this, for some might break their covenants and that would be a sin. . . . I have never made a covenant since I entered this Church only to do good and serve the Lord our God, and in every possible way aid in developing His purposes."[261]

There Is Business and . . .

It is doubtful if Shakespeare himself could surpass the scathing eloquence of Brigham Young whenever he gets on his favorite loathing—lawyers and their ways;[262] but hardly less devastating are his descriptions of businessmen in action—especially merchants. "Our merchants . . . do not ask what they can afford to sell an article for, but they ask

what they can get the people to pay; and as much as the
people will pay, so much will the merchants take—a hundred, or a thousand percent, if they can get it, and then
thank God for their success."[263] But that is simply a matter
of supply and demand—which is wrong, according to
Brigham Young, and especially insidious because it can be
rationalized to a form of righteousness: "They put me in
mind," he says, "of some men I have seen who, when they
had a chance to buy a widow's cow for ten cents on the dollar of her real value in cash, would make the purchase, and
then thank the Lord that he had so blessed them."[264] It is
true, their subconscious fights back and concedes the point
to Brigham: "We frequently hear our merchants say they
cannot do business and then go into the pulpit to preach,"[265]
but in the end the pull of this world is irresistible: "Yet
when we examine the feelings, views, wishes, desires and
aspirations of this people, we see them wandering after
almost everything but that which they should possess."[266]

Now Brigham Young was a practical man and a business man, but he was interested only in this congregation
who are so short-sighted, and so destitute of eternal values
of things—that was the difference:

> There are those in this congregation who are so short-
> sighted, and so destitute of eternal wisdom and knowledge,
> that they believe that brother Brigham is after property—
> after the things of this world. That is a false feeling, a false
> view, and a false faith in such persons. . . . I seek not for the
> world, nor for the things of the world; but God heaps prop-
> erty upon me, and I am in duty bound to take care of it. Do
> you think that I love the world? I do not. Where is the man
> who would more willingly give up his property than I
> would?[267]

"I own property, and I employ the best men I can find

to look after it. . . . But as for spending my own time in doing it, or letting my own mind dwell upon the affairs of this world, I will not do it. I have no heart to look after my own individual advantage, I never have had; my heart is not upon the things of this world."[268] This was no hollow rhetoric—five times Brigham Young had been stripped of all his property, and never so much as a backward look or sigh of regret.

He minced no words on the subject of false values: "It is disgusting to me to see a person love this world in its present organization. . . . Riches take the wings of the morning and fly away; it is beneath the heart of a man who loves God and His spirit."[269] "Oh fools, and slow of heart to understand the purposes of God and his handiwork among the people."[270] "Go to the child, and what does its joy consist in? Toys, we may call them, . . . and so it is with our youth, our young boys and girls; they are thinking too much of this world; and the middle-aged are striving and struggling to obtain the good things of this life, and their hearts are too much upon them. So it is with the aged. Is not this the condition of the Latter-Day Saints? It is."[271]

And what has all this to do with the enemy? A great deal, for it sets forth with great clarity his plan of attack, his strategy and tactics. We must never forget that the devil has more than one arrow in his quiver, and when one does not work he will try another. But the one that works by far the best among all classes of people and in all periods of time is money: he has announced in no uncertain terms that this is his world, and that one can have anything in it for money. The claims are fraudulent, of course: "Satan . . . never owned the earth; he never made a particle of it; his labor is not to create, but to destroy."[272] But then he always works by deception: "The wicked rule all over the earth, and they have had possession . . . so long that they think they are the rightful heirs, and inherit it from the Father,"[273] and so we have in the world of material things a completely inverted scale of values:

> It has been supposed that wealth gives power. In a depraved state of society, in a certain sense it does, if opening a wide field for unrighteous monopolies, by which the poor are robbed and oppressed and the wealthy are more enriched, is power. In a depraved state of society, money can buy positions and titles, can cover up a multitude of incapabilities, can open wide the gates of fashionable society to the lowest and most depraved of human beings; it divides society into castes without any reference to goodness, virtue or truth. It is made to pander to the most brutal passions of the human soul; it is made to subvert every wholesome law of God and man, and to trample down every sacred bond that should tie society together in a national, municipal, domestic and every other relationship.[274]

This little apostrophe on money, delivered as Brigham Young's sermons all were, impromptu, is worthy to stand beside that of Shakespeare's Timon of Athens on the same subject.

. . . Therefore

Does the communist world pose a threat to the peace and security of the human race? Of course it does; the danger cannot be exaggerated. There indeed is an enemy and an extremely dangerous one. The question is not whether the danger exists but how to deal with it. I spent a couple of years in military headquarters at various echelons, and if nothing else, I kept my eyes and ears open. There was nearly always complete agreement among the command as to who the enemy was and what our own objectives were, since both matters had been settled by orders from above. But on the question of just how we were to accomplish our objectives there was very little agreement: every general had his own solution to the problem, and nothing is easier than for one general to say of another (especially if both were bucking for the next promotion), "His plan is insane; it plays right into the hand of the enemy; it gives aid and comfort to the enemy; in fact it is just what the enemy wants us to do." In other words, since my plan is the only one that will work, all others amount to treason.

How then do we deal with the enemy? Brigham Young, who knew as much about as large a variety of enemies as any man who ever lived, has laid it on the line: If we show our Heavenly Father that we trust him to the point of putting aside all feelings of malice and revenge towards our fellowmen, no matter who they may be or how they feel toward us, he will see to it that "the wicked shall destroy the wicked" (cf. Mormon 4:5). That is a promise that has never failed of fulfillment. The alternative to this is the other game, the most dangerous, futile and foolish game in the world, the age-old Asiatic game of world conquest, the madmen's chess match as old as history. It is a game of power, and the rules only exist as tricks to trap one's opponent, and words and courtesies serve only to obfuscate and deceive. The game is endemic to the steppes of Asia, and the Asiatics are better at it than we can ever hope to be: for us to play the game and play it their way is simply suicide. But this vision of world power, of massive armies and machines engulfing the surface of the earth as they grind all opposition to powder, is an intoxicating one; it is the ultimate dream that I have many times heard generals talking about among themselves and to their staff. After all, say these realists, it is power that wins in this world—God is on the side of the big battalions. If we are going to be realists, let us face the facts.

The August 1969 issue of the *Scientific American* was largely devoted to the theme of "Military Technology and National Security," and the leading article, by Herbert F. York, concluded with these words: "There is no technical solution to the dilemma of the steady decrease in our national security that has for more than 20 years accompanied the steady increase in our military power"[275]—a perfect commentary on the repeated assurance of the scriptures that there is no security in the arm of flesh. If there is no technological solution to our dilemma, there is a spiritual one, and Brigham has told us what it is.

Notes

1. *JD* 18:361.
2. *JD* 10:39.
3. *JD* 10:111.
4. Elden J. Watson, *Manuscript History of Brigham Young 1801-1844* (Salt Lake City: Smith Secretarial Service, 1968), 162 (7 March 1844).
5. *JD* 8:143.
6. *JD* 18:360.
7. *JD* 7:56.
8. *JD* 8:156.
9. *JD* 11:111.
10. *JD* 11:267.
11. *JD* 8:175.
12. *JD* 8:325.
13. *JD* 8:358.
14. *JD* 18:361.
15. *JD* 19:5.
16. *JD* 11:134.
17. *JD* 8:36.
18. *JD* 8:166.
19. *JD* 14:40.
20. *JD* 3:257.
21. *JD* 8:358.

22. *JD* 12:177.
23. *JD* 10:256.
24. *JD* 8:285.
25. *JD* 10:32.
26. *JD* 12:311.
27. *JD* 15:6.
28. *JD* 8:285.
29. *JD* 3:222.
30. *JD* 13:4.
31. *JD* 3:356.
32. *JD* 3:207.
33. *JD* 12:128.
34. *JD* 11:251.
35. *JD* 13:251.
36. *JD* 10:2–3.
37. *JD* 8:61.
38. *JD* 3:321.
39. *JD* 3:365.
40. *JD* 3:365.
41. *JD* 9:108.
42. *JD* 10:304.
43. *JD* 17:159.
44. *JD* 8:179.
45. *JD* 3:95.
46. William Shakespeare, *Merchant of Venice,* act IV, scene i, lines 376–77.
47. *TPJS,* 9.
48. J. Grant Stevenson, "The Life and History of Elder Edward Stevenson," master's thesis, Brigham Young University, 1955, 43.
49. *JD* 15:4.
50. *JD* 3:118.
51. *JD* 3:117.
52. *JD* 3:7.
53. *JD* 1:225.
54. *JD* 7:46.
55. *JD* 5:353.
56. *JD* 15:4.
57. *HC* 3:269.
58. *HC* 3:269.
59. *JD* 13:1.
60. *HC* 3:269; see also 18:244.
61. *CHC* 3:349.

62. *JD* 12:202.
63. *JH* (7 December 1848).
64. *JD* 1:78.
65. *JD* 1:252.
66. *JD* 3:119.
67. *JD* 3:223.
68. *JD* 10:3.
69. *JD* 10:329.
70. *JD* 11:216.
71. *JD* 17:38.
72. *JD* 18:238–39.
73. *JD* 17:41.
74. *JD* 8:325.
75. *MS* 16:724.
76. *JD* 8:324.
77. *JD* 8:357.
78. *JD* 11:290.
79. *JD* 11:255.
80. *JD* 8:33.
81. *TPJS*, 179.
82. *JD* 14:149.
83. *JD* 3:256.
84. *JD* 3:195.
85. *JD* 10:191.
86. *JD* 16:28.
87. *JD* 3:207.
88. *JD* 3:207.
89. *MS* 21:823.
90. *JD* 14:156.
91. *JD* 12:218.
92. *JD* 8:287.
93. *JD* 2:180.
94. *JD* 10:20.
95. *JD* 10:41.
96. *JD* 3:195.
97. *JD* 1:360.
98. *JD* 13:155.
99. *JD* 3:255.
100. *TPJS*, 357.
101. *MS* 16:310.
102. *JD* 10:39.
103. *JD* 7:56.

104. *JD* 6:315.
105. *JD* 19:3.
106. *JD* 9:124.
107. William E. Berrett and Alma P. Burton, *Readings in LDS Church History*, 3 vols. (Salt Lake City: Deseret Book, Co. 1953), 1:224.
108. Elden J. Watson, *Manuscript History of Brigham Young 1846–1847* (Salt Lake City: Watson, 1971), 529 (23 February 1847).
109. *TPJS*, 366.
110. *TPJS*, 373.
111. *HC* 7:378.
112. *JD* 5:229.
113. *TPJS*, 365–66.
114. *JD* 8:150.
115. *JD* 8:279.
116. *JD* 8:325.
117. *JD* 10:297.
118. *JD* 14:226.
119. *MS* 33:433.
120. *JD* 2:270–71.
121. *JD* 19:5.
122. *TPJS*, 160–61.
123. *TPJS*, 16.
124. Watson, *Manuscript History of Brigham Young 1846–1847*, 517 (27 January 1847).
125. *JD* 8:324.
126. *JD* 8:325.
127. *HC* 7:256.
128. *JD* 1:105.
129. *JD* 1:165.
130. *MS* 17:675.
131. *MS* 6:197.
132. *MS* 21:303.
133. *JD* 10:250.
134. *JD* 12:120.
135. *JD* 14:226.
136. *JD* 18:362.
137. *JD* 11:239.
138. *MS* 29:564.
139. *JD* 13:149 (emphasis added).
140. *JD* 10:230.
141. *TPJS*, 20.
142. *TPJS*, 358.

143. *TPJS*, 361.
144. *JD* 9:316.
145. Watson, *Manuscript History of Brigham Young 1846–1847*, 91 (17 March 1846).
146. *JD* 10:315.
147. *JD* 7:137.
148. *JD* 8:6–7.
149. *JD* 8:174.
150. *JD* 8:157.
151. *JD* 10:315.
152. Watson, *Manuscript History of Brigham Young 1846–1847*, 541 (26 March 1847).
153. *JH* (9 January 1850).
154. *MS* 16:188.
155. *MS* 17:261.
156. *MS* 19:248.
157. *JD* 5:236.
158. *JD* 11:131–32.
159. *JD* 11:263.
160. *JD* 11:263.
161. *TPJS*, 187.
162. *JD* 13:271.
163. *TPJS*, 9.
164. *JD* 8:160.
165. *TPJS*, 317.
166. *JD* 3:371.
167. *JD* 8:352.
168. *JD* 3:119.
169. *JD* 11:301.
170. *JD* 3:363.
171. *JD* 18:358.
172. *JD* 8:59.
173. *TPJS*, 19.
174. Watson, *Manuscript History of Brigham Young 1801–1844*, 23–24 (22 December 1837).
175. Ibid., 24 (22 December 1837).
176. Ibid., 162 (7 March 1844).
177. *JD* 15:226.
178. *JD* 3:327.
179. *JD* 14:133; cf. *TPJS*, 119.
180. *JD* 2:280.
181. *JD* 3:222–23.

182. *JD* 6:331.
183. *JD* 8:325–26.
184. *JD* 12:259.
185. *JD* 3:222.
186. *JD* 18:359.
187. *JD* 12:309.
188. *JD* 3:226.
189. *JD* 8:132.
190. *JD* 8:132.
191. *JD* 6:347.
192. *JD* 18:305.
193. *JD* 3:50.
194. *JD* 8:128.
195. *JD* 8:261.
196. *JD* 15:18.
197. *TPJS*, 217.
198. *HC* 1:443.
199. *HC* 1:443–44.
200. *JD* 8:287.
201. *JD* 8:37.
202. *JD* 8:128.
203. *JD* 3:119.
204. *JD* 3:363.
205. *JD* 5:229–30.
206. *JD* 19:7 (emphasis added).
207. *JD* 8:118.
208. *JD* 8:181.
209. *JD* 13:178.
210. *TPJS*, 194.
211. *TPJS*, 228.
212. *TPJS*, 240.
213. *TPJS*, 241.
214. *TPJS*, 43.
215. *JD* 17:120.
216. *JD* 14:122.
217. *JD* 1:364.
218. *TPJS*, 49 (emphasis added).
219. *TPJS*, 218.
220. *TPJS*, 43.
221. *TPJS*, 91.
222. *TPJS*, 193.
223. *TPJS*, 212.

224. *TPJS*, 214.
225. *TPJS*, 208.
226. *TPJS*, 18–19.
227. *JD* 7:133–34.
228. Watson, *Manuscript History of Brigham Young 1801–1844*, 44 (4 July 1839).
229. Ibid., 152–53 (4 October 1843).
230. *JD* 13:249.
231. *JD* 8:287.
232. *JD* 14:94–95.
233. *JD* 14:222.
234. *JD* 12:270.
235. *JD* 14:16.
236. *JD* 14:40.
237. *JD* 14:40–41.
238. *JD* 8:150.
239. *JD* 12:173.
240. *JD* 8:155.
241. Watson, *Manuscript History of Brigham Young 1847–1867*, 105 (29 September 1851).
242. *JD* 13:271.
243. *JD* 11:301.
244. *JD* 8:177.
245. *JD* 3:87.
246. *JD* 3:88.
247. *JD* 14:94.
248. *JD* 15:2.
249. *JD* 15:2.
250. *TPJS*, 225.
251. *TPJS*, 155–56.
252. *JD* 14:95.
253. *JD* 8:72.
254. *JD* 10:97.
255. *HC* 7:429.
256. *JD* 8:66.
257. *JD* 4:38.
258. *TPJS*, 146.
259. *JD* 14:225.
260. *MS* 18:679–80.
261. *JD* 11:140.
262. William Shakespeare, *Henry VI*, part II, act IV, scene ii, line 86: "The first thing we do, let's kill all the lawyers."

263. *JD* 17:361.
264. *JD* 17:362.
265. *JD* 13:308.
266. *JD* 12:228.
267. *JD* 8:125.
268. *JD* 11:297.
269. *MS* 12:275.
270. *JD* 8:63.
271. *JD* 18:237.
272. *JD* 10:320.
273. *JD* 11:302.
274. *JD* 10:3; cf. Joe McGinniss, *The Selling of the President* (New York: Washington Square, 1968).
275. Herbert F. York, "Military Technology and National Security," *Scientific American* 221 (August 1969): 29.

8

The Uses and Abuses of Patriotism

The Magnanimous Patriot

The assigned title of our treatise could be misleading. Patriotism is what Aristotle calls a "good of first intent," a thing good and desirable in itself, such as love, joy, or eternal life, whose value needs no argument. Hence to "use" patriotism, treating it as a tool rather than a precious jewel, is to abuse it. Yet like other goods of primary intent, it has a special function. The business of patriotism is to open doors; the abuse of patriotism shuts them.

Patriotism is devotion to the patria, the fatherland, one's own people, the land of one's birth. Thus the genius of patriotism is the sense of identification with others. And the greater the patriot, the wider is the circle of his familial affection. That handful of simon-pure patriots, the makers and saviors of nations who have merited the title of "the Great," from Abraham, Alexander, and Alfred to Washington, Bolivar, and Lincoln, are remembered as the common heroes of all mankind, who "shine as lights in the world . . . in the midst of a crooked and perverse nation" (Philippians

Reprinted by permission from American Heritage: A Syllabus for Social Science 100 (Provo: Brigham Young University Press, 1977), 188–97.

2:15), amazing all observers by their broad humanity, their concern for the weak and downtrodden, and the magnanimous treatment of their enemies. All acted in conscious imitation of those heroes of ancient epic tradition who toiled and suffered to relieve the burdens of weak and erring fellows. The Founding Fathers dedicated their labors to the benefit of the whole human race: "Our Cause," wrote Franklin, "is the Cause of all Mankind. . . . We are fighting for their Liberty in defending our own." The magnanimous brand of patriotism is no more perfectly exemplified than in the person of the Prophet Joseph: "I am the greatest advocate of the Constitution of the United States there is on the earth. In my feelings I am always ready to die for the protection of the weak and oppressed in their just rights."[1] To his mind that was the duty of the patriot, and his behavior confirmed his assertion: "Friendship is one of the grand fundamental principles of 'Mormonism'; [it is designed] to revolutionize and civilize the world, and cause wars and contentions to cease and men to become friends and brothers. . . . It is a time-honored adage that love begets love. Let us pour forth love—show forth our kindness unto all mankind."[2] Brother Joseph opens all the doors:

> There certainly is a tie to those who are of the same faith which is peculiar to itself, but it is without prejudice, gives full scope to the mind, and enables us to conduct ourselves with liberality towards those who are *not* of our faith; this principle, in our opinion, approximates the nearest to the mind of God and is God-like. [With this goes an explicit warning against closing doors:] We further caution our brethren, against the impropriety of the organization of bands or companies; . . . pure friendship always becomes weakened the very moment you undertake to make it stronger by penal oaths and secrecy.[3]

Patriotism is an emotional surge, a "gut feeling," the

generous impulse of those "who more than self their country love and mercy more than life"; hence the moment it
becomes calculating and contrived, its nature is perverted.
Like the priesthood, it works through persuasion and affection, never through coercion. "While we therefore cheer the
Constitution, . . . let us remember that the perpetuity of our
free institutions depends upon"—Let us stop here for a
moment and ask, On what? A strong military posture? But
the most oppressed people on earth have enjoyed the protection of the greatest armed forces. An efficient police
force? And who is to police the police—*quis custodiet cus-
todes?* On what, then? Here is the Prophet's answer:

> There is a duty which we, in common with all men,
> owe to governments, laws, and the regulations in the civil
> concerns of life; these guarantee to all parties and denom-
> inations of religion, equal and indefeasible rights, all alike
> interested; and they make our responsibilities one
> towards another in matters relating to temporal affairs,
> and the things of this life; the former principles do not
> destroy the latter, but bind us stronger, and make our
> responsibility, not only one towards another, but unto
> God also: hence we say, that the constitution of the
> United States is a glorious standard, it is founded in wis-
> dom, it is a heavenly banner.[4]

The Constitution is to be defended by deference and courtesy toward others: the spirit of the thing is all.

Militant Patriotism

Patriotism shows itself in times of crisis: "These are the
times that try men's souls!" is the refrain of the earliest
purely patriotic odes—those of the Greek lyric poets, who
describe the true patriot as one who stands shoulder to
shoulder with his fellow citizens, facing any odds. In this
atmosphere of crisis, an attitude of defense and defiance

naturally associates patriotism with the panoply of war. The classic trappings of patriotism have been inherited by the Western world along with the pageantry of chivalry from the ceaselessly warring tribes of the steppes of Asia. The flag is the bright rallying point that can be seen for miles by the mounted hordes on the open plains, where the trumpet's message and the arrow's flight carry unhindered for great distances. In jungle and forest it is another story, but the formal symbols of European patriotism belong to "the World of the Jaredites," the polarized world of host against host on the darkling plain, of Shiz versus Coriantumr. But does the true patriot destroy his people in his own interests as that previous pair did? Under chivalry the essence of patriotism was to support one's liege lord, who enriched one with a share of his ceaseless looting. There are no more touching stories of loyalty than are found in the literature of the Heroic Ages. Yet Roland, Beowolf, Blondel, etc., stand out precisely because they were those rare souls who remained true while others ran for cover.

There is something wrong with this patriotism, which is based on conflict. As Froissart tells us forcibly, under chivalry the only way to prove one's nobility was by fighting somebody. The tradition survives, and to this day there are many whose patriotism is not a widening but a contracting circle, recalling the defensive-aggressive posture of the Roman *trux et minax* (dour and threatening), the walled towns and castles of the Middle Ages, the family shelter of the Jaredites in which "every man did cleave unto that which was his own; . . . and every man kept the hilt of his sword in his right hand, in the defence of his property and his own life and of his wives and children" (Ether 14:2), and finally, the narrowest circle of all, with every man "walk[ing] in his own way," seeking his own interests amid the rich offerings of Babylon (see D&C 1:16). The passion for security ends in total insecurity, with the would-be patriot fancying himself as a lone frontiersman, facing the world with his long rifle, his keen eyes searching the horizon for enemies and finding them everywhere; until one day as he draws his circle even smaller, we find him coolly keeping his next-door neighbor and fellow countrymen in the sights of his trusty .22, lest the latter make a suspicious move in the direction of his two-years' supply. Can that be patriotism? Yet the sincerity of such people cannot be doubted, and Brigham Young with characteristic insight diagnoses the nature of their condition:

> An individual . . . with [an] abhorrence of evil [joins the Church]. . . . He sets himself upon the watch to detect the failings of others, deeming that he is doing God a service in being so employed [for God and Country], and thus is he decoyed into the occupation of the great master of evil, to be the accuser of the brethren. And during the time thus occupied by him, he considers himself actuated by the purest of motives, arising from a detestation of sin. . . . Yet mark the subtlety of Satan in thus leading men into a false position. Such a course, in the first place, probably arose from the purest of motives, and perhaps the individual was instrumental in rectifying some error; he feels a satisfaction for having done so, his self-esteem is gratified, and ere he is aware, he is seeking for another opportunity of doing the same, . . . continually set[ting] himself up as being capable of sitting in judgment upon others, and of rectifying by his own ability the affairs of the kingdom of God.[5]

There is ample reason for being suspicious if one is so inclined, for "We do live in a devilish and wicked world where men busy themselves in watching for iniquity."[6] But need we join the watchers? "It is the doctrine of the devil to retard the human mind, and hinder our progress, by filling us with self-righteousness [love it or leave it]. . . . We are full of selfishness; the devil flatters us that we are very righteous, when we are feeding on the faults of others. . . . Away with self-righteousness!"[7] Patriotism of this type was the principal weapon used against the Prophet and the Saints; the stock charge against them was treason—they were a danger to America. What was behind it? Brigham knew: "I wish this fact to sink into your hearts, that when men or women have doubts, they also have fear; and when they have fear, they are in danger of what? Of themselves. Want of confidence is the parent of moral imbecility and intellectual weakness."[8]

Stereotyped Patriotism

Without being so grim, there is a stereotyped patriotism into which the less truculent easily subside. For most people, patriotism is a matter of forms and ceremonies. How far can we externalize a noble emotion? Like charity, it vaunteth not itself; the true patriot does not covet medals and badges to be seen of men, fearful less his heroism go unrecognized and unrewarded. The classic display of stereotyped patriotism was the bowing down of the mighty host to the King's image in the Plain of Dura, while the bands played and the banners flew. But Daniel's three friends would not go along; though they were the King's most valued and trusty advisers and bowed down to his person every day, they drew the line at bowing to his image, a mere symbol. They rebelled like Cordelia, who retched at the superloyalist orations of her sisters and protested, "I cannot heave / My heart into my mouth."[9] Daniel was not thrown to the lions because of his religion but because of a superpatriotic law passed by scheming officials who seemed to flatter the King while they betrayed him. Indeed the religious martyrs who died on the stake and the scaffold during the Reformation were executed not for their religion but on technical charges of treason to King and country— always the most convenient weapon for removing one's enemies great and small.

Clichés and heroics can lead to disastrous excesses. The young heroes Hippias and Aristogeiton murdered a tyrant of Athens and lost their own lives in the operation—they became forever after the perfect, nay, romantic, models of ancient patriotism. Result: a rash of terrorism in which no public official was safe from the assassin's knife. The tradition still reverberates in the Middle East, where millions ecstatically hail acts of the most brutal, cowardly, and underhanded terrorism as patriotism of the highest and holiest order. But patriotism, being a state of mind, cannot be equated with any specific pattern of behavior. "Aid and comfort to the enemy?" Every foolish thing we do gives aid and comfort to the enemy, but does that make us all traitors? Only a mind reader could discern the quality of another's patriotism, for which reason we are commanded, "Man shall not smite, neither shall he judge" (Mormon 8:20).

While military action sometimes demands of the patriot a high order of courage, we must not forget that patriotism requires at least all four of the Platonic virtues, and valor is only one of them. The one most likely to be overlooked, and actually the most demanding of these virtues in the patriot, is moderation—restraint and self-control: "We shall go on from victory to victory, and from conquest to conquest; *our* evil passions will be subdued, *our* prejudices depart; we shall find no room in our bosoms for hatred."[10] It is those who "reject milder counsels" who bring "death and sorrow upon the Church";[11] it is "the labors of fanatics" that make

things hang by a thread;[12] the greatest danger to Church *and*
State, according to the prophets, will come from the extremists.[13] "Some of the Elders would much rather fight for their
religion than live it. If any one thinks to get into the kingdom by fighting, . . . they will find themselves mistaken."[14]
The worst disservice one can do to any country is to involve
it in war, if we would follow the prince of military analysts,
Karl von Clausewitz; for, he explains, "There is no other
human activity that stands in such constant and universal
contact with chance as does war"[15]—there is no guarantee
whatever that superior firepower will win; all that we can
be sure of is that there will be waste and destruction, and
the greater the victory, the greater the destruction on *both*
sides.[16] But victory itself, says Clausewitz, is a completely
illusory concept, being purely tactical (local and temporary)
and never strategic.[17] The history of the Church illustrates
the point—it is a long series of tactical setbacks and strategic gains made possible by the remarkable self-control and
moderation exhibited by the Saints in the face of the most
determined provocation. Clausewitz concludes that war is
an act of moral and mental bankruptcy of those who have
no other resources: it is the devil's "own dominion" (D&C
1:35).

And here we have perhaps the worst abuse of patriotism. While "enthusiasm for the cause . . . does *not* constitute
a necessary part of . . . the military virtue of an army"[18] for
officers, according to Clausewitz, it is indispensable for the
"lower ranks." For "in the great combats . . . there is usually
no hostile feeling of individual against individual," so that
the only way they can be induced to shed each other's
blood is by cultivating "national hatred, which . . . becomes
a more or less powerful substitute for personal hostility of
individuals."[19] The stories of the Nephites and Jaredites are

a moving demonstration of this principle at work, and of the horrible consequences to which it leads. Some may protest that Moroni under his title of liberty is a patriot exterminating conscientious objectors. But what did he do? He dispatched only a few Amalekites—a coalition of the very rich, the royalists, ambitious judges, those "who professed the blood of nobility" (Alma 51:21), and some of the misguided members of the Church, all armed to the teeth for military action *against* the government (Alma 46:35, 1–7; 45:23–24). On the other hand, Mormon, that greatest of patriots, "utterly refused to go up against mine enemies" in an unjust war (cf. Mormon 3:11–16). "I have been afraid to ask God to kill my enemies," said Joseph Smith, "lest some of them should, peradventure, repent."[20]

The Self-Serving Patriot

The ancient king was the "gift-giver," who ruled by virtue of being able with his followers to grab and distribute more wealth than other men. He was thus the "Cyning," the man of ability, and as your liege lord who made you rich, he commanded all your loyalty and devotion—as long as he could pay. Thus an economic motive has not been alien to the concept of patriotism since the Age of Fable; *Ubi panis ibi patria*, said the Romans—you are loyal to whatever country feeds you. In a superb demonstration of religious and patriotic zeal (and remember that the ancient state was sacral, with the king as God on earth, so that to be pious was to be patriotic—God and country were inseparable), the Ephesians chanted "Great is Diana of the Ephesians" for two hours on end (cf. Acts 19:34), but Paul is good enough to tell us what was really behind it—the silver business (Acts 19:24–25). (One thinks of other silver businesses operating under the glorious name of the

Constitution.) Cecil Rhodes was so great a patriot that he actually had a country named after him, and his motto was "Philanthropy plus five percent!" Is that so bad, he asks? And yet there is something disturbing about the five percent.

We can never feel quite right about the commercializing of sacred things, including Christmas and the Flag, yet that is the sort of thing that really pays off. "Yes," says Haley the slaveholder in *Uncle Tom's Cabin*, "I consider religion a valeyable thing in a nigger, when it's the genuine article, and no mistake," for Haley "knew the price of everything," and was quite sincere about it. Since the days of Nimrod, ambitious men have known that patriotism of *others* can be a gold-mine. Was there ever a more fervent American than Daddy Warbucks, or more stirring appeals to national sentiment than the advertising of those industries which loudly proclaim their self-sacrificing heroism in converting to wartime economy (with unlimited profits to themselves), or who describe their systematic looting of the most valuable and available of our national resources as a valiant conquest of the wilderness in the manner of the brave pioneers? Today the knack of getting rich by enlisting the willingness of others to make patriotic sacrifices, once a well-kept secret, is becoming common knowledge as we make increasingly heavy drafts upon a rapidly dwindling capital of national virtue. Breaking the rules can be profitable only if others are willing to keep them, for which reason those who exploit patriotism are the sincerest of its advocates— they would be nowhere without it. The idealistic youngster who volunteers for a dangerous mission in war goes out into the dark with the chorus of "So long, sucker!" ringing in his ears. He is the indispensable fall guy without whose heroism the rest would never get home to show their decorations.

"O what a skillful *argumentatrix* self-interest is!" cries Tertullian.[21] With what practiced skill it would convince us that the acquisition of private wealth is a patriotic duty, relieving the nation of the cost of one's upkeep while exercising that independence of mind which the Constitution fosters. True enough, as long as we provide for our wants, which are few—"having food and raiment let us be therewith content" (1 Timothy 6:8); however, beyond that point the economy is reversed, with the individual taking as much as he possibly can and giving as little as he can (this is known as "maximizing profits"), and thus becoming a burden on the government, which he relies on to assist and protect him in the process. The patriot is Plato's hero, one who can be trusted to do the right thing even with the ring of Gyges, which makes the wearer invisible; no rule or official puts restraints on his freedom of speech, press, or assembly, in appreciation of which he knows how to restrain himself from crowding the freedom of others. Everyone is perfectly free to eat twenty meals a day and wear twenty suits—why don't those do so who can afford it? Is it any more sensible or moral to acquire unlimited wealth—a hundred or a thousand times more than one needs for subsistence—especially since money more than anything else empowers one to infringe on the liberty of others? The genius of the Constitution is not that it guarantees every man a chance to "succeed," as we are often told (has there ever been a government under which clever, determined, and unscrupulous men could not get to the top?), but that it gives the same inviolable rights and immunities to rich and poor alike, the only qualification for their enjoyment being their humanity—they are *human* rights pure and simple; because it "guarantees to all . . . equal, coherent, and indefeasible rights," says the Prophet Joseph; ". . . hence we say, that the Constitution of the United States is a glorious standard."[22] It is the human appeal, not the fiscal, that inspired the Prophet's patriotism.

Unlimited Trust

It is all very well to be a trusting soul who believes in the integrity of others, but isn't that both foolish and dangerous in the real world, human nature being what it is? You never know what some people may be up to; is it safe to leave people alone and unsupervised in their kitchens? How do you know they are not busy making bombs? Answer: You don't. You simply have to trust them—a risky proposition, but worth the price: "Rather spare ten iniquitous among you," said Joseph Smith, "than condemn one innocent one."[23] And what is the alternative? Total surveillance—but that is possible only in a Soviet prison. But is the only alternative to that total liberty? What else? "Every man has a natural, and, in our country, a constitutional right to be a false prophet, as well as a true prophet."[24] But a false prophet can do great mischief; does God approve of false prophets? Not of their behavior but of their liberty. He has commanded all men to worship him (Moses 7:33), but by his order, "If a man desired to serve God, it was his privilege; . . . but if he did not believe in him there was no law to punish him," for to pressure him into serving God would be "strictly contrary to the commands of God" (Alma 30:7, 9). "Men must not be constrained against their will to obey the will of God," said President Joseph F. Smith. "They must obey it because they know it to be right, because they desire to do it, and because it is their pleasure to do it."[25] To use the name of God to reinforce patriotism or to use patriotism in the interest of both is an abuse of both religion and patriotism; it is "strictly contrary to the commands of God" (Alma 30:7), to say nothing of the Constitution.

The cornerstone of all coexistence, as Brigham Young often reminded the Saints, is confidence, trust: "Wickedness has submerged the world, and confidence and good faith have fled."[26] A hundred years ago he could say, "The kings on their thrones have to pay for their positions, for they cannot trust themselves in the hands of their attendants, without bribery. Only the semblance of honour, integrity, and confidence are to be found in the world."[27] Was he right? Where are those thrones today? The corridors of history are haunted by the ghosts of kings, magistrates, judges, rulers, and presidents who sought security in suspicion, regimentation, intimidation, surveillance, and coercion. The man who sends the leader of the opposition to the block or the firing squad on Monday, sends his own chief counsellor or brother-in-law on Wednesday, and ends up there himself on Friday. Trust is indivisible. You cannot trust some and mistrust others without constantly rearranging the schedule. The Roman grandee quickly learned that the loyal retainer who murdered his rival one day would just as cheerfully murder him the next. As Joseph Smith said, if you distrust A you will distrust B. If you lie to one man you will lie to another; "the same principle which would trample upon the rights of Latter-day Saints would trample upon the rights of the Roman Catholics, or of any other denomination who may be unpopular and too weak to defend themselves."[28] The Constitution is a bulwark against precisely this type of patriotism.

Granted that we must have trust, the question still remains, how can we be trusting when "he that will war the true Christian warfare against the corruptions of these last days will have wicked men and angels of devils, and all the infernal powers of darkness continually arrayed against him"?[29] Well, for one thing, we do *not* fight fire with fire: "Some pleaded our suffering from persecution and said they were justified in stealing from our enemies because *they* had robbed *us,* but such a course tends to destroy the kingdom of God"[30]—which is just what the enemy wants. No, we can afford the luxury of trusting our fellow man, only because we trust in God, who has assured us that if others let us down, he will make it up to us. Mormon denounced the patriotic fervor of the Nephites, resolved to "go up unto their enemies to battle, and avenge themselves of the blood of their brethren" (Mormon 3:14). What nobler motive? But God absolutely forbids it (Mormon 3:15). He refuses to accept it: when the inhabitants of the Promised Land seek blood and revenge for whatever reason, they must perish like the Jaredites and Nephites before them (Moroni 9:23). As for the wicked enemy, "Behold, the judgments of God will overtake the wicked; and it is *by the wicked* that the wicked are punished" (Mormon 4:5).

The World Patriot

The Founding Fathers were convinced that their liberal teachings were for the benefit of all men, not only for their own times but for endless generations to come, ensuring the blessings of liberty not only to themselves but especially to their posterity, and not only to this land but eventually to the whole world. And indeed, throughout Europe the news of the Declaration of Independence was received by cheering crowds; great English lords refused commissions from their king to fight the Americans, and noblemen came from the Continent to give their active assistance to a cause which their own liege lords found abhorrent. Note the sweeping language of D&C 101:77–80:

> The laws and constitution of the people . . . I have suffered to be established, and should be maintained for the rights and protection of *all flesh*, according to just and holy principles; That *every man* may act . . . according to the moral agency which I have given unto him, that every man may be accountable for his own sins in the day of judgment. Therefore it is not right that *any* man should be in bondage one to another. And for this *purpose* have I established the Constitution of this land, by the hands of wise men whom I raised up unto this very purpose.

"Every" and "all" are the key words:

> We deem it a just principle, and it is one the force of which we believe ought to be considered by *every* individual, that all men are created equal, and that *all* have the privilege of thinking for themselves upon *all* matters relative to conscience. Consequently, then, we are not disposed, had we the power, to deprive *any one* of exercising that free independence of mind which heaven has so graciously bestowed upon the *human family* as one of its choicest gifts.[31]

Trust lies at the root of everything. It is not for us to monitor the freedom of others: "Those who are valiant and inspired with the true independence of heaven . . . will go forth boldly in the service of their God, *leaving others to do as they please*, determined to do right, *though* all mankind besides should take the opposite course."[32] And so the great-hearted Joseph: "It is a love of liberty which inspires my soul—civil and religious liberty to the *whole of the human race.* . . . I will lift them up, and in their own way too, if I cannot persuade them my way is better; and *I will not seek to compel any man* to believe as I do."[33]

The principles of civil and religious liberty enunciated

in the Constitution and now embodied in the constitutions
of most nations carried recognition of man's free agency to
a point which was considered radically dangerous at the
time; but without them the Church could never have been
restored to earth; they are the franchise of the Saints. In any
other country they might have found less persecution ("The
inhumanity and murderous disposition of this people! . . .
It cannot be found among the nations where kings and
tyrants are enthroned"[34]), but in no other country would
their actions be beyond the reach of all legal persecutions.
"It was in this government, formed by men inspired of God,
although at the time they knew it not, . . . that the Lord sent
forth His angel to reveal the truths of heaven as in times
past."[35] "Could that book [of Mormon] have been brought
forth and published to the world under any other government but the Government of the United States? No."[36] No
people ever clung to the Constitution with greater fervor
than the Latter-day Saints; they could not afford to do otherwise, and they knew it. They were convinced that they
were "the only people who know the worth of the
Constitution."[37] An official statement issued in Nauvoo at
the height of crisis illustrates that moderation and restraint
which proved their unswerving patriotism, and the sublime
confidence in God which made it possible:

> To show our loyalty to the institutions of our country
> and preserve peace in the county, as a people, we
> pledged ourselves to . . . abide the decisions of the court,
> not taking vengeance into our own hands [the mob was
> at the time mortally afraid of the Mormons] . . . or com-
> mencing prosecutions . . . [which] would be construed
> into . . . a desire to pick a quarrel on our part, which we
> were and still are determined to avoid, even every
> appearance of evil. . . . We are decidedly for peace, and
> we ever have been.[38]

Such is the patriotism that heals. It was because they trusted in their Heavenly Father that these people could withstand the overpowering temptations to fight, which their enemies' cunning placed in their way: "The plan of raising a battalion to march to California by a call from the War Department was devised with a view to the total overthrow of this kingdom."[39] "I saw the whole plan concocted as plain as I saw the faces then before me, and I felt within myself that my faith in God would out general the wickedness of our enemies. Away went the battalion and the sword fell on the other side; if they had not gone, we would not have been in the valley now."[40] Furthermore they realized that the Constitution, like the gospel, left the doors open to expansion in all directions:

> The signers of the Declaration of Independence and the framers of the Constitution were inspired men from on high to do that work. But was that which was given to them perfect, not admitting of any addition whatever? No. . . . They laid the foundation, and it was for after generations to rear the superstructure upon it. It is a progressive—a gradual work.[41]

So also Joseph Smith: "The Constitution is not a law unto us, but it makes provision for us whereby we can make laws."[42] The Latter-day Saints are in no position to despise the institutions of men but must recognize them as scaffolding.[43] For not only do those institutions embrace eternal principles, but the Saints themselves are still far from rising above them: "You hear men and women talk about living and abiding a celestial law, when they do not so much as know what it is, and are not prepared to receive it. . . . When can you abide a celestial law? When you become a celestial being, and never until then."[44] Meantime, the Constitution, like the gospel, goes on opening doors. "I expect to see the day," said Brigham, "when the Elders of Israel will protect and sustain civil and religious liberty . . . abroad *in connection with the Gospel* for the salvation of *all* nations."[45] For "the cause of God is one common cause; . . . we are all members of one common body. . . . The advancement of the cause of God and the building up of Zion is as much one man's business as another's. . . . Party feelings, separate interests, exclusive designs should be lost sight of in the one common cause, in the interest of the whole."[46]

Our thesis then is that patriotism identifies one's interest with others in a common cause against outsiders; it is thus both inclusive and exclusive. But because it is a generous and spontaneous thing, it tends continually to expand, seeking to include ever greater numbers in its beneficent embrace. What makes it possible to risk extending unlimited credit to outsiders is faith in God. The difference between the inclusive and the exclusive types of patriotism may be best summed up in the words of Brigham Young:

> Very closely allied to this party spirit is the national feeling that some exhibit. This national feeling is another feature of "Gentilism." "Gentilism" breaks up the family of man, and divides them off into parties and nations, having contrary interests. "Mormonism," on the other hand, . . . by drawing them from all nations . . . unites the family of man. . . . There are good and bad . . . qualities in all nations. . . . All real Saints, when they receive the Gospel, will readily relinquish party spirit and national feeling, and count such things as the distinctive ornaments of Satan's kingdom.[47]

"Sustain those principles that do away with and destroy this feeling of nationality that is in the hearts of individuals."[48] And the Lord himself lays down the law: "[I] have heard thy prayers concerning thy brethren. Be not partial

towards them in love above many others, but . . . let thy
love abound unto all men" (D&C 112:11).

Notes

1. *TPJS*, 326.
2. *TPJS*, 316.
3. *MS* 5:72 (emphasis added).
4. *MS* 5:72.
5. *MS* 6:165–66.
6. *TPJS*, 315.
7. *TPJS*, 241.
8. *JD* 10:20.
9. William Shakespeare, *King Lear*, act I, scene i, lines 93–94.
10. *TPJS*, 179 (emphasis added).
11. *TPJS*, 136.
12. *MS* 25:261.
13. Cf. *MS* 39:263.
14. *MS* 33:433.
15. Karl von Clausewitz, *War, Politics, and Power*, tr. and ed. Edward M. Collins (Chicago: Gateway, 1967), 79; cf. 117.
16. Ibid., 108; cf. 96.
17. Ibid., 70–72.
18. Ibid., 182 (emphasis added).
19. Ibid., 151.
20. *TPJS*, 340.
21. Tertullian, *De Spectaculis* II, 16.
22. *TPJS*, 147 (emphasis added).
23. *TPJS*, 239.
24. *TPJS*, 44.
25. Joseph F. Smith, *Gospel Doctrine* (Salt Lake City, UT: Deseret Book, 1973), 65.
26. *JD* 11:256.
27. *JD* 9:316.
28. *TPJS*, 313.
29. *TPJS*, 259.
30. Elden J. Watson, *Manuscript History of Brigham Young 1846–1847* (Salt Lake City: Watson, 1971), 131–32 (4 December 1846; emphasis added).
31. *TPJS*, 49 (emphasis added).
32. *JD* 1:312 (emphasis added).
33. *TPJS*, 313 (emphasis added).

34. *TPJS*, 131.
35. *JD* 2:170–71.
36. *JD* 8:67.
37. *JD* 5:211.
38. *HC* 7:415–16.
39. *JH* (1 October 1848).
40. *JH* (1 October 1848).
41. *JD* 7:14.
42. *TPJS*, 279.
43. *WJS*, 62.
44. *JD* 7:142–43.
45. *JD* 11:262–63 (emphasis added).
46. *TPJS*, 231.
47. *MS* 16:210.
48. *MS* 31:572.

9

Renounce War, or
a Substitute for Victory

Editor:

Recently the doctrine has been propagated hereabouts that there is no substitute for victory—military victory. May I call attention to a very strong statement on the subject in the Doctrine and Covenants: "Therefore, renounce war and proclaim peace, and seek diligently to turn the hearts of the children to their fathers, and the hearts of the fathers to the children; and again, the hearts of the Jews unto the prophets, and the prophets unto the Jews; lest I come and smite the whole earth with a curse, and all flesh be consumed before me" (D&C 98:16–17).

"Renounce" is a strong word: we are not to try to win peace by war, or merely to call a truce, but to renounce war itself, to disclaim it as a policy while proclaiming (that means not just announcing, but preaching) peace without reservation. But if we renounce war, how shall we defend and advance our interests? We are told that, too: after the clear statement of what we must renounce comes the

---

Reprinted from the Daily Universe, *Letter to the Editor, 26 March 1971, entitled "Renounce War."*

equally clear statement of what we must put in its place—
the substitute. Instead of playing with fireworks we are to
"seek diligently" to advance the work of salvation for the
living and the dead, and to make a serious effort to influence the Jews. That is a full-time job and our whole assignment. Next after the prohibition and the command comes
the penalty: if we do *not* take this course "the whole earth"
will be cursed, and all flesh consumed (D&C 98:16–17). The
alternative is not just a substitute suggested for our consideration, but an out-and-out command, accompanied by a
resounding ultimatum: either to renounce war or to be
totally destroyed—there is no third choice.

 Thus we have the mandate to renounce military action,
the order to substitute something very different in its place,
and the terrible penalty for failure to do both. A few years
ago such an extreme proposition sounded quite fantastic;
the consuming of all flesh belonged to the category of wild
apocalyptic nightmares. Today, however, the best scientists
all over the world are repeating the same alternatives with
ominous urgency and insistence: it is to be either no more
war or mutual annihilation. Those two verses of the
Doctrine and Covenants revealed almost 140 years ago are,
standing alone, enough to prove Joseph Smith a true
prophet.

 The Jaredites, thoroughly convinced that there was no
substitute for victory, kept hacking away at each other until
they demonstrated the truth of the maxim "Destroy them
and they will destroy you." When the Nephites, after a
series of brilliant military successes, declared "that they
would go up to battle against their enemies, and would cut
them off from the face of the land" as the only solution
to the Lamanite problem (for there is no substitute for victory), their great general Mormon instantly resigned his

command and "utterly refused" to fight with them, but "did stand as an idle witness" (Mormon 3:16) to record for our benefit what happened next. His message to us is an impassioned plea "to repent and prepare to stand before the judgment-seat of Christ" (Mormon 3:22), substituting the work of salvation for the work of destruction. If we persist in reversing the words of the Savior, Who takes up the sword shall die by the sword (cf. Revelation 13:10), to read, perversely, Who does not take up the sword shall perish by the sword, we shall deserve what happens to us. This is not a protest, just a timely reminder, that we may remember when it happens that we have been warned and fore-warned.

Hugh Nibley
Professor of Ancient Scriptures

10

If There Must Needs Be Offense

It has been a quarter of a century since the end of a war that involved nearly the whole world. And yet there has been no peace since that great tragedy was concluded. Men continue to fight, blood is spilled, lives are lost, and the world totters again on the brink of a massive conflagration. What are the answers to war and peace for Latter-day Saints? Does the Lord suggest a position to be taken by members of the Church?

The word of prophecy is final: "With the sword and by bloodshed the inhabitants of the earth shall mourn; . . . until the consumption decreed hath made a full end of all nations" (D&C 87:6). And yet in the same breath in which he declares that God "foresaw that war should come upon all nations of the world," President Joseph F. Smith declared all this warlike activity to be strictly contrary to the will of God, who "is not pleased, nor was it his purpose or design, or intent, to foreordain the condition [of war] that the world is in today, [since wars come] . . . not to fulfill the purposes of God, but the purposes of the nations of the earth in consequence of their wickedness."[1]

Reprinted from the Ensign 1 *(July 1971): 53–55.*

With the First Vision it was revealed that the two great events lying ahead for mankind in these last days are the building of Zion and the overthrow of Babylon, two developments working in opposite directions and with opposite spirits, excluding compromise. The prophecy on war ends with explicit instructions: "Wherefore, stand ye in holy places, and be not moved, until the day of the Lord come" (D&C 87:8).

But until the day of the Lord comes, we live in a wicked world, and to that degree in which we partake of the sins of Babylon, we must needs receive of her plagues (cf. Revelation 18:4). We may not indulge our covetousness in time of peace and fastidiously disdain to share in the discomforts and perils of war. The saints, by no means immune to the vices of the world, have often had to assume a warlike posture; yet considering the terrible and ceaseless tensions and provocations that surrounded the Church in its early days, and the "wild spirit of ambition" that animated some of its members, "suggesting schemes of blood and empire,"[2] it is a marvel how little fighting was done. The saints were told time and again to stand still and let God fight their battles,[3] and whenever they obeyed they were always saved. Brigham Young's instructions to the Mormon Battalion tell us how to behave when we are forced to fight:

> I instructed the captains to be fathers to their companies, and manage their affairs by the power and influence of their priesthood, then they would have power to preserve their lives and the lives of their companies and escape difficulties. I told them I would not be afraid to pledge my right hand that every man will return alive, if they will perform their duties faithfully without murmuring and go in the name of the Lord. . . . Let no man be without his under garment and always wear a coat or

vest; keep neat and clean, teach chastity, gentility and
civility; swearing must not be admitted, insult no man;
have no contentious conversation with [any type of
people]. . . . Should the battalion engage with the enemy
and be successful, treat prisoners with the greatest civility, and never take life, if it can be avoided.[4]

When Daniel H. Wells, the commander of the Mormon
military army during Johnston's War, issued written orders,
they bore "on the back . . . the usual inscription, 'Shed no
blood.'"[5] What a strange way to wage war!

Recently I received from a Brigham Young University
professor a list of scriptural passages in which God seemed
to favor war; matching it on the other side of the page was
another list of passages in which conflict was forbidden.
This seems like a deadlock, a basic contradiction. But the
contradiction is only apparent, for if one examines the passages on both sides throughout the scriptures, they fall
clearly into two categories: general principles and special
instances. The verses forbidding conflict are of a general
and universal nature, while those which countenance it all
refer to exceptional cases. Karl von Clausewitz, the greatest
of all students of war, says it is all-important in making war
to distinguish between the general principles, which always
apply, and the special instances and exceptions, which are
dictated by expediency and are never exactly the same
twice. It is dangerous and foolish, he says, to lay down rules
based on inference from special cases.[6]

The same applies to the scriptures. It is human nature to
search out of the scriptures special cases to justify whatever
one wants to do; this belongs to what President Joseph F.
Smith calls the dangerous indulging of "religious hobbies."[7]
For example, Nephi beheaded a helpless man, a general in
his country's employ; but he takes great pains to explain

that this was a special case, a painful episode in which he acted only with the greatest reluctance. I may not appeal to this instance, therefore, as justifying the murder of any government official whom I find obnoxious. On the other hand, when Nephi cries out, "Why am I angry because of mine enemy?" (2 Nephi 4:27), he is proclaiming the universal principle that it is wrong to be angry—even with an enemy.[8] When Mormon reports that the Nephites lost their last campaign because they "went up unto the Lamanites," he is reviewing a particular case—there *may* be times when offensive action is indicated in war.

One can easily distinguish between general principles and special exceptions because the former are stated in general terms and as direct commands of God: "Thou shalt not kill" (Exodus 20:13). "Man shall not smite, neither shall he judge" (Mormon 8:20). "Cursed is he that putteth his trust in the arm of flesh" (2 Nephi 4:34). "We believe . . . in doing good to *all* men" (Article of Faith 13). "Contention is not of me, but is of the devil" (3 Nephi 11:29). "Blessed are the peacemakers" (Matthew 5:9). "It is the wicked that stir up the hearts of the children of men unto bloodshed" (Mormon 4:5). "Love your enemies" (3 Nephi 12:44). "Naught but peace, justice, and truth is the habitation of thy throne" (Moses 7:31). Such statements allow of no qualification or modification.

True, there are times when one is forced to drive through a red light in order to avoid disaster or save a life, but such exceptions do not for a moment abrogate the rule against driving through red lights—the law remains in full force, even when it is broken. Even when God recognizes extenuating circumstances, he still gives us a choice, with precedence going always to the general rule. Thus, in Doctrine and Covenants 98 he allows us to fight our enemies under *very special* circumstances; i.e., after they have attacked us and been warned by us three times, they may be repulsed the fourth time. Yet even here, while God acknowledges "I have delivered thine enemy into thine hands" (D&C 98:29), he promises a special blessing if we do *not* choose to take advantage of our option: "*then* if thou wilt spare him, thou shalt be rewarded for thy righteousness" (D&C 98:30); and if the fourth time he still does not repent, but we choose to forgive him, "I, the Lord, will avenge thee of thine enemy an hundred-fold" (D&C 98:45)—his own mighty intervention rewards our forbearance.

The main thing, of course, is the spirit in which things are done. We have Mormon both sparing his enemies every time he gets a chance *and* putting down a coalition by force of arms with some bloodshed. But there is no doubt in the world which course he would prefer. Though they fought a duel, David and Goliath were *not* animated by the same spirit. And why did the first Moroni (about 63 B.C.) give the attitude that he "did not delight in murder or bloodshed" (Alma 55:19)? Because there are people who do delight in it. There were such men even around Joseph Smith, and they were a grief to his soul: "When you find a spirit that wants bloodshed—murder," he said, "the same is not of God, but is of the devil."[9] In the movie *Patton,* that general on a corpse-strewn and stinking field says, "I love it! God forgive me, but I love it!" He delighted in bloodshed—and knew it was wrong, even in wartime. The popularity of that film is a reminder that the Nephites acquired their fatal appetite for bloodshed in a very short time: "And only a few years have passed away, and they were a civil and a delightsome people" (Moroni 9:12). In the course of one long war they became "without principle, and past feeling; . . . without order and without mercy; . . . they have lost their love, one towards another; and they thirst after blood and revenge continually" (Moroni 9:20, 18, 5).

Nothing is easier, Clausewitz notes, than to justify bloodshed.[10] One Latter-day Saint correspondent writes to me that 1 Samuel 15:2–3 is proof that Christ commands a scorched-earth policy for us, and that Matthew 10:34–35 is proof that "Christ . . . advocated war within families." The first instance is a very special case, unique in history; in the second an ambiguous English translation confuses a result-clause (the plain statement of fact that the preaching of the gospel divides families) with a purpose-clause (that Christ came with the express wish and purpose to destroy families); and so a determined exegesis can twist this one verse into making the Prince of Peace an author of contention. Such an act is a clear demonstration not of logic or philology but of the spirit.

Men have even used the expulsion of Satan from heaven, "the peaceable kingdom," as an argument that violence is the order of heaven since Satan was "thrust down in a twinkling" for resorting to violence. There is no limit to the acts of depravity that might be justified and sanctified by appeal to specific instances in scripture. It is best to allow no latitude whatever to individual interpretation, with its easy rationalizations and sophistries, as long as we have an abundance of clear and specific statements of just what pleases and displeases our Heavenly Father (cf. Moses 7:29–34). It is significant that Mormon did not for a moment condone the Nephite search for blood and vengeance because it was directed against the Lamanites; it did not mitigate the shedding of blood for him because it was Lamanite blood that was being shed.

Clausewitz describes the motivating forces and objectives of war and the means by which they are achieved and the spirit in which war must be undertaken (this he considers the most important of all) with the devastating honesty that has made him the prince of military analysts. The same list may be found, exactly reversed, setting forth in the Doctrine and Covenants the nature of that power by which God operates, by which the worlds are created and sustained (D&C 76:24).

Admittedly we are faced with grim situations—these are not called the last days for nothing! How we react to these situations is part of the test we undergo in this time of probation. In the darkest period of the history of the Church, when the saints were nearer than they ever were before or after to extermination by force of arms, Joseph Smith appeared to Brigham Young in a dream with the instructions that alone could save them: "Tell the people to . . . keep the spirit of the Lord," he said three times with great emphasis. "They can tell the Spirit of the Lord from all other spirits; it will whisper peace and joy to their souls; it will take malice, hatred, strife and all evil from their hearts."[11]

In the end the most desperate military situation imaginable is still to be met with the spirit of peace and love.

Notes

1. Joseph F. Smith, *Gospel Doctrine* (Salt Lake City: Deseret Book, Co. 1973), 89–90.

2. *HC* 7:429.

3. D&C 98:37; 105:14; 109:28. On January 24, 1846, Brigham told the official members of the Church, "The Lord has said he would fight our battles, and if this nation still continues to be actuated towards us with a persecuting spirit, vengeance shall come from the Lord upon them, until they shall be utterly wasted; but I intend to preach and do all the good that I can." Elden J. Watson, *Manuscript History of Brigham Young 1846–1847* (Salt Lake City: Watson, 1971), 18, 21.

4. Ibid., 264–65 (July 1846).

5. "Interview with Brigham Young," *Deseret News*, 23 May 1877, 243.

6. Karl von Clausewitz, *War, Politics, and Power: Selections from On War, and I Believe and Profess*, tr. and ed. Edward M. Collins (Chicago: Gateway, 1962), 38–39.

7. Smith, *Gospel Doctrine*, 163–64.

8. Cf. *TPJS*, 358 (King Follett Discourse).

9. Ibid.

10. Clausewitz, *War, Politics, and Power*, 64, 301–4.

11. Watson, *Manuscript History*, 529 (23 February 1847).

11

Warfare and the Book of Mormon

Karl von Clausewitz's great work *Vom Kriege*, or *On War*, has been the Bible of the military for 150 years. The Book of Mormon reads as if it were written by a diligent student of this work. This is another case of Joseph Smith's timing to the split second, because the work wasn't published until 1833. Otherwise, you could accuse him of stealing the whole thing, because it's right out of Clausewitz, who was very active in the Napoleonic Wars. I'm going to read his principal maxims from his two-volume work—the great maxims of war; and you will think of some instances from the Book of Mormon just like those. I could mention a couple and draw out my speech. But one sentence would be enough to show modern applications, because if you've been reading the newspapers or the magazines, you'll know how relevant this all is.

The most famous saying of Clausewitz, the one that everybody knows by heart, is that "War is therefore a

This text was originally presented as "Reflections on War in the Book of Mormon" at the F.A.R.M.S. Symposium on Warfare in the Book of Mormon, 24 March 1989; it was published as "Warfare and the Book of Mormon" in Stephen D. Ricks and William J. Hamblin, eds., Warfare in the Book of Mormon (Salt Lake City: Deseret Book and F.A.R.M.S., 1990), 127–45.

continuation of [state] policy by other means." As he puts it elsewhere, "[War] is . . . a continuation of political intercourse . . . by other means."[1] He is strictly a soldier, dealing only with the technical side, only with how war is conducted. He says he's not going to talk about the causes in the background. And there he spills the beans. This points directly to the causes—the continuation of politics. The Book of Mormon begins with the war in Jerusalem and ends with the war at Cumorah; and in between there are a lot of wars. They all deal with political ambition. We don't have to go into Egypt, Babylonia, and Jerusalem to illustrate this, because we see the territorial ambitions and the political ambitions of Zerahemnah, Amulon, Amalickiah, Ammoron, Laman, Nehor, Zeezrom, Korihor, etc. They were men of political ambitions who wanted to get ahead. They started out with political parties and ended up uniting bodies in war, such as the great coalitions of Amalickiah. Of course we don't need to comment as far as the present world is concerned—what is cold war but politics being carried on? It's a political movement on both sides; it's political systems in conflict.

Another saying of Clausewitz is "War . . . belongs not to the province of arts and sciences, but to that of social existence. . . . It would be better . . . to liken it to business competition . . . and it is still more like politics, which . . . may be regarded as a kind of business competition on a great scale."[2] As I said, Clausewitz is writing back in the eighteenth century, during the Napoleonic Wars. His main study was wars of the eighteenth century, wars of the princes and kings following the grandeur of Louis the Great, "Le Grandeur." It was all-important to be grand. You had to annex as much land as you could, for example, as in the tripartition of Poland between the three great powers. You grabbed not only resources but also a lot of peasants or people, and these strengthened your army. They became your aggrandizement. They strengthened you and enabled you to make further sweeps, which occurred all throughout the seventeenth and eighteenth centuries. Everybody grabbed as much land as they could, the princes doing it in the interest of the state. It was *ratio status*—that would justify anything. (In the nineteenth and twentieth centuries, the great industrial barons were after the same thing—land, because along with that came raw materials, cheap labor, and market.) And so it went on, the territorial wars. Clausewitz continues: "Moreover, politics is the womb in which war is developed." It is "business . . . on a great scale."[3] Nothing describes these days better than that. We don't need to explain, do we?

"The disarming of the enemy—this object of war in the abstract, [is the] final means of attaining the political object."[4] In the Book of Mormon, Moroni often requires the enemy to lay down their arms and lets them go home. There are no reprisals or anything similar (see Alma 44:6, 15, 20; 52:37). The test comes when they lay down their arms—then they know your will has dominated over theirs. So Clausewitz says, the "disarming of the enemy—this [is the] object of war."[5] Moroni was satisfied when the enemy laid down their arms. Likewise in the French and Indian Wars, and in the Mexican Wars, and in the last war when the German and Japanese laid down their arms, the war was over.

Clausewitz's next maxim (and this is an interesting one, too) is "The aggressor always pretends to be peace-loving because he would like to achieve his conquests without bloodshed. . . . Therefore, aggression must be presented as a defensive reaction by the aggressor nation."[6] Nobody ever attacks. You're always just on the defensive. After World

War I, the German War Office, *Kriegsamt,* changed its name to *Wehrmacht,* "defense power." We changed our War Office to the Department of Defense. We're just defensive now, that's all. Both sides must take the defensive position, whether they are aggressors or not. We see good examples in the Book of Mormon in the case of Giddianhi and Lachoneus. Giddianhi writes to Lachoneus, "We wouldn't bother you except you're infringing on our rights of government, our ancient society, which is old and venerable and you've been the aggressor against us" (cf. 3 Nephi 3:9–10). This is true, though; since the loser must always submit to the winner, each side is always fighting for its freedom. I don't want to submit to you and you don't want to submit to me, so I'm defending my freedom and you're defending your freedom. We have a Defense Department, if you please, all throughout the world.

"Those who belong to the profession," says Clausewitz, "will always look upon themselves as a kind of guild. . . . This corporate spirit . . . must exist more or less in every army. . . . Military virtue is a quality of standing armies only."[7] It is professionalism that guarantees the ongoing tradition. But it's also a very dangerous thing: "It is impermissible and even harmful to leave a great military event . . . to *purely military judgment.*"[8] "The influence in the cabinet of any military man except the commander-in-chief is extremely dangerous."[9] That's an interesting remark. It's not the business of military men to meddle in the higher policies of state. The chief military commander is the only one who should be in the cabinet; it's harmful and impermissible for the military to participate.

A good example is Moroni getting on his high horse when he writes to Pahoran. Speaking as a general in the midst of war, he blows his top and writes very indiscreet letters. He doesn't understand what is going on back home; he is writing to Pahoran about conditions he isn't aware of at all. He is going to take over: We'll come and seize the state. We'll expel you. I'll march with my men, and we'll unseat you (cf. Alma 60).

The first maxim is "It's politics by other means." The second maxim is "War is thus an act of force to compel our adversary to do our will. . . . War is nothing but a duel on a larger scale."[10] Alma fights Amlici face-to-face; that's the duel, but they represent the forces (see Alma 2:29). Amalickiah swears to drink Moroni's blood (see Alma 49:27; 51:9). Of course the classic is Shiz versus Coriantumr (see Ether 15:29–30). We still do the same today—we try to destabilize governments which do not favor us or which we do not favor, and we personify them in their leaders. The leader or whoever is in charge becomes the villain, and it becomes a personal duel between this president and that president, whoever they might be. Clausewitz goes on to say, "If the enemy should choose the method of the great decision by arms, our own method *must on that account be changed against our will to a similar one.*"[11] What the enemy does, we must do. "If the enemy should choose the method" he's going to use, "of the great decision by arms," we can't do anything but reply in the same way. We must on that account, against our own will, adopt a similar method. Moroni repeatedly found that the enemy had copied his equipment and tactics. In war, armies come to look alike.

In another place Clausewitz says, "In modern times the armies of European states have arrived very much at a par in discipline and training."[12] You can see why: we can't allow the enemy to get any new gun—whether it's a shepatovka, which we immediately adopted as a bazooka, or whether it's a Mark VI Panzer, which we immediately countered as a Pershing. We can't allow them to hold an edge, whether it's in the type of helmet or camouflage or anything else. We have to copy it if it works better than ours. So armies very quickly come to look exactly alike. Thus the duel, in which the parties are necessarily equal. There will be very little difference between them when they meet. That makes it all very destructive. When the Lamanites tried to encircle the Nephites with the same wine tricks the Nephites had tried, the Nephites then tried other tricks. But their tricks didn't work anymore, because the enemy knew them all by heart; both had adopted each other's methods.

Continuing on with the idea of the duel of the equal parts, Clausewitz writes, "The ruthless user of force who shrinks from no amount of bloodshed must gain an advantage if his opponent does not do the same."[13] Teancum and Amalickiah typify this principle. It's always the wicked against the wicked in the Book of Mormon, never the righteous against the wicked. In the duel between Amlici and Alma (see Alma 2:29–31), wasn't that a good guy against a bad guy? No, when the war was over they mourned terribly because they were convinced that the war had been because of their wickedness. They had brought it on themselves. They weren't fighting bad guys as good guys after all. In the same way, Mormon counsels, Don't worry about the wicked; surely the "judgments of God will overtake the wicked; and it is by the wicked that the wicked are punished" (Mormon 4:5).

Clausewitz describes the old-fashioned wars as punishment wars. We can't afford that luxury now. We must copy the enemy if he is bloody-minded. The Lord gives a rule right at the beginning of the Book of Mormon. The second chapter of the Book of Mormon states that the wicked

Lamanites "shall have no power over thy seed except they shall rebel against me also" (1 Nephi 2:23). When they fight, it is because they are both rebellious against God. Otherwise, there is going to be no fight. "They will have no power over thy seed unless they rebel against me also. I'll keep things going." That was the agreement, and it is repeated throughout the Book of Mormon.

Clausewitz continues: Because we're so equal, "the wastage of our own forces is always the greater the more our aim is directed toward destruction of the enemy's forces."[14] In other words, "the harder we try"—which is represented, of course, by the Book of Mormon's total extermination story, Shiz versus Coriantumr (see Ether 14:17–15:30). They exterminate each other, although such a thing can never happen, according to Clausewitz. But we know that such a thing can. It's kill or be killed. Teancum is an example (see Alma 51, 61, and 62), and the Nephites and the Lamanites, too. The Lamanites decidedly became completely disrupted at Cumorah, we are told, as well as the Nephites; but with that wastage, you must risk your own forces at whatever cost. If you're going to destroy, you must be destroyed. You must accept that, says Clausewitz. That's the rule.

"In the lower ranks the spirit of self-sacrifice is more required [than in others]."[15] You regulate the policy. The general is at a distance; we expect others to sacrifice. "Amalickiah [did not] come down out of the land of Nephi, at the head of his army. . . . He did care not for the blood of his people" (Alma 49:10). Such an attitude so shocks Moroni that he writes to Pahoran, "Can you think to sit on your thrones in a state of thoughtless stupor, while your enemies are spreading the work of death around you" (cf. Alma 60:7). They don't care for the lives of those on the front, and that's a policy which Clausewitz says you can't worry about. Self-sacrifice is what the soldiers are there for.

Then he goes on to the third rule: "We can never introduce a modifying principle into the philosophy of war without committing an absurdity. . . . War is an act of force, and there is no limit to the application of that force."[16] To talk about civilized warfare and the rules of warfare is ridiculous. If you're civilized, you won't start scratching and biting; you'll continue the discussion. And war is even worse. You try to kill the other person, and there's no limit to that. Their death is what you're after. "To introduce a modifying principle is an absurdity." You can't modify it. There's no limit to the application of that force. Alma puts it very well when he says they had exhausted all their resource: "Whatever evil we cannot resist with our words, [then] let us resist them with our swords" (Alma 61:14). That means you must go all the way. There are no more rules in warfare—in "civilized" warfare. And the Lord says (a frequent expression), "Cursed shall be the land . . . unto destruction" (Alma 45:16). Brushfire wars are out of the question.

At the end of World War II, the generals became very discouraged, because there was going to be no fighting for them. The war had been a lark for most of them. But then they discovered the concept of brushfire wars and tried it out in Southeast Asia. I remember very well the day General Taylor, just glowing, discovered brushfire wars; he explained how we could have little wars going on, so the military could get their promotions and always have opportunity for practice—send the officers out to get practice. It doesn't work that way. And this is why Clausewitz explains, "War and peace are ideas which fundamentally can have no gradations."[17] He goes on, "We need not lose sight of the absolute form of war. [War is all the way or nothing. There is no partial war]; rather [the] image [of absolute war] must constantly hover in the background."[18] After a great victory, Alma announces to the people, "I perceive that this very people, the Nephites, . . . shall become extinct" (Alma 45:10–11).

Clausewitz continues: In pursuing the aim of war, "there is only one means: *combat*. . . . All the effects manifested in [war] have their origin in combat."[19] Moroni, in combat, returns the sword to Zerahemnah. Zerahemnah didn't want to discuss terms anymore. Moroni invited him to take his sword back and continue fighting. That's all we can do—it's the only solution. Unless you choose to make a covenant of peace, you'll just have to go on fighting. Military combat is the only effective way—the pursuance of only one means. "All the effects manifested in [war] have their origin in combat." As Moroni hands Zerahemnah his sword back, he says, "We will end the conflict"—if you don't want to discuss it, there's nothing else to do (cf. Alma 44:10–11). Then the only reason, says Clausewitz, for "suspension of military action [is] . . . *to await a more favorable moment for action*."[20] When Zerahemnah puts up his sword, he is merely waiting for a more favorable time to strike back. He tells Moroni quite frankly to hand him back his sword and then adds, "We will not suffer ourselves to take an oath unto you, which we know that we shall break" (Alma 44:8–10). When he got his sword back, he immediately made a mad lunge for Moroni, only to have the top of his head cut off (see Alma 44:12). You suspend your action to wait for more action.

Again from Clausewitz: "The destruction of the enemy's armed forces is the foundation stone of all actions in war, the ultimate support of all combinations."[21] The theme is destruction, and the armed forces now of course extend to everybody. That was unthinkable at the end of the Napoleonic Wars in 1815. Those were gentlemen's wars, but now everybody gets wiped out. The words *destruction* and *destroy* appear 534 times in the Book of Mormon, and nearly always in conjunction with the word *war*. Why with war? We're told that war and plague and pestilence and famine all go together, but the wars are the part you bring on yourselves. You cannot plead innocent victim as you can of famine and plague, for example. You invite war. In the army we were always told that our mission was to search and destroy. So Clausewitz says, "The soldier is levied, clothed, armed, trained—he sleeps, eats, drinks, marches—*merely to fight at the right place and the right time.*"[22] That is the only reason for his existence—just to fight at the particular time and place. In World War II, only eight percent of the armed forces ever saw action. It was the cutting edge units that did the dirty work, and it was pretty nasty. All the others were just for the purpose of supporting them. That was their whole purpose and it still is—to destroy.

And so, quoting Clausewitz again, "If we speak of the destruction of the enemy's forces, we must expressly point out that nothing obliges us to confine this idea to the physical forces."[23] We try to break the enemy down psychologically as well. But of course it was Clausewitz who introduced a doctrine of *Schrecklichkeit*—make yourself as terrible as possible—which the Germans applied so effectively in the first world war. Making yourself an object of utter terror is beautifully described in the Book of Mormon, as do the Lamanites on various occasions (see Enos 1:20; Mosiah 10:8; Alma 3:4–5), and also the Gadiantons in their various trappings (see 3 Nephi 4:7). They make themselves and their uniforms up as hideously as possible, like the trappings of the Middle Ages, which paralyzed resistance by fear. On July 4, 1944, the Allies sent at least five thousand planes over Germany in one bunch to give a display of force. We thought that would show them. Well, people looked up once or twice but didn't pay any attention after that. The planes just went on and on, but who cared? It was a bore. As Tolstoy tells us, war is a crashing bore. All night long you pray for it to be day. All day long you pray for it to be night. That's the whole thing—search and destroy. But you can use more than the physical forces—you can employ *Schrecklichkeit* to make the soldiers objects of terror. Feudal trappings paralyze resistance and create fear. The Lamanites were especially good at that, specializing in it, and it sometimes worked rather well. But it didn't work when the Nephites were praying for the Lord to help them. The armies of Giddianhi—with the red on their foreheads, lambskins on their loins, and all that nonsense—thought the Nephites were praying because the armies' fierce appearance had paralyzed them, but they were only supplicating the Lord for his protection (see 3 Nephi 4:8–10).

There is a fourth point, one on which Clausewitz lays very heavy emphasis. He very decisively states, "There is no other human activity that stands in such constant and universal contact with chance as does war."[24] "He who undertakes war . . . must renounce every absolute certainty of a result."[25] Typical examples are found in Alma 49:10 and Alma 59:5–13, where Moroni, the great military genius, is caught flat-footed time and again. Coriantumr marches right into the center of Zarahemla, catching the Nephites off guard; but in the end, he caught himself in a trap. When he tried to get out of the land, he found that the Nephites had put all their defenses on the periphery, and he couldn't get out (see Helaman 1:25–30). Everybody surprises everybody else in war; nobody is sure of anything. "War is therefore a chameleon," Clausewitz explains, "a strange trinity [three things make it up]. . . . It is composed of [1] the original violence of its essence; [2] the hate and enmity which are to be regarded as blind, natural impulse; . . . [3] the play of probabilities and chance, which make it a free activity of the emotions."[26] In other words, war is a madhouse. Those climactic pages of Mormon describe the final windup. Mormon prays for God to destroy them if they don't change their ways. They're so hopeless: "I saw that the day of grace was passed" (Mormon 2:15). The Nephites had reached the point of no return, and Mormon simply wished they'd get wiped out. There is nothing more terrifying than that, nor more vivid or to the point. It's like today's wars in Lebanon and Central America—madhouses, crazy scenes. "War, of all branches of human activity," says Clausewitz, is "most like a game of cards."[27] Again, only in Hollywood are we sure that the good guys are going to win.

One of the most famous phrases coined by Clausewitz, next to the one on war and politics, is "Three-fourths of the things upon which action in war is calculated lie hidden in a fog of uncertainty"[28]—the fog of battle. Fortunately I was in a position in the front in which I could see everything the Germans did while the battle was going on; all the general could do in his little tiny tent was pace back and forth and chew his nails. He tried to make contact with the walkie-talkie, but he never got through. Everything collapsed. As soon as the battle begins, nobody has any control. Nobody knows what anybody else is doing. I don't know if it would be so now. But you can imagine just a little technical flaw occurring, such as happens to our marvelous computers—how they can be jammed. How that will compound the fog of wars! So Clausewitz observes, "War . . . is the province of

chance. . . . It increases the uncertainty of every circumstance and deranges the course of events." He continues,
"Differences of opinion are nowhere so great as in war [the
generals never agree]. . . . *Strength of character* leads to a
degenerate form of [disagreement—which is sheer] *obsti-
nacy*."[29] Arguments among the staff are terrible—Moroni
versus Pahoran, Patton versus Monty and Eisenhower
(whose main job, his greatest achievement, was to reconcile
clashing plans and personalities, prejudices and pride of the
commanders). They never agreed on any plan, on any project, on anything else. Were you out in one of those CP's
[command posts], you would hear them argue.

And finally, "We shall soon feel what a dangerous edi-
fice war is, how easily it may fall to pieces and bury us in
its ruins."[30] The Nazi SS learned in a hurry. Clausewitz
explains, "Decision[s are based upon] reports [all of which
have] been lies, exaggerations, and errors. . . . Most reports
are false, and the timidity of men gives fresh force to lies
and untruths." Note his frankness and honesty in these
things. This is military "intelligence," part of a joke: "this
difficulty of seeing things correctly . . . is one of the greatest
sources of friction in war"[31] among commanders. Thus
Moroni has no idea what is happening to Pahoran, who is
home with a rebellion on his hands, which could break
everything up. When Pahoran writes back to Moroni and
explains the situation, Moroni realizes he's had it all wrong
from the beginning, yet he was as well informed as anyone
(see Alma 61:1–62:1). What does a general do in a case like
this? "War . . . in its plan—is so often thwarted by [the]
unexpected . . . [that its conduct must] be left to talent [a
person who has a genius for it. Frederick the Great and
Napoleon had the genius. Of course, Clausewitz thought
Napoleon was a great man, though he was really a great

rascal], and less use can be made of a theoretical *guide* [in war] than in any other business."[32] So Clausewitz says to throw away the rule book. You must depend on the genius of the commander.

Of course that's what you learn from Tolstoy's *War and Peace*. Clausewitz says the thing that's surprising about war is that war is supremely simple. That is what fools everybody. That's why a talented genius, the most intelligent person, is not going to be the greatest general. You want a man like Suvarov who has the instinct to do the right thing and knows just what to do.

Here's another of Clausewitz's main doctrines, the central doctrine of strategy and tactics: "The defensive is the stronger form of [making] . . . war. . . . It is . . . contrary to the prevalent opinion— . . . the defensive form of war is in the abstract stronger than the offensive. The absolute defense[, of course,] completely contradicts the conception of war."[33] "All the time which elapses [you spar for time, you see] falls into the scale in favor of the defender."[34] Put confirmation off as long as you can. But of course "every defensive, according to its strength, will seek to change to the offensive."[35]

The defensive screen of the two thousand sons of Helaman is interesting. Helaman leads the Lamanite army on and on. Then finally the Nephites turn on their heels and attack and surprise the daylights out of the Lamanites (see Alma 56:30–54). That's why Clausewitz says, "It is extremely important always to bear in mind that almost the only advantage which the offensive possesses is the effect of surprise."[36] You have to be the innocent aggressor, yet you must make a surprise attack on someone; and there are many surprise attacks in the Book of Mormon.

"Every defensive, according to its strength, will seek to

change to the offensive"[37]—as in the case of the two thousand sons, who turned suddenly in the opposite direction (see Alma 58:25–27). We claim defensive strategy today in Europe, Latin America, Africa, the Near East, Southeast Asia, and elsewhere, showing the flag; but armies don't exist to sit still. Their threatening presence and the power to destroy invite combat; it is a challenge to action in the medieval sense.

So Clausewitz says, "The negative effort . . . must prefer a bloodless decision."[38] And "the only . . . advantage of the negative object is [to] delay . . . [a] decision."[39] It's game to switch to war after all. You can stall all you want, "but everything is subject to a supreme law: *The decision by arms.*"[40] Clausewitz underlines that. "When this is actually demanded by the enemy, such an appeal can never be refused [so it will make the war inevitable]. . . . Accordingly, among all the objects which may be sought in war, the destruction of the enemy's forces appears always to be the one that overrules all others."[41] No matter how you spar, no matter how you wait, no matter how long you delay, no matter how strong your defensive position, this will be your objective—sooner or later you must destroy the enemy. But let him destroy himself. This is not what the Ammonites practiced, but it leads to the policy adopted by the Generalstab in World War II in the blitzkrieg. The blitzkrieg is strictly Clausewitz; that's where it came from. "No conquest can be finished too soon." Don't drag it out. But wars always do drag out, and that's the problem. Six-week wars always turn out to be five-year wars. "No conquest can be finished too soon; . . . spreading it over a *greater period of time* makes it more *difficult*. . . . A speedy and uninterrupted effort toward a decision is essential to [an] offensive war."[42] "Until it [the final result] takes place nothing is decided, nothing won [you may be winning up to the final last minute, and then something will happen and you'll be defeated—that's happened], nothing lost. . . . The end crowns the work. War is an indivisible whole."[43]

At Cumorah, both lost (see Mormon 6:2–22; 8:2). This would be inconceivable to Clausewitz, who says, "Once the great victory is gained, there should be no talk of rest, of pausing for breath, . . . or of consolidating, . . . but only of pursuit."[44] That's the fatal flaw, because every campaign has to slow down somewhere, as ours did in World War II. We could have attacked the Germans very easily, had it not been for our gasoline supplies. Patton couldn't get the gasoline because Monty wanted it, and there was a big fight between them. "Beware . . . of confusing the spirit of an army with its morale."[45] "The highest spirit in the world changes only too easily at the first check into depression."[46] There is always such a check, and that comes in the Book of Mormon, too, when the tide suddenly turns.

Clausewitz's last principle is important: "War is never an isolated act. In the real world, war never breaks out suddenly, and it does not spread immediately."[47] He observes that the modern world, and modern wars, are different. On this point Clausewitz is wrong. He saw that principle in the princes' wars, the gentlemen's wars, in the seventeenth and eighteenth centuries, but the nineteenth and twentieth century wars are something different. And for a good reason, which still applies: "Human organizations" have, because of their inefficiency, "always fall[en] short." There are always the bungling, misunderstanding, and deficiencies. You never get things mobilized instantly, "and these deficiencies, operative on both sides, become a modifying influence."[48] That's why we have cold wars, and the Book of Mormon proceedings of men aspiring for position. The

Nephite-Lamanite wars were sometimes raids, a very common thing. All wars are raids anyway. When Zoram went out, he said it was to obtain those who had been carried away captive into the wilderness. His whole purpose was to get them back, and he did get them back (see Alma 16:6–8). Incidentally, in talking about the defense, the best position, remember that all Book of Mormon wars take place on Nephite property, not on Lamanite. They rarely invade the other. The Nephites are rarely the aggressors, in that sense.

On that point, Clausewitz says something that will amuse us: "If the wars of civilized nations are far less cruel and destructive than those of the uncivilized, the cause lies in the social conditions of these states, internally and in their relations with each other."[49] The various documentaries on TV show that animals and savages do fight, but they know when to stop—before everybody is killed! We don't, as we find in the Asiatic exterminations, among the Jaredites (see Ether 15:25, 29–32), and so forth. They were what Clausewitz had in mind. Thinking of certain wars in Russia, he says they are unthinkable in our society because you can't exterminate a whole nation; a thing like that is out of the question. Yet what is the expression used in the Book of Mormon? "[When] the time . . . come[s] that the voice of this people should choose iniquity, . . . [or] fall into transgression, they would be ripe for destruction" (Alma 10:19). And when the cup is full, they shall be "swept off from the face of the land" (Jarom 1:3), and "ye shall become extinct" (3 Nephi 3:8).

Then Clausewitz says, "Since Bonaparte, war . . . has approached much nearer to its real nature, to its absolute perfection."[50] The Napoleonic Wars were the real wars: "The most violent element of war, freed from all conventional restrictions, broke loose with all its natural force."[51] This is the way it should be. Mormon says, "from this time forth . . . the Nephites . . . began to be swept off by them even as a dew before the sun" (Mormon 4:18). It was a total thing. "The most violent element of war," like a violent "natural force," like a plague sweeping the nation, simply appeared. When "freed from all conventional restrictions, [it] broke loose with all its natural force." That's what happens: war is absolute; war is basic. There are no rules or other restraints; war is much nearer to real nature in absolutes. Bonaparte put the whole nation in arms, and since then it's been the nation with arms. Operation Barbarosa, in June 1941, when Hitler entered Russia, took almost a third of Russia in two weeks, a terrific sweep of a vast land, total destruction. So Clausewitz was wrong—because he didn't have a nuclear bomb.

Finally from Clausewitz: "In the great combats which we call wars . . . there is usually no hostile feeling of individual against individual. . . . National hatred . . . becomes a more or less powerful substitute for personal hostility of individuals. Where this is also absent, . . . a hostile feeling is kindled by the combat itself; an act of violence . . . will excite in us the desire to retaliate and be avenged."[52] This is the circle. Amalickiah has to get the Lamanites to hate so they can go to war, so he has his people preach from towers—gets the propaganda machine going (see Alma 48:1–3). Such hatred is artificial. It has to be stirred up, but once the killing starts, there follows the idea of vengeance— the Green Beret syndrome. The good guy sees his friends bullied; so he seeks vengeance—the theme of almost all TV shows, so many on World War I and II. Every time you turn the TV on, you can see documentaries on World War I and II, which we hang on, because we know how it turns out and we want to see the bad guys get what's coming to them.

Revenge is the whole thing. Mormon, at the end, says, "And now, because of this great thing which my people, the Nephites, had done, they began to boast in their own strength, and began to swear before the heavens that they would avenge themselves of the blood of their brethren who had been slain by their enemies" (Mormon 3:9). What nobler motive can they have than to "avenge themselves of the blood of their brethren." With that, Mormon lays down his arms. He resigns as their commander and says he will have nothing more to do with them. He utterly refuses to avenge his enemy, for the one thing the Lord had absolutely forbidden them to do was to seek vengeance and build up hatred. For Mormon heard the "voice of the Lord . . . saying: Vengeance is mine, and I will repay" (Mormon 3:14–15).

So where does that leave us today? Well, short of Zion. It seems that war is inevitable, according to Clausewitz. President Benson is right—he says it all applies to us. That's why I don't like the wars in the Book of Mormon. They make me ill.

Notes

1. Karl von Clausewitz, *War, Politics, and Power: Selections from On War, and I Believe and Profess*, tr. and ed. Edward M. Collins (Chicago: Gateway, 1962), 83.

2. Ibid., 167–68.

3. Ibid., 168.

4. Ibid., 91.

5. Ibid.

6. Ibid., 33.

7. Ibid., 183, 185.

8. Ibid., 261.

9. Ibid., 264.

10. Ibid., 63.

11. Ibid., 108 (emphasis added).

12. Ibid., 180.
13. Ibid., 64.
14. Ibid., 108.
15. Ibid., 156.
16. Ibid., 65.
17. Ibid., 252.
18. Ibid., 257.
19. Ibid., 100.
20. Ibid., 73 (emphasis added).
21. Ibid., 106.
22. Ibid., 102.
23. Ibid., 107.
24. Ibid., 79.
25. Ibid., 210.
26. Ibid., 86.
27. Ibid., 80.
28. Ibid., 117.
29. Ibid., 122–23.
30. Ibid., 128.
31. Ibid., 129.
32. Ibid., 155.
33. Ibid., 189.
34. Ibid., 190.
35. Ibid., 245.
36. Ibid., 290.
37. Ibid., 245.
38. Ibid., 110.
39. Ibid., 111.
40. Ibid. (emphasis added).
41. Ibid., 112.
42. Ibid., 240.
43. Ibid., 206–7.
44. Ibid., 292.
45. Ibid., 188.
46. Ibid., 187.
47. Ibid., 68.
48. Ibid.
49. Ibid., 64.
50. Ibid., 229.
51. Ibid., 230.
52. Ibid., 151.

PART 3

Education

12

The Day of the Amateur

A boast of Latter-day Saints is that they have never been afflicted with a professional clergy. To this day, what most impresses outside observers is the fact that almost everything the Mormons do is undertaken on a nonprofessional basis—and it is done pretty well at that. Only when they have brought in professional help have they come to grief.

Professionalism is the child of the universities. Its modern rule began with the Sophists of old. Preceding the Sophists were those wise men called *Sophoi*, ancient traveling teachers who gave the modern world its moral and intellectual foundations. They were, to a man, amateurs.

They had to be amateurs, for the same reason that the greatest athletes in the world, the Olympic victors, ancient and modern, were required to be amateurs; and for the same reason that the people who wrote and directed and acted and danced in the greatest dramas the world has ever seen were required by law to be amateurs: because what they were doing was holy business and not to be contaminated by ulterior motives and ambitions.

Then the Sophists, imitation *Sophoi*, took over and

Reprinted from New Era *(January 1971): 42–44.*

professionalized everything to the highest degree. They were the great professors, and since they professed publicly and for a fee, Socrates, the champion of the independent mind and not one of the Sophists, advised students to examine every prospective teacher's credentials very carefully and critically before enrolling with him. That indiscretion cost Socrates his life, for the whole point of professionalism is that one's credentials should never be challenged. Rashdall has shown how the medieval universities, beginning with wild elan and spontaneity in the days when anyone could get into the act, "quickly hardened into the mold of the university system" as administration took over.

Official credentials, a foolproof shield against criticism and scrutiny, were naturally coveted most by those who needed them most: it was the poorly qualified who clamored for the status symbol of the degree. As in the days of the Sophist schools, the great demand for this valuable commodity caused factories to spring up everywhere, competing for degree-seeking customers by making their product ever easier and cheaper to get. At the same time the degree became the object—the sole object—of "education." And when it reached that point, it was, of course, worth nothing.

Learning, forgotten in the universities, was revived in academies, salons, societies, courts, and coffeehouses where amateurs came together to revel in things of the spirit and make the seventeenth and eighteenth centuries the high point of Western civilization. It was the Age of the Amateur.

Beginning around the midnineteenth century, the university staged a comeback, culminating in elephantine growth as twentieth-century technology sends everyone to school. During the first half of the present century, college teaching offered a safe berth for mild and mediocre souls who in time, by the sacred rule of seniority, ended up ruling their institutions.

Here they jealously perpetuated their own kind in office and shut out those talented students who might threaten their own supremacy in any way. The more intelligent students had always seen through professorial sham, but as the university population soared into the millions, the tension between the two mounted dangerously. It is no paradox that some of the most intelligent students at the best schools have been causing the most trouble. In fact, most students have been galled by the artificial restraint of professional status.

If the only way to get a professional certificate was to deserve one, there would be little trouble. But there have always been many ways of winning a prize for which the incompetent are willing to pay almost any price. The time-honored devices for beating the game are legion, but the most reliable one, since the days of the emperors, has always been appointment.

Someone (this writer, in fact) has said that anyone can become a dean, a professor, a department head, a chancellor, or a custodian by appointment—it has happened thousands of times; but since the world began, no one has ever become an artist, a scientist, or a scholar by appointment. The professional may be a dud, but to get any recognition, the amateur has to be good. To maintain his amateur status, moreover, he has to be dedicated, honest, and incorruptible—from which irksome necessity the professional, unless he cares otherwise, is freed by an official certificate.

Do Americans have to apologize for generations of ingenious amateurs from Franklin to Ford, who fathered their modern technology? Or for Ives and Carpenter, their best composers? Or for Parkman, Motley, Prescott, H. C.

Lea, and the rest of their excellent historians? Is science ashamed of Descartes or Priestly, or Sir William Hershel or Father Mendel? Arts, science, and scholarship would be in a sorry way today were it not for patrons who were also first-class practitioners in their own right, i.e, von Bissing, H. Carter, and A. Gardiner in Egyptology.

Of course there has always been protest from the professional side: the greatest discoveries in classical scholarship were made by a German merchant and a young English architect, each of whom in his time was ridiculed by the professors. Emerson, "the wisest American," was banned from the campus of Harvard for his famous "American Scholar" address, which proclaimed that one did not have to be a professional to be a true thinker and scholar.

Not long ago one of the world's greatest violinists was barred from the music faculty of a West Coast university solely because he did not have a degree, while the head of the department in a neighboring university gave whole seasons of dismally mediocre concerts and got away with it, because he did have a degree.

If we have no professional clergy in the Church, it is not because the Church cannot use expert knowledge but because all members should be experts where the gospel is concerned, and as such they should make their contribution. All the same contribution? Not at all! The Church is structured for eternal progression, and that takes place as we all feel our way forward along a broad front. *Seeking* and *searching* are among the most common words in our scriptures; we are all supposed to be seeking all the time. Just as missionaries go forth as an amateur army, searching out the honest in heart in the most scattered and unlikely places on the widest possible front, so the rest of us increase in knowledge, here a little and there a little, not by trusting a few experts to come up with answers but by all of us searching all along the line, finding out a fact here and a document there, and reporting the discovery to the whole body.

When he was editor of the *Times and Seasons*, the Prophet Joseph invited *all* to contribute.

13

Educating the Saints

The compelling mystique of those franchise businesses which in our day have built up enormous institutional clout by selling nothing but the right to a name was anticipated in our great schools of education, which monopolized the magic name of education and sold the right to use it at a time when the idea of a "School of Education" made about as much sense as a class in erudition or a year's course in total perfection. The whole business of education can become an operation in managerial manipulation. In "Higher Education" the traffic titles and forms are already long established: The office with its hoarded files of score-sheets, punched cards, and tapes can declare exactly how educated any individual is—even to the third decimal. That is the highly structured busywork which we call education today; but it was not Brigham Young's idea of education. He had thoughts which we have repeated from time to time with very mixed reception on the BYU campus. Still we do not feel in the least inclined to apologize for propagating

This text appeared as "Educating the Saints—A Brigham Young Mosaic," in Nibley on the Timely and the Timeless (Provo, UT: Religious Studies Center, 1978), 229–59; and in BYU Studies 11 (Autumn 1970): 61–87.

them on the premises of a university whose main distinction is that it bears *his* name.

A big black leather chair stood in Brigham Young's office by the Lion House—it faced the window on the opposite wall and the President's desk in the middle of the room. First-time visitors to the office were invited to sit on that chair, facing the strong light of day and the calm blue eyes of Brother Brigham, who sat there at his desk, his back to the window, quietly waiting for his guest to say something. After all, the man had come to see him, and it was only right to let him state his business. President Young, according to Grandfather,[1] would never say a word for the first three minutes. And at the end of those first three minutes he always knew exactly the sort of man he was dealing with, and the nature—greedy, benign, or sinister—of his business. "And he *never* [here Grandpa smote the arm of his chair] had to change his mind!"—his psychoanalytical techniques, black leather couch and all, were deadly accurate, and always put him on top of the situation. Brigham Young used to say that no man, if allowed to speak, could possibly avoid revealing his true character, "For out of the abundance of the heart the tongue speaketh."

It is important to know this if we would understand Brigham Young himself. No man ever spoke his mind more frankly on all subjects. All his days he strove to communicate his inmost feelings, unburdening himself without the aid of notes or preparation in a vigorous and forthright prose that was the purest antirhetoric. It has been common practice to dismiss any saying of his of which one disapproves (and he makes no effort to please) by observing that he said so much on so many things that he was bound to contradict himself, and therefore need not be taken too seriously all the time. No view could be more ill-advised, for there never was a man more undeviatingly consistent and rational in thought and utterance. But we must let him speak for himself to see that, and that is what his critics stubbornly refuse to do, allowing him only an occasional phrase or two quoted out of context to clinch their case. The few quotations that follow are, it is true, only a tantalizingly small fraction of the Prophet's inspired and resounding utterances on the subject of education, but at least there will be enough of them to establish a definite thesis. Granted that Brigham would admonish the Saints to wear overcoats one day, so to speak, and the next day turn around and advise shirtsleeves, the element of scandal and confusion vanishes if we only get the main idea, which is that it is not the rule-book or the administration but the weather that prescribes the proper dress for the day. All the other apparent contradictions in Brother Brigham's teachings likewise vanish when we grasp the main idea behind them.

What, for example, could sound more worldly and self-centered than a remark such as "I labor for my own dear self, I have self continually before me; the object of my pursuit is to benefit my individual person"? That is, until we read the whole statement, which continues, "Men may think, and some of them do, that we have a right to work for ourselves; but I say we have no time to do that in the narrow, selfish sense generally entertained when speaking about working for self."[2] What can he possibly mean? He explains: The only way properly to serve one's self is to labor "in the . . . kingdom of God"; any other course "is folly in the extreme!"[3] "Do you want the riches pertaining to this world? Yes, we acknowledge we do!" That again seems brutally frank until we read on: "I merely use the term 'rich' to lead the mind along, until we obtain eternal riches in the celestial kingdom of God," which is a very different thing.[4] We seem to hear the credo of the ambitious executive when we read, "We are organized for the express purpose of controlling the elements, of organizing and disorganizing, of ruling over kingdoms, principalities, and powers." But the next phrase completely reverses our verdict: "And yet our affections are often too highly placed upon paltry, perishable objects. We love houses, gold, silver, and various kinds of property, and all who unduly prize any object there is beneath the celestial world are idolators."[5] So it is all along: We may grant that Brigham Young talks like a solid, hard-headed Yankee materialist, but only as long as we understand that the only matter that interests him is the enduring substance of eternity. There is no real paradox when he says: "Then let us seek to extend the present life to the uttermost . . . and thus prepare for a better life."[6] He is thinking of this life *only* in terms of the next.

But very few people have been able to see that: "There are those in this congregation who are so short-sighted, and so destitute of eternal wisdom and knowledge, that they believe that brother Brigham is after property—after the things of this world."[7] Well, what else *could* they think of any man who rolled over all opposition, amassed substance and power, and commanded the absolute obedience that Brigham Young did? To do that in terms of our world, a man must needs be a combination of Tamerlane, Caesar Borgia, and Boss Tweed, and as such even the Latter-day Saints have pictured Brigham Young. How can you explain to the average American that there was once a shrewd Yankee farmer and builder with a passion for thrift ("I never suffered a peach-pit to be thrown away, nor ate an apple without saving the seeds to plant"[8]), who practiced and preached as the watchword of his economy the slogan, "Never count the cost"? How could you make him believe that the same dynamic character whose astounding accomplishments have made his name a synonym for work used to admonish his people: "Work less, wear less, eat less, and we shall be a great deal wiser, healthier, and wealthier people"?[9] How could you ask him to take seriously the multimillionaire who declares, "I have never walked across the streets to make a trade. I do not care anything about such things"?[10] Or the devoted family man who advised missionaries to follow his example and put all thought of family from their minds: "I am not bound to wife or child, to house or farm, or anything else on the face of the earth, but the Gospel of the Son of God"?[11] Here is the great leader who is utterly contemptuous of his "image": "I care not one groat whether they believe all that I say or not, or whether they love me or not; I have no concern about that."[12] Here is the man who worked himself almost to death to get the Nauvoo Temple built on time, and then rejoiced to see it in flames: "I was thankful to see the Temple in Nauvoo on fire. . . . When I saw the flames, I said 'Good, Father, if you want it to be burned up.'"[13]

There is no paradox in all this. Brigham Young was able to master the things of the world because he would not let them master him: he took the measure of a world that could never understand him. It is not a case of physical versus "spiritual" values, but of eternal things, physical or not, versus things we know to be passing and therefore unworthy of our ultimate dedication. "What is this earth in its present condition? Nothing but a place in which we may learn the first lesson towards exaltation, and that is obedience to the Gospel of the Son of God."[14] That makes education the purpose of our life—a special kind of education. "The world are seeking after the paltry, perishable things of time and sense. They are their glory—their pretended comfort—their

god, and their daily study and pursuit."[15] But not for us!
"'Seek FIRST *the kingdom of God*,' . . . and let the gold and
silver, the houses, the lands, the horses, the chariots, the
crowns, the thrones, and the dominions of this world be
dead to you."[16] "The Latter-day Saints have been driven
from their homes, and their goods have been spoiled; but
they esteem this as nothing. What do we care for houses
and lands and possessions? The whole earth is before us
and all the fulness thereof."[17]

That sounds like another paradox: we do not mind the
loss of earthly things as long as we get possession of the
whole earth! Yes, but in the proper way:

> While the inhabitants of the earth are bestowing all
> their ability, both mental and physical, upon perishable
> objects, those who profess to be Latter-day Saints, who
> have the privilege of receiving and understanding the
> principles of the holy Gospel, are in duty bound to study
> and find out, and put in practice in their lives, those prin-
> ciples that are calculated to endure, and that tend to a
> continual increase . . . in the world to come.[18]

"As I said yesterday to a Bishop who was mending a
breach in the canal, and expressed a wish to continue his
labor on the following Sabbath, as his wheat was burning
up, let it burn, when the time comes that is set apart for
worship, go up and worship the Lord."[19] "Let the kitchens
take care of themselves, and let the barns, the flocks and
herds take care of themselves, and if they are destroyed
while you are praying, be able to freely say, 'Go, they are the
Lord's.'"[20] The treasures of the earth are merely to provide
us with room and board while we are here at school, being
"made for the comfort of the creature, and not for his adoration. They are made to sustain and preserve the body
while procuring the knowledge and wisdom that pertain to

God and his kingdom, in order that we may preserve ourselves, and live for ever in his presence."[21]

The astonishing thing is that Brigham Young, as his
behavior demonstrated on innumerable occasions, really
believed what he preached, which goes far to explaining his
brilliant success in surmounting the most terrifying obstacles. "The Gospel of life and salvation reveals to each individual who receives it that this world is only a place of temporary duration, existence, trials, &c. Its present fashion and
uses are but for a few days, while we were created to exist
eternally."[22] That is the basic idea which resolves the paradoxes of Brigham Young's philosophy. No one grants more
readily than this supremely practical man of affairs that
"the things of this world add to our national comfort, and
are necessary to sustain mortal life," and that "we need
these comforts to preserve our earthly existence"; but none
is more emphatic in insisting that

> those things have nothing to do with the spirit, feeling,
> consolation, light, glory, peace, and joy that pertain to
> heaven and heavenly things, which are the food of the
> ever-living spirit within us. . . . This I know by experi-
> ence. I know that the things of this world, from beginning
> to end, from the possession of mountains of gold down
> to a crust of johnnycake, makes little or no difference in
> the happiness of an individual.[23]

So we live two lives at once, taking care to keep our values straight: "I have a being and a life here; and this life is
very valuable; it is a most excellent life! I have a future! I am
living for another existence that is far above this sinful
world."[24]

Brigham Young was the Prophet Joseph's most faithful
disciple; their teachings are one as the minds of the Saints
and prophets have always been one. Before he met Joseph

Smith, Brigham recalls, "the secret feeling of my heart was that I would be willing to crawl around the earth on my hands and knees, to see such a man as was Peter, Jeremiah, Moses, or any man that could tell me anything about God and heaven."[25] And then "when I saw Joseph Smith, he took heaven, figuratively speaking, and brought it down to earth; and he took the earth, brought it up, and opened up, in plainness and simplicity, the things of God; and that is the beauty of his mission."[26] It was a mind-stretching religion: "Thy mind, O man!" said the Prophet Joseph Smith, "if thou wilt lead a soul unto salvation, must stretch as high as the utmost heavens, and search into and contemplate the darkest abyss, and the broad expanse of eternity."[27] The promise he gave to those who took the gospel and the cause of Judah to heart was that "your minds will expand wider and wider, until you can circumscribe the earth and the heavens . . . and contemplate the mighty acts of Jehovah in all their variety and glory."[28] What attests to him the divinity of the Bible is that it is "so much beyond the narrow-mindedness of men, that every man is constrained to exclaim: 'It came from God.'"[29] The Holy Ghost, the ultimate teacher, "has no other effect than pure intelligence. It is more powerful in expanding the mind, enlightening the understanding, and storing the intellect with present knowledge. . . . It is . . . the pure spirit of intelligence."[30] Mind and heart must expand together, according to the Prophet: "You must enlarge your souls towards each other. . . . Let your hearts expand, let them be enlarged towards others."[31] For not only is "the mind or the intelligence which man possesses . . . co-equal with God himself" in time,[32] but "all the minds and spirits that God ever sent into the world are susceptible of enlargement . . . so that they . . . have one glory upon another."[33]

This was what Brigham Young learned from his beloved Joseph as he "continued to receive revelation upon revelation, ordinance upon ordinance, truth upon truth."[34] It was all good news: "What are we here for? To learn to enjoy more, and to increase in knowledge and in experience."[35] Learning is our proper calling: "We shall never cease to learn, unless we apostatize. . . . Can you understand that?"[36] "God has given us mental and physical powers to be improved,"[37] and along with them "our senses, if properly educated, are channels of endless felicity to us."[38] All systems are "go" for the expanding mind: "Let us not narrow ourselves up; for the world, with all its variety of useful information and its rich hoard of hidden treasure, is before us; and eternity, with all its sparkling intelligence, lofty aspirations, and unspeakable glories, is before us."[39] The news is all good—forever: "And when we have passed into the sphere where Joseph is, there is still another department, and then another, and another, and so on to an eternal progression in exaltation and eternal lives. That is the exaltation I am looking for."[40] "When we have lived millions of years in the presence of God and angels, . . . shall we then cease learning? No, or eternity ceases."[41] First and last, the gospel is learning unlimited.

The Mormons were latecomers in the learning game, and it is not hard to see why: "Most of the people called Latter-day Saints have been taken from the rural and manufacturing districts of this and the old countries, and they belonged to the poorest of the poor."[42] "We have gathered the poorest class of men to be found on the continent of America, and I was one of them; and we have gathered the same class from Europe."[43] "I never went to school but eleven days in my life."[44] "I am a man of few words, and unlearned in the learning of this generation."[45] "Brother

Heber and I never went to school until we got into 'Mormonism': that was the first of our schooling."[46] Such men, coming of age in the flowering of their native New England, hungered for the things of the mind, the more so since they had been denied them: "We are all of the labouring and middle classes. There are but few in this Church who are not of the labouring class, and they have not had an opportunity to cultivate their minds,"[47] yet they felt strongly "the necessity of the mind being kept active and having the opportunity of indulging in every exercise it can enjoy in order to attain to a full development of its powers."[48] Mormonism gave them their great chance, as it sought, in the words of Joseph Smith, "to inspire every one who is called to be a minister of these glad tidings, to so improve his talent that he may gain other talents."[49]

If they were late starters, the gospel gave the Saints certain advantages which might even enable them to overhaul the more privileged. For one thing, they had motivating zeal: "Take those who are in the enjoyment of all the luxuries of this life, and their ears are stopped up; they cannot hear; but go to the poor . . . and they are looking every way for deliverance. . . . Their ears are open to hear and their hearts are touched. . . . These are they that we gather."[50] True, "very few of the learned or of those who are high and lifted up in the estimation of the people receive the Gospel";[51] but that is all to the good, since such haughtiness can be paralyzing. God is now working with rough but reliable materials: "The beginning of this dispensation of the fulness of times may well be compared to the commencement of a temple, the material of which it is to be built being still scattered, unshaped and unpolished, in a state of nature."[52] "A spirit and power of research is planted within, yet they remain undeveloped."[53] "When we look at the

Latter-day Saints and remember that they have been taken from the coal pits, from the ironworks, from the streets, from the kitchens and from the barns and factories and from hard service in the countries where they formerly lived, we cannot wonder at their ignorance."[54]

But if their ignorance is not to be wondered at, neither is it to be condoned. Without a moment's delay the newly converted Saints were put to work on a grandiose intellectual project, which was nothing less than the salvaging of world civilization! As Brigham puts it, "The business of the Elders of this Church (Jesus, their elder brother, being at their head) [is] to gather up all the truths in the world pertaining to life and salvation, to the Gospel we preach, to mechanism[s] of every kind, to the sciences, and to philosophy, wherever [they] may be found in every nation, kindred, tongue, and people, and bring it to Zion."[55] The "gathering" was to be a bringing together not only of people but of all the treasures surviving in the earth from every age and culture; "every accomplishment, every polished grace, every useful attainment in mathematics, music, and in all science and art belong to the Saints,"[56] and they "rapidly collect the intelligence that is bestowed upon the nations, for all this intelligence belongs to Zion. All the knowledge, wisdom, power, and glory that have been bestowed upon the nations of the earth, from the days of Adam till now, must be gathered home to Zion."[57] "What is this work? The improvement of the condition of the human family."[58] But why do the poor struggling Saints have to do it? Because "the Lord has taken the weak things of the world to confound the . . . wise,"[59] and especially because the rest of the world is no longer up to it.

It was a daring concept, but one fully justified by history, that once "the Lord has bestowed great knowledge

and wisdom upon the inhabitants of the earth—much truth
. . . in the arts and sciences," it is quite possible for such treasures to be lost: "This wisdom will be taken from the
wicked"—and once it is gone, "I question," says the far-
seeing Brigham Young, "whether it would return again." To
this impressive bit of historical insight he adds an exciting
suggestion: "My faith and my desire are that there should
be a people upon the earth prepared to receive this wisdom.
It should not be so forfeited as to be taken from the earth."[60]
The concept (recalling James Hilton's *Lost Horizon*) is an
ancient one, being the idea, for example, behind the
Cabbala. Repeatedly Brother Brigham admonishes the
Saints that if they are to carry out such a task they must in
time come to equal and even excel the learning of the
world. They can do it if they work like demons: "Put forth
your ability to learn as fast as you can, and gather all the
strength of mind and principle of faith you possibly can,
and then distribute your knowledge to the people."[61] If the
world seems far ahead of us, remember, "we are not as
ignorant as they are" because, like Socrates, we acknowledge our ignorance and know where we stand.[62] If the
Saints "have not had an opportunity to cultivate their
minds," neither had they "been educated in the devilry and
craft of the learned classes of mankind," to hold them
back.[63] Joseph Smith had assured them that "there is a superior intelligence bestowed upon such as obey the Gospel,"[64]
and Brigham promised them, "There is nothing that the
Saints can ask, or pray for, that will aid them in their progress . . . that will not be granted unto them, if they will only
patiently struggle on."[65]

That last point, the patient struggling, was the rub.
President Young kept after his people all the time: "After
suitable rest and relaxation there is not a day, hour or

minute that we should spend in idleness, but every minute of every day of our lives we should strive to improve our minds and to increase in the faith of the holy Gospel."[66] A year after the arrival in the valley, Brigham Young copied down in his journal a letter which Parley P. Pratt had written to his brother back east describing the new society: "All is quiet—stillness. No elections, no police reports, no murders, no war nor little war. . . . No policeman has been on duty to guard us from external or internal dangers. . . . Here we can cultivate the mind, renew the spirit, invigorate the body, cheer the heart and ennoble the soul of man. Here we can cultivate every science and art calculated to enlarge the mind, accommodate the body, or polish and adorn our race; and here we can receive and extend that pure intelligence which is unmingled with the jargon of mystic Babylon."[67] Wonderful to relate, for the ever practical Brigham and the struggling pioneers the improvement of the *mind* always came first. Brigham laid it on the line: "All who do not want to sustain co-operation and fall into the ranks of improvement, and endeavor to improve themselves by every good book" were invited to leave the community.[68] The challenge of nature was not the real issue—"the greatest and most important labour we have to perform is to cultivate ourselves."[69]

What the Church most urgently needed at the start was what might be called "missionary learning." It makes perfectly good sense to insist that "we should be familiar with the various languages, for we wish to send to the different nations and to the islands of the sea,"[70] or that all spend "a certain portion of the time . . . in storing their minds with useful knowledge," by "reading the Bible, Book of Mormon, and other Church works, and histories, scientific works and other useful books."[71] At an early time Brigham Young suggested the formation of independent study groups among the people: "Call in your brethren, and read the Bible, the Book of Mormon, the Book of Covenants, and the other revelations of God to them; and talk over the things contained in those books, and deal them out to your brethren and neighbors."[72] More formal schooling had ever an eye to the mission field: "In our schools, all our educational pursuits are in the service of God, for all these labors are to establish truth on the earth,"[73] specifically, "that our young men, when they go out to preach, may not be so ignorant as they have been hitherto."[74] Good missionaries should know things: "I do not wish to be understood as throwing a straw in the way of the Elders' storing their minds with all the arguments they can gather . . . [or] learning all they can with regard to religions and governments. The more knowledge the Elders have the better."[75] After all, Joseph Smith had said that the mind of one who would "lead a soul unto salvation, must stretch as high as the utmost heavens."[76]

But articulate and informed missionaries do not issue forth from a community of ignoramuses—Zion itself must be the central hearth and home of a broad and flourishing culture: "There is a great work for the Saints to do. Progress, and improve upon, and make beautiful everything around you. Cultivate the earth and cultivate your minds."[77]

> Now, if we can take the low and degraded and elevate them in their feelings, language and manners; if we can impart to them the sciences that are in the world, teach them all that books contain, and in addition to all this, teach them principles that are eternal, and calculated to make them a beautiful community, lovely in their appearance, intelligent in every sense of the word, would you not say that our system is praiseworthy and possesses great merit?[78]

For Brigham, the proper study of mankind is every-thing: "This is the belief and doctrine of the Latter-day Saints. Learn everything that the children of men know."[79] It all comes under the heading of our religion: "Every true principle, every true science, every art, and all the knowl-edge that men possess or that they ever did or ever will possess, is from God. We should take pains and pride to . . . rear our children so that the learning and education of the world may be theirs."[80] "Every accomplishment, every grace, every useful attainment in mathematics, . . . in all sci-ence and art belong to the Saints, and they should avail themselves as expeditiously as possible of the wealth of knowledge the sciences offer to every diligent and perse-vering scholar."[81]

A favorite with LDS schoolmen has been Brigham Young's declaration that "every art and science known and studied by the children of men is comprised within the Gospel."[82] But this does not mean, as is commonly assumed, that anything one chooses to teach is the gospel—that would be as silly as arguing that since all things are made of electrons, protons, neutrons, etc., whenever anyone opens his mouth to speak he gives a lecture on physics. It means rather that all things may be studied and taught in the light of the gospel: "If an Elder shall give us a lecture upon astronomy, chemistry, or geology, our religion embraces it all. It matters not what the subject be, if it tends to improve the mind, exalt the feelings, and enlarge the capacity."[83] It would be quite impossible to improve the mind, exalt the feelings and enlarge the capacity of any man without making him a better candidate for heaven—"it matters not what the subject be."[84] By the same token, the reading of the scriptures if not undertaken in that spirit does *not* belong to our religion: " 'Shall I sit down and read the Bible, the Book of Mormon, and the Book of Covenants all the time?' says one. Yes, if you please, and when you have done, you may be nothing but a sectarian after all. It is your duty to study . . . everything upon the face of the earth, in addition to reading those books."[85]

"Everything on the face of the earth" is a large order, and Brigham was no fool; he knew perfectly well that "the most learned men that have ever lived on the earth have only been able to obtain a small amount of knowledge,"[86] and that time, patience, and method are necessary to bring the Saints around: "As Saints in the last days we have much to learn; there is an eternity of knowledge before us; at most we receive but very little in this stage of our progression."[87] There must be a priority of things to be learned, which is what curriculum is all about: "We wish to have our young boys and girls taught in the different branches of an English education, and in other languages, and in the various sciences, all of which . . . [will] eventually . . . [be] taught in this school."[88] "We also wish them to understand the geography, habits, customs, and laws of nations and kingdoms, whether they be barbarians or civilized. This is recommended in the revelations. . . . Let them become more informed in every department of true and useful learning than their fathers are."[89]

Immediately after arriving in the valley, President Young recommended "securing at least a copy of every valuable treatise on education—every book, map, chart, or diagram that may contain interesting, useful, and attractive matter, to gain the attention of children, and cause them to love to learn to read"; this includes "every historical, mathematical, philosophical, geographical, geological, astronomical, scientific, practical, and all other variety of useful and interesting writings."[90] To train "the whole man" was his object from the first: "Let us make mechanics of our boys, and educate them in every useful branch of science and in the history and laws of kingdoms and nations."[91] He was always fascinated with problems of communication, on which he had some interesting theories, including the improvement of English phonology: "I would also like our school teachers to introduce phonography into every school. . . . This is a delightful study! In these and all other branches of science and education we should know as much as any people in the world."[92]

But curriculum is a game for little minds; the important thing for Brigham is that the Saints use their newfound liberty and revel as he did in the things of the mind. The starving man eats thankfully what he can get and does not quibble for hours over the menu and etiquette. The decisive factor is a passion for the things of the *mind:* "We believe . . . that every man and woman should have the opportunity of developing themselves mentally as well as physically. In the present condition of the world this privilege is only accorded to a few."[93] Learning is a privilege to be eagerly exploited: "If we can have the privilege, we will enrich our minds with knowledge, filling these mortal tenements with the rich treasures of heavenly wisdom."[94] The proper priority of study is not as important as study itself: "If it would do any good, I would advise you to read books that are worth reading," but "I would rather that persons read novels than read nothing"[95]—reading nothing being the normal outcome of waiting on the curriculum committee.

As the strong man loveth to run a race, so Brigham loved to exercise his brains, and constantly appealed to the people to do the same: "We are trying to teach this people to use their brains."[96] "I pray to the Lord for you; I pray for you to get wisdom—worldly wisdom."[97] Every problem was to be approached as a mental problem, an exciting game of wits: "Whatever duty you are called to perform, take your minds with you, and apply them to what is to be done."[98] Proper pioneering takes as much brain as brawn. Intelligence is not only useful, it is a high moral quality, a holy thing, an attribute to God himself: "If men would be great in goodness," Brigham Young wrote in his history, "they must be intelligent," and he records in the same work that Joseph Smith prayed for the leaders of the Church "that God may . . . grant unto them wisdom and intelligence, that his kingdom may roll forth."[99] And so he appeals to the people: "When you come to meeting . . . take your minds with you. . . . I want [your] minds here as well as [your] bodies."[100]

To use one's brains is to think for one's self: "Ladies and gentlemen, I exhort you to think for yourselves, and read your Bibles for yourselves, get the Holy Spirit for yourselves, and pray for yourselves."[101] The appeal has been repeated by every president of the Church. "The catalogue of [a] man's discipline," says Brigham, the sound psychologist, "he must compile [for] himself: he cannot be guided by any rule that others may lay down, but is . . . under the necessity of tracing it himself through every avenue of his life. He is obliged to catechise and train himself."[102] Even virtue is not too high a price to pay for individual responsibility: "Every mortal being must stand up as an intelligent, organized capacity, and choose or refuse the good, and thus act for himself. All must have that opportunity, no matter if all go into the depths of wickedness."[103] We can never grow as long as we are "other-directed": "Pay no attention to what others do, it is no matter what they do, or how they dress."[104] A favorite saying of Brigham Young's was that "men . . . are organized to be just as independent as any

being in eternity."[105] No one was a more passionate advocate
of temperance than he, but when in his youth he was asked
to sign a temperance pledge he absolutely refused: "I said, 'I
do not need to sign the temperance pledge.' I recollect my
father urged me. 'No, sir,' said I, 'if I sign the temperance
pledge I feel that I am bound, and I wish to do just right,
without being bound to do it; I want my liberty.' . . . What
do you say? Is this correct?"[106] "It would be useless for anybody to undertake to drive me to heaven or to hell. My
independence is sacred to me—it is a portion of that same
Deity that rules in the heavens."[107] Again, it was Joseph
Smith who led the way: "All have the privilege of thinking
for themselves upon all matters relative to conscience. . . .
We are not disposed, had we the power, to deprive anyone
of exercising that free independence of mind which heaven
has so graciously bestowed upon the human family as one
of its choicest gifts."[108]

President Young tried to make the meetings of the
Saints stimulating and adult affairs instead of humdrum
routines. For one thing, "it may sometimes be just as good
and profitable to stay at home as to come to meeting. . . . I
do not believe that those who stay at home are, in many
instances, any worse than those who come to meeting, nor
that those who come to meeting are particularly better than
those who stay at home."[109] "If any of you feel that there is
no life in your meetings, . . . then it becomes your duty to
go and instil life into that meeting, and do your part to produce an increase of the Spirit and power of God in the meetings in your locality."[110] And even at conference: "If any of
you are not instructed to your satisfaction, be so kind as to
send up a card to the stand, intimating your desire to speak,
and we will give you an opportunity of doing so, to display

your wisdom; for we wish to learn wisdom and get under-standing."[111]

On the other hand, he rebukes senseless applause and even dampens the patriotic ardor of a Twenty-fourth of July gathering: "I have noticed that people there applaud and the boys whistle when there was nothing to elicit their approbation; and I would say that it would be very gratify-ing to my feelings if such useless, noisy, and uncalled for demonstrations were discontinued."[112] Even high spirits and firecrackers are no excuse for turning off one's brains: "I ask . . . all the boys under a hundred years of age—never to applaud unless they know what they are applauding. It is confusing, bewildering, and making a noise without under-standing."[113] Empty-headed laughter pleases him not: "Never give way to vain laughter. . . . I always blush for those who laugh aloud without meaning."[114] Children at meeting, even to attest to the growth of Zion, do not delight him: "I cannot understand the utility of bringing children into such a congregation . . . just for the sake of pleasing the mothers."[115] "If you cannot, for the space of two or three hours, forego the pleasure of gazing upon the faces of your little darlings, just stay at home with them."[116]

No matter where we begin, if we pursue knowledge diligently and honestly our quest will inevitably lead us from the things of earth to the things of heaven. All science is cosmology, says Karl Popper,[117] and, we add, all cosmol-ogy is eschatology. For Brigham Young, since all knowledge can be encompassed in one whole, the spectrum of secular study blends imperceptibly with the knowledge of the eter-nities: "In our schools, all our educational pursuits are in the service of God, for all these labors are to establish truth on the earth, and that we may increase in knowledge, wis-dom, understanding in the power of faith and in the wisdom of God, that we may become fit subjects to dwell in a higher state of existence and intelligence than we now enjoy."[118] Note well that secular learning is sanctified only if it is approached in a certain spirit. Only that knowledge belongs to the gospel which is viewed and taught as such—as *all* knowledge should be. "God has created man with a mind capable of instruction," according to Joseph Smith, "and a faculty which may be enlarged in proportion to the heed and diligence given to the light communicated from *heaven* to the *intellect*."[119]

There are three factors involved: intelligence, revelation, *and* hard work, and if the spirit may help in earthly learning, the mind is required to operate in celestial matters. The learning process begun in this life carries on into the next: "And when we pass through the veil, we expect still to continue to learn and increase our fund of information."[120] The Saints must "first learn everything that the children of men know," and then go on and "improve upon this until we are prepared and permitted to enter the society of the blessed—the holy angels."[121] This is done by pursuing a steady course that leads from the earthly to the heavenly without a break: "We should not only learn the principles of education known to mankind, but we should reach out further than this, learning to live so that our minds will gather in information from the heavens and the earth until we can incorporate in our faith and understanding all knowledge."[122] "Teach the children, give them the learning of the world *and* the things of God; elevate their minds, that they may not only understand the earth we walk upon, but the air we breathe, the water we drink and all the elements pertaining to the earth; and then search other worlds, and become acquainted with the planetary system." Not stopping there, they are to go on to discover "the dwellings of the angels

and the heavenly beings, that they may ultimately be prepared for a higher state of being, and finally be associated
with them."[123] "It is the privilege of man to search out the
wisdom of God pertaining to the earth and the heavens."[124]
"Learn the wisdom of the world and the wisdom of God,
and put them together and you will be able to benefit yourselves."[125] "We try to so live as to gain more information,
more light, more command over ourselves . . . until we can
comprehend the great principles of existence and eternal
progression."[126]

Such a concept has, of course, no conflict with science.
The motto of the Royal Society, *Nullus in verba*—"we take no
man's word for anything"—is even more strongly
expressed in the first editorial to appear in the *Times and
Seasons*, written by Brigham Young: Remember, Brethren,
"no man's opinion is worth a straw."[127] Brigham is a man who
wants to know: "The object of this existence is to learn. . . .
How gladly would we understand every principle pertaining to science and art, and become thoroughly acquainted
with every intricate operation of nature, and with all the
chemical changes that are constantly going on around us!
How delightful this would be, and what a boundless field
of truth and power is open for us to explore! We are only
just approaching the shores of the vast ocean of information
that pertains to this physical world, to say nothing of that
which pertains to the heavens."[128] "Send the old children to
school and the young ones also; there is nothing I would
like better than to learn chemistry, botany, geology, and
mineralogy."[129] "In these respects we differ from the
Christian world, for our religion will not clash with or contradict the facts of science in any particular. You may take
geology, for instance, and it is a true science; not that
I would say for a moment that all the conclusions and

deductions of its professors are true [opinions are not facts!], but its leading principles are."[130]

The basic common sense of science appeals to Brigham Young as being sound and true. He took the shocking position that God works on scientific principles: "If I had the skill . . . to construct a machine" to pass through "the atmosphere as they do now on *terra firma* on the railway, would there be any harm in acknowledging God in this?"[131] When "'the elements shall melt with fervent heat,' the Lord Almighty will send forth his angels, who are well instructed in chemistry, and they will separate the elements and make new combinations thereof."[132] That was an outrageous statement both from a religious and a scientific viewpoint a hundred years ago. He also propounded a doctrine which has only recently been brought to the fore by such scientists as Giorgio de Santillana:[133] "The people of this day think they know more than all who have preceded them—that this is the wisest generation that ever did live on the earth, . . . but there is no question that many things of great worth known anciently have been lost."[134]

Brigham Young's sanguine discourses on education were meant to stir his people up and shame them out of their intellectual lethargy. No one knew better than he the weaknesses of human nature ("Mankind are weak and feeble, poor and needy; how destitute they are of true knowledge, how little they have when they have any at all!"[135]); the hebetude of minds used to having others think for them ("The great masses of the people neither think nor act for themselves. . . . I see too much of this gross ignorance among this chosen people of God"[136]); the hesitancy of the uprooted, tending either "to hide ourselves up from the world" or "to pattern after the people they had left"—both wrong;[137] the smugness of the chosen people, who "imagine that they must begin and unlearn the whole of their former education,"[138] and who expect God to give them everything on a platter: "Have I any good reason to say to my Father in heaven, 'Fight my battles,' when He has given me the sword to wield, the arm and the brain that I can fight for myself?"[139] The Saints were much too easily satisfied with themselves: "How vain and trifling have been our spirits, our conferences, our councils, our meetings, our private as well as public conversations—too low, too mean, too vulgar, too condescending for the dignified characters of the called and chosen of God," wrote the Prophet Joseph from Liberty Jail.[140] "Condescending" means settling for inferior goods to avoid effort and tension. Brigham hated that: "That diffidence or timidity we must dispense with. When it becomes our duty to talk, we ought to be willing to talk. . . . Interchanging our ideas and exhibiting that which we believe and understand affords an opportunity for detecting and correcting errors"—the expanding mind must be openly and frankly critical, come hell or high council;[141] without that we get "too much of a sameness in this community"[142]—"I am not a stereotyped Latter-day Saint, and do not believe in the doctrine. . . . Are we going to stand still? Away with stereotyped 'Mormons.'"[143]

But the foibles of human nature were but some of the timbers and cobblestones of the real barricade which the adversary has contrived to place in the way of learning. The Saints, gathered "from the poorest of the poor," had good reason to know that the imperious question put to all who presume to set foot on this world where Belial rules is not "Have you any knowledge?" (as in the ancient mysteries), but "Have you any money?" That is Satan's golden question. If the answer is "yes," well and good ("for money answereth all things"), but if it is "no" you might as well be dead. That is the way things are set up here upon the earth; "man has become so perverted as to debar his fellows as much as possible from these blessings, and constrain them by physical force or circumstances to contribute the proceeds of their labour to sustain the favoured few."[144] It is no wonder that the Saints who had momentarily broken free from the system were obsessed with an overpowering drive to seek the only security this earth has to offer—wealth. And this passion, as Brigham Young tells them in a mounting crescendo of warning and appeal through the years, is the one absolute obstacle to their ever acquiring the knowledge they must seek.

Brigham discovered the basic conflict at an early age; he tells how at the age of nineteen he "sought for riches, but in vain; there was something that always kept telling me that happiness originated in higher pursuits."[145] At the very beginning of the Church Joseph Smith noted that "God had often sealed up the heavens because of covetousness in the Church."[146] In 1855 Brigham Young pointed out the way in which love of knowledge and love of wealth, like antipathetical sets of glands, render each other ineffective: "It is possible for a man who loves the world to overcome that love, to get knowledge and understanding until he sees things as they really are, then he will not love the world but will see it as it is."[147] In 1859: "I desire to see everybody on the track of improvement. . . . But when you so love your property . . . as though all your affections were placed upon the changing, fading things of earth, it is impossible to increase in the knowledge of truth."[148] In 1860: "There are hundreds in this community who are more eager to become rich in the perishable things of this world than to adorn their minds . . . with a knowledge of things as they were, as they are, and as they are to come."[149] In 1862: "No man who possesses the wealth of wisdom would worship the wealth of mammon."[150] In 1863: If we go on "lusting after the grovelling things of this life which perish with the handling," we shall surely "remain fixed with a very limited amount of knowledge, and, like a door upon its hinges, move to and fro from one year to another without any visible advancement or improvement. . . . Man is made in the image of God, but what do we know of him or of ourselves, when we suffer ourselves to love and worship the god of this world—riches?"[151] In 1866: "When you see the Latter-day Saints greedy, and covetous of the things of this world, do you think their minds are in a fit condition to be written upon by the pen of revelation?"[152] In 1870: "We frequently hear our merchants say that they cannot do business and then go into the pulpit to preach."[153] In 1872: "A man or a woman who places the wealth of this world and the things of time in the scales against the things of God and wisdom of eternity, has no eyes to see, no ears to hear, no heart to understand."[154] In 1874: "The covetous, those who are striving continually to build themselves up in the things of this life, will be poor indeed; they will be poor in spirit and poor in heavenly things."[155]

Over against the expanding mind, the prophets placed the contracted mind: "You must not be contracted, but you must be liberal in your feelings," Joseph Smith told the people.[156] "How contracted in mind and short-sighted we must be," Brigham reflects, "to permit the perishable things of this world to swerve us in the least degree from our fidelity to the truth."[157] "Let us not narrow ourselves up; for the world, with all its variety of useful information and its rich hoard of hidden treasure, is before us."[158] He illustrates this by the practice of constantly quoting a very limited number of scriptures to the exclusion of others equally

important, and comments: "This same lack of comprehensiveness of mind is also very noticeable at times with some
men who happen to accumulate property, and it leads them
to forsake the Spirit of the Gospel. Does it not prove that
there is a contractedness of mind in those who do so, which
should not be?"[159] Business by its very nature is narrowing:

> Take for instance, the financial circles, the commerce
> of the world, those business men; where they have their
> opponents they, . . . with all the secrecy of the grave, I
> might say, will seek to carry out their schemes unknown
> to their opponents, in order that they may win. Like the
> man at the table with the cards in his hands, unseen by
> any but himself, he will take the advantage as far as he
> can. So says the politician. So say[s] the world of
> Christendom, so say[s] the world of the heathens, and it
> is party upon party, sect after sect, division upon divi-
> sion, and we are all for ourselves.[160]

"In our trading and trafficking we wish to confine the
knowledge of our business in as small a limit as possible,
that others may not know what we are doing. . . . We all
wish to know something that our neighbors do not know.
With scientific men you will often find the same trait of
character: . . . I know more than they know; I treasure this
up to myself, and I am looked upon as a superior being,
and that delights me."[161]

Against this, "you see the nobleman seeking the benefit
of all around him, trying to bring, we will say, his servants,
if you please, his tenants, to his knowledge, to like blessings
that he enjoys, to dispense his wisdom and talents among
them and to make them equal with himself."[162] Brigham
told the well-heeled Saints to "keep their riches, and with
them I promise you leanness of soul, darkness of mind, narrow and contracted hearts, and the bowels of your compassion will be shut up."[163] Even so, Joseph Smith had warned

against "those contracted feelings that influence the children of men" who judge each other "according to the narrow, contracted notions of men," while "the Great Parent of the universe looks upon the whole of the human family with a fatherly care and paternal regard."[164]

For Brigham Young the contracted mind reached its bathos in the world of fashion: "But to see a people who say, 'We are the teachers of life and salvation,' and yet are anxious to follow the nasty, pernicious fashions of the day, I say it is too insipid to talk or think about. It is beneath the character of the Latter-day Saints that they should have no more independence of mind or feeling than to follow after the grovelling customs and fashions of a poor, miserable, wicked world."[165] "To me a desire to follow the ever-varying fashions of the world manifests a great weakness of mind in either gentleman or lady."[166] Again, it is the things of the world versus the things of the mind: "Mothers, . . . we will appoint you to a mission to teach your children their duty; and instead of ruffles and fine dresses to adorn the body, teach them that which will adorn their minds."[167] So the Prophet Joseph had told the sisters at the founding of the Relief Society, "This Society shall rejoice, and knowledge and intelligence shall flow down from this time henceforth," but only if they "don't envy the finery and fleeting show of sinners, for they are in a miserable situation."[168] Status symbols belong to the same category: "A good name! Bless me! what is a name? It may shine like the noon-day sun . . . to-day, and to-morrow be eclipsed in midnight darkness, to rise no more! The glory of the world passes away, but the glory that the Saints are after is that which is to come in the eternal world."[169] "In all nations, or at least in all civilized nations, there are distinctions among the people

created by rank, titles, and property. How does God look
upon these distinctions?"[170]

Misreading the case of the ancient patriarchs, whose
wealth came and went and always hung by a thread, many
of the Saints dreamed fondly of a happy wedding between
the good things of this earth and the blessings of the next,
and sought after the death of Brigham Young to bridge the
unbridgeable gulf between Babylon and Zion. We cannot go
into this here, but it should be clear by now that the search
for knowledge, in Brigham's book, by its very nature must
be pure and disinterested: "Will education feed and clothe
you, keep you warm on a cold day, or enable you to build a
house? Not at all. Should we cry down education on this
account? No. What is it for? The improvement of the *mind*;
to instruct us in all arts and sciences, in the history of the
world, in . . . laws of life, and how to be useful while we
live."[171] It is the things of the mind that are really useful.
"Truth, wisdom, power, glory, light, and intelligence exist
upon their own qualities; they do not, neither can they, exist
upon any other principle. Truth is congenial with itself; and
light cleaves unto light. . . . It is the same with knowledge,
and virtue, and all the eternal attributes; they follow after
. . . each other. . . . Truth cleaves unto truth, *because* it is truth;
and it is to be *adored*, because it is an *attribute* of *God*, for its
excellence, for *itself*."[172] There can be no ulterior motive in the
study of heavenly things; "Knowledge is Power" is the slogan of a rascally world: "What do you love truth for? Is it
because you can discover a beauty in it, because it is congenial to you; or because you think it will make you a ruler, or
a Lord? If you conceive that you will attain to power upon
such a motive, you are much mistaken. It is a trick of the
unseen power, that is abroad amongst the inhabitants of the

earth, that leads them astray, binds their minds, and sub-
verts their understanding."[173]

Here Brigham Young goes all the way: "Suppose that
our Father in heaven, our elder brother, the risen Redeemer,
the Saviour of the world, or any of the Gods of eternity
should act upon this principle, to love truth, knowledge,
and wisdom, because they are all powerful, . . . they would
cease to be Gods; . . . the extension of their kingdom would
cease, and their God-head come to an end."[174] The Saints do
what they do "purely because the principles which God has
revealed . . . are pure, holy and exalting in their nature."[175]
How can there be compromise with the world? "Shame on
men and women, professing to be Saints, who worship and
love the perishing things of earth."[176] "It is disgusting to me
to see a person love this world in its present organization."[177] "Go to the child, and what does its joy consist in?
Toys; . . . and so it is with our youth, our young boys and
girls; they are thinking too much of this world; and the
middle-aged are striving and struggling to obtain the good
things of this life, and their hearts are too much upon them.
So it is with the aged. Is not this the condition of the Latter-
day Saints? It is."[178]

The Latter-day Saints have always had a way of missing the bus: "Take the history of this Church from the commencement, and we have proven that we cannot receive all
the Lord has for us."[179] The trouble is that "these tabernacles
are dull, subject to sin and temptation, and to stray from the
kingdom of God and the ordinances of his house, to lust
after riches, the pride of life and the vanities of the world."[180]
"We may look upon ourselves with shamefacedness
because of the smallness of our attainments in the midst of
so many great advantages."[181] "In things pertaining to this
life, the lack of knowledge manifested by us as a people is

disgraceful."[182] "I have seen months and months, in this city, when I could have wept like a whipt child to see the awful stupidity of the people."[183] "I feel like taking men and women by the hair of their heads, figuratively speaking, and slinging them miles and miles, and like crying, stop, before you ruin yourselves!"[184]

In a now-classic study, Ernst Käsemann showed that God's peculiar way of dealing with the chosen people, ever stiff-necked and slow to learn, was to send them wandering in the wilderness.[185] The last dispensation has proven no exception in this regard: "Some may ask why did we not tarry at the centre stake of Zion when the Lord planted our feet there? We had eyes, but we did not see; we had ears, but we did not hear; we had hearts that were devoid of what the Lord required of his people; consequently, we could not abide what the Lord revealed unto us. We had to go from there to gain an experience. Can you understand this?"[186] "Could our brethren stay in Jackson county, Missouri? No, no. Why? They had not learned 'a' concerning Zion; and we have been traveling now forty-two years, and have we learned our a, b, c? . . . I will say, scarcely."[187] "I never attributed the driving of the Saints from Jackson County to anything but that it was necessary to chasten them and prepare them to build up Zion."[188] "Are we fit for Zion? . . . Could we stay in Independence? No, we could not. . . . What is the matter with all you Latter-day Saints? Can the world see? No. Can the Saints see? No, or few of them can; and we can say that the light of the Spirit upon the hearts and understandings of some Latter-day Saints is like the peeping of the stars through the broken shingles of the roof over our heads."[189]

The prophecies have not been revoked, but their fulfill-ment can be delayed, indefinitely, if need be, until all necessary conditions are fulfilled. The Saints "will take the kingdom, and possess it for ever and ever; but in the capacity they are now, in the condition that they now present themselves before God, before the world and before each other? Never, never!"[190] "We are not yet prepared to go and establish the Centre Stake of Zion. The Lord tried this in the first place. . . . He gave revelation after revelation; but the people could not abide them. . . . They do not know what to do with the revelations, commandments and blessings of God."[191] So though this people will surely go back to Jackson County, they will nonetheless be *held back* until they are ready—which may be a very long time.[192]

"And so we have got to continue to labor, fight, toil, counsel, exercise faith, ask God over and over, and have been praying to the Lord for thirty odd years for that which we might have received . . . in one year."[193] But there was nothing for it but to keep on plugging: "We are so organized that we need preaching to all the time. This is because of our weaknesses, and we shall have to bear with one another until we become stronger and wiser."[194] We may give up and lose the blessings, but the prophecies and promises will all be fulfilled, and "if we do not wake up and cease to long after the things of this earth, we will find that we as individuals will go down to hell, although the Lord will preserve a people unto himself."[195] "We may fail, if we are not faithful; but God will not fail in accomplishing his work, whether we abide in it or not."[196] "If we are not faithful, others will take our places; for this is the Church and people that will possess the kingdom for ever and ever. Shall we do this in our present condition as a people? No; for we must be pure and holy."[197] "If my brethren and sisters do not walk up to the principles of the holy Gospel, . . . they will be removed out of their places, and others will be called to occupy them."[198] It had already happened many times: "Of the great many who have been baptized into this Church, but few have been able to abide the word of the Lord; they have fallen out on the right and on the left, . . . and a few have gathered together."[199] Joseph Smith stated the problem: "I have tried for a number of years to get the minds of the Saints prepared to receive the things of God," but they "will fly to pieces like glass as soon as anything comes that is contrary to their traditions: they still cannot stand the fire at all."[200]

We have felt no necessity in this brief and sketchy survey to point out to the reader how Brigham Young's educational concepts stand out in brilliant contrast against the background of everything that is practiced and preached in our higher schools today. But the moral of our story must not be overlooked: *Brigham was right after all.* As administrative problems have accumulated in a growing Church, the authorities have tended to delegate the business of learning to others, and those others have been only too glad to settle for the outward show, the easy and flattering forms, trappings, and ceremonies of education. Worse still, they have chosen business-oriented, career-minded, degree-seeking programs in preference to the strenuous, critical, liberal, mind-stretching exercises that Brigham Young recommended. We have chosen the services of the hired image-maker in preference to unsparing self-criticism, and the first question the student is taught to ask today is John Dewey's golden question: "What is there in it for me?"

As a result, whenever we move out of our tiny, busy orbits of administration and display, we find ourselves in a terrifying intellectual vacuum. Terrifying, of course, only because we might be found out. But that is just the trouble: having defaulted drastically in terms of President Young's instructions, we now stand as a brainless giant, a pushover for any smart kid or cultist or faddist or crank who even pretends to have read a few books. That puts them beyond our depth and so we (I include myself) stand helplessly and foolishly by, dangling our bonnet and plume, while hundreds of students and missionaries, of members and enemies of the Church alike, presume to challenge and reject the teachings of Joseph Smith on evidence so flimsy that no half-educated person would give it a second thought. How can you hope to make these people see that the documents and discoveries they hail with such reverence and delight for the most part went out of date in the 1930s; that Huxley, Breasted, Wellhausen, and Frazer do not represent present-day scientific thought; that one book does not settle anything: No one has ever told them of the new discoveries which *every month* call for revision of established scientific and scholarly beliefs. No one has ever told them what it means to lay a proper foundation essential to any serious discussion of the things they treat so glibly and triumphantly. No one has ever told them of the millions of unread documents that already repose in our libraries, holding the answers to countless questions that must be asked before they can justify their instant conclusions. An awesome outpouring of newly discovered documents of direct bearing on the history and teachings of the Church is even now in full spate, amazing and confounding Jewish and Christian scholars, but bursting with good news for the Latter-day Saints—who ignore them completely.

It is perfectly natural for the young who discover the world of scholarship for the first time to strike in their sophomoric zeal an intellectual pose, rail in high terms against the Church that has kept them in darkness all these years, and catalogue the defects and miscalculations of the prophets in the light of their own scholarly elevation. That is perfectly natural, and if we had heeded Brigham Young, the urge to study and criticize would be running in fruitful channels. Whether we like it or not, we are going to have to return to Brigham Young's ideals of education; we may fight it all the way, but in the end God will keep us after school until we learn our lesson: "Behold, you have not understood; you have supposed that I would give it unto you, when you took no thought save it was to ask me. But, behold, I say unto you, that you must study it out in your mind; then you must ask me if it be right" (D&C 9:7–8).

Notes

1. Charles W. Nibley. During the winter of 1921, when President Nibley was writing his reminiscences at Ocean Park, California, he used to read the manuscript to the family of the author in the evenings, telling as he went the much better stories left out of the official biography. This was one of them, and has since been repeatedly confirmed by Preston Nibley, who had it from the same source.

2. *JD* 14:101.
3. *JD* 14:101.
4. *JD* 15:35, 37.
5. *JD* 3:357.
6. *JD* 11:132.
7. *JD* 8:125.
8. *JD* 10:335.
9. *JD* 12:122.
10. *JD* 12:219.
11. *JD* 14:19.
12. *JD* 10:302.
13. *JD* 8:203.
14. *JD* 14:232.
15. *JD* 6:40.
16. *JD* 1:266.
17. *JD* 11:16.
18. *JD* 2:91.
19. *JD* 3:331.
20. *JD* 3:53.

21. *JD* 8:135.
22. *JD* 5:53.
23. *JD* 7:135.
24. *JD* 13:220.
25. *JD* 8:228.
26. *JD* 5:332.
27. *TPJS,* 137.
28. *TPJS,* 163.
29. *TPJS,* 11.
30. *TPJS,* 149–50.
31. *TPJS,* 228.
32. *TPJS,* 353.
33. *TPJS,* 354.
34. *JD* 16:42.
35. *JD* 14:228.
36. *JD* 3:203.
37. *JD* 10:231.
38. *JD* 9:244.
39. *JD* 8:9.
40. *JD* 3:375.
41. *JD* 6:344.
42. *JD* 14:103.
43. *JD* 14:121.
44. *JD* 13:149.
45. *JD* 9:287.
46. *JD* 5:97.
47. *JD* 6:70–71.
48. *JD* 13:61.
49. *TPJS,* 48.
50. *JD* 12:256.
51. *JD* 14:75.
52. *JD* 12:161.
53. *JD* 7:1.
54. *JD* 14:38.
55. *JD* 7:283–84.
56. *JD* 10:224.
57. *JD* 8:279.
58. *JD* 19:46.
59. *JD* 14:38.
60. *JD* 8:319.
61. *JD* 8:146.
62. *JD* 14:38.

63. *JD* 6:70–71.

64. *TPJS*, 67.

65. *JD* 11:14.

66. *JD* 13:310.

67. *MS* 11:24.

68. *JD* 13:4.

69. *JD* 10:2.

70. *JD* 8:40.

71. *JD* 18:75.

72. *JD* 1:47.

73. *JD* 13:260.

74. *JD* 12:31.

75. *JD* 8:53–54.

76. *TPJS*, 137.

77. *JD* 8:83.

78. *JD* 13:176.

79. *JD* 16:77.

80. *JD* 12:326.

81. *JD* 10:224.

82. *JD* 12:257.

83. *JD* 1:335.

84. *JD* 1:335.

85. *JD* 2:93–94.

86. *JD* 3:354.

87. *JD* 3:354.

88. *JD* 12:116.

89. *JD* 8:9.

90. *MS* 10:85.

91. *JD* 10:270–71.

92. *JD* 12:32.

93. "Interview with Brigham Young," *Deseret News,* 23 May 1877, 243.

94. *MS* 24:630.

95. *JD* 9:173.

96. *JD* 11:328.

97. *JD* 10:296.

98. *JD* 8:137.

99. Elden J. Watson, *Manuscript History of Brigham Young 1801–1844* (Salt Lake City: Smith Secretarial Service, 1968), 45.

100. *JD* 8:137.

101. *JD* 11:127.

102. *JD* 6:315.

103. *JD* 8:352.

104. *JD* 15:162.

105. *JD* 3:316.

106. *JD* 14:225.

107. *JD* 10:191.

108. *TPJS*, 49.

109. *JD* 10:349.

110. *JD* 10:309.

111. *JD* 12:124.

112. *MS* 31:571.

113. *MS* 30:550.

114. *JD* 9:290.

115. *JD* 13:343.

116. *JD* 13:344.

117. Karl Popper, *Conjectures and Refutations* (New York: Harper and Row, 1958), 136.

118. *JD* 13:260.

119. *TPJS*, 51 (emphasis added).

120. *JD* 6:286.

121. *JD* 16:77.

122. *JD* 12:172.

123. *JD* 14:210 (emphasis added).

124. *JD* 9:242.

125. *JD* 12:313.

126. *JD* 9:254.

127. *Times and Seasons* (November 1839): 13.

128. *JD* 9:167.

129. *JD* 16:170.

130. *JD* 14:116.

131. *JD* 12:260.

132. *JD* 15:127.

133. Giorgio de Santillana and Hertha von Dechend, *Hamlet's Mill: An Essay on Myth and the Frame of Time* (Boston: Gambit, 1969). See, for example, his discussion of the "historical chasm that opened with the adoption of the Copernican doctrine," and the ancient understanding of the Precession of the Equinoxes, 60–69.

134. *JD* 13:305–6.

135. *JD* 3:343.

136. *JD* 9:295.

137. *MS* 29:756–57.

138. *JD* 3:204.

139. *JD* 12:240–41.

140. *HC* 3:295–96.
141. *JD* 6:93.
142. *JD* 13:153.
143. *JD* 8:185.
144. *MS* 17:673–74.
145. Watson, *Manuscript History of Brigham Young 1801–1844* , xiv.
146. *TPJS*, 9.
147. *JD* 3:119.
148. *JD* 7:337.
149. *JD* 8:9.
150. *JD* 10:3.
151. *JD* 10:266–67.
152. *JD* 11:241.
153. *JD* 13:308.
154. *JD* 15:18.
155. *JD* 17:159.
156. *TPJS*, 228.
157. *JD* 11:283.
158. *JD* 8:9.
159. *JD* 11:283.
160. *JD* 15:124.
161. *JD* 17:52.
162. *JD* 15:19.
163. *JD* 12:127.
164. *TPJS*, 218.
165. *JD* 13:4.
166. *JD* 14:16.
167. *JD* 14:220–21.
168. *TPJS*, 229.
169. *JD* 14:77.
170. *JD* 14:83.
171. *JD* 14:83 (emphasis added).
172. *JD* 1:117 (emphasis added).
173. *JD* 1:117.
174. *JD* 1:117.
175. *JD* 16:70.
176. *JD* 7:271.
177. *MS* 12:275.
178. *JD* 18:237.
179. *JD* 11:103.
180. *JD* 18:238.
181. *JD* 12:192.

182. *JD* 11:105.
183. *JD* 2:280.
184. *JD* 3:225.
185. Ernst Käsemann, *Das wandernde Gottesvolk: Eine Untersuchung zum Hebräerbrief* (Göttingen: Vandenhoeck and Ruprecht, 1957).
186. *JD* 11:102.
187. *JD* 15:4.
188. *JD* 13:148.
189. *JD* 15:3.
190. *JD* 15:2.
191. *JD* 11:324.
192. *JD* 3:278–79; 11:324; 13:148.
193. *JD* 11:300.
194. *JD* 8:181.
195. *MS* 39:119.
196. *JD* 8:183.
197. *JD* 8:143–44.
198. *JD* 16:26.
199. *JD* 11:324.
200. *TPJS*, 331.

14

More Brigham Young on Education

I have been asked to speak on the subject of Brigham Young and education. Brother Sidney Sperry and I used to talk long hours about education in the Church, both because our offices were side by side and because we agreed on everything. I have assembled statements by Brigham Young on education before this, but recently, talks by Brothers Boyd K. Packer, Arthur Henry King, Thomas Rogers, Noel Reynolds, and others have brought to the fore matters which we have never discussed and on which Brigham Young had a good deal to say. So this is "new" material.

The keynote of all Brigham Young's thinking and preaching was the wonder and glory of the gospel against the background of a lost and distracted world. Here was the race of mankind living lives of quiet desperation in a lone and dreary world which they firmly believed would eventually pass away and "leave not a rack behind." Into this world of frustrated, restless, unhappy creatures there came one who told them who they really were and bore ample credentials to the bona fides of the great revelations he

This text was originally presented as the Sperry Lecture at the Joseph Smith Auditorium of Brigham Young University, 11 March 1976.

brought them. The news was overpowering, almost too good to be true—from now on everything was going to be different: who could keep such news to himself? Certainly not Brigham Young. He shouted hallelujah all the day long and joyfully urged everyone to come and see. His whole concern was to learn all there was to know about this marvelous message and then pass it on to everyone he possibly could reach. "There was more or less of a gloom over my feelings from the earliest days of my childhood that I have in any recollection, until I heard the everlasting Gospel declared by the servants of God."[1] "The secret feeling of my heart was that I would be willing to crawl around the earth on my hands and knees, to see such a man as was Peter, Jeremiah, Moses, or any man that could tell me anything about God and heaven. But to talk with the priests was more unsatisfactory to me then than it now is to talk with lawyers."[2] Then: "When I saw Joseph Smith, he took heaven, figuratively speaking, and brought it down to earth; and he took the earth, brought it up, and opened up, in plainness and simplicity, the things of God."[3] "Under that preaching the gloom vanished, and has not since troubled me for a moment."[4] Nothing else mattered: "I gave away what I had, and I started to preach the Gospel. I was obliged to do it, for I felt as though my bones would consume within me if I did not, consequently I devoted my time to preaching."[5]

So there you have it: "Outside of the religion we have embraced, there is nothing but death, hell and the grave."[6] What an educational project lay before those who accepted the glad message! The gospel is knowledge, and its recipients had first to acquaint themselves with it as quickly and as fully as possible and then disseminate it with all possible skill and speed. "Put forth your ability to learn as fast as you can, and gather all the strength of mind and principle of faith you possibly can, and then distribute your knowledge to the people."[7] "We are here to live to spread intelligence and knowledge among the people. I am here to school my brethren, to teach my family the way of life."[8] "Remember, too, the great principle of improvement. Learn! learn! learn! Continue to learn, to study by observation and from good books!"[9]

That was the assignment: "What are we here for? To learn to enjoy more, and to increase in knowledge and in experience."[10] Eternity begins here and now: "'Education is our motto.' This will be my text. We are here that we may learn to improve."[11] The curriculum, of course, is unlimited: "We should not only learn the principles of education known to mankind, but we should reach out further than this, learning to live so that our minds will gather in information from the heavens and the earth until we can incorporate in our faith and understanding all knowledge which is useful and practicable in our present condition."[12]

This concept of education is implicit in Mormonism. Once we categorically assume a career of eternal progression, no other way lies open. For the course ahead absolutely requires sustained, progressive, ever-increasing mental power and exertion. To be alive is to be conscious, and to be conscious is to think, and to think is to think about something: "The brain craves for information as the body craves for food."[13] The gospel not only requires such application of the mind, but facilitates and guarantees it.

> There is no position a man can occupy in this world . . . wherein he can learn so much of that which is truly valuable and worthy of acceptation as that of an elder in the Church of Jesus Christ in the active discharge of his calling. The present is the day of your opportunities, to mold

your characters, to strengthen your faith, to develop your powers of mind and thought.[14]

For Brigham Young, knowledge was what Aristotle calls a good of first intent, a thing good and desirable in itself, needing no argument or excuse for its existence.[15] Goods of secondary intent are good for something else. A hammer, a watch, a pair of shoes, a ladder, a knife—each is good because it helps us get some other good thing we are after; but there are goods whose value does not depend on anything else but is intrinsic and immediate, and knowledge is one of them. Joseph Smith feasted on knowledge. He said it tasted good to him.[16] Paradoxically, things of primary intent are actually the most useful goods—in fact, the only useful ones in the long run. We can and do get along without many of the goods of secondary intent and never really miss them; as Brigham Young said many times, life without them may be inconvenient, but it is always possible. Without goods of primary intent, on the other hand, life is by no means possible: without them we wither and die. They are incorporated in our very nature:

> The things of this world add to our national comfort, and are necessary to sustain mortal life. We need these comforts to preserve our earthly existence. . . . But those things have nothing to do with the spirit, feeling, consolation, light, glory, peace, and joy that pertain to heaven and heavenly things, which are the food of the ever-living spirit within us. . . . This I know by experience. I know that the things of this world, from beginning to end, from the possession of mountains of gold down to a crust of johnnycake, makes little or no difference in the happiness of an individual.[17]

The poor man's johnnycake is no more to be prized than the rich man's gold. "Nothing is calculated to satisfy the mind of an intelligent being, only to obtain principles that will preserve him in his identity, to enable him to increase in wisdom, power, knowledge, and perfection."[18] "Truth cleaves unto truth, because it is truth; and it is to be *adored*, because it is an *attribute* of *God*, for its *excellence*, for *itself*."[19]

> Will education feed and clothe you, keep you warm on a cold day, or enable you to build a house? Not at all. Should we cry down education on this account? No. What is it for? The improvement of the mind; to instruct us in all arts and sciences, in the history of the world, in the laws of nations; to enable us to understand the laws and principles of life, and how to be useful while we live.[20]

Brigham Young often repeated the maxim "'Mormonism' embraces all truth that is revealed and that is unrevealed, whether religious, political, scientific, or philosophical."[21] But we cannot cross the bounds of knowledge into new territory until we've traversed the expanse of ground that lies between us. "We, as a people, have in the future to excel the nations of the earth in religion, science, and philosophy."[22]

But to surpass them we must first catch up with them! In short: "This is the belief and doctrine of the Latter-day Saints. Learn everything that the children of men know, and be prepared for the most refined society upon the face of the earth."[23]

But Brigham Young is known before all else as a solid practical, commonsense man, a pragmatic genius. And this leads us to the common fallacy of classing one kind of activity as practical by nature and the other as impractical by nature. Brigham Young has been accused of inconsistency in insisting that knowledge should be sought for its own sake on one hand but primarily for its practical application on the other. Inconsistent he is not. He knows that the person who does not regard the most practical task primarily as a mental exercise is going to botch it; he's going to be a waster, and a bungler, and not do it properly. He says, "You will almost invariably find that people who are industrious in the common pursuits of life, are industrious in improving their minds as far as they have opportunity."[24] Intelligence is not a monopoly of a particular kind of work, or a particular class or age or stage of advancement. A smart baby is far more edifying company than a stupid dean. I've spent many hours in the company of both. Consider this quotation:

> And while you delight in raising flowers, &c., do not neglect to learn how to take care of the cream, and how to make of it good wholesome butter, and of the milk good healthy nutritious cheese; neither forget your sewing, spinning, and weaving; and I would not have them neglect to learn music and would encourage them to read history and the Scriptures, to take up a newspaper, geography, and other publications, and make themselves acquainted with the manners and customs of distant kingdoms and nations, with their laws, religion, geographical location on the face of the world, their climate, natural productions, the extent of their commerce, and the nature of their political organization; in fine, let our boys and girls be thoroughly instructed in every useful branch of physical and mental education. Let this education begin early.[25]

Now in a passage like that, try to separate the book learning from the other. It can't be done. For Brigham Young it is all practical, and it is all a wonderful adventure of the mind.

On "Sunday, August 12th, President Brigham Young addressed the people from the stand. He observed that our business was with the things immediately before us, and not with the glories of the eternal worlds."[26] Again he says, "The Kingdom we are talking about, preaching about and trying to build up is the Kingdom of God on the earth, not in the starry heavens."[27]

> My mission to the people is to teach them with regard to their every-day lives. I presume there are many here who have heard me say, years and years ago, that I cared very little about what will take place after the millennium. . . . My desire is to teach the people what they should do *now,* and let the millennium take care of itself. To teach them to serve God and to build up His Kingdom is my mission.[28]

For Brigham Young what was practical was the task at hand, the thing that had to be done right now, whether it was praying, bathing, dancing, sleeping, or shoeing a horse—all were equally practical, including dancing, but they are practical because each one at the proper time helps us on the way to our objective—always the same objective for all of them. There are indeed two categories of goods, but the distinction is *not* between the practical and the impractical; they are both practical and both spiritual; there is no difference in spiritual and temporal labors—all are one.[29]

Brigham is teaching the Saints how to climb Jacob's ladder—how to do it in a sensible, practical way, grasping firmly the next rung above, and not grabbing wildly for something up near the top; and thus proceeding carefully and surely step by step, line upon line, and precept upon precept. This does not mean, as many suppose, that he is telling them to forget the ultimate goal, the Spirit, the Millennium, or the eternities, and come down to earth and devote themselves to the commonsense everyday activities of life. No—that is an entirely different ladder. Brother

Packer's figure of the ladder is a very instructive one: how we go about climbing the ladder is important, but even more important is *which* ladder we choose to climb.[30] Both ladders, the one to heaven and the one to the executive suite, are to be climbed in the same way. The rules of success are the same in business, the arts, science, crime, and the military—but the ladders are by no means the same. Brigham Young never allowed the Saints to forget which ladder they were climbing.

> This is the lesson we should study. The powers of our minds and bodies should be governed and controlled in that way that will secure to us an eternal increase. While the inhabitants of the earth are bestowing all their ability, both mental and physical, upon perishable objects, those who profess to be Latter-day Saints, who have the privilege of receiving and understanding the principles of the holy Gospel, are in duty bound to study and find out, and put in practice in their lives, those principles that are calculated to endure, and that tend to a continual increase in this, and in the world to come.[31]

"And thus we teach the people how to live. This is our business. If you do not learn to live here, how can you live hereafter? If you do not understand the things of this life, how can you understand the things pertaining to the life to come?"[32]

All business must be undertaken with an eye to the eternities, but how rarely do we take that view! I remember how disturbed my mother was when a visiting General Authority at our house (we lived in the mission field and were often visited by them) announced at the dinner table that it was more important for a girl to learn how to make a pot of soup than to recite Shakespeare. As he saw it, the one thing was practical and the other was not, and no girl could do both. Actually both belong to the building of the

kingdom and need not be mutually exclusive: the girl has
learned to make soup by the time she is ten years old, and if
that is all she does for the rest of her life, she doesn't even
have a ladder. If people insisted on thinking in such terms,
however—if it must be a matter of soup or Shakespeare—
for Brigham it was the soup that would have to go.

> Make good houses [soup]; learn how to build;
> become good mechanics and business men, that you may
> know how to build a house, a barn, or a storehouse, how
> to make a farm, and how to raise stock, and take every
> care of it. . . . On the other hand, the neighbourhood or
> community that adorns its city, farms, gardens, and
> supremely loves and sets its affections upon these things,
> had better never have seen or had anything to enjoy.[33]

If it is a choice between Mary's work and Martha's,
there can be no doubt what the Lord recommends (Luke
10:38–42). Again and again statements of Brigham Young
that seem to be as solid and earthy as a handbook on gar-
dening end up pointing us to the stars and the eternities:

> We cannot marvel at a man's talking about paper
> rags in a religious meeting, and saying that it is the word
> of the Lord or at least the word of wisdom that we should
> save our rags. . . . When the Lord has gathered together a
> people to be a chosen people to him, he has always begun
> to educate them by instructing them in the little things
> pertaining to life.[34]

If paper rags were a spiritual quantity, Shakespeare was
no less a practical one, and Macbeth and Hamlet saw the
Saints through more than one hard winter in the valleys.
"Instead of trying to find out how God is made, or how
angels are made, I wish you would try to learn how to sustain yourselves in your present existence, and at the same
time learn the things of God—the things that await you,

that you may begin to prepare to dwell to all eternity."[35] "Then what is this earth in its present condition? Nothing but a place in which we may learn the first lesson towards exaltation, and that is obedience to the Gospel of the Son of God."[36] "[The things of the earth] are made for the comfort of the creature, and not for his adoration [i.e., they are of second, never of first intent]. They are made to sustain and preserve the body while procuring the knowledge and wisdom that pertain to God and his kingdom, in order that we may preserve ourselves, and live for ever in his presence."[37]

Practical knowledge is any knowledge that is put to use, as all knowledge should be. A favorite teaching of Brigham Young was that we should use everything we have: money is meant to be spent, not stored in a vault;[38] food is meant to be distributed and eaten, not hoarded for speculation. Remember what happened to the manna that some far-seeing Israelites stored up as a business investment—it promptly became foul and stinking (Exodus 16.19–20). Mere accumulation of anything is the act of the miser, the most miserable of men, who has so little faith in God that he must ever build up walls of security around himself. "Keep [your] riches," cries Brother Brigham, "and with them I promise you leanness of soul, darkness of mind, narrow and contracted hearts."[39] All knowledge must be put to use if only to beget more knowledge. Why? To fill a need— constant, urgent, and vital. Remember, "the brain craves for information as the body craves for food,"[40] and if true knowledge is withheld from it, it will manufacture all manner of false doctrine; without a steady diet of learning the person sickens and withers, being false to his own nature. What we need is *constant* nourishment for both body and spirit, not terminal degrees.

But we treat knowledge today exactly as we do precious

metals and negotiable papers which, as Brigham Young often reminds us, are in themselves not only worthless but most pernicious in their effect. We exchange knowledge for tokens—marks on paper, punched holes in cards, impressions on tape, and then we lock them up in a safe like a Swiss bank, and make a law that no one may even see our transcript without special permission! The bank then gives us a token, a doctor's degree, which we wear publicly at all times. We never let our fellowmen forget for a moment that we are sitting on all that knowledge, but make careful provision that they shall never take too close a look at it or ask us to draw upon it at short notice—that simply is not done.

This sort of thing is, of course, death to knowledge. For intelligence, the glory of God, is a moral quality. It is defined by the psychologists as "problem-solving ability." And how do you solve any problem? The first step for me is to discover what I do *not* know about it—I must search out the weak and defective spots in my knowledge, for that ignorance is what makes the problem. The next step is to find out the next things in order that I do *not* know but should; and thus I move forward in my quest, progressively laying bare dark new areas of ignorance, looking for the blank spaces on the map, the areas of which I know nothing, or where I have been deceived, where my vanity or enthusiasm have led me astray. It is a humiliating experience, and the checks, corrections, revisions, deletions, weary retracing, and new beginnings never end. There is no terminal degree. Only the truly humble can take it; in fact, it is the very sort of thing that our institutional bookkeeping, poker-chip credits, and computed degrees are designed to avoid. The first words I ever heard spoken in a class at BYU (the only class I ever took here) was the opening statement of a professor at the old Aspen Grove summer school, way

back in 1927. He had just come from the coast with his
brand new doctor's degree, and he introduced himself to
the class by reporting how the chairman of the committee a
few days before had shaken his hand at the conclusion of
his oral exams with the ringing congratulation: "Now you
will never have to take another examination as long as you
live!" And he firmly believed it! Degrees, honors, appointments, awards, emoluments, offices—all are forlorn attempts to give a sense of enduring value to what Brigham
Young calls the "grovelling things of earth," which have
nothing in common with the gospel.[41]

> That Spirit, with the Gospel of Christ, interrupts the
> whole world in their common career, in every capacity of
> life. That Spirit does not chime in and harmonize with
> any earthly kingdom or government, either in their polit-
> ical or religious institutions; but it seems to put a check
> upon every thing, to throw into disorder the best laid
> plans of the wise and far-seeing among men; in short, it
> turns the whole current of earthly calculations back upon
> the world, and deluges it in the dark waters of confu-
> sion.[42]

"We expect to be a stumbling block to the whole world,
and a rock of offence to them."[43] "And to the natural man we
are taking an unwise, an unnatural course, wherein our religion is obnoxious to the Christian world. . . . They can see
nothing more than natural things; they do not understand
the ways of God; they are unacquainted with His doings,
with His kingdom, and with the principles of eternity."[44]
Having made their choice, the Latter-day Saints should forget the ways of the world:

> But to see a people who say, "We are the teachers of
> life and salvation," and yet are anxious to follow the
> nasty, pernicious fashions of the day, I say it is too insipid
> to talk or think about. It is beneath the character of the

Latter-day Saints that they should have no more independence of mind or feeling than to follow after the grovelling customs and fashions of a poor, miserable, wicked
world.[45]

So there are at least two ladders, and you cannot climb
them both. We have been hypnotized into thinking that
there is only one, the conventional ladder of success, but for
Brigham that is out:

> No one supposes for one moment that in heaven the
> angels are speculating, that they are building railroads
> and factories, taking advantage one of another, gathering
> up the substance there is in heaven to aggrandize them-
> selves, and that they live on the same principles that we
> are in the habit of doing. No Christian, no sectarian
> Christian, in the world believes this; they believe that the
> inhabitants of heaven live as a family, that their faith,
> interests and pursuits have one end in view—the glory of
> God and their own salvation, that they may receive more
> and more. . . . We all believe this, and suppose we go to
> work and imitate them as far as we can.[46]

"Instead of reflecting upon and searching for hidden
things of the greatest value to them, they [the Latter-day
Saints] rather wish to learn how to secure their way through
this world as easily and as comfortably as possible. The
reflections [upon] what they are here for, who produced
them, and where they are from, far too seldom enter their
minds."[47] Such is the ladder the Saints are inclined to
choose, and it is the wrong one: "We are engaged in a
higher-toned branch of business than any merchants or railroad men, or any institution of an earthly nature."[48] "He
[Abraham] obtained the promise that he should be the
father of lives. In comparison with this, what did Abraham
care about machinery, railroads, and other great mechanical
productions?"[49] We remember that "railroads and telegraph

lines and cables . . . will increase our facilities and accelerate the progress of the work of the Lord."[50] We also remember that they are only temporary and are not justified on any other grounds. To his son John W. Young, Brigham wrote, "I will . . . not tear and wear my strength and life to shreds promoting any private enterprise."[51] "I have never walked across the streets to make a trade," he said. "I do not care anything [much] about such things."[52] This attitude set him off sharply from his competitors in the gilded age. He comments on this in a letter in 1870 to his son on a mission in Switzerland:

> We are constantly receiving communications from the elders laboring in the States, but how different is their testimony with regard to the work of God there. There is a coldness in the minds of the people, a total indifference to the gospel and its glorious truths and the whole sum of their inquiries [is] how and where we can make the most money. Of course there are a few exceptions, but what a condition of things does this indicate! Every species of wickedness is on the increase. . . . The people are fast ripening for destruction. And why is this? The gospel door was opened on this land, . . . but these ordinances have been held in derision, the truth has been rejected, prophets and apostles have been slain for the testimony of Jesus, and now the people have become hardened in iniquity and are led captive to the will of that evil power they prefer to serve.[53]

A good summary of Brigham's attitude toward what we call education for success is given in one of his many statements on the study of the law, i.e., specialization:

> It is hard for a man to study law without forsaking the spirit of the Gospel. This proves that there is a lack of sound knowledge in the individual who permits himself to be thus led away. There are many among the inhabitants of the earth who . . . can only look upon one thing

at a time [not for the moment but during an extended period of interest and activity]; and they forsake the contemplation of everything else for the one idea which occupies the mind [this is the whole secret of success set forth in the how-to-get-rich books!]. There are some of our Elders who will argue themselves into false doctrine by giving an undue preference to one scripture and passing over others equally as important. [This is what President J. F. Smith called "Religious Hobbyism."] This same lack of comprehensiveness of mind is also very noticeable at times with some men who happen to accumulate property, and it leads them to forsake the Spirit of the Gospel. Does it not prove that there is a contractedness of mind in those who do so, which should not be? . . . How contracted in mind and short-sighted we must be to permit the perishable things of this world to swerve us in the least degree from our fidelity to the truth. It shows that we lack knowledge which we should possess.[54]

He puts his finger on the spot as he comments on the unbridgeable gulf that lies between the search for knowledge and the search for success.

How difficult it is for our Elders to go forth and contend with the learning of the age. . . . When a false theory has to be maintained, . . . it requires study, and learning, and cunning sophistry to . . . give it the semblance of truth, and make it plausible and congenial to the feelings of the people [i.e., to sell it]. . . . A child can tell you the truth, in child-like language, while falsehood . . . requires a scholastic education to make falsehood pass for truth. . . . Men are educated to promulgate and sustain false theories to make money. . . . But if the profession of a lawyer is chosen, . . . he needs to be educated in all the learning of the age to be successful—. . . to make things appear what they really are not.[55]

Let us recall that "making things appear what they really are not" is Plato's definition of Rhetoric: making false appear true and true appear false by the skillful use of words.[56] With the recognition of the profession of Rhetoric of Public Relations as a legitimate activity, any civilization proclaims its moral bankruptcy.

It was natural that the Latter-day Saints should gravitate toward "education for success." Brother Brigham knew his people only too well. For him the purpose of education was to take the measure of the world, but for the poor Saints who had lived their lives among the ignorant and oppressed, its great promise was to find a place in the world. Being human, the Mormons followed the course of least resistance and defined success like everyone else as getting what you want, which in its ultimate terms means power and gain with fame and popularity as a bonus—all of which are exactly the things which God has categorically forbidden us to seek. The Saints were not yet ready for the higher school.

Brigham Young knew the material he had to work with: "We gather a few scientific and learned men, but the great majority are the poor and the ignorant."[57] "Very few of the learned or of those who are high and lifted up in the estimation of the people receive the Gospel."[58]

> In the due time of the Lord, the Saints and the world will be privileged with the revelations that are due to them. They now have many more than they are worthy of, for they do not observe them. . . . If guilt before my God and my brethren rests upon me in the least, it is in this one thing—that I have revealed too much concerning God and his kingdom, and the designs of our Father in heaven. If my skirts are stained in the least with wrong, it is because I have been too free in telling what God is, how he lives, the nature of his providences and designs in creating the world.[59]

Having been given great knowledge, the Saints were in

constant danger of underestimating their own ignorance. It was necessary to remind them again and again that if God's gifts are treated lightly they will be lightly withdrawn. The Mormons have constantly slipped into the dangerous complacency of the student who feels superior because he has the only answerbook in the class. Had they been given too much light? When would they be ready for more?

A year before his death, the Prophet Joseph wrote:

> I could explain a hundred fold more than I ever have of the glories of the kingdoms manifested to me in the vision, were I permitted, and were the people prepared to receive them. The Lord deals with this people as a tender parent with a child, communicating light and intelligence and the knowledge of his ways as they can bear it. The inhabitants of the earth are asleep; they know not the day of their visitation.[60]

And Wilford Woodruff recalled: "His mind was opened by the visions of the Almighty, and the Lord taught him many things by vision and revelation that were never taught publicly in his days; for the people could not bear the flood of intelligence which God poured into his mind."[61]

And Brigham himself: "This people have not received, improved, grown, and enlarged in their capacities as fast as they should have done."[62] "We may look upon ourselves with shamefacedness because of the smallness of our attainments in the midst of so many great advantages."[63] "It is mortifying that the children of this world should know more about these things than the children of light. . . . The lack of knowledge manifested by us as a people is disgraceful."[64] The trouble was that the Latter-day Saints were insistent on combining Zion and Babylon in a new concept of success. This combination as we have frequently seen is utterly impossible. To try to combine the ways of the world and the law of the gospel can only lead to disaster, as Brigham Young often noted:

> The man or woman who enjoys the spirit of our religion has no trials; but the man or woman who tries to live according to the Gospel of the Son of God, and at the same time clings to the spirit of the world, has trials and sorrows acute and keen, and that, too, continually. This is the deciding point, the dividing line. They who love and serve God with all their hearts rejoice evermore, pray without ceasing, and in everything give thanks; but they who try to serve God and still cling to the spirit of the world, have got on two yokes—the yoke of Jesus and the yoke of the devil, and they will have plenty to do. They will have a warfare inside and outside, and the labor will be very galling, for they are directly in opposition one to the other.[65]

So we are forced, whether we like it or not, to take up our position on one side of the line or the other. The conflict between the two projects is summed up by Brigham Young in a powerful passage:

> What do you love truth for? . . . Because you think it will make you a ruler, or a Lord? If you conceive that you will attain to power upon such a motive, you are much mistaken. It is a trick of the unseen power, that is abroad amongst the inhabitants of the earth, that leads them astray, binds their minds, and subverts their understanding. Suppose that our Father in heaven, [or] our elder brother, the risen Redeemer, the Saviour of the world, or any of the Gods of eternity should act upon this principle, to love truth, knowledge, and wisdom, because they are all powerful [i.e., for what they could get out of them], . . . they would cease to be Gods; . . . the extension of their kingdom would cease, and their God-head come to an end.[66]

Why should concern for the economy be especially

pernicious to the cause of education? Aristotle's famous formula gives us the answer, *ou to zein alla to eu zein:* our object is not to stay alive but to live as we should. Our real interests and concerns begin where the economy leaves off. Dogs, mice, cockroaches, elephants, and oysters have through the long ages managed to solve the problem of staying alive and reproducing, the problem of survival. So far God has always provided. He has also promised to provide for us as for the sparrows. The question of how much will I get paid is the last question any student should ask, so with us at the BYU it is invariably the first. In the words of Samuel the Lamanite, "Ye do always remember your riches" (Helaman 13:22)—always the economy, the economy, all the day long. Brigham Young with his Puritan upbringing knew as much about the work ethic as anybody, and he despised it. Again he insisted it's the objective that's contemptible. Commendable zeal should not be wasted on the wrong ladder. We admire the billionaire who takes his lunch to work in a paper bag. He is seeking to project the image of the true work ethic, while all his life's goals belie it. The real work ethic is dedicated to a life of austerity and plain living and high thinking precisely because its goal is not to accumulate substance. "Work less, wear less, eat less, and we shall be a great deal wiser, healthier, and wealthier people than by taking the course we now do. . . . Our artificial wants, and not our real wants, and the following of senseless customs subject our sisters to an excess of labor."[67] "But you find the mechanics that can go to with an old three-cornered file, a jack-knife, a spike-gimlet, and an inch augur, and build a waggon in a workmanlike manner, and you would say that he is a superior workman."[68]

This is the type of economy and resourcefulness that Brigham admires, not that aimed at the accumulation of a lot of stuff to have power over others. The work ethic is only a method. The objective is the important thing. Which ladder are you climbing? "After suitable rest and relaxation there is not a day, hour or minute that we should spend in idleness, but every minute of every day of our lives we should strive to improve our minds and to increase in the faith of the holy Gospel."[69]

This is the typical Brigham Young twist: what seems to begin as the typical routine admonition of the millionaire on "the secrets of success" turns out to be a call to the improvement of the mind. "If we all labor a few hours a day, we could then spend the remainder of our time in rest and the improvement of our minds."[70] That is the real work we are called to do and the real wealth we are to accumulate individually. "The laboring man, the ingenious, industrious and prudent man, the man who lays himself out to advance the human family in every saving principle for happiness, for beauty and excellency, for wisdom, power, greatness and glory is the true benefactor of his race; . . . he is a civilized man."[71]

A measure of the avoidance of real work in our day is the universal surrender to kitsch. What is kitsch? It is a more established international term for what we also call corn and camp. Kitsch is the lowest common denominator in art and style, what is supposed to have the widest popular appeal and therefore the widest market. The ultimate in kitsch is the "commercial." Applied to the gospel, kitsch puts everything on the telestial level, easy of access to all, no effort required. But kitsch runs counter to everything the gospel stands for, for it seeks to escape the impact of reality by limiting our vision to safe and familiar objects. Every close view of eternity has a terrifying effect on mortals, who must always be reassured by visiting angels whose presence makes them "sore afraid." To the extent to which the gospel influences a creative artist, something of this culture-shock carries over. This means, paradoxically, that there is something to be said for kitsch where the gospel is concerned.

In the study of early Christian and Jewish art, it is notable that the nearer one gets to the pure primitive community of Saints, the clumsier and less beguiling their art becomes. At the same time, however, it becomes ever more symbolic. It is as if they knew perfectly well that the fourth dimension that gives the gospel its power and its glory simply cannot be captured in any two- or three-dimensional medium. Any attempt to depict celestial glory in any of the limited media at the artist's disposal is doomed to be a dismal failure. Religious art and music reached their height in the Baroque, and even then all is painfully artificial, contrived, forced, theatrical, operatic—*Theatrum Dei* was Bernini's expression to describe his own work. For the real gospel that will never do. It is better not to try to depict the glories of the eternities than to fall flat on one's face and make them ridiculous. The Egyptians perhaps had the answer. They made no attempt at realism or impressionism but presented a carefully thought-out arrangement of symbols, mere abstractions, but symbols so intimate and familiar to the beholder that the sight of any of them had a direct impact on his mind and his emotions. The greatness of a presentation would have to be all in the beholder's eye. The avowed purpose of kitsch is to settle for the safe and commonplace—music, art, science, literature, religion, all-for-family fare, G rated: the kiddies must enjoy it as much as you do.

It is Joseph Smith who puts his finger on the spot when he says, "Our spirits, our conferences, our councils, our meetings, our private as well as public conversations [have been] too low, too mean, too vulgar, too condescending for the dignified characters of the called and chosen of God."[72] *Condescending* is what kitsch is. Webster defines the verb as "to come down; descend; accommodate one's self to an inferior." Dale Carnegie's maxim, "If the customer says 'ain't,' you say 'ain't,'" is not an index of humility or a common humanity but merely a trick to get money from people. Kitsch is out for the general market and deliberately chooses to appeal through the commonplace, ordinary, conventional, things that disturb nobody. In art it is realistic, obvious, shallow, sentimental, ordinary, insipid, requiring the least possible amount of effort to produce a predictable reaction.

Brigham Young, on the other hand, insisted that the Saints should stretch their minds and work hard at cultivating taste, never settling for kitsch. "Let us . . . show to the world that we have talent and taste, and prove to the heavens that our minds are set on beauty and true excellence, so that we can become worthy to enjoy the society of angels."[73]

> We enjoy because we have sensibility. Promote this sensibility, seek to get more and more knowledge, more wisdom, and more understanding. . . . This will give us greater sensibility, and we shall know how to enjoy, and how to endure. I say, if you want to enjoy exquisitely, become a Latter-day Saint, and then live the doctrine of Jesus Christ.[74]

"The greatest and most important labour we have to perform is to cultivate ourselves."[75] "Our senses, if properly educated, are channels of endless felicity to us, but we can devote them to evil or to good."[76]

It is an Article of Faith (No. 13) with the Latter-day Saints that the world has good things to offer and that the Mormons possess no monopoly of taste.

If there is anything that is great and good and wise among men, it cometh from God. If there are men who possess great ability as statesmen, or as philosophers, or who possess remarkable scientific knowledge and skill, the credit thereof belongs to God, for He dispenses it to His children whether they believe in Him or not, or whether they sin against Him or not; it makes no difference.[77]

This is the belief and doctrine of the Latter-day Saints: Learn everything that the children of men know, and be prepared for the most refined society upon the face of the earth, then improve upon this until we are prepared and permitted to enter the society of the blessed—the holy angels that dwell in the presence of God.[78]

What could be more foolish than to reject such gifts because they are found outside the Church? Just as the King James Version of the Bible is worthy of our reverent attention until the day when we can excel it, so it is no disgrace that the Church has not produced a Bach, Michelangelo, or Shakespeare—the whole world has hardly produced a handful of such men in a thousand years. We should receive their gifts with gratefulness before we presume to supplant them with our own poor talents.

Many think that all which was taught them by their fathers and mothers, school teachers and priests, ought to be removed, laid aside, dispensed with, and that they should begin anew to learn every principle of civilization. This is a great mistake. . . . Some imagine that they must begin and unlearn the whole of their former education, but I say, cling to all the good that you have learned, and discard the bad.[79]

Accordingly, no Latter-day Saint can be justified in setting up standards of taste until he has had the widest possible experience. Brigham comments on the well-known phenomenon of the young Latter-day Saint who had no inkling of how great the gospel is and how much it offers until he goes out in the world and makes extensive comparisons:

> Our children do not know the greatness of their blessing and privileges. . . . They do not know that they possess the light of the Holy Spirit until they go out into the world and learn the great contrast. . . . They hear their fathers pray, and they hear the Apostles and Prophets preach, but they cannot know that "Mormonism" is true for themselves until they have had the privilege of being placed in circumstances to exercise faith for themselves, and to pray to God for themselves for testimony and knowledge.[80]

It was this absorption in the larger scene that drew Brigham toward the stage as a vehicle of culture, though his Puritan ancestors would have been horrified at the thought.

> The Lord knows all things; man should know all things pertaining to this life, and to obtain this knowledge it is right that he should use every feasible means; and I do not hesitate to say that the stage can, in a great degree, be made to subserve this end. . . . Can we not even make the stage of a theatre the platform upon which to exhibit truth in all its simple beauty?[81]

But this was no mere holding up of the mirror to society as the stage depicted it. The great geniuses of art and literature are timeless; but to heed the voice of fashion is another matter entirely. He wanted the Saints to create what he called a "style of our own."[82]

> To me a desire to follow the ever-varying fashions of the world manifests a great weakness of mind in either gentleman or lady. We are too apt to follow the foolish fashions of the world; and if means were plentiful, I do not think that there are many families among the Latter-day

Saints but what would be up to the highest and latest fashions of the day.[83]

If I do not say much about such customs and fashions, I shall probably skip over some naughty words. In my feelings they are positively ridiculous, they are so useless and unbecoming. . . . I take the liberty of saying that these fashions are displeasing in the sight of truth, mercy and justice.[84]

Nothing could be more retrograde to this philosophy than the present-day practice of combining the splendor of the gospel with the lowest fashionable idiom of the day, the kitsch of the Broadway stage, as a means of selling inferior compositions in the Church market. The facile, sentimental Broadway melody tolerable in its place is set to equally mawkish words and exalted to the realm of high art simply by assigning it the subject of the First Vision or the Temple. This is definitely hitting below the belt. It is like trying to raise the standard and status of a school simply by giving it the cheap and easy title of "the Lord's University." Indeed, when that expression was first used about 1950, some of the General Authorities found it foolish and offensive—clearly a case of claiming the prize before one has earned it. When Laman and Lemuel affected superior virtue by pointing out that they and their friends were the Chosen People, Nephi rebuked them sharply: "Behold, the Lord esteemeth all flesh in one; he that is righteous is favored of God" (1 Nephi 17:35). Wherever the honest in heart seek knowledge that is the Lord's school.

The very essence of taste is that it is not to be prescribed by any authority. It is one of those things in which every individual is required to exercise his own judgment. "We are not disposed," said Joseph Smith, "had we the power, to deprive anyone of exercising that free independence of mind which heaven has so graciously bestowed upon the human family as one of its choicest gifts."[85] Brigham Young spoke often on this theme: "Ladies and gentlemen, I exhort you to think for yourselves, and read your Bibles for yourselves, get the Holy Spirit for yourselves, and pray for yourselves."[86] "The catalogue of man's discipline," says Brigham Young, the sound psychologist, "he must compile himself: he cannot be guided by any rule that others may lay down, but is placed under the necessity of tracing it himself through every avenue of his life. He is obliged to catechise and train himself."[87]

"Pay no attention to what others do, it is no matter what they do, or how they dress."[88] Brigham deplored the idea of following fashion for fashion's sake no matter who said it: "I am not a stereotyped Latter-day Saint," he cried; "away with stereotyped Mormons!"[89]

Yet he knew that there is no stronger temptation at all levels of authority than to prescribe taste—which is under no circumstances a leader's prerogative:

> It is no more natural for your lungs to expand and contract in breathing than it is for you to wish others to be like yourselves. . . . All of these classes act according to their faith and traditions, and each one of them says, "If you are not as I am, you are not right." This is just as natural as it is to breathe vital air. I wish this trait in the Saints to be done away. I want the Elders of Israel to learn to take people as they are.[90]

If decisions must be made in such matters he recommends the broadest base of communication:

> When it becomes our duty to talk, we ought to be willing to talk. If we never exhibit the knowledge within us, the people will not know really whether we have any. Interchanging our ideas and exhibiting that which we believe and understand affords an opportunity for

detecting and correcting errors and increasing our stock of valuable information. I have frequently thought that I should be very happy if I could hear the Elders of Israel speak their feelings and impart their knowledge pertaining to their fellow-beings, to earthly things, to heavenly things, to godliness, and God.[91]

Thus we are to advocate our ideas, but never force them on others:

No person has a right to say to another, "Why do you eat wheat bread, corn bread, or no bread at all? why do you eat potatoes, or why do you not eat them? why do you walk, or why do you sit down? why do you read this or that book? or why do you go to the right or the left?" ... If the Elders of Israel could understand this a little better, we would like it, for the simple reason that if they had power given them now they manifest the same weaknesses in the exercise thereof as any other people.[92]

If we do not prescribe to others in matters of taste, neither may we depend on them to prescribe for us: "Now those men, or those women, who know no more about the power of God, and the influences of the Holy Spirit, than to be led entirely by another person, suspending their own understanding, and pinning their faith upon another's sleeve, will never be capable of entering into the celestial glory."[93] Granted "there never was and never will be a people in heaven nor on earth, in time nor in eternity, that can be considered truly and entirely independent of counsel and direction."[94] Still the law of agency requires them only to follow the counsel they ask for and accept: "If they do not believe in my advice, teachings, and counsel, they are at perfect liberty to disbelieve them, and I will not find one word of fault with them for so doing."[95] "We have history enough to prove that when [men] have the power their motto is, 'You shall.' But there is no such thing in the economy of heaven."[96]

Of course we run the risk of being confronted by all manner of false doctrine and ideas, if left thus to ourselves, but that is part of the plan. Brigham Young's son Willard very shrewdly observed in a letter to his father in 1876 that his friends who had left the Church did not do so because of "instructions they got that misled them, so much as the *want* of proper instructions."[97] The trouble was not that they had heard too much but that they did not hear enough.

In short, Brigham's teaching "breathes that spirit of liberty in the pursuit of knowledge characteristic of the work of God in the last days."[98] Everyone was free to go his own way: "'To mind your own business' incorporates the whole duty of man."[99]

Let me conclude at last with a sentimental journey which I took the other night. It began when I found in my overstuffed mailbox (alas for the forests of America!) an impressive flyer from the BYU Travel Study—an elegantly inscribed Hebrew version of Orson Hyde's prayer dedicating the Holy Land in 1841, along with an invitation "to be instructed more perfectly . . . of things both in heaven and earth." "What better way to be instructed," said the flyer, "than by a scholar from the Church Education System while standing on the Mount of Olives where Orson Hyde's dedicatory prayer was offered." With this the customer was provided with a list of almost twenty experts to chose from; the question arises: which of these could best read and interpret the Hebrew prayer? Can *all* of them? Can *any* of them? I leave it to you to discover.

Intrigued by this, I went over to the Travel Study office for more information, and as I left was attracted by an impressively drawn placard announcing a series of courses in a certain department in which I could choose to take "Primitive Pottery," "NRA Hunter Safety," or "Interim classes." Having been long at the BYU, I was neither shocked nor surprised by this sort of thing, which I have seen a thousand times—the impressive facade with nothing behind it is the rule, not the exception, with us. I was reminded of the announcers over KBYU speaking with oh-so-cultured accents as they elaborately mispronounce all the proper names they are reading off from the record covers. As I left the place I picked up another brochure inviting the public to enter into a great "Adventure into Learning"—this surely is the real thing: I opened the brochure and was challenged to extend my questioning mind through courses in Slimnastics, Cake Decorating, Auto Maintenance, and A More Feminine You. From there I passed to the bookstore and was reminded both of what Brother King has recently said about it (a vulgar place and a monopoly), and of the fact that for upwards of one hundred years Provo has been a university town without a single bookstore. What on earth could the students have been doing all the time? To find out, listen to their conversation among themselves, as I have for the past thirty years: one thing you would never guess from such conversation is that you are at an institution of learning. The subjects are (1) jobs and money, (2) cars, and (3) social activity—religious and romantic. Quite recently Brother Thomas Rogers, speaking from a higher and more official level of observation, has announced the same verdict: BYU students simply are *not* interested in things of the mind. From the bookstore by a natural transition I passed to the library, where without the new addition we already have shelf-space for over a million volumes; but here any thought of serious research is out of the question, because the officials, to save themselves time and trouble and make room for new acquisitions, simply took all bound periodicals earlier than the year 1970 and locked them up in a warehouse. Now the heart of any program of serious study in almost any field is the periodical literature of the past century—but can you make a librarian see that? Never mind—the books will not be missed: that became apparent to me as I left the library late at night and walked home through an empty and deserted campus, as I have done thousands of times in the past—the lights do *not* burn late on Temple Hill; they never have.

Descending the steps that take me home, I remembered President Harris and his interest in making a lovely natural preserve on the south side of campus: now what we have is the carefully manicured, groomed, trimmed, regimented landscaping where nothing is allowed to grow in its wild or natural state. Nature must observe our dress standards—the look comes first, nothing else really matters. I noticed as I always do the smoke pouring from the power plant and asked myself again: What is it we produce that is worth the price of all that pollution? Certainly not knowledge. I was reminded that most of our smartest students are now working with computers: they are not discovering or absorbing knowledge, but simply processing it, neither producers or consumers of the precious stuff, but middlemen, dutifully attendant on machines. And if knowledge, then not character; Woodrow Wilson said that character is a by-product, the by-product of hard work well done.

So I have come full circle. My first day in Provo, thirty years ago, President Joseph Fielding Smith was on the campus and made a remark to Leroy Robertson that I have never forgotten: "We are rapidly coming to be known as a mediocre people." Why must this be? In a letter written just

one hundred years ago, Brigham Young clearly states his
purpose in founding the BYU at Provo:

> We have enough and to spare, at present in these
> mountains, of schools where young infidels are made
> because the teachers are so tender-footed that they dare
> not mention the principles of the gospel to their pupils,
> but have no hesitancy in introducing into the classroom
> the theories of Huxley, of Darwin, or of Miall and the
> false political economy which contends against co-oper-
> ation and the United Order. This course I am resolutely
> and uncompromisingly opposed to, and I hope to see the
> day when the doctrines of the gospel will be taught in all
> our schools, when the revelation of the Lord will be our
> texts, and our books will be written and manufactured by
> ourselves and in our own midst. As a beginning in this
> direction I have endowed the Brigham Young Academy
> at Provo and [am] now seeking to do the same thing in
> this city.[100]

The purpose of the BYU, then, is to challenge the reign-
ing philosophies of Darwinism and what today is commonly called Social-Darwinism (see Alma 30:17)—not to
forbid their teaching but to present the gospel alternatives
to it. Instead of which we still embrace both with uncriti-
cally open arms, and as a result remain to this day "fixed
with a very limited amount of knowledge, and, like a door
upon its hinges, move to and fro from one year to another
without any visible advancement or improvement. . . . Man
is made in the image of God, but what do we know of him
or of ourselves, when we suffer ourselves to love and worship the god of this world—riches?"[101]

I pray that the Lord may enlighten all our minds with a
fuller understanding of his purposes.

Notes

1. *JD* 8:129.
2. *JD* 8:228.
3. *JD* 5:332.
4. *JD* 8:129.
5. *JD* 16:69.
6. *JD* 10:352.
7. *JD* 8:146.
8. *JD* 8:282.
9. *JD* 19:64.
10. *JD* 14:228.
11. *JD* 12:238.
12. *JD* 12:172.
13. Nigel Calder, *The Mind of Man* (London: British Broadcasting Corp., 1970), 33.
14. Dean C. Jessee, *Letters of Brigham Young to His Sons* (Salt Lake City: Deseret Book, Co. 1974), 158.
15. Aristotle, *Metaphysics* V, 2, 1–3.
16. *TPJS*, 82–83.
17. *JD* 7:135.
18. *JD* 7.202.
19. *JD* 1:117.
20. *JD* 14:83.
21. *JD* 9:149.
22. *JD* 12:122.
23. *JD* 16:77.
24. *MS* 31:571.
25. *JD* 9:189.
26. Elden J. Watson, *Manuscript History of Brigham Young 1846–1847* (Salt Lake City: Watson, 1971), 120.
27. *JD* 10:328–29.
28. *JD* 12:228 (emphasis added).
29. *JD* 13:270 reads: "It will be hard for any divine that now lives to draw the line between the law of carnal commandments and the law of divine commandments."
30. Boyd K. Packer, "The Arts and the Spirit of the Lord," *Brigham Young University Studies* 16 (Summer 1976): 576, says, "There are many who struggle and climb and finally reach the top of the ladder, only to find that it is leaning against the wrong wall."
31. *JD* 2:91.
32. *JD* 12:261.

33. *JD* 8:289.

34. *JD* 10:26.

35. *JD* 8:68.

36. *JD* 14:232.

37. *JD* 8:135.

38. *JD* 1:254; for example, Brigham Young says, "If a man comes in the midst of this people with money, let him use it in making improvements, in building, in beautifying his inheritance in Zion, and in increasing his capital by thus putting out his money to usury. Let him go and make a great farm, and stock it well, and fortify all around with a good and efficient fence. What for? Why for the purpose of spending his money."

39. *JD* 12:127.

40. Calder, *The Mind of Man,* 33.

41. *JD* 2:124–25; cf. *JD* 10:266, "grovelling things of this life"; 13:151, "grovelling things of the world."

42. *JD* 1:190.

43. *JD* 4:77.

44. *JD* 5:53.

45. *JD* 13:4.

46. *JD* 17:117–18.

47. *JD* 7:282.

48. *JD* 15:34.

49. *JD* 8:63.

50. Jessee, *Letters of Brigham Young to His Sons,* 106.

51. Ibid., 121.

52. *JD* 12:219.

53. Jessee, *Letters of Brigham Young to His Sons,* 138.

54. *JD* 11:283.

55. *JD* 11:214–15.

56. Plato, *Phaedrus* 267A.

57. *JD* 13:148.

58. *JD* 14:75.

59. *JD* 8:58.

60. *TPJS,* 305; *HC* 5:402.

61. *JD* 5:83–84.

62. *JD* 8:134.

63. *JD* 12:192.

64. *JD* 11:105.

65. *JD* 16:123.

66. *JD* 1:117.

67. *JD* 12:122.

68. *JD* 8:353.
69. *JD* 13:310.
70. *JD* 19:47.
71. *JD* 10:359.
72. *TPJS*, 137.
73. *JD* 11:305.
74. *JD* 18:246–47.
75. *JD* 10:2.
76. *JD* 9:244.
77. *JD* 11:123.
78. *JD* 16:77.
79. *JD* 3:203–4.
80. *JD* 11:215.
81. *JD* 9:243.
82. Cf. *JD* 14:16.
83. *JD* 14:16.
84. *JD* 15:161–62.
85. *TPJS*, 49.
86. *JD* 11:127.
87. *JD* 6:315.
88. *JD* 15:162.
89. *JD* 8:185; cf. 10.153.
90. *JD* 9:121, 123.
91. *JD* 6:93.
92. *JD* 14:94–95.
93. *JD* 1:312.
94. *JD* 10:19.
95. *JD* 8:11.
96. *JD* 14:95.
97. Jesse, *Letters of Brigham Young to His Sons*, 202.
98. *HC* 4:234.
99. *JD* 11:107.
100. Jessee, *Letters of Brigham Young to His Sons*, 199.
101. *JD* 10:266–67.

15

Mediocre Meditations on the Media

The Great Malaise

Few will challenge the proposition that there is a universal malaise in the world today, a restlessness, impatience, insecurity, smoldering anger, explosive violence, etc. We have become a danger to each other. It may be inevitable, for experiments have shown that overcrowding of animal populations has the same effect. Well, what else can you expect? How long do we have to be told that these are the Last Days? But now for the first time few will laugh at the proposition, least of all the more sophisticated who once took the Last-Days syndrome as a quaint and old-fashioned delusion. Not anymore.

Freud made the discovery (which was known to all the ancient poets) that we are all neurotics living by repressions that make it possible to deny the horrible reality. In a new prize-winning book by a worshipful disciple of Freud, we are given what he calls the New Freud, and this is it: "Consciousness of death is the primary repression, not sexuality."[1] Freud himself, we are told, was "always unhappy,

This address was delivered on 13 September 1991 at Snyder's Mill in Park City, Utah, to representatives of the LDS Church Communications Department.

helpless, anxious, bitter, looking into nothingness with fright."[2]

So that is what is wrong with us; we are all scared to death with what lies ahead for each of us. "The iceman cometh," but today he seems to be drawing closer than ever and young people have a morbid fascination with fatality, a perverse passion for chain saw murders, zombies, guns, and roses, etc. There is a prosperous business in manufacturing realistic trashing, gouging, smashing of bodies with oozing, festering, gory, slimy effects.

More sophisticated adults display an insatiable appetite for blood and revenge with unspeakably vile and cynical crimes countered by mandatory shootouts, car chases, and, of course, the final explosion night after night over almost every channel.

We are like sulky children wrecking and smashing things because at last we know what we really want and we can never have it ("I want it all and I want it now").[3] (What they really want is the gospel, but that comes later.) Today the word to conjure with is *career*—there is your answer; a career will pretty well take care of everything—security, respectability, the future is yours, and, of course, this is the biggest letdown of all. A career is just once around the track, a carrière. Studs Terkel's interviews with our most successful men report the bitterness and disillusionment, because careers must always end and nothing is more forlorn than a has-been. The other response to the perennial threat of the future is the hedonism of Marcuse or Robert Brown, thought to be very modern—eat, drink, and be merry. Alma said it best: Korihor preached of the real world to the people, "causing them to lift up their heads in wickedness, yea, leading them to commit whoredoms—

telling them that when a man was dead that was the end thereof" (Alma 30:18).

It is the Terrible Question that has us all intimidated and acting like characters out of E. T. Hoffman. And the Terrible Question is: "Is this all there is?" Is there to be an abrupt end of the good life before it is even started? Or of the unhappy life before there has been a chance for happiness? Or as the psychiatrist tells us, are we with our immense endowment and endless capacities to be shut off before we have had a chance to experiment in even one direction, etc.?

The Church Fathers believed in an afterlife but not in a resurrection of the flesh. Are we to settle with St. Jerome with being absorbed into "the nothing from which we came"?

We do hear of ghosts, live spirits; very recently there has been a sudden flood of movies dealing with spirits, ghosts, other lives, and the other world.

But only Moroni has something of real consequence to give us. There is that clinical description of just what he was like and what happened when he came. And then there is that handing over of solid metal plates—we didn't see them, but they were translated in a work of such staggering prodigality that it may risk challenging to call it the most remarkable achievement of the human mind—that is, if Joseph Smith was not telling the truth.

The Fulness

After all, what everyone really wants is "life and that more abundant," as the Lord says, and not only more abundant than we are getting, but it should be eternal, not cut off in the middle or running down to imbecility the way it always is. "To be thus is nothing," said a man who had reached the pinnacle of success, "but to be safely thus . . ."[4]

Only the gospel can offer us that. Today only the gospel even pretends to. It is a *shulḥan arukh,* a table spread for a banquet, a full-course dinner, and we are sent out to invite the world to a feast. Are we holding back? Are we telling them what they are missing? The guests have failed to appear in numbers in other dispensations: "[But they] that were bidden to the wedding . . . would not come. . . . Tell them which are bidden, Behold, I have prepared my dinner. . . . Come unto the marriage. . . . But . . . they went their ways, one to his farm, another to his merchandise, . . . but when the king heard thereof, he was wroth" (Matthew 22:3–7). They all preferred the *real world*—that is the other word by which we conjure today. The king might have said, "The menu doesn't attract you? Then we will make it a businessman's lunch or even a prayer breakfast, if you will, and let you order just what you want."

Why do we hang back and temporize? Why the cautious approach, the soft sell? Are we waiting for more favorable conditions? Does not that argue a lack of faith in ourselves?

Just what is it they all want today? It is the things which the two Nephis state explicitly that men should not seek after.

1 Nephi 22:23: Gain, power over the flesh, to become popular, and finally, lusts of the flesh.

3 Nephi 6:15: Power, and authority, and riches, and the vain things of the world.

You will note that this pretty well covers our prime TV and our glitzy advertising. By a singular necessity these are also four attributes of God who is All Powerful, to whom all things belong, whom all things praise, and who rejoices in his world and in his creatures. What they all want (Kierkegaard, Heidegger, and the psychoanalysts agree on this) is simply to be like God! Freud admitted that more fantastic than any science fiction was "man's own inner yearning to be good." And if you think of it, that is the case. Today even "in the crooked currents of this world," everyone has a ready explanation for his behavior, which somehow is always made out to be virtuous. It has become one of the great mass products of our time, the stamp of our culture—the easy, ready, earnest, innocent, reasonable explanation, with graphs and charts if necessary to make any outrageous action, collusion, broken promise, betrayal, etc., not only excusable but commendable. We could began with Saddam and Abu Nidal and go right down the list to much nearer home.

Since everyone wants to be virtuous, we should have an easy time selling our products, but it is not so. Consider what we have been born to or accepted: "The Spirit of God like a fire, . . . latter-day glor[ies], . . . visions and blessings of old, . . . angels are coming to visit the earth, . . . the Lord is extending the Saints' understanding, . . . the knowledge and power of God are expanding; the veil o'er the earth is beginning to burst."[5]

Is that the real picture today? Where is the hunger? Why are people so complacent?

The key word to this dispensation is *fulness*. The word appears sixty-three times in the Doctrine and Covenants and thirty-one times in the Book of Mormon. After all, this is the dispensation of the *fulness* of times; go down the list:[6] "The *fulness* of mine intent" (1 Nephi 6:4), "received the *fulness* of the gospel" (1 Nephi 10:14), "through the *fulness* of the Gentiles" (1 Nephi 15:13), "the *fulness* of the wrath of God" (1 Nephi 17:35), "may God grant, in his great *fulness*" (Helaman 12:24), "the *fulness* of these things" (3 Nephi 16:7), "I will bring the *fulness* of my gospel" (3 Nephi 16:10), "knowledge of the *fulness* of my gospel" (3 Nephi 16:12), "my joy is great even unto *fulness*" (3 Nephi 27:30), "the Father has given me *fulness* of joy" (3 Nephi 28:10), "the *fulness* of my scriptures" (D&C 42:15), "which rest is the *fulness* of his glory" (D&C 84:24), "he receives not of the *fulness* at the first" (D&C 93:13), "the *fulness* of the record of John" (D&C 93:18).

The doctrine of the *fulness* has not been on earth until now. It cannot be received all at once, but our obligation is to receive everything we possibly can so that we can be ready for more. The *fulness* is not that infinity of knowledge stretching into the eternities which we envisage in the eternities, but the *fulness* of what one is capable of receiving. Not to receive all that one can comprehend is to "reject the *fulness* of my gospel" (3 Nephi 16:10).

How that word *fulness* binds and commits us! If we want to know how we should begin to deliver the message, we have all the admonitions of the early Saints to go by. It is from the first the voice of warning: "Say nothing but repentance unto this generation" (D&C 6:9).

Nothing but repentance? They are not going to like that: "He that exercises no faith unto repentance is exposed to the whole law of the demands of justice [the *fulness*]; therefore only unto him that has faith unto repentance is brought about the great and eternal plan of redemption. . . . Yea, cry unto him for mercy; for he is mighty to save. . . . Cry unto him when you are in your fields, yea, over all your flocks, . . . in your houses, yea, over all your household, both morning, mid-day, and evening, . . . against the power of your enemies, . . . against the devil, . . . over the crops of your fields, . . . over the flocks of your fields [this is poetry, hence the repetition. Professor Fecht has recently shown that virtually all Egyptian writings are in verse!], that they may increase. . . . Ye must pour out your souls in your closets, and your secret places, and in your wilderness. . . . And now, . . . after ye have done all these things, if ye turn away the needy . . . and impart [not] of your substance, . . . behold, your prayer is vain. . . . Therefore if ye do not remember to be charitable, ye are as dross" (Alma 34:16–29).

This a fulsome and passionate appeal, you will agree. But is it not exactly the sort of thing that comes up to the demands of these desperate times? Of course this sort of thing does not go well over the air; it guarantees a swift shifting of channels. Why not try it? Why not a bold experiment just to see what happens?

This being the last time, what is rejected of the *fulness* will not be handed on but taken elsewhere. Here we should pay closer attention to what is presented by the Lord as a lively possibility that concerns us. As he was about to take his leave of the Nephites for the last time, Jesus told them that there was one last thing of great importance that he must leave with them for the later inhabitants of the land.

"I command you that you shall write these sayings after I am gone, . . . that these sayings which ye shall write shall be kept and shall be manifested unto the Gentiles, that through the *fulness* of the Gentiles, the remnant of their seed [the Jews and other tribes of Israel], who shall be scattered forth upon the face of the earth . . . may be brought to a knowledge of . . . their Redeemer. . . . And blessed are the Gentiles, because of their belief in me, . . . in the latter day shall the truth come unto the Gentiles, . . . notwithstanding they have . . . scattered my people who are of the house of Israel; and my people who are of the house of Israel . . . have been trodden under feet by them, . . . smitten, . . . afflicted, . . . slain, . . . cast out from among them, . . . hated by them, . . . to become a hiss and byword. . . . And thus commandeth the Father that I should say unto you: At that day when the Gentiles shall sin against my gospel [and they cannot sin against a gospel that they have not first received], . . . and shall be lifted up in the pride of their hearts above all nations, and above all the people of the whole earth, and shall be filled with all manner of lyings, and of deceits [note what vices head the list of horrors], and of mischiefs, and all manner of hypocrisy, and murders [we lead the world 10 to 1 in that], and priestcrafts, and whoredoms, and of secret abominations [BCCI, a contemporary banking scandal, qualifies here]; and if they shall do all those things and shall reject the *fulness* of my gospel, behold, saith the Father, I will bring the *fulness* of my gospel from among them" (3 Nephi 16:4–10).

That is an unpleasant topic for discussion. Still, it does not have to be: "But *if* the Gentiles will repent and return unto me, saith the Father, behold they shall be numbered among my people, O house of Israel" (3 Nephi 16:13).

But if they don't repent, he tells us, "I will bring my gospel from among them" (3 Nephi 16:10), and, remembering the house of Israel, says, "I will bring my gospel unto them" (3 Nephi 16:11).

Readers of the Book of Mormon are puzzled by the long and repetitious fifth chapter of Jacob. I have heard speakers complain of its length and boredom. It is easily one of the most important discourses in the book, laying down with great clarity the justice of the preaching and the policy of distributing it throughout the world to those places where a *fulness* will be accepted. The Lord of the vineyard is willing to take his prize fruit to whatever patch of ground will receive it. He goes further than that; he makes every effort to make the precious trees flourish in every part of the globe where it proves at all possible. If it does not work in one place, he takes it to another; if that one turns back, he moves it. If things have improved in a former spot, he goes back to work on that. It is a policy of endless patience, training, adaptation, experimentation, cultivation, grafting, transplanting, fertilizing, watching and waiting, etc.

The Lord instructed his disciples to follow his own practice: "When they persecute you in this city, flee ye unto another" (Matthew 10:23).

Here we have a best case and a worst case. The best case is that the Gentiles repent and are taken in with the rest of the adopted house of Israel. It has happened both with the Nephites and the Jaredites. So we don't give up hope. The thrust of the message is that the Lord is leaving the door open to the very end. But there are disturbing undertones in the message which has the flavor of the rest of the Book of Mormon—too much of the human tragedy. But still, God is leaving the door open for us to the very end.

The worst case is presented as a distinct possibility; it would not be there or be so powerfully emphasized—delivered by specific command of the Father as the last and most emphatic message to the descendants of the Nephites and the Gentile successors on the land. "And wo be unto him that will not hearken unto the words of Jesus, and also to them whom he hath chosen and sent among them. . . . It would be better for them if they had not been born" (3 Nephi 28:34–35). So ends the message.

No matter which way things go, as I tell myself repeatedly, the admonition of Mormon to his son holds to the very end, delivered as it was after all was lost: "And now, my beloved son, notwithstanding their hardness, let us labor diligently; for if we should cease to labor, we should be brought under condemnation; for we have a labor to perform whilst in this tabernacle of clay, that we may conquer the enemy of all righteousness [what happened to Communism?], and rest our souls in the kingdom of God" (Moroni 9:6).

Whether we are spreading the gospel from a permanent center or transplanting it to more fertile soil, it is all the same work. There is nothing said about taking the gospel away from the earth; on the contrary, we are told it is now restored for the last time; but with the *fulness* it is another matter.

With Fear and Trembling

The ancient apostles had no choice but to give it to them straight, even though that guaranteed mobs and imprisonments. The word imposes an awful responsibility with those who make it their profession.

A phenomenon viewed with solemnity in what are traditionally the two most ancient writings in existence, the Shabako text of the Memphite Theology (though transmitted in a Nineteenth Dynasty text, it is of predynastic content), and the *Sefer Yetzirah,* which was held by most of the earliest rabbis to be the world's oldest book and a composition of Abraham.

Both writings tell of the seven openings of the head, the seven orifices or receptors—two eyes, two ears, two nostrils, and one mouth. The Egyptian account tells how these receptors receive impulses, energy quanta from the world outside, organize it in the brain, give it meaning in the breast where values are imparted, the *thymos* of the Greeks, the seat of emotion. When the individual has thus composed images and impressions of the outside world he is prepared to communicate to others.

What comes in by seven receptors goes forth by the one powerful projector, which is the sacred word of mouth. The *logos* is more than a myth; it is actually the only way with which we convey our thoughts and beliefs and convictions to others; the only way in which they can have any image of the world we are experiencing. By the word alone we make a common universe of discourse.

So we can easily see why we should watch our words with fear and trembling, and why a lie is the most heinous of all crimes. Joseph Smith said that the devil will tell a thousand truths to put over one falsehood because that one falsehood can disrupt and destroy the whole structure of truth. To distort my picture of the world by a lie is to render real communication impossible and human relationships the hopeless morass they have become.

We risk lying when we exaggerate and misrepresent any product. Should we treat the gospel as a product? Should we strive to make it attractive to an indifferent public? Or preach the straight gospel to the few who will listen?

When surveys by the *Wall Street Journal,* cover stories by *Newsweek* and *Time,*[7] expose us as a nation of liars, we can take it as an invitation to go against the stream. But that way you will never sell anything. And that is the problem.

Rhetoric Today

The ancient Apostles did not break the news gradually. What they had was the best possible news, and they came right out with it even if that meant getting mobbed and thrown in jail. Their policy was to give the whole message and let those susceptible to it react: "My sheep hear my voice" (John 10:27). "I am the good shepherd, and know my sheep, and am known of mine" (John 10:14).

If we saturated the air with the straight gospel, some would certainly hear it and might even take action. But what would happen to the ratings? We have never risked trying to find out.

What put Brother Edwards onto my trail, he has told me, is an article I wrote thirty-five years ago on ancient rhetoric and its ravages.[8] It destroyed ancient society. Defined as "the art of pleasing the many," it followed public taste and therefore always pushed downhill—rhetoric cannot lose: It is the ever *victoriosa loquacitas*, but the civilization that accommodates and adapts itself like a chameleon cannot win. Rhetoric is not to be cured of its vices by any technical or electronic refinements, for those vices are its very nature—the healthy cancer cells are the ones that kill, and rhetoric is a cancer. An example of this skillfully adaptive parasite is the manner in which commercials follow styles. Many of the big ones now have strong religious undertones. Recent commentators have noted the strong leaning toward spirits, ghosts, revenants, postdeath experiences, and the like in popular movies. In advertising the trend has been to sensitivity—a lengthy illustrating of heroic and climactic moments in the life of Winston Churchill culminating in celebrating those same sterling qualities of character animating the Southern Bell Telephone Company. We are now told that life simply cannot get better than following up some minor achievement, such as making a sale or winning a game or contemplating the future of one's children as successful doctors, with a visit to McDonald's. And the point is that they really think that is the best that life has to offer. Babies are exploited shamelessly, with a crooning, husky, cracked, affectionate, slightly choked-up voice of an elderly gent to sell the product, which can be a truck, or a tire, or a power mower— somehow the baby shames you into buying it. The key word is *message*. What all these pitchmen have for the world

is a message. It necessarily works by the principle of perverted values, Aristotle's doctrine of the mountain reflected
in the lake; the less necessary an object is, the more it must
be praised to sell it so that those who watch thousands of
ads end up with a complete reversion of values, the most
important things in life being deodorants, manageable hair,
a sexy car, things to eat and drink, and, above all, the
achievement of an absolutely perfect body without which
the individual can never cease to be a reliable customer.
This is what the Book of Mormon calls being carnally
minded, the mainstay of all public relations. If you are perfect, then *carefree* is the operative word. To be youthful,
beautiful, and at the beach where nobody does anything
and nobody wears anything has become the common
denominator. It is also the perfect Freudian escape to be free
from the anxiety of age and death. What we want is a
Paradise, and that is what Madison Avenue is out to give
us.

Here is a surprise. What the gospel promises is exactly
the same. Joseph Smith has given us in the Standard Works
the news that should make millions deliriously happy. As a
matter of fact that has been the actual effect that the message has had on almost everyone who has accepted it. Why
are we then holding back? Why do we offer sitcom family
skits, meet the Mormons, Mr. Nice Guy. It is a bid for acceptance, and what people most accept is the ordinary. They
are, in Kierkegaard's expression, seeking refuge in the trivial. Refuge from what? From the gospel, from the culture
shock of bonding with eternity.

The uncompromising nature of the gospel makes it
impossible to play around in this manner: "Wo unto him . . .
that wasteth the days of his probation, for awful is his state"
(2 Nephi 9:27). We used to sing the old sectarian hymn

"From Greenland's Icy Mountains" in which we expressed awareness that the blind heathen desperately need exactly what we have—and can we hold it back? Can we deny it to them? They don't know how badly they need it. But today the need is becoming desperate.

For us, seeking comfort in the conventional, it is above all acceptance of the big-time. A son of mine who once worked in the Church medium had a friend working with Karl Malden as his personal assistant. To help Mike out, he asked him to send his manuscripts to him in Hollywood, and he would send them back to Utah with a Hollywood postmark. That would make them acceptable to a reader, for, as Mike said, those in Salt Lake were completely cowed by the industry. He calls it our helplessness, and it is very crippling. For example, when they got Jimmy Stewart to play in a Christmas drama, everybody thought that we had arrived—there was just one catch—the film itself was dismally amateurish. What could be done about that? Must we prove that we are slick and professional? Does the typical priesthood or Sunday School manual carry the impact of the scriptures with a dozen or so disconnected excerpts for four or five minutes' discussion in a half-hour lesson? Must we go into ecstasies of self-congratulation any time the outside media take notice of the Mormons? Many were thrilled when *Time* magazine recently characterized Mormons as spending their days praying, having children, and making money.

Recently, a speaker at Ricks College told his audience how to sell the gospel. He had his guitar and he sang jingles; the jingles had no merit and made very little sense, but he did not apologize for that, for the point of his talk was that in selling the gospel the only thing that really counted was the Barnum principle—to have something stick in people's heads, no matter what, that would remind them of your business.

When I started writing things down years ago, Richard L. Evans used to admonish me to follow the rule he always followed: "Always think of yourself as addressing the tiredest farmer in Koosharem." It was the equivalent of Napoleon's advice to one writing military dispatches to make sure that the stupidest corporal could understand them—only then were they really clear. I am afraid I have not followed Brother Evans's advice, though I admit it is the general rule in the Church.

But how can we possibly avoid these tried and true tricks and devices? The way one of my sons did. He had a good job teaching filmmaking at BYU discussing the merits and weaknesses of various films, naturally the most significant ones. But one day he received an order never to show or even discuss any R-rated film in his class—no matter how eminent the drama or how unqualified the judges. I hasten to add that this restriction did not come from any department in the BYU or the University itself. Some student had written home complaining that an R-rated movie was discussed, whereupon his parents had written to someone in Salt Lake City, and you know the rest. What was he to do? He promptly resigned his good job, family or no family, because to him the issue was instantly clear, and I have never known a more honest person. I have a niece who gave up a job in the media when it became clear that she would have to assist in doctoring a documentary.

Through the years I have seen many changes in teachings and practices in the Church. All have been in the direction of convenience, efficiency, accommodation, taste, fastidiousness. It was exactly such accommodation as the great church historian Louis Duschesne showed which turned the ancient church into a popular world-church to which it had only distant resemblance.

Can the media be led to the honest in heart or must missionary contact be eye to eye, spirit to spirit, mind to mind? From the very beginning in the days of Adam the written word was revealed to implement the spreading of the gospel. Then why not the broadcasting of voice and image? Hear O Israel! Is it because the speaker does not really come into your home? He does not see you and you do not look at him reading from the teleprompter.

But the book is something else. All you need is a smooth surface and something to scratch it with, and you are in a position to communicate to the ends of the earth and the end of time. As Galileo said, no other invention can compare. We believe it began with Adam as a gift to Adam. By it the most delicate nuances of thought, the subtlest feelings, the profoundest insights can be conveyed over any span of time and space from one thinking person to another. The only catch is that the message must be read. And here the media do their greatest disservice, even where broadcasting rules it is simply the script, the written word, that is being conveyed.

One hears increasing complaint, e.g., via *Sunstone,* of the shallow and insipid nature of our teaching materials today. Actually, it has always been that way. Joseph Smith laid it on the line: "How vain and trifling have been our spirits, our conferences, our councils, our meetings, our private as well as public conversations—too low, too mean, too vulgar, too condescending for the dignified characters of the called and chosen of God, according to the purposes of His will, from before the foundation of the earth."[9]

It is quite inconceivable that the gospel should ever be under condemnation, though the Church has been from time to time. They are not the same thing. The one is a teaching; the other, an organization to foster that teaching. Is the organization free to adjust and control the doctrine? Can it decide on the basis of public relations what would be most appropriate for what audience and for what occasion? What to emphasize and what to play down? Does any organization through its officers have that discretion? This is where the fulness comes in.

When the time is *full*, or the cup is full, or the fruit is fully ripe, we must accept it in that condition. Nothing can be added because it is *full*. If ever there was a single package, it is the gospel teaching we have heard from childhood: faith, repentance, and baptism. The first includes the Articles of Faith, the second includes all our moral precepts and practical covenants, the third is the passage from one condition to another, one world to another, one life to another. All accept the great scenario in its *fulness*.

The principal guide is certainly the Book of Mormon. The divinity of that work can be sustained by one argument alone, if that were all we had, namely, the sheer prodigality of the thing: a tapestry unequalled in all the library for its richness and detail, an inexhaustible well of knowledge, and the prophetic book of the age.

Even the Book of Mormon confesses limitations: "O that I had the voice of an angel!" Some consider the miraculous powers of the media to come close to that condition. What then would the angel say? What angels always say when they appear to men. First, don't be afraid, fear not, I bring good news. This is necessary because the gospel always has that culture-shock when our collective consciousness runs into the brick-wall requirements of righteousness.

Psychotherapy can cure you of the neurotic lies you live by to block out the real horror of your condition—we are all hiding in the broom closet. Freud said he could liberate you from that but only to face a worse horror—your actual condition. So that is the content of the media.

But we offer a third way—one that the world knows not of. Let us not withhold it from them any longer out of fear of offending sensibilities. When the prophet Elijah appeared to announce the restoration of the glorious work for the dead, his first words were "The time has fully come!" It is folly to pretend that it is not simply because we are frightened of the obligation. Yet we know that everyone will stall and "rather bear the ills they have than fly to others that they know not of." Yet everywhere the message is matched to the capacity of the hearer to receive it, leaving all, as the Lord says, "without excuse." No one may say, as we still tend to do today, "Come back later and we will consider your offer."

What would it take to convince me if I were an outsider? I spend my days thinking about evidence. Have I absolute proof of the gospel? Not that I can thrust my testimony upon you, yet there are things that I can assert with absolute certainty. It has nothing to do with people who have turned their lives around, found happiness, a new life, new success—Oh joy, oh rapture unforeseen, the cloudless skies are all serene! The things we talk about in our conferences and journals are the common fare of all churches, but ours must go beyond that; when we ride off into the sunset, we will be riding off into the darkness.

It is comforting to know that the Lord is doing his own work and his agents improving the time, regardless of adverse conditions of spreading the gospel around the world, moving on a broader front than ever before. They are fulfilling the plans of the Lord of the vineyard, transplanting the gospel in its *fulness*, leaving behind them a trail of the Standard Works, ready to fulfill the Saints and expand their minds until they can receive more. We see this principle of expansion when Christ instructs the Nephites (3 Nephi 17:2): "I perceive that ye are weak, that ye cannot understand all my words. . . . Therefore go ye unto your homes, and ponder upon the things which I have said, and ask the Father, in my name, that ye may understand, and prepare your minds for the morrow."

A fundamental rule of the Rhetorician has always been to put over your point any way you can; turn every situation, accident, device, and contraption to your advantage and make use of it.

Thus Paul takes advantage of a special situation on the Areopagus, just as Jesus does in the Temple, or on the seashore, preaching from a boat.

Amalickiah takes advantage of the media when he spreads his warmongering talks from a series of towers. But an even more sophisticated use of media was Benjamin's address from the tower, augmented by written leaflets circulated among the crowd beyond hearing range.

So the Latter-day Saints have taken advantage of such opportunities—as when Joseph Smith stood on the scaffolding of the new school in Far West to preach a resounding sermon.

Needless to say, in more recent times the authorities have been quick to consider the opportunities offered by new advances in mass communication.

My point is that these have done more harm than good because they block off more than they convey. Consider the seven sensory passages and the single projector, the human voice. Modern electronics have made the former more sensitive than ever and amplified the voice ad infinitum.

But has this made any change in content? It has, as all

students admit, by reducing the message to the lowest common denominator. That is natural and inevitable. But it has had disastrous effects. It would seem that the mass media is a broken reed to lean on, especially where the gospel is concerned.

Here is an article less than a month old by a specialist in public communication: "The broadcast television networks appear to be dying right before our glazed eyes. Revenue is sinking, their once enormous audience is deserting them for the expanding competition and what viewers the networks do have keep zapping in and out of the wretched shows. Last season's hot TV trend, 'creativity,' . . . didn't work, and the network programmers seem to have no idea what to do next. The news this season is that the hour-long TV drama is as moribund as the news documentary. . . . So what? Who cares if they *all* stop broadcasting? Network programming is usually so stupefying that it's not even worth pausing to criticize it." [10]

But the author confronts us with a dilemma. Without TV, he says, "We'll have nowhere to turn for a unifying culture. Television is our common cultural ground. . . . If you want to address Americans in general, and you want to be understood by as many of them as possible, you are safest taking your subject from the tube. If you doubt this, why don't you attempt, say, a scriptural allusion sometime and see how many people know what you are talking about?"

And that is where we come in. Who's going to recognize the Book of Mormon over the air? This author believes that the appeal must necessarily be to separate types of audiences. "People make their own cultures; you can't design one for them." "In the future," he writes, "different demographic groups will likely be spending much of their time with programming targeted toward them and only them: Sports fans with ESPN, rock music fans with MTV, older audiences with The Lifetime Network, ethnic groups with material produced specifically for them, etc. . . . The result threatens to be increasingly discrete subcultures that are rarely if ever exposed to the stuff of each other's subculture. The stuff of American life is going to be niche-marketed." And to which of these groups will our Latter-day Saint message be directed? "Each targeted audience will move into its own TV neighborhood, rarely to emerge. Why should it? It's comforting to be addressed continually in one's own terms; it's annoying to deal with challenges."

These have always been the great obstacles to broadcasting the gospel effectively through the media. The great days of Hollywood are past. Most of those products of the thirties, except the great ones, seem quaint to us now. How incredibly artificial the acting was, the sets, the lighting. The fabulous success of Hollywood depended entirely on the commitment of the audience, and this was obtained by subtle titillation of the senses, the Oriental splendor of the gigantic movie mosque—or medieval castle, Egyptian temple; the colorful prologues of Barnum and Bailey proportions, and above all the musical accompaniment put the thing over. Alexander Schreiner moved to Portland from Nürnberg when he was nineteen years old and became the organist at the Page Theatre. Whether a movie was a hit or a flop depended in no small part on his performance; his business was to put people into the proper mood. He let me play the organ sometimes, and it was awesome. Those weren't silent movies at all; the Wurlitzer never ceased its relentless manipulation of our emotions. And after that came the full-size symphony orchestra, which never let up during any major production.

That world has vanished. Who misses it except sentimentally? Does the gospel lend itself to such manipulation and presentation? The Byzantine tricks of Constantine's successor may have worked on some barbarians from the Steppes, and the baroque approach properly impressed the German peasants, but I have never heard of anyone being converted by the glories of St. Peters. One thing is certain, the First Vision will not lend itself to any amount of hype—any attempt to sell it that way will fall flat every time.

In a recent review of a book entitled *The Brief Wonderful Life of Network News,* Reuven Franks notes that we have entered "an age of drastically lowered expectations and drastically lowered budgets."[11] He goes down the list of the great producers, the whiz-kids, and the money managers: "All come off badly. The book is not venomous, however, but dismaying. . . . There used to be a solid, dependable contingent [of news hawks; shall we say news specialists?]. It helps that these newsniks were not raised on television, but instead on print and radio. Today, they are almost extinct." After all, it *is the word* that conveys the message as of old.

Here is a new book by Ken Auletta, *Three Blind Mice: How the TV Networks Lost Their Way.* It is based on 1,500 interviews with 350 people. To quote the reviewer, "The inescapable conclusion of this book is that new technologies and market forces, not greed or stupidity, are killing off network television."[12] Again it is technology to blame. Because of it, the author says, "Network news began its slow but steady decline into the realm of entertainment several years before the barbarians reached the gate."[13]

This gives us pause. Should we try to make our communications with the world entertaining? Every attempt to do so without the skill of a J. Golden Kimball is counterproductive. The author foresees that "Sleazy programs . . . will increasingly monopolize the schedule," given the "dwindling audiences and plunging profits facing network television today." The book is called "a valuable requiem for a dying industry."[14]

A few of the great films of the thirties and forties are seen over and over again. The most persistent déjà vu is, of course, *It's a Wonderful Life*. So what would somebody do but bring Jimmy Stewart to Salt Lake to do it again.

In the case of the Book we have a demonstrable miracle. In fact, God has made it clear, and at considerable length in the Book of Mormon, that he intends to use the Book as the proper means of transmitting the gospel through time and space. Nothing else will do. Years ago I left a three-hundred-year-old copy of Appian's *Roman History* lying on our front lawn, a hillside in California (the big white house you can still see right at the end of Normandy Avenue). Every day for two weeks while we were away the sun would bake the book, and then the automatic sprinklers would come on and drench it thoroughly, then the sun would break through again, and so the process continued. Here is the book, and it is in perfect condition. What other equipment could stand up to such punishment?

Quite apart from that, even if it were more vulnerable than our hypersensitive electronic gadgets, it is still infinitely more effective in delivering, as Galileo pointed out. Over an infinite stretch of time and space it not only conveys information, but like Homer or the deeply sincere writings of the Old Kingdom of Egypt, it can still stir in the reader the same emotions experienced by the author.

It should be enough to note that the gift of writing was given to man by God for the express purpose of recording his communications with men. Quite recently a number of articles have confirmed what I demonstrated years ago; it would seem that all the earliest known writings are quotations given by the Deity to mankind.

Today a strange situation has arisen. To make a joke one must speak about things the hearer is acquainted with. Gore Vidal recently wrote: "Few Americans have ever been able to cope with wit or irony, and even the simplest jokes often cause unease, especially today, when every phrase must be examined for covert sexism, racism, ageism." Several years ago I began to notice that my best jokes failed to go over; and today, though I teach an honors class of supposedly literate upperclassmen, it is absolutely impossible to get a laugh—they seem to think it is risky; they wonder if they are getting the point, because, to put it bluntly, they are uneducated.

Notes

1. Ernest Becker, *The Denial of Death* (New York: Free, 1973), 96.

2. Ibid., 122, citing Zilboorg, *Psychoanalysis and Religion* (London: Allen and Unwin, 1967), 242.

3. In "Citizen Kane." Can that account for the unaccountable sheer vandalism?

4. William Shakespeare, *Macbeth*, act III, scene i, 48.

5. "The Spirit of God," in *Hymns of The Church of Jesus Christ of Latter-day Saints* (Salt Lake City: The Church of Jesus Christ of Latter-day Saints, 1985), no. 2.

6. R. Gary Shapiro, comp., *An Exhaustive Concordance of the Book of Mormon, Doctrine and Covenants, and Pearl of Great Price* (Salt Lake City: Hawkes, 1977), 363.

7. Cf., for example, Paul Gray, "Lies, Lies, Lies," *Time* (5 October 1992): 32–38.

8. Hugh W. Nibley, *"Victoriosa Loquacitas:* The Rise of Rhetoric and the Decline of Everything Else," *Western Speech* 20/2 (Spring 1956): 57–82; reprinted in *CWHN* 10:243–86.

9. *TPJS,* 137.

10. Charles P. Freund, "Save the Networks! They May Be a Wasteland, but They're the Wasteland We Share," *Washington Post,* 28 July 1991, C1.

11. Tom Shales, "Back When the Networks Were Newsworthy,"

review of Reuven Franks, *Out of Thin Air: The Brief Wonderful Life of Network News*, in *Washington Post* National Weekly Edition, 12–18 August 1991, 35–36.

12. Barbara Matusow, "Changing TV's Golden Age into Lead," review of Ken Auletta, *Three Blind Mice: How the TV Networks Lost Their Way*, in *Washington Post* National Weekly Edition, 2–8 September 1991, 35.

13. Ibid.

14. Ibid.

PART 4

Leadership

16

Criticizing the Brethren

This is a talk on criticizing the Brethren, and I have decided to let Joseph Smith do most of the talking. After all, criticism of the Church and its leaders has always centered around him. It began before the Church was founded, and to this day he is still the main object of attack. The astonishing fulfillment of Moroni's prophecy to a country kid living out in the backwoods, that his name would be known for good and evil among men everywhere, is enough in itself to prove that Joseph Smith was a true prophet. Critics attacking the Church still assail Joseph Smith with a sort of private vindictiveness, as if he personally were responsible for their own woes and frustrations. Remember the great contempt he met with from the ministers when he was but fourteen and fifteen years old? The report of his first vision says that it "excited a great deal of prejudice against me among professors of religion and was the Cause of great persecution."[1] Before the Church existed, not only Joseph, but his brethren, were under heavy attack. The *Painesville Telegraph* reported the shocked and scandalized neighborhood and described

This Sunstone Symposium talk was given in Salt Lake City at the University Park Hotel on 29 August 1989. A similar talk was delivered at the Church Educational System Symposium at Brigham Young University on 18 August 1989.

the family of Smiths as rude, ignorant, simple-minded, gullible, superstitious, and of course sly, scheming, prevaricating, and immoral. It was rich soil for rural gossip, but why the passionate and relentless attacks on Joseph Smith? And why do they continue to this day?

It was mostly Moroni's fault. The night he visited Joseph Smith, he widened the yawning gulf which the First Vision had placed between Joseph and normal people and removed him from the sphere of established theology and rational thinking. Henceforth, if Joseph was right, the world was in total darkness: "This world is a very wicked world; . . . the world grows more wicked and corrupt."[2] Joseph took an uncompromising position, for the Lord had told him: "Behold the world lieth in sin at this time and none doeth good no not one, . . . and mine anger is kindling against the inhabitants of the earth to visit them acording to th[e]ir ungodliness."[3] He adopted the frame of mind of one who, after a glimpse into yonder heavens, once and for all took the measure of the world. While he was still a child, he said: "My mind become excedingly distressed [sic]."[4] When he viewed the yawning gulf between the world of men and the world which God had given men, he reflected upon "the earth also upon [which] I stood and the beast of the field and the fowls of heaven and the fish of the waters and also man walking forth upon the face of the earth in ma[j]esty and in strength of beauty";[5]—and compared that with the shambles men had made of it—the "contentions and divi[si]ons [and] the wicke[d]ness and abominations and the darkness which pervaded the minds of mankind . . . and I felt to mourn for my own sins and for the sins of the world."[6] He saw that gulf ever widening: "I behold the manifest withdrawal of God's Holy Spirit, and the veil of stupidity which seems to be drawn over the hearts of the people."[7] "Mankind will persist in self-justification until all their iniquity is exposed."[8]

When he first tried to tell his story, he found all communication severed. "My soul was filled with love, and for many days, I could rejoice with great Joy and the Lord was with me. But [I] could find none that would believe the he[a]venly vision."[9] As one tutored from above, he reached a conclusion: "The opinions of men, so far as I am concerned, are to me as the crackling of the thorns under the pot, or the whistling of the wind."[10] What he had done was to reintroduce a new dimension into the world, or rather as Eduard Meyer so impressively sets forth: He reintroduced the very same universe of discourse which had existed in the days of the apostles and prophets.[11] It was no mere rhetoric when he said, "No man knows my history. . . . I don't blame any one for not believing my history. If I had not experienced what I have, I could not have believed it myself."[12] "Have we increased in knowledge or intelligence? . . . Our nation, which possesses greater resources than any other, is rent, from center to circumference, with party strife, political intrigues, and sectional interest. . . . Our tradesmen are disheartened, our mechanics out of employ, our farmers distressed, and our poor crying for bread, our banks are broken, our credit ruined."[13] "What is the matter? Are we alone in this thing? Verily no. . . . The world itself presents one great theater of misery, woe, and 'distress of nations with perplexity.' All, all, speak with a voice of thunder, that man is not able to govern himself, to legislate for himself, to protect himself, to promote his own good, nor the good of the world."[14]

It was not a speculative religion that Joseph brought; like John, he spoke only of what he had seen with his eyes, heard with his ears, and felt with his hands. In contrast to that, the whole Christian doctrine, as Brigham Young put it, "simmered down ... into a snuffbox, ... but, when I found 'Mormonism,' I found that it was higher than I could reach, ... deeper than I was capable of comprehending and calculated to expand the mind ... from truth to truth, from light to light, ... to become associated with the Gods and angels."[15] In 1831 Joseph reported: "The conference voted that they prize the revelations to be worth to the Church the riches of the whole earth";[16] the Book of Mormon and the revelations are worth the riches of eternity. In short, as Joseph put it, "The difference between [the] Saints and [the] world is that Saints know [the truth, and] the world do[es] not."[17] To say the least, that attitude is going to invite criticism. Incidentally, this quotation is from a new book by Scott Faulring, *An American Prophet's Record: The Diaries and Journals of Joseph Smith,* being circulated by Jerald and Sandra Tanner as an anti-Mormon book as if that passage damned the Church. It's actually a very strong defense of Joseph Smith. He was a realist. He recognized the truth when he saw it. I hope the book circulates far and wide. It testifies to the absolute honesty of Joseph Smith.

The word *criticize* is from the same root as the Latin *cerno*—"to sift, separate, decide"—and the Greek *krino*—"to separate, decide, judge." The Latin *discerno* means "to distinguish between two things exactly alike." The Latin *interlegere,* from which we get our word "intelligence," is the power to distinguish or judge between two or more things (it's the binary process; in fact, *bayana* is the reconstructed Semitic form, and *bîn* is the Hebrew form).

It may seem surprising that the critics from the beginning to the present did not attack Joseph Smith on moral grounds—that would have been counterproductive; naughty boys were a dime a dozen, and scandal-mongering works both ways. While the stock phrases from Hurlbut and Howe, down to Brodie, were *lazy, indulgent, money-digging, superstitious,* the specific attacks of the super-offender were, and still are, all on intellectual grounds. This is only fair. He saw them behind a "veil of stupidity."

Webster defines criticism as "the art of evaluation or analyzing with knowledge and propriety [the beauties and faults of] works of art or literature, . . . [of] moral values or the soundness of scientific hypotheses and procedures."[18] Notice "with knowledge and propriety": the critics necessarily assume intellectual and moral superiority to the things they're criticizing. As Aristotle says, the observer feels superior to the observed even when the observer is the cat and the observed is the king. Since Joseph frankly stated that because of his family's indigence, he was denied the advantages of an education, the critics have rejoiced to find themselves holding all the cards, under no obligation to pay serious attention to anything that an ignorant farmer might say.[19] To this day, they have worked their alleged intellects to advantage for all they were worth.

Critics within the Church have done the same thing; they still take the position of high academic advantage. There were always those among the Brethren themselves who, resenting Joseph Smith's towering ascendency in view of his limited education, tried to bring him down with terrible affidavits, which they later admitted were false. Some of "the first Elders of this Church," reported Brigham, "decided that Joseph did not understand temporal matters."[20] The first bishops of the Church said they believed with all their heart that they understood the temporal matters far better than the Prophet Joseph. "I have seen men who belonged to this kingdom, and who really thought that if they were not associated with it, it could not progress."[21]

So the critics magnanimously volunteer their superior intellectual powers and put them at the disposal of the Church.

This brings us to a fundamental issue. The Prophet's advantage over the world lay of course in revelation; but in the Church, every follower has an equal right to revelation. How could the Prophet stand up and be the leader, when everyone could have his own claim to revelation? They immediately started doing it as soon as they joined the Church. It was Joseph himself who insisted most emphatically on everyone's right to inspection. He said, "Search the scriptures—search . . . and ask your Heavenly Father, in the name of His Son Jesus Christ, to manifest the truth unto you; . . . you will then know for yourselves and not for another. You will not then be dependent on man for the knowledge of God; nor will there be any room for speculation."[22]

This is a point upon which the Prophet Joseph himself placed the greatest emphasis. No office or calling in the Church qualifies its holder as an official interpreter of the scriptures. That's the prerogative of a conventional priest or minister who has been to college and studied for the ministry. The boast of the Latter-day Saints is that they have no professional clergy, even in matters of doctrine. Joseph said, "It is the privilege of every Elder to speak of the things of God."[23] The Lord has declared "that the people should each one stand for himself and depend on no man or men, . . . that righteous persons could only deliver their own souls."[24] If the people departed from the Lord, they must fall; they were dependent on the prophet and hence were darkening their minds in consequence of neglecting the duties evolving upon themselves. "The people should each one stand for himself, and depend not on man or men. . . . Righteous persons could only deliver their own souls."[25]

"Fellow sojourners upon earth, it is your privilege to purify yourselves and come up to the same glory, and see for yourselves, and know for yourselves. Ask, and it shall be given you."[26] Let us recall that the scripture which put Joseph's feet on the path was the statement in James, "Let him ask of God, that giveth to all men liberally, and upbraideth not; and it shall be given him" (James 1:5). God won't rebuke you for asking. "God hath not revealed anything to Joseph," he said, "but what he will make known unto the Twelve, and even [to] the least Saint."[27] They know all things as fast as they are able to bear them. For the day must come when no man need say to his neighbor, "Know ye the Lord?" for "all shall know [him], . . . from the least unto the greatest" (D&C 84:98). How is this to be done? By the sealing power and the other comforter spoken of, which would be manifest by the revelations. But wouldn't that sort of thing lead people to all sorts of confusion, all kinds of crazy ideas, and the like? Of course it did; right from the first we had crazy ideas, but we don't preach them. Joseph said you do not do that. When old Brother Brown was brought up before the High Council, Joseph stated the case:

> I never thought it was right to call up a man and try him because he erred in doctrine, it looks too much like methodism and not like Latter day Saintism. Methodists have creeds which a man must believe or be kicked out of their church. I want the liberty of believing as I please, it feels so good not to be tramelled. It dont prove that a man is not a good man, because he errs in doctrine. The High Council undertook to censure and correct Br. Brown because of his teachings in relation to the beasts [in Revelation], and he came to me to know what he should do about it.[28]

Joseph Smith said that Brother Brown's teachings were absolutely ridiculous. He could not keep from laughing at his ideas. But Brother Brown had a right to them, and the elders shouldn't attack Joseph for defending him. He said, "I . . . qualify my declaration which I am about to make so that the young Elders who know so much may not rise up and choke me like hornets."[29] The elders liked to dictate doctrine to each other, and he didn't reserve to himself even the mysteries. He said, "There is no salvation in believing an evil report against our neighbor [instead of criticizing]— I advise all to go on to perfection and search deeper and deeper into the mysteries of Godliness."[30]

"It has always been my province to dig up hidden mysteries—new things—for my hearers."[31] "I never hear of a man being damned for believing too much; but they are damned for unbelief."[32] But let us always bear in mind that a mystery, by definition, is something that you keep to yourself; the Greek *muō* means "to shut up." A mystery is something you've been initiated into, and you don't convey that to the general public:

> We deem it a just principle . . . that all men are created equal, and that all have the privilege of thinking for themselves upon all matters relative to conscience. Consequently, then, we are not disposed, had we the power, to deprive any one of exercising that free independence of mind which heaven has so graciously bestowed upon the human family as one of its choicest gifts.[33]

"If others' blessings are not your blessings, others' curses are not your curses; you stand . . . agents unto yourselves, to be judged according to your works. . . . Every man lives for himself."[34] This applies in politics and everything else:

> I have not come to tell you to vote this way, that way, or the other in relation to National matters. I want it to

[go] abroad to the whole world that every man should stand on his own merits. The Lord has not given me Revelation concerning politics—I have not asked the Lord for it.—I am a third party [and] stand independent and alone—I desire to see all parties protected [under the laws]. . . . I utterly forbid these pol[i]tical demagogues from using my name hereafter forever.[35]

Parties were doing just that. "If 10000 men testify to a truth you know would it add to your faith? No, or will 1000 testimonies destroy your knowledge of a fact? No.—I do not want anyone to tell [that] I am a prophet or attempt to prove my word."[36] He says, quite strongly, with regard to elections, "Some say we all vote together . . . as I say. But I never tell any man how to vote or who to vote for. . . . Joseps Duncan said if the people would elect him he would exterminate the mormons & take away their charters. As to Mr Ford he made no such threats."[37] In such a uniquely clear-cut case, open and shut, there was no need for Joseph or anybody else to give advice. In all other cases Joseph absolutely refused to, and so he wrote in a letter to the editor of the *Wasp:* "My feelings revolt at the idea of having anything to do with politics. I have declined in every instance in having anything to do on the subject. I think it would be well for politicians to regulate their own affairs. I wish to be let alone, that I may attend strictly to the spiritual welfare of the church."[38] That was another arena, another ball game, another area of experience in power that has nothing to do with the eternities. For Joseph, it was a distraction he was pushed into; he did not like it. Government was never by compulsion; even in the Church no man is forced against his will. He said,

> People acting together are the foundation of the authority of the church. "I informed the people [that in]

the government of the church, in business transactions, every man should have a voice in the matter as if the whole responsibility were on his shoulders."[39]

When "every one of them shall see for themselves, and prophesy for themselves, have vision to themselves,"[40] only then will they have "undivided feelings"[41] and be able to dispense with present teachers because they'd all have the same visions then, but for themselves; but even when they act with such unity "every man must act according to the wisdom he can command. No man can be condemned for voting in the negative."[42]

One can see that this newfound freedom was bound to go to the heads of some people. Until they became Mormons they never dreamed of such a prospect for advancement. Pioneer types were always looking for the big bonanza. New members of the Church almost overnight would start having dreams of personal glory and claiming authority of personal revelation. When Brother Joseph put restraints on their claims and their plans, they would often declare him a fallen prophet and offer their own revelation as the way to go.

A surprising number of people follow that course today. You would think this would put the Church at a terrible risk. In fact, it would have destroyed any man-made organization many times, and indeed the scores of defectors have loudly proclaimed that their newly discovered evidence and powerful arguments would once and for all bring Mormonism down in ruins. Brodie made that very same boast. When the great theologian Krister Stendahl, now Lutheran Bishop of Lund, was in Provo, I had a conversation with him. He was very much upset with Joseph Smith's statement, "I never hear of a man being damned for believing too much; but they are damned for unbelief."[43] No man was ever damned for believing too much. But if you're damned for believing too much, then we are all damned. All of us believe things that aren't true, things that will be proven false in time to come. Scientists like Galileo, Newton, Heisenberg, Planck, Hawking, and Penrose all have had differing beliefs about the very nature of our existence, the most fundamental doctrines of reality. Einstein used to bring God into it. But they all respected each other and didn't damn each other for wrong ideas. Yet throughout history, men have damned and persecuted and banished and imprisoned and burned others on a vast scale, not for any crimes they committed, but purely for having the wrong ideas. The only crime for which persons were brought to trial during the inquisition was heresy. Joseph said, "If any man is [authorized] to take away my life who say I am a false teacher so I [should] have the same right to all false teacher[s] & [then] where [would] be the end of the blood & there is no law in the heart of God that [would] allow any one to interfere with the rights of man; every man has the right to be a false as well as a true prophet. If I [show] verily that I have the truth of God & [show] that ninety nine of 100 are false [prophets,] it [would] deluge the whole world with blood."[44]

That's exactly what it has done. Consider the Christians and Muslims of Lebanon, for example, living together for centuries with each other, sharing the same customs and values. Each knows the other not as a bad person, yet for years they've been slaughtering each other purely for having the wrong beliefs; and within that group, the Sunni and the Shiites are both good Muslims who disagree on but one point of tradition, and for that the car bombs and artillery fire have reduced their beautiful city to rubble.

How should one deal with unbelievers, critics, and

heretics? Joseph Smith wrote the book on that. The Book of Mormon sets it all forth in exceeding plainness. In the reign of King Mosiah, after the time of prosperity, a rising generation could not understand the words of King Benjamin. The resurrection especially they found incomprehensible and unbelievable (as do most Christians), because they would not make an effort to believe. Benjamin had said they could not understand, and so their hearts were hardened. They used that as an excuse, of course, for escaping the moral restraints of their behavior, a behavior which the gospel required. They adopted their own lifestyle, "and they were a separate people as to their faith, and remained so ever after, even in their carnal and sinful state" (Mosiah 26:4). They embraced a much more permissive moral doctrine, which became very popular. The popularity of that easygoing church, the religion of Nehor, made it the dominant religion almost to the end of the Book of Mormon. This is no wonder since it allowed them, as we're told, to live in a "carnal and sinful state."

The numbers of dissenters grew, due to criticism within the Church. There were dissensions among the brethren, while the outsiders kept working on the members to accept the new moral emancipation (Mosiah 26:1–6). What was to be done? Members of the Church who had begun to make trouble were brought by local members before local priests and teachers; but those officers didn't know what to do, except to send the culprits on to Alma, since Mosiah recognized Alma as the head of the Church, the high priest (Mosiah 26:7). Mosiah felt it should be Alma's problem, but Alma didn't know what to do either. In fact, he had no idea of what had been going on. That's very interesting: Alma, the head of the Church, hadn't heard of it at all. He was the only one who didn't know.

Couldn't Alma be criticized for that? Remember, Moroni criticized Pahoran unfairly because he [Moroni] didn't know the score, and he didn't know the score because Pahoran hadn't told him the bad news, lest it discourage the soldiers at the front. Who was to blame in a case like that? As to the new subversives, Alma, we're told, "was troubled in his spirit," and he referred the matter back to the king (Mosiah 26:10–11). The immoral conduct of certain members of the Church was confirmed and admitted by them. They had no intention of repenting: Civil law could only punish them "according to their crimes" (Mosiah 26:11). Couldn't this disruption of the Church by making sport of people's beliefs be punished? Mosiah washed his hands of it. He said, "Behold, I judge them not," and tossed the hot potato right back to Alma: "I deliver them into thy hands to be judged" (Mosiah 26:12).

Alma was helpless. He "was again troubled; and he went and inquired of the Lord" (Mosiah 26:13), and the answer was clear and explicit: "He that will not hear my voice, the same shall ye not receive into my church" (Mosiah 26:28). Excommunication was the limit of their authority and is the only power to punish which the Church has ever had. It is not the same power of excommunication claimed by the Roman church, where excommunication means the same as damnation. It is for God alone to judge and pronounce a sentence of eternal salvation or damnation, and that only when the time comes, as the Lord told the disciples at Capernaum (cf. Mark 3:28–29). The Lord told Alma that after being cut off from the Church, any who confessed and repented were to be forgiven out of hand, even as often as they repented (Mosiah 26:30–31). After that they were not to be judged or criticized by other members of the Church for what they had done.

Then something much worse happened. Alma's eldest son and four of Mosiah's sons rebelled. One gets the feeling that Alma had been perhaps too strict. Extreme severity with youth doesn't go over well in prosperous times, as leading lights among the young, like Alcibiades (a fifth-century B.C. Athenian playboy, politician, and general), or the Algonquin crowd[45] who flourished when I was young, have shown. The younger Alma, an impressive and persuasive personality, as we learn from his later career, became all the rage with the youth, making fun of their beliefs, deriding them for the old-fashioned ways of their parents. With their public showing off, they mixed private parties and conclaves, deliberately seeking to break down the Church and the government (cf. Mosiah 27:8–9).

We know it took an angel to stop them. But their fathers were the monarch himself and the head of the Church. Why didn't they do more? Why didn't they simply lock up the troublemakers until they learned to behave? It was because the young protestors were making a religious statement, however offensive and negative. The king had laid down the law: No persecution either of believers by unbelievers, of unbelievers by believers or of believers by other believers, or unbelievers by other unbelievers (cf. Mosiah 27:1–3). In short, there was to be no persecution, and the purpose of all this was so that "there should be an equality among all men" (Mosiah 27:3). When one group can bring social pressure one against another, you do not have equality. Just imagine the king and the high priest both allowing criticism, dissension, and propagandizing to go on and on, doing nothing about it until the lax and easy church of the dissenters became Nehors and began taking over everything! The fact that the young men behaved so insolently certainly suggests that they had been either somewhat spoiled, overdisciplined, or neglected. Remember, Alma didn't know what was going on.

Nevertheless, obnoxious as they made themselves, they were within their rights. They were making a religious statement, and no one could deny them that privilege. Why not? "For it was strictly contrary to the commands of God that there should be a law . . . against a man's belief" (Alma 30:7, 11), including atheism, whose believers are often as fervid as any fundamentalist. We are told in Alma, "If a man desired to serve God, it was his privilege, . . . but if he did not believe in him there was no law to punish him" (Alma 30:9). It was under the protection of this Bill of Rights that the infamous Korihor was able to carry on with perfect impunity. Only a miracle stopped him, and the only punishment he received was at the hands of a Zoramite mob after he left the country (Alma 30:59). Korihor had been brought before Ammon, the high priest at Jershon (Alma 30:19–20), who passed him on to Giddonah, the high priest in the land of Gideon, who sent him on to Alma at Zarahemla (Alma 30:21–30). What were all those leading authorities so helpless against? Against abridging the right of free speech and freedom of religion as "laid down by the commandments of God" (cf. Alma 30:7). These are the words of the Book of Mormon. There was punishment for crimes, of course, and the crimes are listed. "Nevertheless, there was no law against a man's belief; therefore, all men were on equal grounds." No one was subject to any social pressure or group disapproval. If you did not want to participate in public prayer, for example, or if you agreed with Isaiah that such displays of piety were usually an abomination before God (cf. Isaiah 1:13), that was your privilege. Only God is in a position to say which nations are really under God and which are not.

Let me insert a quotation from a news dispatch of a couple of years ago. "In Charlottesville, Virginia, at the National Council of Boy Scouts of America, a local scout official has ruled that a youth who does not believe in God must be expelled from the organization. Paul Trout, 15, was denied a Life Scout promotion several months ago when he said he didn't believe in a supreme being. Now [he] will be forced to leave the organization, following the ruling by the national scout leaders, an official said Friday."

Going back to the Nephites again: "If [a man] did not believe, . . . there was no law to punish him. . . . Therefore all men were on equal grounds" (Alma 30:9, 11). No one will deny that the smart-aleck criticism of Alma and his friends was bad, unfair, foolish, and injurious. What could be done about it? The answer is always the same. One replies by preaching the gospel with increasing fervor, and that is what the young Alma learned for himself.

> Do not you wish sometimes you had some power to pinch their ears? Do not you wish you had power to stop them in their mad career? Let the Lord Almighty do this. You think his eye is upon the work of his hands? It is. His ears are open to the prayers of his children, he will hear their prayers, he will answer their desires; and when we as a people possess the abundance of that patience, that long-suffering and forbearance that we need, to possess the privileges and the power the Lord has in reserve for his people, we will receive to our utmost satisfaction. We shall not have it now.[46]

The Lord says, I cannot give it now. We are not tolerant enough.

> Now, suppose that we were to issue our edicts to the whole world of mankind for them to obey the Gospel we preach, and had the power to compel them to obey, could we do it according to the dictates of our religion? We

could not. We could invite them, and could tell them how, but we could not say, and maintain the faith that we have embraced, you must bow down and profess our religion and submit to the ordinances of the kingdom of God.[47]

A principle as strong as that of free agency itself exists from eternity to eternity. We read about that principle in the book of Abraham—There is a head. There must always be a head: "In the spirit of my calling, and in view of the authority of the Priesthood that has been conferred upon me, it would be my duty to reprove whatever I esteemed to be wrong."[48] Joseph did not hesitate to cut off the highest authorities in that capacity. Would any impostor have dared to excommunicate such powerful and ambitious men as William E. McLellan, Thomas B. Marsh, David W. Patten, William W. Phelps, John Whitmer, Orson Hyde, and others—men who knew all about the personal affairs of Joseph and whether there had been any serious transgressions in his past? He said, "We do not consider ourselves bound to receive any revelation from any one man or woman [everybody has a perfect right to revelation—all he wants] without his being legally constituted and ordained to that authority, and giving sufficient proof of it."[49] Many should take this to heart today. Many a character has come up to me and said, "Brother Nibley, the Lord has revealed to me that you should give me an 'A.'" Well, all I have to say is that we do not feel bound by any such revelation. No member of the Church has any right to publish any doctrine of the Church. You can have all the ideas you want but may not publish them as doctrines of a church without first submitting them to the leaders for their approval. This does not cramp anyone's style. "Any person," Joseph Smith said, "can ask the Lord for a witness concerning himself, and get an answer, but not to lead the Church."[50] That belongs to the head of the Church. This doesn't make a tyrant of the leader. The keys of the priesthood were committed to Joseph to build up the kingdom, but when he was called to preside over the Church, it was by the voice of the people. This is strong stuff: "Leaders are not to be blindly followed."[51] "Suppose that the people were heedless, that they manifested no concern with regard to the things of the kingdom of God, but threw the whole burden [of leadership] upon the leaders of the people, saying, 'If the brethren who take charge of matters are satisfied, we are,' this is *not* pleasing in the sight of the Lord."[52] Nothing is automatic. The Spirit must always lead.

In recent years, one frequently hears (especially in testimony meetings) such things as, "We are thankful for having a prophet who can tell us exactly what we have to do and think every moment of the day." The prophet is a convenient time and trouble saver. Actually, people pester him to death for these things (they always have), as someone ready to bail us out no matter what silly things we've done or what a fool you've made of yourself. We're not going learn anything that way. Let us recall Joseph's warning the people who "were depending on the Prophet, hence were darkened in their minds, [and] . . . neglecting the duties devolving upon themselves"[53] as much as the prophet; but he was not to be called on for every emergency. "It is a great thing to inquire at the hands of God, or to come into His presence; and we feel fearful to approach him, . . . especially about things [which] . . . men ought to obtain in all sincerity . . . for themselves, in humility by the prayer of faith."[54] Don't ask me for revelation in your own affairs, says the leader. You have just as much right to it as I have.

Joseph was not told everything. He said that the three

things he wanted to know more than anything else were withheld from him, and he said regarding the Missouri affair, "[I] dare not advise, not knowing what shall befall us, as we are under very heavy and serious threatenings from a great many people in this place."[55]

Did the people believe Joseph Smith, Jr., to be a prophet? Yes, and every man who has a testimony of Jesus. When Brigham Young was asked in an interview with a representative of the *New York Herald*, "[Do] you, like the old prophets, receive direct revelation from God?" he answered, "Yes, and not only me, but my brethren also." "Does that extend to all the Church without reserve or rank?" "Yes, and it is just as necessary for the mother to possess this spirit in training and rearing her children as for any one else." "It is not absolutely necessary, then, that each person receive revelation through you?" "Oh, no; through the spirit of Christ, the Holy Ghost; but to dictate the Church is my part of it"[56]—what the Brethren say is the word and the will of the Lord (cf. D&C 84), but only, as President Clark pointed out no fewer than twenty-seven times in a speech on the subject, when they are so moved upon by the Holy Ghost. "How can we know that?" asked Brother J. Reuben Clark, Jr. By following the oft-repeated principle that everyone must so live that the Holy Ghost will reveal to him whether the others are speaking by the spirit or not.[57]

> Do you know whether I am leading you right or not? Do you know whether I dictate you right or not? Do you know whether the wisdom and the mind of the Lord are dispensed to you correctly or not? . . . I have a request to make of each and every Latter-day Saint, or those who profess to be, to so live that the Spirit of the Lord will whisper to them and teach them the truth. . . . In this there is safety; without this there is danger, imminent

danger [you otherwise get a tyrant or a dictator]; and my
exhortation to the Latter-day Saints is—Live your religion
[and you'll know for yourself].[58]

Does this fit us in the position of critics, then? Yes, critics
of our own behavior. Before I question another or make a
direct appeal to God, I must be perfectly sure of my own
purity and integrity, because what I'm asking for is the
same revelation.

For myself, there's where the real criticism starts. This is
the paradox of freedom of the individual in society. The first
check on criticism is this: "Be [not] so certain that you comprehend the things of God, when all things with you are so
uncertain."[59] That's the first step: You don't know so damn
much. In fact, you know very little that is true and proven:
How high is Timpanogos? The figure changes from time to
time, which makes me something of a dupe. This is something the *New York Herald* reported: Brigham Young at a
dance; the reporter was bemused. The *Herald* said he
couldn't get away with it: "From his position as a leader,
such familiarity would, in most cases, be fatal to great
claims. . . . Strange world, strange folks!"[60] A wonderful
man, Brigham. No other man dared to speak to such men
as he did. Yet they took it in good part. Talking of the
brethren, he said, "They wince under it at the time, but once
chastened they are even more devoted than ever." "Most of
the Elders who preach in this stand ought to be kicked out
of it, and then kicked into it again, until they overhaul
themselves and find out what is the matter with them."[61]
That's criticism, but it's constructive criticism. He wanted
them kicked out, but then kicked back again. That was the
paradox.

Of course, one can't be certain about anything. Joseph
said that "we . . . live in a wicked world where men busy

themselves watching for iniquity";[62] and what is to be gained by it? But the spirits of good men cannot interfere with the wicked beyond prescribed bounds. For "Michael, the archangel dared not bring a railing accusation against the devil, but said, the 'Lord rebuke thee Satan'" (cf. Jude 1:9).[63]

A characteristic and familiar situation occurred in the year the Prophet was martyred:

> An individual . . . with . . . [an] abhorrence of evil [joins the Church]. . . . He sets himself upon the watch to detect the failings of others, deeming that he is doing God [a] service in being so employed, and thus is he decoyed into the occupation of the great master of evil, to be the accuser of the brethren. And during the time thus occupied by him, he considers himself actuated by the purest motives, arising from a detestation of sin. . . . Yet mark the subtlety of Satan in thus leading men into a false position. Such a course, in the first place, probably arose from the purest of motives, and perhaps the individual was instrumental in rectifying some error; he feels a satisfaction in having done so, his self-esteem is gratified, and ere he is aware, he is seeking for another opportunity of doing the same, . . . continually set[ting] himself up as being capable of sitting in judgment upon others, and of rectifying by his own ability the affairs of the kingdom of God.[64]

Joseph said, "The eagerness to accuse is from the devil."[65] But Joseph recognized that at all times the defects of the Church are the same we find today. But that's not the point. "Notwithstanding this congregation profess to be saints yet I stand in the midst of all characters and classes of man. . . . Yes, I am standing in the midst of all kinds of people. Search your hearts & see if you are like god."[66]

"We have thieves among us, adulterers, liars, hypocrites. . . . As far as we degenerate from God, we descend to the devil and lose knowledge, and without knowledge we cannot be saved, and while our hearts are filled with evil, and we are studying evil, there is no room in our hearts for good, or studying good. . . . The Church must be cleansed, and I proclaim against all iniquity. A man is saved no faster than he gets knowledge."[67] Hence we need revelation to assist us and give us knowledge. We are helpless otherwise. "Ignorance," Joseph said, "superstition and bigotry placing itself where it ought not, is oftentimes in the way of the prosperity of this Church."[68] Why don't the Church's enemies circulate Brother Joseph Fielding Smith's *Teachings of the Prophet Joseph Smith* as an anti-Mormon book? It has such strong statements in it.

What would Joseph Smith do about evil? He didn't worry, because God was in charge. "Notwithstanding we are rolled in the mire of the flood for the time being, the next surge peradventure, as time rolls on, may bring to us the fountain as clear as crystal, and as pure as snow."[69] With that perfect confidence, he never panicked, he never worried. As Eduard Meyer said, "He never shows a moment of doubt," as every other religious leader necessarily must. After his vision, he never showed any signs of doubting where it all would end. Though Thomas B. Marsh was president of the Twelve, still he was told, "Therefore, see to it that you trouble not yourselves concerning the affairs of my Church in this place [it wasn't his business], . . . but purify your hearts before me and then go ye into all the world and preach my gospel."[70] Heber C. Kimball, when he visited Kirtland after the debacle, found it a bleak and doleful prospect. He said, "But the faults of our brethren is poor entertainment for us. We have no accusation to bring, for the Lord has shown us that he has taken the matter into his own hands."[71]

During the past two weeks, the beginnings of phenomenal spread of religious scams throughout the country, a major item in national news, has been traced to Utah. So what else is new? Ever since Moroni told Joseph Smith that greedy men would be after the plates and that he, too, would be tempted, the problem of exploiting the Church and the gospel has been with us. "There have been frauds and secret abominations and evil works of darkness going on, leading the minds of the weak and unwary into confusion and distraction, and all the time palming it off upon the Presidency,"[72] Joseph Smith reported. "Where a crowd is flocking from all parts of the world of different minds, religions, &c., there will be some who do not live up to the commandments; & there will be designing characters who would turn you aside & lead you astray, speculators who would get away your property."[73] This is nothing new. Therefore it is necessary that we have an order, and it is the heads of the Church who are best qualified to advise us. "Many, when they arrived here, were dissatisfied with the conduct of some of the Saints, because everything was not done perfectly right, and they get angry, and thus the devil gets advantage over them to destroy them. . . . But if they would bear with my infirmities and the infirmities of the brethren, I would likewise bear with their infirmities."[74]

Men whose questionable business prospects he rebuked would go over and find allies among the mob. Joseph Smith was never safe a moment. When he gave a speech to some newly arrived immigrants who had just come to Nauvoo very much impressed, he ended by saying, "I told them it was likely I would have again to hide up in the woods, but they must not be discouraged."[75] He had come out of the woods to preach, and he would have to hide up in the woods. This is a man who was not going to get a big head.

"The First Presidency returned at Evening all sound and well. . . . They were chased some 10 or 12 miles by some Evil designing persons but escaped out of their hands."[76] Such were the special privileges of the President of the Church—hiding out in the woods and being chased. What a business!

Franklin D. Richards reported Joseph Smith as saying that "He intended to do his duty before the Lord and hoped that the brethren would be patient as they had a considerable distance [to go]. . . . Until we have perfect love we are liable to fall. . . . That God had often sealed up the heavens because of covetousness in the Church. . . . And except the Church receive the fulness of the Scriptures, . . . they would yet fail."[77]

Isn't this exactly the situation today? President Benson pleads with us to read the scriptures, so we gingerly pick our way through the Book of Mormon, as if we were tiptoeing through a minefield instead of taking each passage to heart. What a trial it must have been for one who had conversed with angels and with the prophets of old to find himself surrounded by a bunch of yahoos who considered themselves very important. In the 1840s, important men swarmed on the frontier; everybody seemed to be a "botanic" doctor who either prescribed calomel or lobelia (those were the two schools of medical thought); or a general, someone who had mustered troops at one time or another, or you were a judge, someone who had read the law sometimes.[78] Joseph Smith said, "All ye doctors who are fools, . . . stop your practice. And all ye lawyers who have no business, only as you hatch it up, would to God you would go to work or run away!"[79] Joseph was surrounded by such men. How could he get through to them? How could he get them to react? "How vain and trifling have been our spirits, our conferences, our councils, our meetings, our private as well as public conversations—too low, too mean, too vulgar, too condescending for the dignified characters of the called and chosen of God."[80]

But because people have faults, we do not rebuke them unless some good can come of it. What we call "constructive criticism," meaning approval, is not criticism at all. To be constructive, criticism must reach the person for whom it is meant and, of course, he must have a chance to reply—but that is discussion, not criticism. "They frequently accused the brethren, thus placing themselves in the seat of Satan, who is emphatically called 'the accuser of the brethren.'"[81] The word *devil* derives from the Greek *diabolos,* which simply means "accuser," and there are many tales of how Satan goes before the Lord bringing accusation against his erring children. The interesting point is that Satan does not make *false accusations*—he doesn't need to with men behaving the way they do, it is for making these real accusations that the Lord rebukes and dismisses the devil from his presence.

We can always count on the critics: "False and wicked misrepresentations [by members] . . . have caused thousands to think they were doing God's service when persecuting the children of God."[82] The splinter group was another phenomenon that began with the Church itself and is still flourishing. The leaders of such, who go off by themselves to live the gospel in its purity, as they think, have discredited the Church, their cause, by breaking the basic rule on which the Church is founded: "No man has any liberty to lead away people into the wilderness."[83] There were various "Rechabite" departures in the Book of Mormon, and such defections are still going on, always based on someone's personal revelation.

People must be proven guilty by positive evidence, or they stand clear. Let no one presume to say this or that General Authority is fallen, or anything else. "No man is capable of judging a matter, in council, unless his own heart is pure; . . . we frequently are so filled with prejudice, or have a beam in our own eye, that we are not capable of passing right decisions."[84] "Every man, before he makes an objection to any item, . . . should be sure that he can throw light upon the subject rather than spread darkness."[85] Joseph set forth to the people "the evils that existed, and that would exist, by reason of hasty judgment, . . . upon any subject given by any people, or in judging before they had heard both sides of a question."[86] "If I esteem mankind to be in error, shall I bear them down? No. I will lift them up, and in their own way too, if I cannot persuade them my way is better; and I will not seek to compel any man to believe as I do, only by the force of reasoning."[87] No matter what the provocation, "let the Elders be exceedingly careful about unnecessarily disturbing and harrowing up the feelings of the people. . . . Avoid contentions and vain disputes with men of corrupt minds, who do not desire to know the truth. . . . If they receive not your testimony in one place, flee to another, remembering to cast no reflections, nor throw out any bitter sayings."[88]

"Leave the kingdom alone, the Lord steadies the ark; and if it does jostle, and appear to need steadying, if the way is a little sideling sometimes and to all appearance threatens its overthrow, be careful how you stretch forth your hands to steady it; let us not be too officious in meddling with that which does not concern us. Let it alone, it is the Lord's work. I know enough to let the kingdom alone, and do my duty. It carries me, I do not carry the kingdom."[89] It's interesting that people who find fault do not want to be excommunicated. They'd lose their clout with the Gentiles if they were not members of the Church, and of course if they were excommunicated they wouldn't carry much weight in the Church anyway. "Many who have left this Church have tried the experiment of building up the kingdom of God by their learning, saying, 'When we have established our Church it will then be the kingdom of the Lord.'"[90] So what do you do if you see folly and error all around you? You continue to think for yourself. That's the first rule, which means to think *to* yourself. Thought is an inner process. It never reaches finality. "Theories can't be proved," says Hawking, the eminent physicist of our time.[91] Joseph said, "We build our own kingdoms and obtain by our own faithfulness our own crowns that will exactly fill us."

So it is with Brother Joseph's advice on the subject. "Let us be faithful and silent, brethren, and if God gives you a manifestation, keep it to yourselves. . . . Do not watch for iniquity in each other, if you do you will not get an endowment, for God will not bestow it on such."[92] In an organization made up so largely of nonconformists, conflicts are inevitable, and the leader told them this was one of the ways in which they were being tested. "His personal presence we have not, therefore we have need of greater faith, . . . and I am determined to do all that I can to uphold you, although I may do many things inadvertently that are not right in the sight of God."[93] Within the Church itself, said Joseph, "Indeed, the adversary is bring[ing] into requisition all his subtlety to prevent the Saints from being endowed by causing division among the 12 [apostles] also among the 70 and bickerings and jealousies among the Elders and official members of the Church."[94] So he covenanted with the Twelve: "I will not listen [to] nor credit any derogatory report against any of you nor condemn you upon any testimony beneath the heavens, short of that testimony which is infal[l]ible, untill I can see you face to face and know of a surity. . . . I ask the same of you[!]"[95] This was a peculiarity of Joseph Smith—to love and esteem people deeply, but at the same time be perfectly aware of all their terrible faults. "Brethren, I am not a very Pieus man," he said. "I do not wish to be a great deal better than any body else. If a Prophet was so much better than any body else was he would inherit a glory far beyond what any one else would inherit and behold he would be alone, for who would be his company in heaven."[96] Then he added, "Righteousness is not that which men esteem holiness. That which the world call righteousness I have not any regard for. To be righteous is to be just and merciful. If a man fails in kindness justice and mercy he will be damed."[97]

"Brother Sidney is a man whom I love."[98] When a conference by a vote of the Church restored him to the First Presidency after Joseph had dismissed him, Joseph took him back and said, "Notwithstanding these things, he is a very great and good man."[99] A typical example appears in two successive entries in Joseph Smith's journal. Several elders united with Joseph Smith and prayed "that the Lord would grant that our Brother Joseph [Smith] might prevail over his enemy, even Doctor P[hilastus] Hurlbut, who has threatened his life."[100] The next entry, recalling an earlier event, states that, "Doctor P[hilastus] Hurlbut came to my house. . . . He was ordained to the office of an Elder in this Church. . . . I heard him say . . . that if he ever became convinced that the Book of Mormon was false, he would be the cause of my destruction."[101] And he tried to prove that the rest of his life, with false affidavits, etc. Notice that Joseph always gives the enemy, the other person, the benefit of the doubt. How could he meet such depravity, as in the case of his brother William?[102]

A final point: The main object of jealousy and rivalry in organizations is rank and office:

> Let the Twelve be humble, and not be exalted, and beware of pride, and not seek to excel one above another, but act for each other's good, and . . . make honorable mention of . . . [our brother's] name [in our prayers before the Lord and before our fellow men], and not backbite and devour our brother. . . . Must the new ones that are chosen to fill the places of those that are fallen, [of] the quorum of the Twelve, begin to exalt themselves, until they exalt themselves so high that they will soon tumble over and have a great fall, and go wallowing through the mud and mire and darkness, Judas-like, to the buffetings of Satan, as several of the quorum [of the Twelve] have done?[103]

Joseph said that from the commencement of this work, he had to surmount difficulties in "consequence of aspiring men, 'Great big Elders,' as he called them, who [had] caused him much trouble. . . . He had been trampled under foot by aspiring Elders, for all were infected with that spirit. . . . He said we had a subtle devil to deal with, and could only curb him by being humble."[104]

"He spoke of the disposition of many men to consider the lower offices in the Church dishonorable, and to look with jealous eyes upon the standing of others who are called to preside over them. . . . It was the folly and nonsense of the human heart for a person to be aspiring to other stations than those to which they are appointed of God for them to occupy"[105] (cf. D&C 104; cf. 1 Corinthians 12:21). "Let not the head say unto the feet it hath no need of the feet" (D&C 84:109; cf. 1 Corinthians 12:21). Many already have been ordained. This personal ambition is natural, the

tendency to form exclusive groups and cliques, as bestow-
ing prestige and influence. "Concerning thy brethren, . . . be
not partial towards them in love above many others but let
thy love . . . abound unto all men and unto all who love my
name."[106] "Personal feelings of friendship and association
ought to sink into comparative insignificance and have no
force in view of consequences so momentous to the people
of the kingdom of God." Hence "the advancement of the
cause of God and the building up of Zion is as much one
man's business as another's. . . . Party feelings, separate
interests, exclusive designs should be lost sight of in the one
common cause, in the interest of the whole."[107] Joseph Smith
did his best to invest the brethren with his own magnanimous spirit. He "addressed [the Twelve] . . . against self-
sufficiency, self-righteousness, and self-importance, . . .
especially teaching them to observe charity, wisdom and . . .
love one toward another in all things and under all circumstances."[108]

But all men are not alike in stature, temperament,
or endowment. That's why the Lord, in the revelations, lays
such emphasis on gifts. It is through the various gifts distributed among us that we are able to get into the act. We
are told repeatedly both to *ask* for gifts and *seek* for gifts
(cf. D&C 42, 46). Among the last words of the Book of
Mormon are "Do not deny the gifts, do not reject the gifts"
(cf. Moroni 10:8). On the other hand, we are commanded
not to ask for or seek for office. Yet nobody seems particularly interested in asking or seeking for gifts, while men
constantly plan, scheme, and aspire to office. Martin Harris
and others actually left the Church because their services
were not recognized by high office. Martin Harris, who had
the privilege of standing in the presence of an angel and
turning over the plates, wanted an office in the Church,

something which would only be temporary and a nuisance. Why, let me talk to Moroni for five minutes and I'll give you the pleasure of sitting on the stand forevermore!

Why this craving for office? Because office necessarily has high profile and prestige. High seats in the synagogue are attended by what Shakespeare calls the "insolence of office."[109] Gifts, on the other hand, are secret and private. According to Joseph Smith, "The greatest, the best, and the most useful gifts would be known nothing about by an observer." It's the gifts you should want. What does the world know about prophesying? Our gifts are to be put to the use of the Church as part of a mix (D&C 46). Offices are distributed and balanced among the members, and that's why the Church, with a crew of pushy and assertive people, always sails with an even keel. Plots to bring it to sudden and brilliant worldly success have been matched by equally ambitious schemes to bring it to a complete halt, to accomplish complete dissolution. What Brigham Young calls the "Good Ship Zion" has sailed on in complete disregard of both—it has neither exploded in growth nor collapsed in dissolution.

While "it is the privilege of every Elder to speak of the things of God,"[110] says Joseph, God calls or elects particular men for particular works on whom to confer special blessings. He's aware of their defects. "If others' blessings are not your blessings, others' curses are not your curses."[111] So if you think any of the Brethren seem to be underendowed in any particular gift or knowledge, know that God has chosen that brother for other gifts, and God will endow him with the gifts he needs as the occasion arises.

How often have we seen quite ordinary men called to responsibility in the Church suddenly grow to stature almost beyond recognition? They become giants, so to speak. So let the intellectuals criticize the Brethren. The critics have always been right about the lack of intellectual, artistic, and literary savvy in the Church. We have always treasured the trash and trashed the treasures in the Church. Brigham Young said, "I could have wept like a whipt child to see the awful stupidity of [the Latter-day Saints] in not realizing the blessings bestowed upon them."[112]

Joseph Smith, for example, was an impassioned scholar; he hungered for learning; he revelled in it when he had a chance; and he never tired of showing and explaining the papyri to his visitors. His own curiosity was typically the most lively of all. "I . . . spent the day in translating the Egyptian records. . . . President [Oliver] Cowdery returned from New York bringing with him a quantity of Hebrew books for the benefit of the school. He presented me with a Hebrew Bible, lexicon and grammar, also a Greek Lexicon and Webster's English Lexicon."[113] Joseph threw himself with passion into the study of ancient Hebrew writings, and he made great progress through the year 1835, especially in Hebrew. It would be easy to underestimate his progress. By the end of the year, I'm sure he certainly would have qualified for graduate study in Hebrew. He knew much more about it than we give him credit for.

Joseph Smith had good advice for scholars. He said, "I discovered in this debate, . . . to[o] much zeal for mastery, to[o] much of that enthusiasm that characterizes a lawyer at the bar who is determined to defend his cause right or wrong. I . . . advise[d them] that they might improve their minds and cultivate their powers of intellect in a proper manner."[114] The critics are really just showing off, which is what we do in sessions like this [the Sunstone Symposium]. The next day he said he organized the School of the Prophets as a direct result of the manuscript find. "Spent this [day] in indeavering to treasure up know[l]edge for the be[n]ifit of my Calling."[115] "O may God give me learning even Language and indo[w] me with the qualifycations to magnify his name while I live."[116] "At home stud[y]ing the Greek Language. . . . In the afternoon visited . . . with the relatives of Bro[ther] Oliver Cowdery,"[117] who were obnoxious fundamentalists.

Why have we not followed Joseph Smith's lead in this search for learning? Our naiveté has brought the Church into embarrassing situations from time to time, and this is where the gifts are important. The Church is a school in which we all take the same basic courses. All are free then to branch out into specialities, which are important and necessary for some to pursue, lest we lose by default when we are noisily attacked in some directions. Joseph, had he lived, might have been a specialist. "My Soul delights in reading the word of the Lord in the original and I am determined to p[u]rsue the study of languages untill I shall become master of them if I am permitted to live long enough."[118] Always that "if"; he knew it. He made allowance for other plans, and the Lord did have other plans. Had Joseph and the Brethren followed the line of study that fascinated him, we would be up to our ears today in hair-splitting discussions and recondite speculation. If science never reaches any conclusions, scholarship never even makes a beginning. As it is, a General Authority recently told me that he found more snobbery and rank-consciousness among the religion faculty of the BYU than anywhere else in the Church. If a very, very little learning can have that effect on devoted brethren, what would it have done among the real brethren?

The Brethren have their work cut out for them, and strenuous work it is. It calls for studying the gospel and to see that the greatest possible number of people in all parts of the world get to hear the first principles. This requires constant repetition of first principles to fresh audiences wherever General Authorities go; they cannot be expected to set forth advanced ideas or front-line research. This poses a dilemma, for no men are more in touch with developments in various fields where the Church might be benefitted. On my first day in Provo, President Joseph Fielding Smith was having lunch with LeRoy Robertson at Edna Mae's [a Provo cafeteria on Fifth North and University], where I later joined them; and during the lunch, Joseph Fielding made a remark I will never forget: "We are rapidly coming to be known as a mediocre people." Since then we have made giant strides in the direction of mediocrity! But whose fault is that?

That very same first week, I had my first meeting with some of the faculty. Some of them complained of the mediocrity of our literature and art—the Harry Anderson school in the Church. I took the liberty to point out to the speaker, one of the most eminent on the faculty, that the Brethren would have no objection at all to his writing an immortal drama or poem or even a great American novel; in fact, nothing would delight them more than to have the present company produce an outpouring of those masterpieces whose absence they so deplored. They, not the Brethren, were responsible for the famine. That was rather surprising; they had not thought about it that way. But the knee-jerk reaction was, when upset, to blame the Brethren.

Joseph Smith retained his sanity by dealing with this type of situation in high good humor. We have some examples. "Don't be limited in your views with regard to your neighbor's virtue, but beware of self-righteousnes, and be limited in the estimate of your own virtues. . . . You must enlarge your souls towards each other. . . . We must bear with each other's failings, as an indulgent parent bears with the foibles of his children."[119] You see, we're at school. We must be allowed to make mistakes. "There are mistakes in the essays and the reports that are handed in," you say. So should we disband the schools? These mistakes are the whole point of it. We're here to search out the nitty-gritty. We need to find out where we're wrong and why. Such a practice will prepare us for the long pull ahead and here-after. Overriding all else is that grand feeling of love which makes life a joy, and everything I read about Joseph Smith reflects that promise. "I see no faults in the church," he said. "Let me be resurrected with the Saints, whether to heaven or hell."[120] The Church, taken as a whole, is the way things stand right now. A particular fault is neither here nor there. "What do we care if the society is good? . . . Friendship is the grand fundamental principle of Mormonism, to revolu-tion[ize and] civilize the world, [to] pour forth love. . . . I do not dwell upon your faults. You shall not [dwell] upon mine. . . . [If] Presbyterians [have] any truth, embrace that. Baptist, Methodist, &c. Get all the good in the world. Come out a pure Mormon."[121]

Then he gives a good description of our world: "The only polishing I get is when some corner gets rubbed off by coming in contact with something else, striking with accel-erated force against religious bigotry, priest-craft, lawyer-craft, doctor-craft, lying editors, suborned judges and jurors, and the authority of perjured executives, backed by mobs, blasphemers, licentious and corrupt men and women—all hell knocking off a corner here and a corner there."[122] Now isn't that our society today? Yet note well what follows: "It is with difficulty that I can keep from complaining and murmuring against this dispensation; but I am sensible that this is not right."[123] Nobody had better reason for knowing what was going on than Joseph because he was the object. All the brickbats were coming his way, and he was tempted to murmur, "but I am sensible that this is not right."[124] "The power over the minds of mankind, which I hold, . . . is . . . the power of truth in the doctrin[e]s. . . . I ask did I ever exer[c]ise any compulsion over any man. Did I not give him the liberty of disbelieveing any doctrin[e] I have preached if he saw fit, why do not my enemies strike a blow at the doctrin[e], they cannot do it, it is truth."[125] Joseph showed that his power was in the doctrines that he taught. He defied all men to upset that. The *Willard Richards Pocket Companion* says that the "final key deliver[e]d by Joseph [was] in the following Language: . . . It is an eternal principle that has existed with God from all Eternity that that man who rises up to condemn others, finding fault with the Church [the whole system], saying that they are out of the way while he himself is righteous, then know assuredly that that man is in the high road to apostacy and if he does not repent will apostatize as God lives."[126]

You might say that that person has already apostatized if he doesn't trust God to know what God is doing. But critics don't think of it that way. They want to be *in* the Church. A body of such people came together to complain to the Prophet of various annoyances; his reply was this: "These things are of too trivial a nature to occupy the attention of so large a body. I intend to give you some instruction on the principles of eternal truth. . . . Those who feel desirous of sowing the seeds of discord will be disappointed, on this occasion. It is our purpose to build up, and establish the principles of righteousness, and not to break down and destroy."[127] The case of William E. McLellan is typical. He "said he had no confidence in the heads of the Church, believing that they had transgressed. . . . Consequently he left of[f] praying [had he been praying until then?] and keeping the commandments of God and went his own way and indulged himself in his lustfull desires [what he wanted to do all along—to show disapproval of them?]. . . . O! foolish Man! . . . because thou hast heard of some *man's* transgression that thou Shouldest leave *thy* God and forsake *thy* prayers."[128]

This has always been the familiar scenario in the Church—people using perceived imperfections of the Church as a pretext for them to relax their own personal moral standards. The psychologists tell us regarding our own emotional feelings not to keep these feelings bottled up too tight, because it can lead to an explosion. So what should we do? Be like the importunate widow and complain; itemize your griefs, your doctrinal objections, your personal distastes to yourself, and then lay them all out in full detail before the Lord and get it out of your system. (You may wonder why people see me talking so much to myself.) With this understanding—you will do all this before the only Person qualified to judge either you or your tormentors. As you bring your complaints, be fully aware that he knows everything already—including everything there is to know about you.

I must mention reverse criticism here—flattery, which flourishes in our society. When I flatter someone, I'm telling him that he is better than I really think he is to get on his good side. There is a cynical twist to that; it's opportunistic. Actually, I am snidely mocking the man, manipulating him in my interest. I end with this admonition against flattery, lest I be accused when I say that I cannot imagine a body of men less likely to go astray or to lead anyone else astray than the present leaders of the Church.

When I first came to BYU, the division of Religion was

small, and Wilkinson's plan was to send the faculty out to stake conferences with the Brethren to recruit students for the school. I had the privilege of making a number of visits with quite a few General Authorities—S. Dilworth Young, young Milton R. Hunter, and others. How they worked their lifelong assignments, living in a goldfish bowl, ever-lastingly meeting appointments, and carrying out routine duties! True, there is nothing like the joy of doing the Lord's work, but anyone can have that privilege anytime. Don't envy them that.

I spent a week with Apostle Spencer W. Kimball visiting his home stake in Arizona. We were gone ten days. We went by train in those early days. We came back to the old Los Angeles station, and in that part of Los Angeles, there were a lot of bookstores, which I knew very well. I bought a whole set, a very rare collection, of Alfonsus De Lingorio, the seventeenth-century Redemptorist writer on probabilism, a very valuable set of ten volumes. I barely made it back to the train by running across a lot. I jumped on the train, plunked down beside Brother Kimball, who was already on the train, and staggered into the drawing room, my arms full of the complete set, which I greatly valued.

As we sat talking about the books, Brother Kimball casually took an immaculate linen handkerchief from the breast pocket of his jacket, and, stooping over, vigorously dusted off my shoes and trousers. It was the most natural thing in the world, and we both took it completely for granted. After all, my shoes were dusty in the race for the train, and Brother Kimball had always told missionaries to keep themselves clean and proper. It was no great thing—*pas d'histoire*. Neither of us said a thing about it, but ever since, that has conditioned my attitude toward the Brethren. I truly believe that they are chosen servants of God.

Notes

1. Milton V. Backman, Jr., *Joseph Smith's First Vision* (Salt Lake City: Bookcraft, 1971), 164.

2. *TPJS*, 196.

3. Dean C. Jessee, ed., *The Personal Writings of Joseph Smith* (Salt Lake City: Deseret Book, Co. 1984), 6.

4. Ibid., 5.

5. Ibid.

6. Ibid.

7. *TPJS*, 13.

8. *TPJS*, 18.

9. Scott H. Faulring, ed., *An American Prophet's Record: The Diaries and Journals of Joseph Smith* (Salt Lake City: Signature Books, 1989), 6.

10. *WJS*, 205.

11. Cf. Eduard Meyer, *The Origin and History of the Mormons*, tr. H. Rahde and Eugene Seaich (Salt Lake City: University of Utah, 1961), 54, 64, 99.

12. *TPJS*, 361.

13. *TPJS*, 249.

14. *TPJS*, 250.

15. Brigham Young, cited in Leland R. Nelson, comp., *The Journal of Brigham* (Provo, UT: Council Press, 1980), 29.

16. *TPJS*, 8.

17. Faulring, *Diaries and Journals of Joseph Smith*, 227.

18. *Webster's Third New International Dictionary* (Springfield, MA: Merriam Webster, 1986), 538.

19. Faulring, *Diaries and Journals of Joseph Smith*, 4.

20. *JD* 1:74.

21. *JD* 11:252.

22. *TPJS*, 11–12.

23. *TPJS*, 8.

24. *WJS*, 120; cf. *TPJS*, 237–38, *HC* 5:19.

25. *WJS*, 120; cf. *TPJS*, 237–38, *HC* 5:19.

26. *TPJS*, 13.

27. *TPJS*, 149.

28. *WJS*, 183–84.

29. *WJS*, 184.

30. *WJS*, 365–66.

31. *TPJS*, 364.

32. *TPJS*, 374.

33. *TPJS*, 49.

34. *TPJS*, 12.

35. *WJS*, 236–37.

36. *WJS*, 237.

37. *WJS*, 228.

38. *TPJS*, 275.

39. *JD* 3:89.

40. *JD* 3:89.

41. *JD* 3:89.

42. President Orson Pratt in *MS* 12:322.

43. *TPJS*, 374.

44. *WJS*, 349.

45. A group of New York intellectuals who met at the Algonquin Hotel in the 1920s.

46. *JD* 15:2.

47. *JD* 14:94.

48. *HC* 2:340.

49. *TPJS*, 21.

50. *HC* 5:551.

51. Cf. *JD* 1:244; 3:45, 157; 6:100; 9:150; 12:66, 96; 13:171; 14:205; 17:51; 18:248.

52. *JD* 3:45.

53. *TPJS*, 237.

54. *TPJS*, 22.

55. *HC* 1:455.

56. "Interview with Brigham Young," by a representative of the *New York Herald*, in *Deseret News* 26 (23 May 1877): 242.

57. J. Reuben Clark, Jr., "When Are the Writings or Sermons of Church Leaders Entitled to the Claim of Scripture?" second part of an address delivered 7 July 1954 at Brigham Young University, 5–17.

58. *JD* 17:51.

59. *WJS*, 238.

60. *MS* 22:701.

61. *JD* 3:223.

62. *TPJS*, 315.

63. Elden J. Watson, *Manuscript History of Brigham Young 1801–1844* (Salt Lake City: Smith Secretarial Service, 1968), 44.

64. *MS* 6:165–66.

65. Cf. *MS* 8:45: "The spirit that seeks only to accuse, that can only delight itself in the failings and errors of mankind, so born of hell as only to find delight in the defects of humanity. . . . It is the very work of Satan, and his servants."

66. *WJS*, 113.

67. *TPJS*, 217.
68. *TPJS*, 138.
69. *TPJS*, 138.
70. Faulring, *Diaries and Journals of Joseph Smith.*, 208.
71. Ibid., 189.
72. *TPJS*, 127–28.
73. *WJS*, 191.
74. *TPJS*, 268.
75. *TPJS*, 268.
76. Faulring, *Diaries and Journals of Joseph Smith*, 204.
77. *TPJS*, 9.
78. Cf. *WJS*, 277, nn. 16 and 17.
79. *WJS*, 329.
80. *WJS*, 137.
81. *WJS*, 212.
82. *HC* 2:255.
83. *HC* 7:254.
84. *TPJS*, 69.
85. *TPJS*, 94.
86. *TPJS*, 118.
87. *TPJS*, 313.
88. *TPJS*, 13.
89. *JD* 11:252.
90. *JD* 1:198.
91. Stephen W. Hawking, *A Brief History of Time* (New York: Bantam, 1988), 167.
92. *TPJS*, 91.
93. *TPJS*, 90.
94. Faulring, *Diaries and Journals of Joseph Smith*, 94.
95. Ibid., 110.
96. *WJS*, 206.
97. *WJS*, 206.
98. *TPJS*, 30.
99. *TPJS*, 30.
100. Faulring, *Diaries and Journals of Joseph Smith*, 19.
101. Ibid., 20.
102. Ibid., 94–95.
103. *TPJS*, 155.
104. *TPJS*, 225.
105. *TPJS*, 223–24.
106. Faulring, *Diaries and Journals of Joseph Smith*, 207; cf. D&C 112:11.

107. *TPJS*, 231.

108. Faulring, *Diaries and Journals of Joseph Smith*, 237.

109. William Shakespeare, *Hamlet*, act III, scene i, line 73.

110. *TPJS*, 9.

111. *TPJS*, 12.

112. *JD* 2:280.

113. Faulring, *Diaries and Journals of Joseph Smith*, 66.

114. Ibid., 65–66.

115. Ibid., 96. The School of the Prophets was organized before this, but it was the next day (18 November 1835) that the school voted to send for a Hebrew teacher. On 4 January 1836, his diary says that they "[met] and organized our Hebrew School," but it was not until January 26 that their accepted professor, Joshua Seixas, arrived and began to teach.

116. Ibid., 91.

117. Ibid.

118. Ibid., 133.

119. *TPJS*, 228.

120. Faulring, *Diaries and Journals of Joseph Smith*, 398–99; cf. *TPJS*, 316.

121. Faulring, *Diaries and Journals of Joseph Smith*, 399; cf. *TPJS*, 316.

122. *WJS*, 282.

123. *TPJS*, 35.

124. *TPJS*, 35.

125. *WJS*, 337.

126. *WJS*, 413.

127. *WJS*, 339.

128. Faulring, *Diaries and Journals of Joseph Smith*, 182 (emphasis added).

17

Brigham Young as a Leader

For some years I've been collecting material on Brigham
Young, and now have a collection of pretty well everything
Brigham Young ever said on anything.[1] The computers will
have to get to work now and index it. If you arrange these
materials in topical order, you get some very interesting
results. I will be presenting his principal statements in
regard to leadership. He made an enormous number of
statements, thousands. And why Brigham Young? Well,
he's the one thing we have to be proud of at BYU, and he
certainly is, in my opinion, the greatest leader of modern
times. It would be hard to imagine any leader who faced
more terrible obstacles and more hopeless odds than
Brigham Young, or any leader who overcame them more
brilliantly. What he did was marvelous, and it is also very
relevant to our times.

   He led in a spirit of calm benevolence and was rarely
upset, and we can take great comfort in his example. We
want to find out how he did it, and he tells us. No matter
how bad our situation may be, individually and collectively,
in this modern world it can't conceivably be as bad as the

This talk was given 6 June 1967 at Brigham Young University.

situations in which the Mormons found themselves in the thirty years during which Brigham Young led them. How did he always manage to come out on top? How, with his tremendous achievements, against tremendous odds, did he manage to avoid all signs of wear and tear on himself, and turn the most intensely dangerous and unpleasant situations into amusing episodes, as far as he was concerned?

All the commentators, no matter how hostile, concede that Brigham Young was one of the great leaders of all time, one of the supremely practical men of his age, a hard-headed, even-keeled, no-nonsense realist who got things done. From this it is only too easy to reconstruct the character of Brigham Young as a hard, uncompromising, driving, materialistic businessman—and you could not find anyone more different from that, for there are limits beyond which such men can't accomplish, and Brigham Young went far beyond those limits. He was unique, and we are very fortunate to be able to learn just what made him tick. He himself tells us clearly and often just what it was. For along with his practical attainments and mechanical skills, he was one of the most discursive and lucid of men. He had a passion for teaching. His great attainments are accompanied by a running commentary that enables us to learn just what was really going on.

For him, getting things done was incidental. The important thing was that the people should know what they were doing and why. His orders and recommendations are never without full and persuasive explanation. He wanted everyone to know what was going on. That's one of the great secrets of his leadership, as we'll see. It was one of his theories that if any man would allow himself to talk, he would infallibly reveal his true nature. As he says, "No man can hide [himself] if he is allowed to talk; he will be sure to manifest his true feelings."[2] He had a black leather couch in his office, opposite the window. His desk was at the window, so he sat with his back to the window, and anyone who came to visit him to make any requests for the first time would have to sit on that couch. For three minutes, Brigham wouldn't say a word. He'd just sit there and let them talk. If they didn't want to talk, that was fine. This was a nondirective interview. Here was Brigham Young, the window behind him, here was the couch, and he just sat at the desk sizing up his visitor. My grandfather was a passenger agent for Brigham Young's railroad, and he said that Brigham Young was the smartest man he ever knew. It was he who told me about this little black leather couch—real psychoanalysis. Within three minutes, Brigham knew perfectly the kind of person he was dealing with. If the person had come to swindle or otherwise damage him, he could see right through him by that time. And he never had occasion to change his judgment, my grandfather added. It took just three minutes, and all Brigham did was sit there without a sound, without a word; and before you knew it, he knew just whom he was dealing with, and he dealt with him accordingly. It showed his marvelous insight, and what a psychologist this man was.

He talks a lot and has a lot to say about everything, so it's a pleasure to read his vigorous, forthright, imaginative, picturesque prose. He swings from the shoulder with quick and powerful blows. Here's a man who has something to say with something behind it. He isn't a doctrinaire, a person giving us theory, a preacher who can be wise, or a professor in the four walls of an institution. This is a man who was tried seven times seven in the fire and who knew what he was talking about.

In the first place, since he was, above all, a leader, we

ask what he considers to be the general principles of leadership. So from now on you can listen to Brigham Young and not me. First of all, he notices that he has tough and rebellious people to lead. He says, "The Lord Almighty could resuscitate a corpse lying before us a thousand times easier than He could control the congregation in this house."[3]

> The sons of Ephraim are wild and uncultivated, unruly, ungovernable. The spirit in them is turbulent and resolute; they are the Anglo-Saxon race, and they are upon the face of the whole earth, bearing the spirit of rule and dictation, to go forth from conquering to conquer. They search wide creation and scan every nook and corner of this earth to find out what is upon and within it. I see a congregation of them before me to-day. No hardship will discourage these men; they will penetrate the deepest wilds and overcome almost insurmountable difficulties to develop the treasures of the earth, to further their indomitable spirit for adventure.[4]

> Now, that these people are governed at all is a great miracle in our estimation.[5]

> I fully believe that we are naturally a little rebellious, and that we are practically so; we are a little disposed to have our own way too much.[6]

And he deplores the lack of leadership for this group, this people. Good leaders are hard to find; they don't grow on trees, and he knew that. He says, "There are but few men that know how to govern in temporal things; fewer still who know how to control the feelings of the people, how to guide the power of any kingdom that was ever organized on the earth."[7]

> There are men here, by the score, who do not know their right hands from their left, so far as the principle of

justice is concerned. Does our High Council? No, for they
will let men throw dust in their eyes, until you cannot
find the hundredth millionth part of an ounce of common
sense in them. You may go to the Bishops' courts, and
what are they? A set of old grannies. They cannot judge
a case pending between two old women, to say nothing
of a case between man and man. We have already
dropped many of them, and we are picking up young
men. We will train them, and tell them to serve God or
apostatize.[8]

But there are some of our great men who are so ignorant that a personal favor will so bias their minds that
they will twist the truth and sustain a person in evil. This
principle is to be found, more or less, in the old, middle-
aged and youth. Some, with a trifling consideration, can
so prejudice the mind of a High Councillor, a High Priest,
a Bishop, or an Apostle, that he will lean to the individual instead of the truth.[9]

So he was out to find leaders, and the first principle of
leadership, as he declares it, is to lead. You do not drive.
Leadership is the antithesis of compulsion. "There never
was; and never will be a people in heaven nor on earth, in
time nor in eternity, that can be considered truly and
entirely independent of counsel and direction."[10] They must
have it. "You can gain and lead the affections of the people,
but you cannot scare them, nor whip them, nor burn them
to do right against their wills. The human family will die to
gratify their wills. Then learn to rightly direct those wills,
and you can direct the influence and power of the people."[11]
"Gather the Saints, but do not flatter; invite, but do not
urge, and by no means compel any one."[12] He then quotes
Joseph Smith: "I do not govern them at all. The Lord has
revealed certain principles from the heavens by which we
are to live in these latter-days. . . . The principles which He

has revealed I have taught to the people and they are trying to live according to them, and they control themselves."[13] "Gentlemen," Brigham Young resumes, "this is the great secret now in controlling this people. It is thought that I control them, but it is not so. It is as much as I can do to control myself and keep myself straight and teach the people the principles by which they should live."[14] "If they do not believe in my advice, teachings, and counsel, they are at perfect liberty to disbelieve them and I will not find one word of fault with them for so doing."[15] "We cannot make laws like the Medes and Persians. We cannot say you shall never drink a cup of tea, or you shall never taste of this, or you shall never taste of that; but we can say that Wisdom is justified of her children."[16] "We have paid our tithing. . . . But if your consciences and my conscience do not accuse us, why, I will not accuse you."[17] "We have history enough to prove that when [men] have the power their motto is, 'You shall.' But there is no such thing in the economy of heaven."[18] There is no "you shall." He asked them if they would or not. "I have not come here to say that you have got to join this order or we will cut you off [from] the Church, or you must join this order or we will consider you apostates [this is towards the end of his life, when he was going up and down preaching the United Order]; no such thing, oh no, the Saints are not prepared to see everything at once. They have got to learn little by little, and to receive a little here and a little there."[19] "I am not for cutting people off from the Church that worship their property instead of their God, but for bearing with them until they shall gain light and knowledge so as to see their errors and turn to the God of truth."[20]

A very consistent character emerges here in Brigham

Young: his broad tolerance and his sanity, but there's more than that behind it. He says,

> Now, suppose that we were to issue our edicts to the whole world of mankind for them to obey the Gospel we preach, and had the power to compel them to obey, could we do it according to the dictates of our religion? We could not. We could invite them, and could tell them how, but we could not say, and maintain the faith that we have embraced, you must bow down and profess our religion and submit to the ordinances of the kingdom of God. . . . It would prove that God is in fault in not making them do so [if he wanted them automatically to obey, he would have created them that way, as Dante says in "Paradise"]. . . . If we become Godlike we will be just as full of charity as he is. We would let pagans worship as they please, and to the Christians and Mohammedans, and all sects and parties in the world we would say, "Do just as you please, for your volition is free, and you must act upon it for yourselves before the heavens." Our religion will not permit us to command or force any man or woman to obey the Gospel we have embraced.[21]

"If a person wishes to know my religion, I am willing that he should know the whole of it. There is nothing secret or hidden in it. . . . But I am not disposed to compel any person to partake of that which they dislike, or have aversion for."[22]

"In our day it seems that the Spirit will actually prompt people," he says in 1871, "to liberal thinking, to liberal actions and to liberal government, and not to be as suppressive as they were in the days of the Jewish nation and other nations that then bore rule."[23] So he recognizes the futility of compulsion, and he has good reason for knowing it, too. "You cannot break down the indomitable will of the human family. I have known children to be so abused and whipped as to render them almost or entirely worthless, and still the indomitable will remained. How came it there? God organized us to become absolutely independent, and the will I am speaking about is implanted in us by him; and the spirit of every intelligent being is organized to become independent according to its capacity."[24]

Brigham Young said in 1859:

> When did tyranny ever cause repentance of evil? Never. It produces crime. When men are infringed upon in their rights and tyrannized over, they are prone to rise in their might and declare, "We will do as we please, and will let you know that we will have the ruling of our own rights and dispositions." Tyrannical power may possess the ability to behead them, hang them, or sentence them to prison; but resolute men will have their will.[25]

> They are willing to stand in the front of the battle, to go to the ends of the earth to preach the Gospel, or to do anything they are called upon to perform, yet, when you examine their morality, it highly outrages the feelings of those who are strictly moral and honest in all their ways. Do you believe this? Yes, and many of you know it.[26]

Leadership, then, means understanding men as they are, so you can't try to cast them into your mold. He says this is very important. You must deal with people as individuals:

> Then let us take a course to understand men as they are, and not endeavour to make them precisely as we are, for this you cannot do. . . . I am not going to drive a man or a woman to heaven. A great many think that they will be able to flog people into heaven, but this can never be done, for the intelligence in us is as independent as the Gods. People are not to be driven, and you can put into a gnat's eye all the souls of the children of men that are driven into heaven by preaching hell-fire.[27]

And then he speaks for himself: "Should I be told that it is time to wash my face and eat my breakfast, I should be strongly inclined to notify my informant that I knew that as well as he did. [But, there are people in the world who like to be told and need to be told.] There are [some] . . . who would not embrace the truth, unless they were ordered to do it."[28] Look at the difference between men.

> You may, figuratively speaking, pound one Elder over the head with a club, and he does not know but what you have handed him a straw dipped in molasses to suck. There are others, if you speak a word to them, or take up a straw and chasten them, whose hearts are broken; they are as tender in their feelings as an infant, and will melt like wax before the flame. You must not chasten them severely; you must chasten according to the spirit that is in the person. Some you may talk to all day long, and they do not know what you are talking about. There is a great variety. Treat people as they are.[29]

And he abhorred regimentation, as a true leader does. He recognized that God intends variety in all spheres of life. If you want to lead, the first thing you must never do, he says, is regiment.

> Inasmuch as the spirits of men have wisely been organized as diverse in power and peculiarities as their number, it is not expected, possible, or desirable, that the thoughts and actions of mankind be run in the same mold.[30]

> You cannot find two twigs alike. [He used to talk in this vein a lot.] You may examine any tree of the forest and see whether you can find any two leaves that are precisely alike. You cannot. Then you may go to a meadow, and see whether you can find two spears of grass just alike in shape and form. There are no two precisely alike.

Examples of that endless variety are now before me [in the tabernacle].[31]

> The Gospel will teach us all that variety that we see before us in nature—the greatest variety imaginable. One sister would get up a certain fashioned bonnet [he's talking about the millennium now—we'll all be different in the millennium], and another one another fashion; one would trim it in a certain way, and another in another way. When the brethren build their houses, the styles would be different. . . . The same variety would exist in the internal arrangements of the houses. We should see this variety with regard to families—here is one's taste, and another's taste, and this constant variety would give beauty to the whole. Thus a variety of talent would be brought forth and exhibited of which nothing would be known, if houses and dresses and other things were all alike.[32]

He was a great builder, and he was very ingenious, in his way. He built over two hundred houses, with never any two alike. Many are still displayed with pride in Pennsylvania—the ingenuity of the staircases, the cabinets, the cunning cupboards, and so forth. All sorts of Yankee ingenuity in display, but also great variety. He never got stereotyped; he didn't like it.

"There are not two faces alike [he says in 1862]; no two persons tempered alike; we have come from different nations of the world, and have been raised in different climates, educated and traditioned in different and, in many instances, in opposite directions, hence we are tried with each other."[33] It's hard to get along because we're so different. Of course it was true. This was one of his big problems. But he says, Let's make a virtue of that.

"And large drafts are made upon our patience, forbearance, charity, and good will—in short, upon all the higher and god-like qualities of our nature."[34] That's what we want to do. We have to live with this. "How many glories and kingdoms will there be in eternity? You will see the same variety in eternity as you see in the world."[35] "I conclude that there is as great a variety in the spiritual as there is in the temporal world, and I think that I am just in my conclusion."[36] He mentions this: "I have built a great many houses, both for myself and for others. I have never built two houses alike, and I do not expect to in time or eternity, but I mean to improve every time I begin. Build the best houses you can imagine."[37]

"I am not surprised that there are those who do not understand things as I do. I expect people to have their own peculiar views, forms, principles, and notions. In consequence of this great variety, we should not be astonished if all do not believe the Gospel—do not love the truth."[38] "The leader's business is to get people to want to do things, to place desirable objects before them, so that each will strive, entirely on his own, for that objective." The individual is not being driven, just being pulled into a vacuum. If you can put something more desirable in front of him than he has, something he wants very much, and make him want it, then your leadership takes care of itself. It's automatic. You are not driving, you are leading.

"I wish to say to you," he says without compulsion, "do not do it unless you want to."[39] This is the main thing. It's better not to do it at all than to do it grudgingly, as Mormon says: "If a man being evil giveth a gift, he doeth it grudgingly; . . . wherefore he is counted evil before God" (Moroni 7:8). "I wish to say to you, and I wish you to tell your neighbors, if there is any man or woman who do not want to pay their tithing, we do not want they should. It is for your particular benefit, and that of every individual upon the face of the earth."[40] "People are not compelled to pay their tithing, they do as they please about it, it is urged upon them only as a matter of duty between them and their God."[41]

> In all your transactions in these public matters, do
> not do, unless you want to. . . . We say to the Saints, Do
> not pay Tithing, unless you want to; do not help to build
> up this Temple unless you want to; do not put forth your
> hands to one day's work, unless you want to. . . . If you
> grudgingly put forth your means to help to gather the
> Saints, it will be a curse to you.[42]

We don't want your means. We want it to be your idea. "Then pay your tithing, just because you like to, not unless you want to. They say we cut people off the Church for not paying tithing; we never have yet."[43] "As far as these are concerned they have a right to get drunk; but we have rights, and have a right to disfellowship them, or cut them off from the Church and we calculate to do it whenever it ought to be done."[44]

"But we, in and of ourselves, ought to be independent; every son and daughter in Israel should say, we will keep the 'Word of Wisdom' independent of father, mother, or any elder of the church. [You don't do it because they tell you to, or even because they set the example.] We know what is right, and we will do it."[45]

> No person has a right to say to another, "Why do you
> eat wheat bread, corn bread, or no bread at all? [They had
> their food faddists, too.] why do you eat potatoes, or why
> do you not eat them? why do you walk, or why do you
> sit down? why do you read this or that book? or why do
> you go to the right or the left?" . . . If the Elders of Israel
> could understand this a little better, we would like it, for
> the simple reason that if they had power given them now
> they manifest the same weaknesses in the exercise thereof
> as any other people.[46]

Brigham Young says that when he was young someone wanted him to sign a temperance pledge. Well, he believed in temperance, but he refused to sign the pledge. "Even then I said, 'I do not need to sign the temperance pledge.' I recollect my father urged me. 'No, sir,' said I, 'if I sign the temperance pledge I feel that I am bound, and I wish to do just right, without being bound to do it; I want my liberty'; and I have conceived from my youth up that I could have my liberty and independence just as much in doing right as I could in doing wrong. What do you say? Is this correct?"[47] He would sign no pledges.

"One of the simplest things in the world is to control a people. Is there any particular art in making this people obedient? There is just one. If you Elders of Israel can get the art of preaching the Holy Ghost into the hearts of the people, you will have an obedient people. This is the only art required. Teach the people truth, teach them correct principles; show them what is for their greatest good and don't you think they will follow in that path? They will."[48] You don't need to push them.

"Pay no attention to what others do, it is no matter what they do, or how they dress."[49] Nobody, even if it is your father or mother or the elders of the Church, he said.[50] That isn't the reason. You do it because you want to do it. You are self-directed, you are inner-directed, you are not other-directed. This is what makes a great leader.

This is the secret of Brigham Young's power and his calmness. He tells us,

> It's basic to realize that we don't run things. We are not in control. We can't make people do anything, and so we have nothing to lose. So don't get flustered and don't worry. Your Heavenly Father is in control. The Lord reigns and rules in the armies of the heavens, and does

His pleasure among the inhabitants of the earth. He sets up a kingdom here, and pulls down another there, at His pleasure. He walks in the midst of the people, and they know it not. He makes Kings, Presidents, and Governors at His pleasure; hence I conclude that I shall be Governor of Utah Territory, *just as long as He wants me to be; and for that time* [there had been rumors that he was going to be deposed in 1855], neither the President [and Buchanan did send someone out to take his place] of the United States, nor any other power, can prevent it.[51]

He said, "Don't worry about it. I'll be governor as long as he wants." This is one of the few passages which he underlines in the *Journal of Discourses*.

True, to a certain permitted degree, we rule, govern, and control circumstances, in a great many instances, but, on the other hand, do not circumstances control us? [We make the decisions we have to make. We have very little choice, actually.] They do. Who has guided all these circumstances, which neither we nor the Prophet [Joseph] knew anything about? [There were a lot of things they didn't know about.] Was it in the power of a single man, or of any set of men, to create and control the circumstances which caused this people to be planted within these mountains? The moment that you say it was not, you acknowledge the workings of a Supreme Power.[52]

God is at the helm of this great ship, and that makes me feel good. When I think about the world, and the enemies of the cause of God, I care no more about them than I do for a parcel of musketoes.[53]

All people are in the hands of the Almighty, and He governs and controls them, though they cannot perceive, neither do they acknowledge, His handy-work. He exalts the President to be the head of the nation, and places kings upon their thrones. There is not a man that escapes

His cognizance, and He brings forth His purposes in the latter days.[54]

"I am in the hands of God, so is the President of our nation, and so are kings, and emperors, and all rulers. He controls the destiny of all, and what are you and I going to do about it? Let us submit to Him, that we may share in this invisible, almighty, God-like power, which is the everlasting Priesthood."[55] "I have labored faithfully over forty years," he says in 1873, "to convince the children of men that God rules in the heavens and that he will rule upon the earth."[56] "I believe in the one-man power. Who is that man? Our Father in heaven, God, the eternal Father."[57] The great difficulty we have to surmount is to bring ourselves to a condition of perfect submission. The flesh is so contaminated with evil that it is hard for us to submit entirely to the will of God.

Therefore, he can afford to be forbearing, and he was anything but overbearing. He never forces anyone, and that's true. Notice that all the personal biographies that deal with Brigham Young, written about him by his children and others close to him, always give the same thing: a totally different picture from what all the other biographies paint—Brigham the Tyrant, and that sort of thing. He never was that. He was always gentle. He could be pushed around by his wives and children. It was almost laughable. Although he wasn't pushed around, the fact is that he never used any force—perhaps he was too permissive. He accused himself of being so.

But "if a man asks you to go with him one mile, go two, and then you can say, 'You only asked me to go one mile, but I have gone two.' That is the counsel Jesus Christ gave. If you sit down and calmly reason the case, you cannot but discover that it gives you an influence over that man, which you could not gain by contending with him in anger. All the power which is gained by contending with people is usurped power."[58] "My father taught me in my youth that light knocks would split great blocks."[59] Don't go about it in super, all-out, crash programs. We're in his book. If it is going to take forty years for this temple, let it take forty years. But "light knocks will split great blocks" was one of his maxims. There's no danger in this neglect. Never worry about the Church, that it might be overcome, or anything. God's in charge of it, so Brigham says it doesn't worry him in the least. "The Lord stands at the helm that guides Zion's ship. He is its Dictator; and unless we work exactly to the line that is marked out by him, our works will be in vain."[60] So the breath of the Almighty can scatter our enemies to the four winds, and blow them to oblivion if we have faith. "That individual, neighborhood, people, or nation that will not acknowledge the hand of God in all things, but will squander their blessings, and thus pour contempt upon his kind favors, will become desolate and wasted away."[61] "You know the history of 'Mormonism'; and if this is not the Lord's work,"[62] I want it to be taken away. There's nothing to lose, anyway. There's nothing to worry about. If the Church should be overcome, well, plain enough, the Lord didn't support it. Then why shouldn't it be overcome? Then it is a fraud.

He continues: "If this is not the Lord's work, we had better quit it, for we should derive no benefit from remaining in it. If this is the Church of Christ, God will take care of his people and carry on this work. Brother [George Q.] Cannon stated that one gentleman he conversed with said that there is a power in this work beyond the power of Brigham Young. If we did not know this, we should quickly

scatter."[63] Not only did God foreknow the wicked and pre-
destinate them, but he also foreknew the righteous and pre-
destinated them. "I depend not upon human wisdom or
human power. I occupy the position that God our Heavenly
Father has placed me in, and . . . I tremble not, I fear not,
neither do I care for the insults of the world, for the Lord is
my bulwark, my shield and my deliverer."[64]

> What earthly power can gather a people as this
> people have been gathered, and hold them together as
> this people have been held together? It was not Joseph, it
> is not Brigham, nor Heber, nor any of the rest of the
> Twelve, nor any of the Seventies and High Priests that
> does this, but it is the Lord God Almighty that holds this
> people together, and no other power.[65]

So there's no problem of leadership at all, after all. God
will overrule the acts of the children of men in this kingdom
as well as among the nations. "Be ye reconciled to God, and
ask for the things that you want."[66] "We have not the influence and power necessary to refute the falsehoods circulated about us. We depend on God, who sits in the heavens."[67] "He has not committed the keys of the results of the
acts of the nations of the earth to any man on the earth; but
that power he retains to himself."[68] "All is right. God can
carry on his own work. This kingdom will stand forever.
You have heard brother [Heber C.] Kimball testify that this
kingdom will stand forever."[69] "The Lord dictates, governs,
and controls: I do not, neither do I wish to."[70]

So this is the foundation, the first practical rule of leadership. This is the theoretical, you see. God is in charge;
therefore, don't worry. It's very important not to. "It is a
great mystery to many people, and especially to strangers,
how I have preserved myself. . . . I am neither iron nor
immortal. But a great many marvel at my preservation. I

have revealed the secret a great many times, and can now—
I never worry about anything. I try to live so as to know my
business and understand my duty and to do it at the
moment without a long study."[71] He never broods over anything. "I say to a farmer or a merchant, if you want to live
so as to prolong your days, never worry about anything;
but have the Spirit of the Lord so as to know what to do,
and when you have done or counseled right never fret
about the result. It is in the hands of the Lord."[72] That's that,
you see. "We ought not to speak lightly of and undervalu-
ate the life we now enjoy, but so dispose of each passing
day that the hours and minutes are spent in doing good, . . .
cultivating the principle of kindness to every being pertaining to our earthly sphere; . . . and overcome every
ungovernable passion by a constant practice of cool judgment and deliberate thoughts."[73] "Do not worry. All is right,
for God reigns. Trust in him."[74]

> Keep as calm as a summer's evening; no harm can
> come to him who serves God with all his heart and trusts
> in Him for future results. "But" some say, "cannot they
> kill us?" Yes, they can kill you and me, if the Lord per-
> mits; but if He does not, I reckon they cannot. And sup-
> pose they do kill us! Do we want to stay in this world in
> our present condition forever? O, no.[75]

"Whether the world is going to be burned up within a
year [in 1856], or within a thousand years, does not matter a
groat to you and me. We have the words of eternal life, we
have the privilege of obtaining glory, immortality, and eternal lives, now will you obtain these blessings?"[76]

"Be not discouraged," he says, "for it is a joyful time."[77]
And he always kept a joyful countenance, in all the reverses
of the Saints. "There is not that man or woman in this congregation, or on the face of the earth, that has the privilege

of the holy Gospel, and lives strictly to it, whom all hell can make unhappy. You cannot make the man, woman, or child unhappy, who possesses the Spirit of the living God; unhappiness is caused by some other spirit."[78]

Brigham Young said during a grave crisis:

> I am as unconcerned, and just as happy as a man can be. It is no matter if the whole world is against us, God is for us. Could not they kill you? Yes, if it be the Lord's will. If it be the will of the Lord for the people to live, they will live. Had it been the will of the Lord that Joseph and Hyrum should have lived, they would have lived. It was necessary for Joseph to seal his testimony with his blood. Had he been destined to live he would have lived. The Lord suffered his death to bring justice on the nation.[79]

He says, "Instead of crying over our sufferings, as some seem inclined to do, I would rather tell a good story, and leave the crying to others," which he always did.[80] "I did not produce myself—I did not cause my existence. A being superior to me has done this; and if I do as well as I know how, I will then risk all in his hands, and be perfectly contented and satisfied. I shall go with a cheerful countenance, and shall pass through the world as cheerfully as I can, making the best of it."[81] "This people are to the world an object of derision and hatred; to God, of care and pity. There are but few of us [in 1857, when they had just announced that Johnston's Army had arrived], we compare ourselves with the rest of the inhabitants of the earth. We now have a day of trial. It has been observed that the Saints feel well: they never felt better."[82] "Rejoice evermore, pray without ceasing, and in everything give thanks, even if you have nothing but buttermilk and potatoes."[83]

"Often have I looked at individuals passing to and fro through our Territory, and heard them say, 'These are the jolly Mormons; these are the merry Mormons, I never saw such a society!' Why is this? Simply because they enjoy themselves, because they take so much comfort."[84] He likes this.

"Cast all bitterness out of your own hearts—all anger, wrath, strife, covetousness, and lust, and sanctify the Lord God in your hearts, that you may enjoy the Holy Ghost, and have that Spirit to be your constant companion day by day, to lead you into all truth, and then you will have good doctrine, good feelings, good wives, good children, a good community; and, finally, you will be Saints in the fullest sense of the word, but not yet. I believe we shall be saints, through the grace of God."[85]

So he's a regular Pollyanna, all for the best. But again, this isn't somebody sitting in a study and writing about this, or a popular preacher, somebody in an expensive pulpit sounding forth on these matters, and sounding very uplifting in his positive thinking. This was right in the midst of Johnston's Army, right on the doorstep. He could take this quite coolly.

And this: "If the wicked come here they do not wish to stay, no matter how well they are treated, and I thank the Lord for it; and I want hard times, so that every person that does not wish to stay, for the sake of his religion, will leave."[86]

> Do you ask if I rejoice [he says in 1852] because the Devil has the advantage over the inhabitants of the earth, and has afflicted mankind? I most assuredly answer in the affirmative; I rejoice in this as much as in anything else. I rejoice because I am afflicted. I rejoice [he was laid up with mountain fever then] because I am poor. I rejoice because I am cast down. Why? Because I shall be lifted up again. I rejoice that I am poor, because I shall be made rich; that I am afflicted, because I shall be comforted, and

prepared to enjoy the felicity of perfect happiness, for it is impossible to properly appreciate happiness, except by enduring the opposite.[87]

"Marvel not that we have what are called troubles: marvel not that our enemies seek to destroy us and the kingdom of God from the earth. These persecutions are to prepare the humble and faithful to dwell in the presence of God the Father and his Son."[88] He really means it.

"The Lord leads His people in this way expressly to give them trials which they have not passed through before, and which it is necessary they should have."[89] "There is not a hardship, there is not a disappointment, there is not a trial, there is not a hard time, that comes upon this people in this place, but that I am more thankful for than I am for full granaries."[90]

"I would be happy, exceedingly happy, to let our past experience and afflictions sleep forever; but the Lord will not suffer me to let them sleep. I would be willing to forget them, but I cannot. The Lord will never suffer this people to dwindle down, and be hid up in a corner; it cannot be; neither does He want any person to help them but Himself."[91] He wants us to be dependent on no one but himself. But he wants us to be dependent on him. That's why he keeps hitting them with these hardships. So don't get upset, keep cool. "Cultivate an even, unruffled temper, until you can perfectly control yourselves at all times, in all places, and under all circumstances."[92] "There is not a man in this house [Salt Lake Tabernacle] who has a more indomitable and unyielding temper than myself."[93] It was not his natural temper to be calm.

"Consider well before you suffer your minds to be irritated in the least. Suffer them not to be agitated until your blood is boiling with rage before you are aware; but stop and reflect."[94] In the morning, when he heard that Johnston's Army had arrived, he announced in the Tabernacle, and it happened to be during conference, "I am too angry this morning to preach."[95] Later, he apologized for it, saying, "Do not be angry. I will permit you to be as angry as I am. Do not get so angry that you cannot pray: do not allow yourselves to become so angry that you cannot feed an enemy—even your worst enemy, if an opportunity should present itself."[96] And here was the enemy at the gates.

"I mean to correct my own faults, and it is for you to do the same. It is an individual business, over which each man must preside. . . . If your neighbour suffers his cattle or his children to trespass upon your property, never retaliate or speak an angry reply. . . . Consider well before you suffer your minds to be irritated in the least; . . . stop and reflect; coolly consider, and quietly reason with the person . . . who [has] trespassed upon you."[97] "There is not a person in this community that can bring to mind or mention the time whenever I exhibited one particle of sorrow or trouble to them."[98] He never showed his emotions. You don't do that. "I calculate to carry my own sorrows just as long as I live upon this earth, and when I go the grave, I expect them all to go there, and sleep with me in eternal silence."[99] So everybody thought everything was wonderful whenever they met Brigham. He made them feel good. He was never downcast. He never showed it at all. He says, "I am careful to keep my tears to myself."[100] And here was a man—who believed he shouldn't worry, since he trusted his Heavenly Father—who didn't worry. So the others didn't worry either. He always came out on top.

The only power you can acquire in this life [this was a favorite doctrine of Brigham Young] was power over yourself. "Never let anger arise in your hearts. No, Brigham, never let anger arise in your heart, never, never!"[101] Emma Lucy Gates [Bowen] used to tell a story of when she was a little girl. There was a barn out behind the Beehive House, and Brigham Young had fine horses. One night one of the saddles fell down from the peg, a rather expensive saddle, and got trampled in the filth all night long. When Brigham Young came out in the morning, he was furious. He called all the help together and gave them a real dressing down. Then he stormed down the hall and into his office. Emma Lucy Gates, being a little girl, was standing outside the door listening, and she heard him say, "Down on your knees, Brigham, get down on your knees!" He'd lost his temper; he had to learn how to control himself.

And as he says in 1867,

> I will say, there is not a man in this house who has a more indomitable and unyielding temper than myself. But there is not a man in the world who cannot overcome his passion, if he will struggle earnestly to do so. If you find passion coming on you, go off to someplace where you cannot be heard; let none of your family see you or hear you, while it is upon you, but struggle till it leaves you; and pray for strength to overcome.[102]

"Watch yourselves day by day, hour by hour and minute by minute. Keep a guard over yourselves so that you will never do or say anything that you will regret hereafter."[103] "If you feel evil, keep it to yourselves until you overcome that evil principle. This is what I call resisting the devil, and he flees from me. I strive not to speak evil, to not feel evil, and if I do, to keep it to myself until it is gone from me, and not let it pass my lips."[104] "It would be better for you to chew up a whole plug of tobacco than to have a real quarrel with your tongues."[105]

He used to hand out plugs of India rubber for people to chew—his teamsters and others; so they chewed the India rubber rather than swear—chew, chew, chew. He says, "Had I not better let it out than to keep it rankling within me?" No, Brigham Young was a psychologist, he knew all about this principle. You have to release the tensions, or something bad's going to happen. "No," he says, "I will keep bad feelings under and actually smother them to death, then they are gone."[106] "If you keep silent, you can master your feelings, can subdue your passions, and ultimately become masters of them and banish them from you. If you give way to your unbridled tongues, you increase anger within you."[107] You're not letting off steam at all. You're not going to feel better, and first because it's a two-way affair. Oh, you can go out alone, by yourself. "That's it," he says, "and work it out there." Let nobody see you; then you're all right. But you don't do it in the presence of another, that will just make more trouble. It's not being a great leader. "If you give way to your unbridled tongues, you increase anger within you, and the first you know your blood is boiling with wrath. . . . If you find that you cannot keep your tongue still, get some India-rubber and chew it with all your might."[108] "A man must first learn to rightly rule himself, before his knowledge can be fully brought to bear for the correct government of a family, a neighborhood, or nation, over which it is his lot to preside [but first himself]."[109]

"In all our daily pursuits in life, of whatever nature and kind, Latter-day Saints, and especially those who hold important positions in the kingdom of God, should maintain a uniform and even temper, both when at home and when abroad."[110]

There was, in Brigham's philosophy and his actions, no

place for heroics and hysterics. This sounds like a strange thing for the Lion of the Lord to say. "I have always acknowledged myself a coward, and hope I always may be, to make me cautious enough to preserve myself and my brethren from falling ignobly by a band of Indians."[111] Be a coward, keep clear of them. Don't go out and stir up something. He says again, "I am a great coward myself, I do not wish to rush into danger imprudently."[112] But on the other hand, there is no sense in getting hysterical about things. Talking to the Saints, he says, "Imagined danger always produces the most trouble."[113] This was before the Walker War, too.

"I should have more fear in consequence of the ignorant and foolish audacity of the Elders, than of their being afraid. I should fear they would rush into danger like an unthinking horse into battle."[114] And he said there were many courageous characters. This was a danger he always had to watch, that the elders didn't go out and start something. Look out, he said—"they would rush into danger like an unthinking horse into battle. So I will not find fault with regard to their courage. On that point, I am a coward myself, and if people would do as I tell them, I would not only save my own life, but theirs likewise."[115] And where they followed his cowardly advice, they survived.

There is also no place for contention in his book. He insists on that: "There is no need of debate and contention in regard to truth and error, for debate tends to create a spirit of bitterness."[116] There is no need for war and blood-shed—of course the Lord says the same thing in the eleventh chapter of 3 Nephi, in his first command to the Nephites: "There shall be no contentions among you, there shall be no more disputations among you" (3 Nephi 11:28). Then what should one do? He goes on to say, "For [the principles of eternal life—a man's testimony] must be revealed from our Father which is in heaven."[117] Not from me, not from anybody else. He can't impose it, he can't give it to another person. Another person can't give it to him, so there's nothing to argue about. You can let your conversation be "yea, yea," and "nay, nay." You can bear your testimony, but you can't force it on anyone. So there can be no contention.

He mentions an atheist who has come to Salt Lake and tried to stir things up: "I do not want to say much about it, it is too vain! In my travels and labors I have met a great many persons who have desired to contend about the principles I taught, though I am happy to say I have passed through the world thus far without a discussion."[118] It is a remarkable thing, for a man as rambunctious as Brigham Young. "It is natural for me to contend," he says, "and if I am opposed to oppose in return [when he was hit, he was tempted to hit back], and if a sharp word is spoken to me to give a sharp word back, I have done so but rarely. It is wrong, and we must subdue the inclination."[119] What a man for self-mastery! No illusions of grandeur or anything like that. It was always Brigham he was correcting.

"Let contention, *all* contention cease; cease finding fault with and casting reflections upon those who are not exactly with us. Let us show by our daily walk and doings that we have something better than they have."[120] "Some of the Elders would much rather fight for their religion than live it. If any one thinks to get into the kingdom by fighting for it, . . . they will find themselves mistaken. We expect opposition, and the quicker the war of principle commences the better. . . . I do not want contention, but I do say let the divines compare their doctrines with ours."[121] "Contention is not my calling; it is no part of the Gospel of Christ; that is peace, life, light, and salvation."[122]

One of his major points, strangely enough, was, don't be in a hurry. "Now from this time, henceforth, *pause,* and, whatever you do, let it be done in a spirit of reflection, never again act in haste, but let your actions always be the result of mature consideration. 'Do not hurry me,' is one of the prominent characteristics of my history. I frequently exhort the brethren *not to be in a hurry,* for we shall not stop here, we are only hunting for the grave, and there is no fear but we shall find it."[123]

"Do not be in a hurry," Brigham says in 1857. "Let us stay together and fight the devil a little longer. Some of you think that by next fall you must obtain all that the Elders preach, if you do, you will go behind the vail, and we cannot have your society,"[124] so please stay around a while. "I am not going into the details, to instruct my brethren particularly how to get wealth; but in the first place, do not be in a hurry."[125] "If we will not be in a hurry, and will pray in our families, pray in secret, attend our meetings, . . . and live so that the Spirit of the Lord will dwell within us, and witness to God every day of our lives, by faithful obedience to his requirements, that we are his, I will say we are bound to get the wealth of the world. . . . But one thing I can say of a truth, I have not been in a hurry, I have taken things moderately, kindly, calmly, and have 'kept my dish right side up.'"[126] "This is the counsel I have for the latter-day Saints to-day. Stop, do not be in a hurry. . . . [Some people say], 'Fortune is somewhat against me.' I will tell you the reason for this—you are in too much of a hurry; you do not go to meeting enough, you do not pray enough, you do not read the Scriptures."[127]

Here is what he means by being in a hurry in your regular business:

> You do not pray enough, you do not read the
> Scriptures enough, you do not meditate enough, you are
> all the time on the wing, and in such a hurry that you do
> not know what to do first. This is not the way to get rich.
> I merely use the term "rich" to lead the mind along, until
> we obtain eternal riches in the celestial kingdom of God.
> . . . Be calm and composed; you are in too much of a
> hurry. Hold on, be easy, never let your nervous system
> rise above your judgment. . . . It is just so with men. I see
> them through the world, I have watched their progress
> for many years, and I see that many of them are too much
> in a hurry. If we are not in too much of a hurry we can
> attend these two-days' meetings, and talk to each other.
> Are you full of faith? You can tell whether I am or not by
> looking at me. . . . I wish there was a little more patience
> and obedience.[128]

Do not be in a hurry—it's an important principle.

And he deplores the common failing of the Saints who
volunteer to steady the ark. You think you have to do something, you think you have to come to the rescue. Well,
notice this splendid psychological study he puts in here.

> An individual . . . with [an] abhorrence of evil [joins
> the Church]. He sets himself upon watch to detect the
> failings of others, deeming that he is doing God [a] service in being so employed. And thus he is decoyed into
> the occupation of the great master of evil, to be the
> accuser of his brethren. And during the time thus occupied by him, he considers himself actuated by the purest
> motives, arising from detestation of sin. . . . Yet mark the
> subtlety of Satan in thus leading men into a false position.
> Such a course, in the first place, probably arose from the
> purest of motives, and perhaps the individual was instrumental in rectifying some error; he feels a satisfaction for
> having done so; his self-esteem is gratified; and ere he is

aware, he is seeking for another opportunity of doing the same, . . . continually set[ting] himself up as being capable of sitting in judgment upon others, and of rectifying by his own ability the affairs of the kingdom of God.[129]

Now, I ask a question: who is there that can know the things of God; who can discern the truth from the error? Where is the man; where are the people now in the world that can do it? They do not exist.[130]

So don't try to run things. This is one of Brigham Young's favorite slogans:

Let the kingdom alone, the Lord steadies the ark; and if it does jostle, and appear to need steadying, if the way is a little sidelong sometimes, and to all appearance threatens its overthrow, be careful how you stretch forth your hands to steady it; let us not be too officious in meddling with that which does not concern us; let it alone, it is the Lord's work. I know enough to let the kingdom alone, and do my duty. It carries me, I do not carry the kingdom. . . . If every bishop, every president, every person holding any position of the holy priesthood, every person who holds a membership in this church and kingdom would take this course the kingdom would roll without our help.[131]

When you are called to do things, that's different. But steadying it is another thing: "Experience . . . teaches us absolutely that we need never undertake to guide the ship of Zion, or dictate, by our own wisdom [this is the President of the Church talking, note well], to the kingdom of God on the earth. It teaches definitely and emphatically that the Lord Almighty can do His own work, and no power of man can stay the potency of His wonder-working hand."[132] "I have seen men who belonged to this kingdom, and who really thought that if they were not associated with it, it could not progress."[133]

"'How is it, brother Brigham, that you manage affairs, and dictate and guide and direct this kingdom as you do?' The secret is I know enough to let the kingdom of God alone, and it goes of its own accord."[134] "Where you find a man who wishes to steady the ark of God, without being called to do so [by special appointment], you will find a dark spot in him. The man [who is] full of light and intelligence discerns that God steadies his own ark, dictates his own affairs, guides his people, controls his kingdom, governs nations, and holds the hearts of all living in his hands."[135] That's why it is improper for people to give advice on the Negro question or anything else. They are trying to steady the ark. They don't really believe. The people who are full of light know that God will manage these things. There are others who wish to destroy.

> I am very thankful that it is not our province, in our present condition, to judge the world; if it were, we would ruin everything. We have not sufficient wisdom, our minds are not filled with the knowledge and power of God; the spirit needs to contend with the flesh a little more. . . . And we must also acquire the discretion that God exercises in being able to look into futurity, and to ascertain and know the results of our acts away in the future, even in eternity, before we will be capable of judging.[136]

"There are men who . . . wish to destroy every power in Heaven and on earth that they do not hold themselves. This is the spirit of Satan that was made so visibly manifest in Heavens and which proved his overthrow, and he now afflicts this people with it [officious people]; he wants to dictate and rule every principle and power that leads to exaltation and eternal life."[137] Notice that he doesn't say "every principle and power that leads to downfall and destruction";

it is Satan who afflicts this people with a desire to dictate every principle that leads to exaltation and eternal life.

There is no place for ambition in the Church. Brigham kept hammering away, because he had no ambition himself. "Should every man be a President?" he asks. This also shows his love of variety.

> Should every man be a member of the Quorum of the Twelve? Should every man be the President of our Government, or a King? No; but each should possess the Spirit of the Lord; and through observing its teachings, every one will be rewarded and enjoy according to his capacity. Each vessel will be filled to overflowing, and hence all will be equal, in that they are full. Every man and woman will receive to a fulness, though the quantity will vary according to the extent of their capacity, and each will be crowned with glory and eternal life, if faithful.[138]

When one is eager to preside, "such a spirit . . . [makes] them altogether unfit to preside over themselves."[139] Of course this is what Plato says in the *Law*, isn't it? A man's fitness to preside is in inverse proportion to his desire to be in charge.

> Such a spirit . . . [makes] them altogether unfit to preside over themselves, or over the least one of God's creations. Brethren, let us mind our own business, that is, the calling the Lord has called us to—never ask how big we are, or inquire who we are; but let it be, 'What can I do to build up the kingdom of God upon the earth?' [Some say,] 'O what a glory it is to me, . . . how grand to think that I am the first lady in the kingdom!' They are just like their brother the devil, precisely.[140]

He's alluding to some of his wives.

"You will often see it thus among the brethren: 'I wish I was ordained president of the High Priests Quorum.' Why?

. . . What nonsense! . . . These little sanctified preachers . . .
will give their views as to whom to call, and whom not to
call. I tell you, you had better stay at home and keep your
noses clean"[141]—and this applies throughout the Church,
including among the women. "I feel sometimes that I could
cuff every Elder's ears—at other times I could cry over their
follies. I have good reason for these remarks. . . . As for
myself, I would rather sit down in the poorest house in this
place, and converse on the things of God, than go to ninety-
nine out of one hundred parties that are got up—and these
are my real feelings. I go to please my brethren." He went
to the parties—everyone was giving parties and fancy balls
for Brigham, but he would rather sit and talk with the
humble about the gospel. And he meant it. My grand-
mother tells some interesting stories about that.

He adds that mothers are too ambitious for their children. "Momism," he says, "can be very destructive."[142] This
man is a real psychologist. You know how apt mothers are
to be full of extreme desire for their children. I've known
mothers to actually ruin their posterity through giving way
to the inordinate desires of their own hearts.

It follows, as you can well imagine, that men have no
power except over themselves; self-discipline is the only
discipline, and who is the enemy? None. What's the danger? he keeps asking. There is just one danger: "I am afraid
of only one thing. What is that? That we will not live our
religion, and that we will partially slide a little from the
path of rectitude, and go part of the way to meet our
friends."[143] "The only things I ever feared were the discord,
discontent, confusion, and apostacy in the midst of this
people."[144] "You are taught from Sabbath to Sabbath what to
do; and if you do that, all will be well. There is only one
thing to fear, and that is, that you will not be faithful to the

kingdom of God."[145] "[We] have to learn to trust in him who has promised to fight our battles, and crown us with victory, if we are faithful as was faithful Abraham. The contest which we have now on hand is chiefly against sin in ourselves."[146] Brother Brigham has but one fear concerning this people: "I do not fear all the devils in hell, or all the mobs that could be raised; but if I have any fear, it is upon this ground—that the people, in their blessings, should forget the Lord their God. . . . There is danger to be anticipated, it is in the slackness of the people to remember the Lord, when the fostering hand of Providence is pouring out blessings upon them and round about them all the day long."[147]

The Church is led by inspiration. This is the point I wanted to get to. He tells some very interesting things about his own troubles. He once thought that Joseph Smith was anything but a born businessman, whereas he was. So what did he do about it? He didn't believe in steadying the ark. He explains, "I prayed and reflected about it, and so did others. I became satisfied that, when a revelation came to Joseph for the people to perform any labor or duty, it was their privilege to go to with their might and do it collectively and individually, not waiting for the manifestations of the Spirit to me, but believing that the Prophet knew more than I knew, that the Lord spoke through him, and that He could do as He pleased about speaking to me."[148]

"I went into the Temple . . . and just challenged [the Brethren] to show wherein the Lord ever conferred upon any man in the world the power to dictate in spiritual affairs, that he did not in temporal affairs. They could not do it. I told them they could not draw the line between the spiritual and the temporal."[149] They were going to follow him in spiritual affairs, but not in temporal. Then he adds, "He was called of God; God dictated him, and if He had a mind to leave him to himself and let him [the Prophet] commit an error, that was no business of mine. And it was not for me to question it, if the Lord was disposed to let Joseph lead the people astray, for He had called him and instructed him to gather Israel and restore the Priesthood and kingdom to them. . . . If He should suffer him to lead the people astray, it would be because they ought to be led astray."[150] It wasn't that he would deny that Joseph Smith could lead the Saints astray. But if he did, it meant that they ought to be.

His theme here is confidence, but the key to the problem of leadership, is, of course, revelation. Not only the leader, but everyone, must receive revelation. He hammered away at that point. He used to ask all the time in conference, "Do you know whether I am leading you right or not? Do you know whether I dictate you right or not? Do you know whether the wisdom and the mind of the Lord are dispensed to you correctly or not? . . . I have a request to make of each and every Latter-day Saint, or those who profess to be, to so live that the Spirit of the Lord will whisper to them and teach them the truth. . . . In this there is safety; without this there is danger, imminent danger; and my exhortation to the Latter-day Saints is—Live your religion [find out for yourself]."[151] Three years earlier, he said,

> "How are you going to know about the will and commands of heaven?" By the Spirit of revelation; that is the only way you can know. How do I know but what I am doing wrong? How do I know but what we will take a course for our utter ruin? I sometimes say to my brethren, "I have been your dictator for twenty-seven years—over a quarter of a century I have dictated this people; that ought to be some evidence that my course is onward and upward. But how do you know that I may not yet do wrong?" . . . I can say this for the Latter-day Saints, and I will say it to their praise and my satisfaction,

if I were to preach false doctrine here, it would not be an hour after the people got out, before it would begin to fly from one to another, and they would remark, "I do not quite like that! It does not look exactly right! What did Brother Brigham mean? That did not sound quite right, it was not exactly the thing."[152]

"Go to with your might, seek unto the Lord your God until you have the revelations of the Lord Jesus Christ upon you, until your minds are open, and the visions of heaven are plain to you. Then follow the dictations of the spirit, and watch Brother Brigham, and see if he counsels you wrong."[153] This is the theme he refers to again and again. "There is not a single Saint deprived of the privilege of asking the Father, in the name of Jesus Christ, our Savior, if it is true that the Spirit of the Almighty whispers through His servant Brigham to urge upon the Latter-day Saints to observe the Word of Wisdom. All have this privilege from the apostle to the lay member. Ask for yourselves."[154]

"Now let me ask you, if you trust to my faith, to my words and teachings, counsel and advise [sic], and do not seek after the Lord to have His Spirit to guide and direct you, can I not deceive you, can I not lead you into error? Look at this and see to what mischief it would lead, and what an amount of evil could be done to a people if they did not live so that the Spirit of the Lord would dwell with them that they might know these things for themselves."[155] A year after, he says, "Now, let me ask the Latter-day Saints, you who are here in this house this day, how do you know that your humble servant is really, honestly, guiding and counseling you aright, and directing the affairs of the kingdom aright?"[156] He always brings up a perfectly legitimate question.

Let you be ever so true and faithful to your friends

and never forsake them, never turn traitor to the Gospel which you have espoused, but live on in neglect of your duty, how do you know but I am teaching false doctrine? How do you know that I am not counseling you wrong? How do you know but I will lead you to destruction? And this is what I wish to urge upon you—live so that you can discern between truth and error, between light and darkness, between the things of God and those not of God, for by the revelations of the Lord, and these alone, can you and I understand the things of God.[157]

Without revelation direct from heaven, it is impossible for any person to fully understand the plan of salvation:

We often hear it said that the living oracles must be in the Church, in order that the kingdom of God may be established and prosper on the earth. I will give another version of this sentiment. I say that the living oracles of God, or the Spirit of revelation must be in each and every individual, to know the plan of salvation and keep in the path that leads them to the presence of God.[158]

The First Presidency have of right a great influence over this people; and if we should get out of the way and lead this people to destruction, what a pity it would be! How can you know whether we lead you correctly or not? Can you know by any other power than that of the Holy Ghost? I have uniformly exhorted the people to obtain this living witness each for themselves; then no man on earth can lead them astray.[159]

That was the principle of his leadership. What a great and marvelous man!—a man completely devoid of humbug, showing contempt for flattery by people who came to him to build him up. He couldn't be bought, he couldn't be shaken, he couldn't be impressed, he wasn't tempted by the things of this world. They're just a lot of toys, unimpressive. He said he'd never walk across the street to make a business deal with anybody; it was beneath his dignity. "When I left Nauvoo, I again left all I had . . . in the hands of the mob, and, said I, 'Eat it up, destroy it, or burn it down, as quick as you please, "for the earth is the Lord's and the fulness thereof."' "[160] "They have had the pleasure"—and again, he wasn't just speaking to be smart—"of driving me five times from my comfortable home; that is nothing."[161] In reference to the burning of the Nauvoo Temple, he said: "When I saw the flames, I said, 'Good, Father. If you want it to be burned up.' . . . I was glad when I heard of its being destroyed by fire, and of the walls having fallen in, and said, 'Hell, you cannot now occupy it.'"[162]

> If you can bring yourselves, in your affections, your feelings, your passions, your desires, and all that you have in your organization, to submit to the hand of the Lord, to his providences, and acknowledge his hand in all things, and always be willing that he should dictate, though it should take your houses, your property, your wives and children, your parents, your lives, or anything else you have upon the earth, then you will be exactly right; and until you come to that point, you cannot be entirely right.[163]

Imagine, people animated by those ideas and led by a man of that calibre—could any obstacle stop them? I think it's plain enough why Brigham Young is the greatest leader of modern times. No man ever proved himself so, or ever spoke with greater authority, and he sought nothing. His whole conviction, his whole strength, lay in the Lord. If people wanted to obey him, it was all right; if they didn't, they didn't. That was none of his concern. Always it came back to the same thing: God was ruling things, and for that reason there was nothing to worry about. That's the only way you'll ever win. Isn't that a useful thing to know, in the world we're living in today? I think it is; I think it's a great comfort.

How people flocked to him as a leader! In times of great danger and stress, he was the Rock of Gibraltar. This was a man you could trust; nothing would throw him off the track. He couldn't be bought, he couldn't be intimidated, he couldn't be moved at all, because he knew exactly where he stood, and he's told us why he couldn't be bought or intimidated. He simply wasn't impressed with anything else. Man didn't move him.

Notes

1. Our main sources are the *Brigham Young History*, the *Times and Seasons*, the *Journal of Discourses*, and the *Millennial Star*. One man chased Brigham Young around for twenty-eight years, taking down everything he said. It's interesting that Brigham Young never prepared a speech; he never talked from notes or anything else—it was all off the cuff. And here's a man who went to school but eleven days in his life. Yet what mastery of language! What vigorous and powerful prose! He knew exactly what he wanted to say, and he knew how to say it. This is part of his great blessing—a man completely devoid of anything phony or any fraud, any personal desire, any shortness of temper, any of the things we think of as weakness. It's a marvelous way to be. Of course it can be very annoying, in a normal society, to have a man like that around.

2. JD 3:237; cf. JD 6:74.
3. JD 13:33.
4. JD 10:188.
5. Cf. JD 13:33.
6. JD 11:253.
7. JD 4:267.
8. JD 3:225–26.
9. JD 10:42.
10. JD 10:19.
11. JD 8:363.
12. JD 8:72.
13. JD 13:176–77.
14. JD 13:177.
15. JD 8:11.

16. *JD* 14:20.
17. *JD* 16:169.
18. *JD* 14:95.
19. *JD* 18:245.
20. *JD* 6:196–97.
21. *JD* 14:94.
22. *JD* 9:248.
23. *JD* 14:201.
24. *JD* 6:332.
25. *JD* 6:332.
26. *JD* 3:275.
27. *JD* 9:124.
28. *JD* 9:248.
29. *JD* 8:367.
30. *MS* 17:120.
31. *JD* 8:334.
32. *JD* 11:305.
33. *JD* 9:293.
34. *JD* 9:293.
35. *JD* 6:293.
36. *JD* 4:268.
37. *JD* 2:284.
38. *JD* 8:131.
39. Cf. *JD* 8:345, 355–56.
40. *JD* 1:278.
41. *JD* 12:36.
42. *JD* 8:355.
43. *JD* 14:89.
44. *JD* 14:224.
45. *JD* 13:3.
46. *JD* 14:94–95.
47. *JD* 225.
48. *JD* 12:257.
49. *JD* 15:162.
50. Cf. *JD* 13:3.
51. *JD* 2:183.
52. *JD* 3:258.
53. *JD* 4:111.
54. *JD* 2:183.
55. *JD* 3:259.
56. *JD* 16:76.
57. *JD* 18:234.

58. *JD* 1:273.
59. *JD* 16:27.
60. *JD* 6:315.
61. *JD* 9:169.
62. *JD* 8:144.
63. *JD* 8:144–45.
64. *JD* 19:4.
65. *JD* 10:305.
66. *JD* 14:136.
67. *JD* 13:177.
68. *JD* 8:31.
69. *JD* 8:69.
70. *JD* 5:351.
71. *JD* 13:308.
72. *JD* 13:308.
73. *JD* 9:291.
74. *JD* 8:39.
75. *JD* 13:317.
76. *JD* 4:53.
77. *JD* 8:151.
78. *JD* 3:343.
79. *JD* 13:94–95.
80. *JD* 12:287.
81. *JD* 8:129.
82. *JD* 5:350.
83. *JD* 3:159.
84. *JD* 1:114.
85. *JD* 8:33.
86. *JD* 4:32
87. *JD* 1:359.
88. *JD* 8:151.
89. *JD* 12:163.
90. *JD* 4:51.
91. *JD* 1:364.
92. *JD* 6:316.
93. *JD* 11:290.
94. *JD* 6:316.
95. *JD* 5:226.
96. *JD* 5:228.
97. *JD* 6:316.
98. *JD* 1:31.
99. *JD* 1:31.

100. *JD* 1:49.
101. *JD* 14:156.
102. *JD* 11:290.
103. *JD* 13:252.
104. *JD* 3:195.
105. *JD* 6:75.
106. *JD* 3:195.
107. *JD* 6:75.
108. *JD* 6:75.
109. *JD* 3:256.
110. *JD* 11:136.
111. *JD* 1:106.
112. *JD* 1:105.
113. *JD* 1:105.
114. *JD* 1:165.
115. *JD* 1:165.
116. *JD* 9:316.
117. *JD* 7:7.
118. *JD* 13:143.
119. *JD* 14:149.
120. *JD* 17:120.
121. *MS* 33:433.
122. *JD* 14:122.
123. *JD* 1:92.
124. *JD* 4:270.
125. *JD* 15:37.
126. *JD* 15:41.
127. *JD* 15:36.
128. *JD* 15:36–37.
129. *MS* 6:165–66.
130. *JD* 3:92.
131. *JD* 11:252.
132. *JD* 1:198.
133. *JD* 11:252.
134. *JD* 11:252.
135. *JD* 8:66.
136. *JD* 19:7–8.
137. *JD* 10:97.
138. *JD* 7:7.
139. *MS* 16:327.
140. *MS* 16:327.
141. *MS* 16:326–27.

142. Cf. *JD* 12:174.
143. *JD* 12:272.
144. *JD* 12:54.
145. *JD* 5:228.
146. *JD* 11:13.
147. *JD* 6:266.
148. *JD* 12:105.
149. *JD* 18:243.
150. *JD* 4:297–98.
151. *JD* 17:51.
152. *JD* 14:205.
153. *JD* 15:6.
154. *JD* 12:117–18.
155. *JD* 13:171.
156. *JD* 14:204.
157. *JD* 14:204.
158. *JD* 9:279.
159. *JD* 6:100.
160. *JD* 2:20.
161. *JD* 10:316.
162. *JD* 8:203.
163. *JD* 5:351–52.

18

Leaders to Managers: The Fatal Shift

Twenty-three years ago today, if you will cast your minds back, on this same occasion I gave the opening prayer in which I said: "We have met here today clothed in the black robes of a false priesthood . . ." Many have asked me since whether I really said such a shocking thing, but nobody has ever asked what I meant by it. Why not? Well, some knew the answer already; and as for the rest, we do not question things at "the BYU." But for my own relief, I welcome this opportunity to explain.

Why a *priesthood?* Because these robes originally denoted those who had taken clerical orders; and a college was a "mystery," with all the rites, secrets, oaths, degrees, tests, feasts, and solemnities that go with initiation into higher knowledge.

But why *false?* Because it is borrowed finery, coming down to us through a long line of unauthorized imitators. It was not until 1893 that "an intercollegiate commission

This speech was delivered at the Brigham Young University commencement ceremony on 19 August 1983 after Nibley had received an honorary doctor of letters degree; it was published as "Leaders to Managers: The Fatal Shift," Dialogue: A Journal of Mormon Thought *16/4 (Winter 1983): 12–21.*

was formed . . . to draft a uniform code for caps, gowns, and hoods" in the United States.[1] Before that there were no rules. You could design your own; and that liberty goes as far back as these fixings can be traced. The late Roman emperors, as we learn from the infallible DuCange, marked each step in the decline of their power and glory by the addition of some new ornament to the resplendent vestments that proclaimed their sacred office and dominion. Branching off from them, the kings of the tribes who inherited the lands and the claims of the empire vied with each other in imitating the Roman masters, determined to surpass even them in the theatrical variety and richness of caps and gowns.

One of the four crowns worn by the Emperor was the mortarboard. The French kings got it from Charlemagne, the model and founder of their royal lines. To quote DuCange:

> When the French kings quitted the palace at Paris to erect a Temple of Justice, at the same time they conferred their royal adornments on those who would preside therein, so that the judgments that came from their mouths would have more weight and authority with the people, as if they were coming from the mouth of the Prince himself. [That's the idea of the robe of the prophet descending on his successor.] It is to these connections that the mortarboards and the scarlet and ermine robes of the Chancellors of France and the Presidents of Parlement are to be traced. Their gowns or *epitogia* [the loose robe thrown over the rest of the clothing, to produce the well-known greenhouse effect] are still made in the ancient fashion. . . . The name "mortarboard" is given to the diadem because it is shaped like the mortarboard which serves for mixing plaster, and is bigger on top than on the bottom.[2]

But where did the Roman emperors get it? For one thing, the mortarboard was called a *Justinianeion*, because of its use by the Emperor Justinian, who introduced it from the East. He got his court trappings and his protocol from the monarchs of Asia, in particular the Grand Shah, from whom it can be traced to the khans of the steppes and the Mongol emperors, who wore the golden button of all wisdom on the top of the cap even as I do now. The shamans of the North also had it, and among the Laplanders it is still called "the Cap of the Four Winds." The four-square headpiece topped by the golden tassel—the emergent Flame of Full Enlightenment—also figures in some Buddhist and Lamaist representations. But you get the idea: this Prospero suit is pretty strong medicine—"rough magic" indeed![3]

Another type of robe and headdress is described in Exodus and Leviticus and the third book of Josephus's *Antiquities*, i.e., the white robe and linen cap of the Hebrew priesthood, which have close resemblance to some Egyptian vestments.[4] They were given up entirely, however, with the passing of the temple and were never even imitated after that by the Jews. Both their basic white and their peculiar design, especially as shown in the latest studies from Israel, are much like our own temple garments. This is not the time nor the place to pursue a subject in which Brother Packer wisely recommends a judicious restraint. I bring it up only to ask myself, "What if I appeared for an endowment session in the temple dressed in this outfit I'm wearing now?" There would be something incongruous about it, perhaps even comical. But why should that be so? The original idea behind both garments is the same—to provide a clothing more fitting to another ambience, action, and frame of mind than that of the warehouse, office, or farm. Doctrine and Covenants 109 describes the function and purpose of the temple as much the same as those of a university: A house where all seek learning by study and faith, by a discriminating search among the best books (no official list is given—you must search them out), and by constant discussion—diligently teaching *"one another* words of wisdom"; everybody seeking greater light and knowledge as all things come to be "gathered in one"—hence *university* (D&C 109:7, 14; 42:36).

Both the black and the white robes proclaim a primary concern for things of the mind and the spirit, sobriety of life, and concentration of purpose removed from the largely mindless, mechanical routines of your everyday world. Cap and gown announced that the wearer had accepted certain rules of living and been tested in special kinds of knowledge.

What is wrong, then, with the flowing robes? For one thing, they are somewhat theatrical and too easily incline the wearer, beguiled by their splendor, to masquerade and affectation. In the time of Socrates, the Sophists were making a big thing of their special manner of dress and delivery.[5] It was all for show, of course, but it was "dressing for success" with a vengeance, for the whole purpose of the rhetorical brand of education which they inaugurated and sold at top prices to the ambitious youth was to make the student successful as a paid advocate in the law courts, a commanding figure in the public assemblies, or a successful promoter of daring business enterprises by mastering those then irresistible techniques of persuasion and salesmanship which the Sophists had to offer.

That was the classical education which Christianity embraced at the urging of the great St. Augustine. He had learned by hard experience that you can't trust revelation because you can't control it—the Spirit bloweth where *it listeth* (John 3:8); and what the church needed was something more available and reliable than that, something *commodior et multitudini tutior* ("handier and more reliable for the public") than revelation or even reason, and that is exactly what rhetorical education had to offer.

At the beginning of this century, scholars were strenuously debating the momentous transition from *Geist* to *Amt*, from spirit to office, from inspiration to ceremony in the leadership of the early church, when the inspired leader, Peter, was replaced by the typical city bishop, an appointed and elected official—ambitious, jealous, calculating, power-seeking, authoritarian, an able politician, and a master of public relations. We have an immense literature on this in the *Patrologia*. This was St. Augustine's trained rhetorician. At the same time, the charismatic gifts (the gifts of the Spirit), not to be trusted, were replaced by rites and ceremonies that could be timed and controlled, all following the Roman Imperial model, as Alföldi has shown, including the caps and gowns.[6]

And down through the centuries the robes have never failed to keep the public at a respectful distance, inspire a decent awe for the professions, and impart an air of solemnity and mystery that has been as good as money in the bank. The four faculties of theology, philosophy, medicine, and law have been the perennial seedbeds, not only of professional wisdom, but of the quackery and venality so generously exposed to public view by Plato, Rabelais, Molière, Swift, Gibbon, A. E. Housman, H. L. Mencken, and others. What took place in the Greco-Roman as in the Christian world was that fatal shift from leadership to management that marks the decline and fall of civilizations.

At the present time, that grand old lady of the Navy, Captain Grace Hopper (the oldest commissioned officer in the Navy), is calling our attention to the contrasting and conflicting natures of management and leadership. No one, she says, ever managed men into battle. She wants more emphasis in teaching leadership. But leadership can no more be taught than creativity or how to be a genius. The *Generalstab* tried desperately for a hundred years to train up a generation of leaders for the German army; but it never worked, because the men who delighted their superiors, i.e., the managers, got the high commands, while the men who delighted the lower ranks, i.e., the leaders, got reprimands.

Leaders are movers and shakers, original, inventive, unpredictable, imaginative, full of surprises that discomfit the enemy in war and the main office in peace. For the managers are safe, conservative, predictable, conforming organization men and team players, dedicated to the establishment.

The leader, for example, has a passion for equality. We think of great generals from David and Alexander on down, sharing their beans or *matzah* with their men, calling them by their first names, marching along with them in the heat, sleeping on the ground, and being first over the wall. A famous ode by a long-suffering Greek soldier, Archilochus, reminds us that the men in the ranks are not fooled for an instant by the executive type who thinks he is a leader.[7]

For the manager, on the other hand, the idea of equality is repugnant and even counterproductive. Where promotion, perks, privilege, and power are the name of the game, awe and reverence for rank is everything, the inspiration and motivation of all good men. Where would management be without the inflexible paper processing, dress standards, attention to proper social, political, and religious affiliation, vigilant watch over habits and attitudes, that gratify the stockholders and satisfy security?

"If you love me," said the greatest of all leaders, "you will keep my commandments." "If you know what is good for you," says the manager," "you will keep *my* commandments and not make waves." That is why the rise of management always marks the decline, alas, of culture. If the management does not go for Bach, very well, there will be no Bach in the meeting. If the management favors vile sentimental doggerel verse extolling the qualities that make for success, young people everywhere will be spouting long trade-journal jingles from the stand. If the management's taste in art is what will sell—trite, insipid, folksy kitsch—that is what we will get. If management finds maudlin, saccharine commercials appealing, that is what the public will get. If management must reflect the corporate image in tasteless, trendy new buildings, down come the fine old pioneer monuments.

To Parkinson's Law, which shows how management gobbles up everything else, he added what he calls the "Law of Injelitance": Managers do not promote individuals whose competence might threaten their own position; and so as the power of management spreads ever wider, the quality deteriorates (if that is possible). In short, while management shuns equality, it feeds on mediocrity.

On the other hand, leadership is an escape from mediocrity. All the great deposits of art, science, and literature from the past, on which all civilization has been nourished, come to us from a mere handful of leaders. For the qualities of leadership are the same in all fields, the leader being simply the one who sets the highest example; and to do that and open the way to greater light and knowledge, the leader must break the mold. "A ship in port is safe," says

Captain Hopper, speaking of management, "but that is not what ships were built for," she says, calling for leadership.

To quote one of the greatest of leaders, the founder of this institution, "There is too much of a sameness in this community. . . . I am not a stereotyped Latter-day Saint and do not believe in the doctrine . . . away with stereotyped 'Mormons'!"[8] Good-bye, all. True leaders are inspiring because they are inspired, caught up in a higher purpose, devoid of personal ambition, idealistic, and incorruptible.

There is necessarily some of the manager in every leader (what better example than Brigham Young himself?), as there should be some of the leader in every manager. Speaking in the temple to the temple management, the scribes and pharisees all in their official robes, the Lord chided them for one-sidedness: They kept careful accounts of the most trivial sums brought into the temple; but in their dealings they neglected fair play, compassion, and good faith, which happen to be the prime qualities of leadership.

The Lord insisted that both states of mind are necessary, and that is important: "These ought ye to have done [speaking of the bookkeeping], and not to leave the other undone." But it is the blind leading the blind, he continues, who reverse priorities, who "strain at a gnat, and swallow a camel" (Matthew 23:23–24). So vast is the discrepancy between management and leadership that only a blind man would get them backwards. Yet that is what we do. In that same chapter of Matthew, the Lord tells the same men that they do not really take the temple seriously, while the business contracts registered in the temple they do take very seriously indeed (Matthew 23:16–18). I am told of a meeting of very big businessmen in a distant place, who happened also to be the heads of stakes, where they addressed the problem of "How to stay awake in the temple." For them what is done in the house of the Lord is a mere quota-filling until they can get back to the real work of the world.

History abounds in dramatic confrontations between the two types, but none is more stirring than the epic story of the collision between Moroni and Amalickiah—the one the most charismatic leader, the other the most skillful manager, in the Book of Mormon. This is both timely and relevant—that's why I bring it in here. We are often reminded that Moroni "did not delight in the shedding of blood" and would do anything to avoid it, repeatedly urging his people to make covenants of peace and to preserve them by faith and prayer. He refused to talk about "the enemy." For him they were always "our brethren," misled by the traditions of their fathers. He fought them only with heavy reluctance, and he *never* invaded their lands, even when they threatened imminent invasion of his own. He never felt threatened, since he trusted absolutely in the Lord. At the slightest sign of weakening by an enemy in battle, Moroni would instantly propose a discussion to put an end to the fighting. The idea of total victory was alien to him—no revenge, no punishment, no reprisals, no reparations, even for an aggressor who had ravaged his country. He would send the beaten enemy home after battle, accepting their word for good behavior or inviting them to settle on Nephite lands, even when he knew he was taking a risk. Even his countrymen who fought against him lost their lives only while opposing him on the field of battle. There were no firing squads, and former conspirators and traitors had only to agree to support his popular army to be reinstated. With Alma, he insisted that conscientious objectors keep their oaths and not go to war even when he desperately needed their help. Always concerned to do the decent thing, he would never take what he called unfair advantage of an enemy. Devoid of personal ambition, the moment the war was over he "yielded up the command of his armies . . . and he retired to his own house . . . in peace" (Alma 62:43), though as the national hero he could have had any office or honor. For his motto was, "I seek not for power" (Alma 60:36), and as to rank he thought of himself only as one of the despised and outcast of Israel. If all this sounds a bit too idealistic, may I remind you that there really have been such men in history, hard as that is to imagine today.

Above all, Moroni was the charismatic leader, personally going about to rally the people, who came running together spontaneously to his title of liberty, the banner of the poor and downtrodden of Israel (Alma 46:12, 19–21). He had little patience with management. He let himself get carried away and wrote tactless and angry letters to the big men sitting on their "thrones in a state of thoughtless stupor" back in the capital (Alma 60:7). And when it was necessary, he bypassed the whole system and "altered the *management* of affairs among the Nephites," to counter Amalickiah's own managerial skill (Alma 49:11). Yet he could apologize handsomely when he learned that he had been wrong, led by his generous impulses into an exaggerated contempt for management; and he gladly shared with Pahoran the glory of the final victory, one thing that ambitious generals jealously reserve for themselves.

But if Moroni hated war so much, why was he such a dedicated general? He leaves us in no doubt on that head— he took up the sword only as a last resort. "I seek not for power, but to pull it down" (Alma 60:36). He was determined to "pull down [the] pride and . . . nobility" (Alma 51:18) of those groups who were trying to take things over. The "Lamanite brethren" he fought were the reluctant auxiliaries of Zoramites and Amalickiahites, his own countrymen.

They "grew proud . . . because of their exceedingly great riches," and sought to seize power for themselves (Alma 45:24), enlisting the aid of "those who were in favor of kings . . . those of high birth . . . supported by those who sought power and authority over the people" (Alma 51:8). They were further joined by important "judges [who] had many friends and kindreds" (the right connections were everything) plus "almost all the lawyers and the high priests," to which were added "the lower judges of the land, and they were seeking for power" (3 Nephi 6:27; Alma 46:4).

All these Amalickiah welded together with immense managerial skill to form a single ultraconservative coalition who agreed to "support him and establish him to be their king," expecting that "he would make them rulers over the people" (Alma 46:5). Many in the church were won over by Amalickiah's skillful oratory, for he was a charming ("flattering" is the word used in the Book of Mormon) and persuasive communicator. He made war the cornerstone of his policy and power, using a systematic and carefully planned communications system of towers and trained speakers to stir up the people to fight for their rights, meaning Amalickiah's career. For while Moroni had kind feelings for the enemy, Amalickiah "did care not for the blood of his [own] people" (Alma 49:10). His object in life was to become king of both the Nephites and Lamanites, using the one to subdue the other (Alma 46:4–5). He was a master of dirty tricks, to which he owed some of his most brilliant achievements as he maintained his upward mobility by clever murders, high-powered public relations, and great executive ability. His competitive spirit was such that he swore to drink the blood of Alma, who stood in his way. In short, he was "one very wicked man" (Alma 46:9), who stood for everything that Moroni loathed.

It is at this time in Book of Mormon history that the word *management* makes its only appearances (three of them) in all the scriptures. First there was that time when Moroni on his own "altered the *management* of affairs among the Nephites" (Alma 49:11) during a crisis. Then there was Korihor, the ideological spokesman for the Zoramites and Amalickiahites, who preached that "every man fared in this life according to the *management* of the creature; therefore every man prospered according to his genius [ability, talent, brains, etc.], and . . . conquered according to his strength; and whatsoever a man did was no crime" (Alma 30:17). He raged against the government for taking people's property, that "they durst not enjoy their rights and privileges, Yea they durst not make use of that which [was] their own" (Alma 30:27–28). Finally, as soon as Moroni disappeared from the scene, the old coalition "did obtain the sole *management* of the government," and immediately did "turn their backs upon the poor" (Helaman 6:39), while they appointed judges to the bench who displayed the spirit of cooperation by "letting the guilty and the wicked go unpunished because of their money" (Helaman 7:5). (All this took place in Central America, the perennial arena of the Big People versus the Little People.)

Such was the management that Moroni opposed. By all means, brethren, let us take Captain Moroni for our model, and never forget what he fought for—the poor, the outcast, and the despised; and what he fought against—pride, power, wealth, and ambition; or *how* he fought—as the generous, considerate, and magnanimous foe, a leader in every sense.

At the risk of running overtime, I must pause and remind you that this story of which I have given just a few small excerpts is supposed to have been cooked up back in the 1820s and somewhere in the backwoods by some abysmally ignorant, disgustingly lazy, and shockingly unprincipled hayseed. Aside from a light mitigation of those epithets, that is the only alternative to believing that the story is *true*; for the situation is equally fantastic no matter what kind of author you choose to invent. This must be a *true* story.

That Joseph Smith is beyond compare the greatest leader of modern times is a proposition that needs no comment. Brigham Young recalled that many of the brethren considered themselves better managers than Joseph and were often upset by his economic naiveté. Brigham was certainly a better manager than the Prophet (or anybody else, for that matter), and he knew it; yet he always deferred to and unfailingly followed Brother Joseph all the way while urging others to do the same, because he knew only too well how small is the wisdom of men compared with the wisdom of God.

Moroni scolded the management for their "love of glory and the vain things of the world" (Alma 60:32), and *we* have been warned against the things of this world as recently as the last general conference.[9] But exactly what are the things of the world? An easy and infallible test has been given us in the well-known maxim, "You can have anything in this world for money." If a thing is of this world you can have it for money; if you cannot have it for money, it does not belong to this world. That is what makes the whole thing *manageable*—money is pure number. By converting all values to numbers, everything can be fed into the computer and handled with ease and efficiency. "How much?" becomes the only question we need to ask. The manager "knows the price of everything and the value of nothing," because for him the value is the price.

Look around you here. Do you see anything that cannot be had for money? Is there anything here you couldn't have if you were rich enough? Well, for one thing you may think you detect intelligence, integrity, sobriety, zeal, character, and other such noble qualities. Don't the caps and gowns prove that? But hold on! I have always been taught that those are the very things that managers are looking for. They bring top prices in the marketplace.

Does their value in this world mean, then, that they have no value in the other world? It means exactly that. Such things have no price and command no salary in Zion; you cannot bargain with them because they are as common as the once-pure air around us; they are not negotiable in the kingdom because there everybody possesses all of them in full measure, and it would make as much sense to demand pay for having bones or skin as it would to collect a bonus for honesty or sobriety. It is only in our world that they are valued for their scarcity. "Thy money perish with thee," said Peter to a gowned quack (Simon Magus) who sought to include "the gift of God" in a business transaction (Acts 8:20).

The group leader of my high priests' quorum is a solid and stalwart Latter-day Saint who was recently visited by a young returned missionary who came to sell him some insurance. Cashing in on his training in the mission field, the fellow assured the brother that he knew that he had the right policy for him just as he knew the gospel was true. Whereupon my friend, without further ado, ordered him out of the house, for one with a testimony should hold it sacred and not sell it for money. The early Christians called *Christemporoi* those who made merchandise of spiritual gifts or church connections. The things of the world and the things of eternity cannot be thus conveniently conjoined;

and it is because many people are finding this out today that I am constrained at this time to speak on this unpopular theme.

For the past year I have been assailed by a steady stream of visitors, phone calls, and letters from people agonizing over what might be called a change of majors. Heretofore the trouble has been the repugnance that the student (usually a graduate) has felt at entering one line of work while he would greatly prefer another. But what can they do? "If you leave my employ," says the manager, "what will become of you?" But today it is not boredom or disillusionment, but conscience that raises the problem. To seek ye first financial independence and all other things shall be added, is recognized as a rank perversion of the scriptures and an immoral inversion of values.

To question that sovereign maxim, one need only consider what strenuous efforts of wit, will, and imagination have been required to defend it. I have never heard, for example, of artists, astronomers, naturalists, poets, athletes, musicians, scholars, or even politicians coming together in high-priced institutes, therapy groups, lecture series, outreach programs, or clinics to get themselves psyched up by GO! GO! GO! slogans, moralizing clichés, or the spiritual exercises of a careful dialectic, to give themselves what is called a "wealth mindset" with the assurance that (in the words of Korihor) "whatsoever a man did was no crime" (Alma 30:17). Nor do those ancient disciplines lean upon lawyers, those managers of managers, to prove to the world that they are not cheating. Those who have something to give to humanity revel in their work, and do not have to rationalize, advertise, or evangelize to make themselves feel good about what they are doing. It is only when their art and their science become business oriented that problems of ethics ever arise. Look at TV. Behind the dirty work is always money. There would be no crime on Hill Street if people didn't have to have money. Paul was absolutely right: The drive for money is "the root of all evil" (1 Timothy 6:10); and he's quoting, incidentally, the old book of Enoch.

In my latest class, a graduating honors student in business management (who is here today) wrote this—the assignment was to compare one's self with some character in the Pearl of Great Price, and he quite seriously chose Cain:

> Many times I wonder if many of my desires are too self-centered. Cain was after personal gain. He knew the impact of his decision to kill Abel. Now, I do not ignore God and make murderous pacts with Satan; however, I desire to get gain. Unfortunately, my desire to succeed in business is not necessarily to help the Lord's kingdom grow [now there's a refreshing bit of honesty]. Maybe I am pessimistic, but I feel that few businessmen have actually dedicated themselves to the furthering of the Church without first desiring personal gratification. As a business major, I wonder about the ethics of business—"charge as much as possible for a product which was made by someone else who was paid as little as possible." You live on the difference. As a businessman will I be living on someone else's industry and not my own? Will I be contributing to society or will I receive something for nothing, as did Cain? While being honest, these are difficult questions for me.

They have been made difficult by the rhetoric of our times. The Church was full of men in Paul's day teaching that gain is godliness and making others believe it. Today the black robe puts the official stamp of approval on that very proposition. But don't blame the College of Commerce! The Sophists, those shrewd business- and showmen, started that game 2,500 years ago, and you can't blame others for wanting to get in on something so profitable. The learned doctors and masters have always known which side their bread was buttered on and have taken their place in the line. Business and "Independent Studies," the latest of the latecomers, have filled the last gaps; and today, no matter what your bag, you can put in for a cap and gown. And be not alarmed that management is running the show—they always have.

Most of you are here today only because you believe that this charade will help you get ahead in the world. But in the last few years things have got out of hand. The economy, once the most important thing in our materialistic lives, has become the *only* thing. We have been swept up in a total dedication to the economy which, like the massive mudslides of our Wasatch Front, is rapidly engulfing and suffocating everything. If President Kimball is "frightened and appalled" by what he sees, I can do no better than to conclude with his words: "We must leave off the worship of modern-day idols and a reliance on the 'arm of flesh,' for the Lord has said to all the world in our day, 'I will not spare any that remain in Babylon' (D&C 64:24)."[10] And Babylon is where we are.

In a forgotten time, before the Spirit was exchanged for the office and inspired leadership for ambitious management, these robes were designed to represent withdrawal from the things of this world—as the temple robes still do. That we may become more fully aware of the real significance of both is my prayer.

Notes

1. *Encyclopedia Americana*, International Edition, 30 vols. (New York: Americana, 1965), 8:49.

2. D. P. Carpenter, "Des Couronnes des rois de France," Dissertation 24 of *Dissertations ou réflexions sur l'histoire de Saint Louys,* in Charles du Fresne DuCange, *Glossarium Mediae et Infimae Latinitatis,* 10 vols. (Paris: Didot, 1840–50; reprinted Graz: Akademische Druck- und Verlagsanstalt, 1954), 10:83; cf. essays on crowns in the supplement.

3. William Shakespeare, *The Tempest,* act V, scene i, line 57.

4. Cf. Exodus 28:4; 39:1–31; Leviticus 8:7–9; and Josephus, *Antiquities* III, 7, 1–7.

5. Plato, *Protagoras* 309a-d.

6. András Alföldi, *A Conflict of Ideas in the Late Roman Empire,* tr. Harold Mattingly (Oxford, Clarendon: 1952).

7. Archilochus, frag. 58.

8. *JD* 13:153, 55.

9. For example, see Thomas S. Monson, "Anonymous," *Ensign* 13 (May 1983): 55–57.

10. Spencer W. Kimball, "The False Gods We Worship," *Ensign* 6 (June 1976): 4, 6.

19

"Exemplary Manhood"

I cannot refuse this honor without being churlish, and I cannot accept it without being ridiculous. Given the choice between being deliberately offensive or my own natural self, of course I choose the latter. Ridiculous? ". . . man, proud man, drest in a little brief authority, most ignorant of what he's most assured, his glassy essence, like an angry ape, plays such fantastic tricks before high heaven as make the angels weep; who, with our spleens would all themselves laugh mortal."[1] If they were not well-behaved angels, they would laugh themselves sick over our antics.

The expression "exemplary manhood" has a quaint old-fashioned ring, rather pleasant turn-of-the-century. I think of Oliver Wendell Holmes's view of himself as "The Last Leaf": "I know it is a sin for me to sit and grin at him here. But the old three-cornered hat and the breeches, and all that are so queer."[2] Who is going to take an octogenarian for a role model? "Exemplary" has a touch of irony. If you are sincerely seeking a role model you will not find him among the living; the best men "carrying, I say, the stamp of one

Nibley presented this keynote address on 11 April 1991 when he was presented the Exemplary Manhood Award at the Associated Students Awards Assembly at Brigham Young University.

defect . . . shall in the general censure take corruption from that particular fault."[3] Already I have betrayed a particular fault which disqualifies me for "exemplary," a weakness for quoting somebody else at the drop of a hat. To be a true role model today means having the right labels on your jackets, jeans, and sneakers. The producers of these items maintain that they are endowing the youth with a sense of self-worth and identity. To this Jesse Jackson replies: They are "exploiting the ethos of mindless materialism. . . . For my inadequate feeling about myself I must at least identify with the best. So I cover up my inadequate feelings with $200 tennis shoes."[4] Jackson is speaking of young blacks, but the Book of Mormon tells us that it is by no means the underprivileged who find fulfillment in costly apparel. Indeed, a notice in last week's paper reports that at BYU students learn that they should try to acquire the most expensive clothing because it does truly give a sense of self-worth, amounting, we might say, to exaltation. I lack the stature of the revered exponents of high-priced sneakers by at least fifteen inches, but then a dislocated knee or shoulder can eclipse their glory in an instant.

Most of you will hardly recognize those quaint values from the early twentieth century—debating, middy-blouses, Indian clubs, the disapproval of cheating, and the reading of Plutarch. Plutarch, as you know, spent his days analyzing and comparing the qualities of greatness in particular men. Our civilization still lives on the capital his great Greeks and Romans have left us. It was the Greeks who won all the prizes, and their secret, as we learn from Plutarch, is their fascination with man's capacity for greatness. That is the *megalopsychia*, that greatness of mind which Aristotle discusses in the fifth book of the *Nicomachean Ethics*.

Perhaps the star role model of all time, as he certainly was of his own time, was Oedipus. He had a fatal flaw, for as we learn from his opening speech of *Oedipus the King*, everybody thought he was *kleinos*, glorious, number one, and he warmly approved their judgment. The fatal flaw was that he would not admit a flaw; he had committed a horrible crime, but an unintentional one, and he was repeatedly told that he would be freely forgiven if he would only admit to the sin. So we come to the famous closing chorus:

> Citizens of Thebes, look at your Oedipus here, the man who solved the world-famous riddle and was unquestionably the ablest man of his time. There wasn't a single man anywhere who didn't look with envy upon his fabulous success. Well, this is the total shipwreck to which he had come. In view of which let every mortal consider how he ended up, and understand that nobody is to be viewed as exemplary manhood (*olbizein*) until he has gone through life without having been cut down to size.[5]

The greatest role model in history is certainly Alexander the Great, who, as you know, conquered the world. But for Plutarch his greatness was not measured quantitatively as greatness is measured today by Malcolm Forbes's richest 400 or the top 500 corporations, strictly in dollars. What Alexander shows at every turn is that nobility of mind which never stoops to anything mean or base, never takes advantage of the weak or the beaten, never seeks vengeance; with him all is humanity and chivalry. It was not his blitzkrieg blows but his generosity and magnanimity to his enemies and to everybody else that enabled him to subdue the world. His first victory was over the horse Bucephalus, a magnificent beast which no one could approach; it simply ate men alive. Alexander, at the age of twelve, wanted the horse and loved it and subdued it with extreme gentleness—and caution, of course.

In the opening sentence of his *Life of Alexander,* Plutarch puts him side by side with Caesar, not as romantic and exciting a figure, but showing the same greatness of spirit; Caesar's first rule was always to deal fairly with the enemy—treat him as you would be treated. He was indeed something like the Caesar of Antony's funeral oration, and his methods worked in subduing all Gaul as all the imperial and barbarian tactics of brutality could not.

Alexander had his own hero, none other than Diogenes, the one who went around looking for an honest man and lived in a tub. He had an absolute passion for honesty that seemed to lead sometimes to rudeness, but Alexander understood it. In the famous anecdote, Alexander came to visit Diogenes and asked him, as he often asked others, whether there was anything he could do for him. Diogenes replied that the only favor he asked was for Alexander to step aside and let him enjoy his sun bath. As he walked away from this memorable interview, Alexander said to those who were with him, "If I was not Alexander, the man I would want to be is Diogenes."[6] What could the two men have had in common and what did he so admire in the old man? It was absolute independence of mind, and the luxury of honesty. In Athens, as we know, everybody was busy making money, or at least being very busy—*chrema chremet' aner*—the business ethic with a vengeance. So on some days one could see Diogenes busily rolling his tub up and down the street, and when people asked what on earth he was doing he would reply, "I am rolling my barrel in the Metroum," i.e., I am being busy like everybody else. It was an object lesson to all those busy people, and surprisingly it got across the point so well that to this day Diogenes is

perhaps the most admired exemplar of manhood among
the Greeks. Diogenes Laertius said that Diogenes' own
model in turn was Heracles, "because he prized independence above all things." He was not impressed by the pre-
tensions of men and would heartily applaud the teachings
of King Benjamin.

You will recall that the people of King Benjamin met in a
great national assembly to celebrate the completion of the
long, victorious, and prosperous reign of their great king. It
was a time for pride and patriotism. So what does Benjamin
do? He devotes his two great addresses to pouring cold
water on every display of enthusiasm: "Now, it came to
pass that when king Benjamin had made an end of speaking . . . that he cast his eyes round about on the multitude,
and behold they had fallen to the earth, for the fear of the
Lord had come upon them. And they viewed themselves in
their own carnal state even less than the *dust of the earth*"
(Mosiah 4:1–2), hardly a case of standing tall, to say the
least! "If the knowledge of the goodness of God at this time
has awakened you to a sense of your nothingness, and your
worthless and fallen state, . . . believe that ye must repent of
your sins . . . and humble yourselves before God. . . . I
would that ye should remember, and always retain in
remembrance, the greatness of God, and your own nothingness, and his goodness and long-suffering towards you,
unworthy creatures" (Mosiah 4:5, 10–11). Along with that,
he kept reminding them that he was no better than the rest
of them.

If Diogenes reminds us of Benjamin, Alexander reminds
us of Moroni, a youthful military genius of great dash and
imagination, but above all of great humanity and empathy
with his fellows. Moroni always calls the enemy "our
brethren." He is always eager to stop the battle the moment

he sees a weakening on the other side and to suggest talking things over. As we are often reminded, he took no pleasure in the shedding of blood and never sought vengeance or even any reprisals or reparations from the enemy—no preventive arrest, not even for Zerahemnah, who frankly told Moroni that if he let his people go they would most certainly break any oaths or promises they made to him. In one revealing situation Moroni refuses to take advantage of a disabled enemy: "But had they awakened the Lamanites, behold they were drunken and the Nephites could have slain them. But behold, this was not the desire of Moroni; he did not delight in murder or bloodshed, but he delighted in the saving of his people from destruction; and for this cause he might not bring upon him *injustice,* he would not fall upon the Lamanites and destroy them in their drunkenness" (Alma 55:18–19). He would not take advantage of those disgusting people who had done all manner of wicked things. How would Alexander and Moroni have responded to General Powell's remark that the number of dead Iraqis "is not a number I'm terribly interested in," or to Mr. Fitzwater's insistence that we should feel not the slightest guilt or responsibility for any of the destruction in the Gulf in "a war caused by Saddam Hussein"?

Moroni has been held up to us as a prime example of exemplary manhood: "If all men had been, and were, and ever would be, like unto Moroni, behold, the very powers of hell would have been shaken forever; yea, the devil would never have power over the hearts of the children of men" (Alma 48:17). You do not deliver the hearts of men from the power of the devil by high explosives, for "this was the faith of Moroni, and his heart did glory in it; not in the shedding of blood but in doing good, in preserving his people, yea, in keeping the commandments of God, yea,

and resisting iniquity" (Alma 48:16). There was the enemy
—the only place you can resist iniquity is in yourself. Alma
sums up all the virtues of Moroni in the ringing pro-
nouncement, "Behold, he was a man like unto Ammon, the
son of Mosiah, yea, and even the other sons of Mosiah"
(Alma 48:18). This is not Ammon, the mightiest warrior in
the Book of Mormon, but explicitly Ammon the missionary
with his companions. Ammon humbled himself as a servant and groom to a king and put on a stunning display of
martial arts in the rough games at the Waters of Sebus. But
the one achievement in which he glories is the true measure
of his greatness, when he subdued an indescribably cruel
and uncompromising enemy. "For if we had not come up
out of the land of Zarahemla, these our dearly beloved
brethren . . . would still have been racked with hatred
against us, yea, and they would also have been strangers to
God. . . . Yea, I know that I am nothing; as to my strength I
am weak; therefore I will not boast of myself but I will boast
of my God" (Alma 26:9, 12). Then he tells his story. He and
the sons of Mosiah had this wild idea of going on a mission
to the enemy: "They said unto us: Do ye suppose that ye
can bring the Lamanites to the knowledge of the truth? Do
ye suppose that ye can convince the Lamanites of the incor-
rectness of the traditions of their fathers, as stiffnecked a
people as they are; whose hearts delight in the shedding of
blood; whose days have been spent in the grossest iniquity;
whose ways have been the ways of transgressor from the
beginning? Now my brethren, ye remember that this was
their language" (Alma 26:24). The idea was so absurd that
"they laughed us to scorn" (Alma 26:23). They had the well-
known and unanswerable arguments that we hear so often:
"Let us take up arms against them, that we may destroy
them and their iniquity out of the land, lest *they* overrun us

and destroy us" (Alma 26:25). It was the open-and-shut case of kill or be killed; if we don't fight them now we will have to fight them later.

What were Ammon's strategy and tactics? "We have . . . been forth amongst them; and we have been patient in our sufferings, and we have suffered every privation; yea, we have traveled from house to house. . . . And we have entered into their houses and taught them, and we have taught them in their streets; yea, and we have taught them upon their hills; and we have also entered into their temples and their synagogues and taught them" (Alma 26:28–29). And what was the reaction? "And we have been cast out, and mocked, and spit upon, and smote upon our cheeks; and we have been stoned . . . and bound . . . and cast into prison. . . . And we have suffered all manner of afflictions" (Alma 26:29–30). How humiliating! How embarrassing! How infuriating for the mightiest man of them all to let himself be pushed around like that. Where was his pride? Why did he put up with it? What was there in it for him? He explains: "And all this, that *perhaps* we *might* be the means of saving *some* soul; and we supposed that our joy would be full if perhaps we could be the means of saving some" (Alma 26:30). They just wanted the chance to try to bring the gospel to some honest soul who just might listen to them. Results were by no means guaranteed as they are by the John Wayne and Rambo approach in which the solution of every problem is the big man with the gun that never misses.

I find "exemplary manhood" paradoxical if not ironic because the qualities we would most like to imitate are by their very nature unique to the individual; the men and women who possess them are truly singularities. This is exceptionally clear in the arts; the greater the artist the more unique and inimitable are his works or performances. I am thinking of the two greatest men of our dispensation, the one the devoted disciple and boundless admirer of the other—Joseph Smith and Brigham Young. They are practically out of reach as exemplary figures since they can no more be duplicated or cloned than Mozart and Houdini.

Why do I say that Joseph Smith is the greatest? For one thing, he was the only man qualified for his task. We get a fresh portrait of him and the things he went through in his newly published letters and papers. As we know, he gave the world in the Latter-day Saint scriptures the most astonishing collection of writings ever put forth by an individual. This was not his own work, of course—"Joseph could do nothing of himself," as he and his friends often noted—so it wouldn't do much good to imitate him. But what he did was beyond the scope of other mortals; as a transmitter no other human being could take the voltage that he did. Reading the early history of the Church from New York on, I find the strongest possible testimony to the divinity of the work in the fact that it did not fold up in five years or ten. At Kirtland no one would have bet the Church could survive for a decade. Joseph made no secret of his own limitations, and the envious brethren, to say nothing of the Gentiles, spared him no rebuff, threat, or indignity. Such men as Rigdon, Cowdery, Phelps, F. G. Williams, the Laws, the Higbys, etc., in fact, "Of the Twelve Apostles chosen in Kirtland, and ordained under the hands of Oliver Cowdery, David Whitmer, and myself, there [are] but . . . two but what have lifted up their heel against me."[7] "Great big Elders," he called them, caused him much trouble. "He said he had been trampled under foot by aspiring Elders, for all were infected by that spirit."[8] "I do not think there have been many good men on earth since the days of Adam. . . . I do not want you to think I am very righteous, for I am not."[9] And would you believe it, all but Frederick G. Williams sooner or later returned to apologize, beg Joseph's forgiveness, and be taken back into the Church. And he always forgave them on the spot. His greatness—uniquely his own—was the overflowing love that invests whatever he does and says. No man ever stood more alone against the world. The hundreds of vicious tales that were told against him cannot be matched by a single story or report which he may have told against others in rebuttal. One of his worst enemies wrote that Joseph, with all the provocation he faced, never did or said an *unkind* thing to anyone. I wonder if there is anyone else of whom that could be said. Whom would Joseph Smith recommend as his model? "The great and wise of ancient days have failed in all their attempts to promote eternal power, peace, and happiness. . . . They proclaim with the voice of thunder, those imperishable truths—that man's strength is weakness, his wisdom is folly, his glory is his shame. . . . History records their puerile plans, their short-lived glory, their feeble intellect and their ignoble deeds."[10] "All are subjected to vanity while they travel through the crooked paths and difficulties which surround them. Where is the man who is free from vanity?"[11] "It is a love of liberty which inspires my soul—civil and religious liberty to the whole of the human race. . . . And if by the principles of truth I succeed in uniting men of all denominations in the bonds of love, shall I not have obtained a good object? . . . I ask, Did I ever exercise any compulsion over any man? Did I not give him the liberty of disbelieving any doctrine [that] I have preached?"[12] "Every man has a natural, and, in our country, a constitutional right to be a false prophet, as well as a true prophet."[13]

Joseph saw that independence requires tolerance: "We

deem it a just principle . . . to be duly considered by every individual, that all men are created equal, and that all have the privilege of thinking for themselves upon all matters relative to conscience. Consequently, then, we are not disposed, had we the power, to deprive any one of exercising that free independence of mind which heaven has so graciously bestowed upon the human family as one of its choicest gifts."[14] It all goes back to the ultimate role model: "Who told you that man did not exist in like manner upon the same principles (as God)? The mind or the intelligence which man possesses is coequal with God himself. . . . The intelligence of spirits had no beginning, neither will it have an end."[15] Who is exemplary for you? "If others' blessings are not your blessings, others' curses are not your curses; you stand . . . agents unto yourselves to be judged according to your works."[16]

In terms of his accomplishments in the face of the obstacles that man and nature threw in his way, Brigham Young is certainly the greatest leader that America has produced. Where does his greatness show through? Not in the overpowering bulldozing personality some people imagine, but in his intelligence and uncanny insight and understanding of human nature. I am thinking of the man with the bucket. Every year Brigham would invite all the Saints to a big Twenty-fourth of July celebration at Brighton. One year (in 1860), a reporter from Horace Greeley's *New York Herald* observed the scene. He tells how when the party was over and night was falling and the dust had settled on the road back to town, a solitary figure could be seen going around among all the campfires with a bucket, carefully putting out the last glowing embers—it was the leader, Brigham Young, practicing what he preached. At the beginning of the celebration the usual officious people had come

forth with a carefully planned agenda of all events—rising
at 5:00 to the bugle, falling into formation, lights out at
10:00, etc. When the experts had laid down the rules,
Brigham Young rose and said that as far as he was concerned he intended to go on dancing until the small hours
of the morning. (And this was the founder of the Brigham
Young University?)

There is one story I must tell because it is strictly first-
hand; I heard it from Emma Lucy [Gates Bowen] during a
dinner at her home when I first came to Utah. There used to
be a barn behind the Lion House where Brother Brigham
kept his horses. One day when Emma Lucy was nine years
old she heard her father out in the barn giving the grooms a
royal dressing down for having allowed a fine saddle to fall
from its peg to the floor where it got trampled in the dirt.
She waited until Brigham came back to the house and
stormed down the hall to his office. Then she listened at the
door and actually heard him say, "Down on your knees,
Brigham! Get down on your knees!" He was ashamed of
himself for having embarrassed the grooms and so lost control over his temper. He recommended that the Brethren
keep handy a piece of India rubber to chew whenever they
got angry, to avoid swearing.

High military officers tell me that the most coveted
medal among them is the familiar red-and-white good conduct ribbon, for which any Beetle Bailey is qualified. It is
prized by the high brass because it shows that the wearer
has come up from the ranks. In itself there is no lower
degree of glory; its secondary message is what is important.
So let it be with this award, the recognition of the unspeci-
fied tribulations of another enlisted man.

This is the day of our probation. In this life no one is
saved and no one is damned. The days of our probation are

prolonged so that we can repent and avoid damnation as long as we are here; while only he who endures to the *end* will be saved, that is, saved only after this life is over. To his followers the Lord said, "Why callest thou me good? There is none good but one, that is, God: but if thou wilt enter into life, keep the commandments" (Matthew 19:17). This is not a confession of weakness by the Lord, but a reprimand to those who judge prematurely, or rather who judge at all— "Man shall not judge neither shall he smite"—what do you know about it? So far as we are concerned there is but one standard of goodness, and that is our Heavenly Father. Shouldn't we seek our role model at a lower level, to say the least? Not at all, says the Lord, when we consider that all good comes from him and to whatever degree we do good we are pleasing him and we are the pattern and example he sets. "A man being evil cannot do that which is good; neither will he give a good gift" (Moroni 7:10). On the other hand, "I would exhort you, my beloved brethren, that ye remember that every good gift cometh of Christ" (Moroni 10:18). "Therefore, what manner of men ought ye to be? Verily I say unto you, even as I am" (3 Nephi 27:27). And as we all know, he did only what he saw the Father do. But what about his own ascendancy? The supreme lesson in humility was given to the brother of Jared; though the sight of the Lord's finger knocked him flat, when the Lord revealed himself fully, as he reports it: "Then shall ye know that I have seen Jesus, and that he hath talked with me face to face, and that he hath told me *in plain humility,* even as a man telleth another in mine own language, concerning these things" (Ether 12:39).

Notes

1. William Shakespeare, *Measure for Measure,* act II, scene ii, lines 117–23.

2. Oliver Wendell Holmes, "The Last Leaf" (Cambridge: Houghton Mifflin—Riverside, 1886), 8.

3. William Shakespeare, *Hamlet,* act I, scene iv, lines 31, 35–36.

4. Jesse Jackson, *Washington Post* National Weekly Edition, 1–7 April 1991, 8–9.

5. Sophocles, *Oedipus Tyrannos,* ed. Richard C. Jebb (Cambridge: Cambridge University Press, 1933), 1524–30.

6. Plutarch, *Life of Alexander* XIV, 3.

7. *TPJS,* 307.

8. *TPJS,* 225.

9. *TPJS,* 303.

10. *TPJS,* 249.

11. *TPJS,* 187.

12. *TPJS,* 313, 341.

13. *TPJS,* 344.

14. *TPJS,* 49.

15. *TPJS,* 353.

16. *TPJS,* 12.

Index of Passages

Index of Subjects

What Is F.A.R.M.S.?

The Foundation for Ancient Research and Mormon Studies (F.A.R.M.S.) encourages and supports research about the Book of Mormon, Another Testament of Jesus Christ, and other ancient scriptures.

F.A.R.M.S. is a nonprofit educational foundation, independent of all other organizations. Its main research interests include ancient history, language, literature, culture, geography, politics, and law relevant to the scriptures. Although such subjects are of secondary importance when compared with the spiritual and eternal messages of the scriptures, solid research and academic perspectives alone can supply certain kinds of useful information, even if only tentatively, concerning many significant and interesting questions about the ancient backgrounds, origins, composition, and meanings of scripture.

The Foundation works to make interim and final reports about this research available widely, promptly, and economically. As a service to teachers and students of the scriptures, research results are distributed both in scholarly and popular formats.

It is hoped that this information will help all interested people to "come unto Christ" (Jacob 1:7) and to understand and take more seriously these ancient witnesses of the atonement of Jesus Christ, the Son of God.

For more information about F.A.R.M.S., call toll free 1-800-327-6715, or write to F.A.R.M.S., P.O. Box 7113, University Station, Provo UT 84602.